THE
ELECTRONICS
PATHWAY

IN ADVANCED GNVQ ENGINEERING

Barry Lewis

The Further Education Funding Council

and

Tim Strickland

Brighton College of Technology

MACMILLAN

First published 1996 by
MACMILLAN PRESS LTD
Houndmills, Basingstoke, Hampshire RG21 2XS
and London
Companies and representatives
throughout the world
ISBN 0–333–59914–4

A catalogue record for this book is available from the
British Library.

10 9 8 7 6 5 4 3 2 1
05 04 03 02 01 00 99 98 97 96

Typeset by Florencetype Ltd, Stoodleigh, Devon

Printed in Great Britain by Unwin Brothers Ltd,
The Gresham Press, Old Woking, Surrey
A member of the Martins Printing Group

Acknowledgements

The authors and publishers wish to thank the following
sources for permission to reproduce photographs:

Analog Devices pp. 173, 300; AVO International p. 304;
British Telecommunications plc pp. 259, 261; Fluke (U.K.)
Ltd pp. 84, 92; General Instrument p. 142; Inmarsat p. 264;
Maplin Professional Supplies pp. 10, 15 (preset resistor), 16
(bead thermistor), 40, 41, 42 (variable air-spaced capacitor),
56, 57, 59, 110, 115, 125; Metrix Electronics plc p. 312; Sarah
Norris pp. 2, 3; Philips Semiconductors p. 282; RS
Components UK pp. 15 (ORP12), 16 (disc thermistor), 42
(trimmer capacitor), 102, 106, 107, 108, 111, 112, 113, 132,
174, 240; Sony p. 127; John Wisden p. 5.

Every effort has been made to trace all the copyright
holders but if any have been inadvertently overlooked the
publishers will be pleased to make the necessary
arrangement at the first opportunity.

Contents

Preface

In recent times greater focus has been placed upon vocational qualifications according them their rightful place as a relevant high quality alternative to the conventional academic route.

This textbook is written for students who have chosen to study an area that appeals to them and one in which they show a genuine interest. It is targeted at students who are studying Units that group together to form the electronics pathway to obtaining an Advanced GNVQ in Engineering.

The approach adopted is user friendly with formulae explained and repeated to reinforce essential points. Both of the authors are experienced lecturers in electronics in further education and have used this experience to include a wealth of practical investigations and circuits that will appeal to all students. These are presented so that they are suitable for use as class

demonstrations or for assignment research and planning. Where appropriate, results tables are included to assist practical investigations. A large number of worked examples with additional explanation are included and the majority of chapters are followed by multiple choice questions which are designed to reinforce the topics introduced in the preceding pages and can be used for individual or class testing purposes.

In addition to GNVQ students this book is eminently suitable for those who are studying BTec National Diploma, City and Guilds Electronic Servicing/Telecommunications courses and A-level Electronics.

Barry Lewis
Tim Strickland

Optional units covered by this book

1
DC circuits

1.1 Characteristics of DC circuits

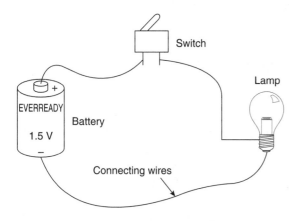

Figure 1.1   A simple typical electrical connection

Electric circuits are made up of parts or components connected to a source of voltage known as the supply. The supply may take the form of a battery or a power supply unit. A simple typical electrical connection is shown in Figure 1.1. Normally, the circuit is drawn using symbols – a form of diagrammatic shorthand. The circuit in Figure 1.1 consists of a battery, switch and lamp and would be drawn as shown in Figure 1.2. For a full list of symbols see the inside back cover.

Current

The effects of connecting a lamp (or load) to the battery (or supply) is that current will flow through

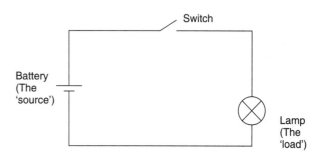

Figure 1.2   A simple circuit diagram of the connection illustrated in Figure 1.1

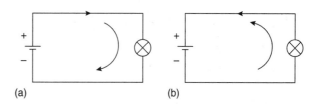

(a)   (b)

Figure 1.3   Direction of (a) conventional current flow and (b) electron flow

the switch and the bulb and back to the other terminal of the battery.

Current is defined as a flow of electrons and we know that these carry a negative charge. Early pioneers of electricity assumed that current flowed from positive to negative. This is known as the direction of **conventional current flow** (see Figure 1.3(a)). However, as unlike charges attract, electrons flow from negative to positive. As an electric current is a flow of electrons its true direction is negative to positive (see Figure 1.3(b)). The opposition offered to the flow of current is known as resistance. We shall return to the subject of resistance later.

The effects of current

When a current travels around the circuit in Figure 1.1

(a) it causes power to be dissipated in the resistance of the lamp which is given off as light (and heat as the lamp warms up), and
(b) a magnetic field is present around the conductors through which the current flows.

Note that current cannot exist unless a source of voltage is present.

The unit of current

Current is measured in amperes, usually shortened to amps (symbol A). It is normally measured with an ammeter, which should have as low a resistance as possible.

When current is smaller than 1 A it is usual to express it in sub-units. The milliamp is equal to one-thousandth of an amp. It is normally written mathematically as

$$1 \text{ mA} = 1 \times 10^{-3} \text{ A} = 0.001 \text{ A}$$

The microamp is one-millionth of an amp and is written mathematically as

$$1 \text{ μA} = 1 \times 10^{-6} \text{ A} = 0.000\ 001 \text{ A}$$

In formulae, current is allocated the abbreviation I, voltage V and resistance R. For example, current equals voltage divided by resistance would be expressed as

$$I = \frac{V}{R} \text{ amps}$$

Current in a series circuit

In Figure 1.4(a) the lamps L_1 and L_2 are connected one after the other and are therefore said to be in series. The current flows from the battery via L_1 and L_2 and is the same at any point in the circuit. For example, the three meters M_1, M_2 and M_3 in Figure 1.4(b) will all show the same reading. If the circuit is broken at any point both of the lamps will go out as there is no longer a complete path for the current to flow from the battery through the lamps and back to the battery. The total current that flows can be calculated from Ohm's law (see page 8) and is dependent on the supply voltage and the total resistance present in the circuit.

Christmas tree lights are well known for giving trouble as they are connected in series. When one lamp is loose in its holder all the lamps fail to light as the current path is interrupted

Current in a parallel circuit

In Figure 1.5 the ends of L_1 are connected directly across the ends of L_2 which, in turn are connected directly to the supply. The current leaves the battery and then splits, some of it flowing via L_1 and some via L_2. It then recombines to flow back to the source. The amount of current which flows via each lamp is dependent on the resistance of the lamp and hence its power rating.

The meter readings will now be different depending on where in the circuit they are placed. In Figure 1.5(b) meter M_1 indicates the total circuit current. Meters M_2 and M_3 show that the current has split equally and is flowing via the lamps. As expected, M_4 gives the same reading as M_1 as the total current that left the supply returns to it.

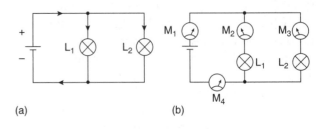

(a)   (b)

Figure 1.5   Current in a parallel circuit: (a) two lamps connected in parallel; (b) current meters give readings indicated

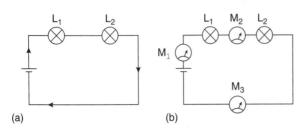

(a)   (b)

Figure 1.4   Current in a series circuit: (a) two lamps connected in series; (b) each current meter will give the same reading

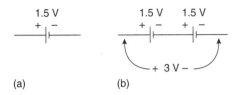

(a)   (b)

Figure 1.6   (a) A single cell; (b) cells in series form a battery

Voltage

Voltage, or potential difference, cannot be present without a supply, which can take the form of a battery, generator, power supply unit or some other device. The voltage produced by the supply provides the force to drive current around the circuit. This voltage is known as the electromotive force (e.m.f.). The term potential difference is used when referring to a voltage developed in DC circuits. The unit of voltage is the volt (symbol V).

The voltage of a normal torch battery is 1.5 volts. A battery consists of a number of cells. Batteries can be joined in series, as shown in Figure 1.6, to give a total supply of, for example, 3 V.

In drawing a DC circuit it is usual to label the supply in one of two ways, i.e. positive and negative or +6 V and 0 V (see Figure 1.7).

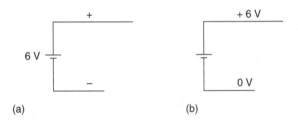

(a)   (b)

Figure 1.7   Two ways of labelling the voltage supply

Electronics technicians refer only to lamps. Bulbs grow in gardens!

Practical 1

Proving the split of voltage and current in series and parallel circuits

In a series circuit the current is common to components and the voltage divides itself between them. This practical will prove this without the use of meters. Note that both lamps used must be of 6 V rating.

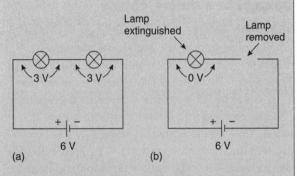

(a)   (b)

Figure 1.8   (a) Both lamps light with equal brightness but at half their full intensity; (b) when one lamp is removed the connection is 'open circuit' and the second lamp is extinguished

In the circuit shown in Figure 1.8 both lamps are identical and they will light with equal brightness. Verify this by constructing the circuit. Disconnect either of the lamps from the circuit and the other will go out. This is because the current cannot pass through the open circuit that has been made.

Rearrange the circuit so that it is connected as shown in Figure 1.9. Each lamp will be twice as bright as before. This is because the 6 V supply no longer has to divide itself between the two lamps. Each

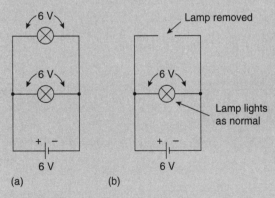

(a)   (b)

Figure 1.9   (a) Both lamps light with equal brightness and at their full intensity; (b) when one lamp is removed the second lamp is unaffected

lamp has 6 V across it and lights to its full brightness. In the series circuit each lamp was only supplied with 3 V and hence lit with half the intensity.

If either of the lamps is removed from the circuit the other will not be extinguished. The total current, however, will halve.

Voltage in a series circuit

The supply voltage (e.m.f.) in a series circuit is equal to the sum of the individual potential differences around the circuit. This is illustrated in Figure 1.10. In Figure 1.10(a) the voltage across L_1 is equal to 1.5 V which is equal to the supply voltage. In Figure 1.10(b) the voltage across L_1 equals the voltage across L_2 (assuming the lamps are identical) which equals 1.5 V. In Figure 1.10(c) the measured voltage equals the supply voltage applied across L_1 and L_2 which equals 3 V.

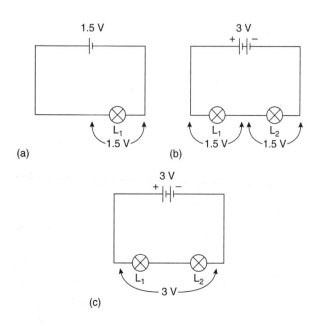

Figure 1.10   Voltage in a series circuit

Practical 2

Voltage and current in a series circuit

This practical is to get you used to measuring voltage and current in a series circuit and, which is very important, to give you an idea of what readings to expect on a meter.

Connect up a circuit as shown in Figure 1.11 and switch on. Set the meter to measure

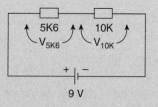

	Voltages	
Resistor	Measured	Calculated
5K6		
10K		

Figure 1.11

voltage and connect it across each resistor in turn. Enter the result in the table.

Now switch off the supply, set the meter to a current range and connect it as shown in Figure 1.12. Again enter the reading in the table.

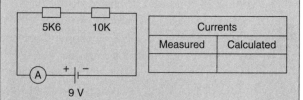

Currents	
Measured	Calculated

Figure 1.12

You should be able to compare your practical answers with those obtained mathematically. These theoretical answers are calculated as follows:

$$R_T = 5.6 \text{ k}\Omega + 10 \text{ k}\Omega$$

$$= 15.6 \text{ k}\Omega$$

$$I = \frac{V}{R_T} = \frac{9 \text{ V}}{15.6 \text{ k}\Omega} = 0.58 \text{ mA}$$

Therefore,

$$V_{5K6} = I \times R$$

$$= 0.58 \text{ mA} \times 5.6 \text{ k}\Omega$$

$$= 3.2 \text{ V}$$

and

$$V_{10K} = I \times R$$

$$= 0.58 \text{ mA} \times 10 \text{ k}\Omega$$

$$= 5.8 \text{ V}$$

NB: When using a meter to measure voltage or current always start on the highest range possible and switch the meter range down until the display is easy to read.

Self-check

Add the two voltages together. They should approximately equal the total circuit voltage, i.e.

$$3.25 + 5.8 = 9.05 \text{ V} \approx 9 \text{ V}$$

Voltage in a parallel circuit

In the parallel circuit shown in Figure 1.13 the lamps L_1 and L_2 are connected across each other and across the supply. It therefore follows that the voltage across each of the lamps is the same.

If more than two lamps are placed in parallel the same principle holds true and the voltage across them is equal to the supply voltage. The battery, however, has to supply a greater amount of current and therefore discharges more quickly.

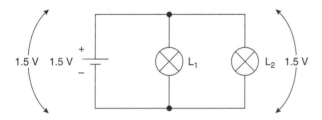

Figure 1.13   Voltage in a parallel circuit

Practical 3

Voltage and current in a parallel circuit

This practical is to get you used to how voltage and current behave in a parallel circuit and what to expect your meter to read. You will need the 5K6 and 10K resistors used in Practical 2 on page 4.

Connect up the circuit shown in Figure 1.14. If you measure the voltage across the resistors you will obtain the same reading for each one. This is because the circuit is parallel and the voltage is common. Remember that this is unlike a series circuit where the voltage is split.

As the circuit is parallel the total current drawn from the supply will split into the two branches of the circuit. Connect the meter as shown in Figure 1.15, taking care to switch first to a high current range. Measure the current via the 5K6 resistor and record it in the table. Now change the wiring so that the meter is connected as shown in Figure 1.16 to determine the current via the 10K resistor. Once again record the reading and enter it in the appropriate part of the table.

For public events where servicing is not easy, lamps are normally connected in parallel so that if one lamp goes out the others are not affected

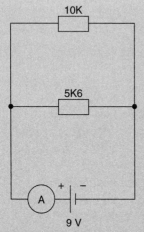

Figure 1.14   The ammeter measures the total current drawn from the 9 V supply. This should equal the sum of the readings from the ammeters in Figures 1.15 and 1.16

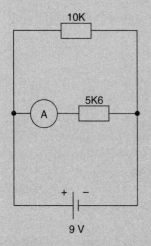

Figure 1.15   The ammeter measures the current via the 5K6 resistor

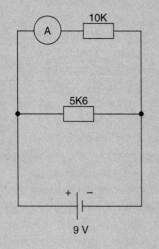

	Meter reading	Calculated
Current via 5K6		
Current via 10K		
Total current		

Figure 1.16   The ammeter measures the current via the 10K resistor

It is possible, of course, to calculate the theoretical results using Ohm's law (see page 8) as follows:

$$R_T = \frac{10 \times 5.6}{10 + 5.6} \text{ k}\Omega$$

$$= \frac{56}{15.6} \text{ k}\Omega$$

$$= 3.59 \text{ k}\Omega$$

$$I_T = \frac{V}{R_T} = \frac{9 \text{ V}}{3.59 \text{ k}\Omega}$$

$$\therefore I_T = 2.5 \text{ mA}$$

$$I_{5K6} = \frac{V}{R} = \frac{9 \text{ V}}{5.6 \text{ k}\Omega} = 1.6 \text{ mA}$$

$$I_{10K} = \frac{V}{R} = \frac{9 \text{ V}}{10 \text{ k}\Omega} = 0.9 \text{ mA}$$

Self-check

$I_{5K6} + I_{10K}$ should equal I, i.e. 1.6 mA + 0.9 mA = 2.5 mA.

Power

When current flows through an imperfect conductor, i.e. one which has some resistance, the electrical energy is changed into other energy forms. In the case of a lamp this is energy which manifests itself as light and heat.

The unit of power is the watt (W) and a power of 1 W will be developed if a current of 1 A flows via a resistance of 1 Ω.

If the power level is large then we talk in thousands of watts or kilowatts (kW). Electrical power engineers are used to calculating in millions of watts, which is more normally referred to as the megawatt (MW).

Electronics engineers are more likely to talk of power in units of less than a watt, such as the milliwatt (mW) and the microwatt (μW).

Two of the most obvious uses of electrical power are the domestic electric heater and a lamp lighting a room in a house. Whenever current flows via an electronic component it will dissipate some power. If the wrong *power rating* of a component is used the component will get hot and eventually burn out. You should remember this when selecting resistors in the design of a circuit as the amount of power dissipated needs to be considered. For further information on the power rating of a resistor see page 11.

Power in a circuit can be calculated using any one of three formulae:

power = current × voltage

$$P = I \times V \qquad (1)$$

power = (voltage)^2 divided by resistance

$$P = \frac{V^2}{R} \qquad (2)$$

power = (current)^2 × resistance

$$P = I^2 R \qquad (3)$$

The decision of which one to use in a particular case depends on the characteristics of the problem being examined.

Guided examples

1   In the circuit shown in Figure 1.17 both the current and the voltage of the circuit are known. Using formula (1) the amount of power dissipated can be calculated as

$$
\begin{aligned}
P &= I \times V \\
&= 0.25 \times 9 \\
&= 2.25 \text{ W}
\end{aligned}
$$

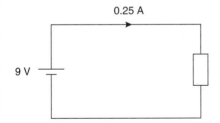

Figure 1.17

NB: 0.25 A could be written as 250 mA. It has exactly the same meaning.

2   In Figure 1.18 the value of the resistance in which the power is developed is given, as is the voltage level of the battery (or source). We can use formula (2) to determine the power that is dissipated:

$$P = \frac{V^2}{R} = \frac{1.5^2}{100} = \frac{2.25}{100}$$

$$= 0.0225 \text{ W}$$

This answer would normally be written as 22.5 mW.

Figure 1.18

3   In Figure 1.19 the circuit current is known, as is the resistance. It is therefore possible to calculate the power that is developed in the load. This can be calculated by using formula (3):

$$
\begin{aligned}
P &= I^2 \times R \\
&= (0.1)^2 \times 1000 \\
&= 0.01 \times 1000 \\
&= 10 \text{ W}
\end{aligned}
$$

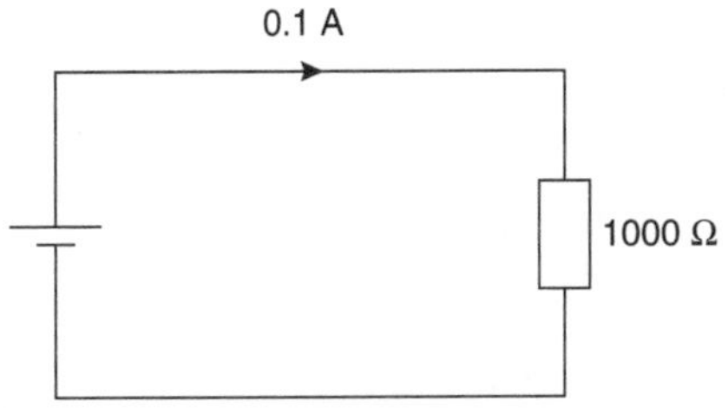

Figure 1.19

Power in a series circuit of more than one element

In the circuit shown in Figure 1.20 the load consists of two resistors in series. The total power developed in the resistors is equal to that drawn from the supply. It can be calculated by adding the resistors together to find the total resistance and then using the appropriate formula:

$$
\begin{aligned}
\text{total resistance } R_{\text{T}} &= R_1 + R_2 \\
&= 330 + 220 \\
&= 550 \ \Omega
\end{aligned}
$$

$$\text{power} = \frac{V^2}{R}$$

$$= \frac{9^2}{550} = \frac{81}{550}$$

$$= 0.147 \text{ W} = 147 \text{ mW}$$

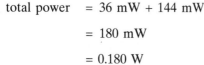

Figure 1.20

Power in a parallel circuit

As the circuit shown in Figure 1.21 is parallel the voltage across each resistor is the same. The total circuit power may therefore be found by working out the power in each component and then adding the individual totals together:

$$\text{power in } R_1 = \frac{V^2}{R_1}$$

$$= \frac{6^2}{1000}$$

$$= 0.036 \text{ W}$$

$$= 36 \text{ mW}$$

$$\text{power in } R_2 = \frac{V^2}{R_2}$$

$$= \frac{6^2}{250}$$

$$= 0.144 \text{ W}$$

$$= 144 \text{ mW}$$

$$\text{total power} = 36 \text{ mW} + 144 \text{ mW}$$

$$= 180 \text{ mW}$$

$$= 0.180 \text{ W}$$

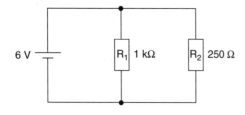

Figure 1.21

1.2 Ohm's law

Current, which can be defined as a flow of electrons, passes through some materials more easily than others. The opposition to the flow of electrons through a material is called the resistance.

> Resistance is defined as the opposition to the flow of electric current.

This means that the greater the resistance the less the current present in a circuit and, conversely, the less the resistance the greater the current in the circuit.

For example, copper, gold, silver and platinum are all good conductors and therefore have a low resistance. On the other hand, carbon, dry wood, china and PVC will not readily allow current to flow and are therefore said to have a high resistance. These are known as insulators.

The relationship that resistance has to current and voltage was investigated by Georg Ohm in 1827. The relationship is summarised by Ohm's law:

> The current through a conductor is directly proportional to the applied voltage and inversely proportional to the resistance of the conductor provided that the conductor is at a uniform temperature.

Mathematically, this can be written

$$I \propto \frac{1}{R} \quad \text{and} \quad I \propto V$$

Therefore

$$I = \frac{V}{R} \quad V = I \times R \quad \text{and} \quad R = \frac{V}{I}$$

If you find maths difficult, the triangle trick, shown in Figure 1.22, will help you when using

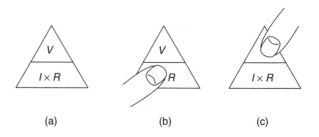

Figure 1.22 Diagrammatical representation of Ohm's law

Exercise 1

Complete the following:

1 (i)   25 µA + 0.296 A + 300 mA   = _____

(ii) 6.2 kΩ + 1.0 MΩ + 220 Ω   = _____

(iii) 16 kV + 3000 V + 0.8 kV   = _____

(iv) 0.8 Ω + 4 × 10⁻³ Ω + 16 Ω   = _____

(v) 392 mA + 0.0079 A + 1800 µA = _____

2

Standard form	Decimal	Engineering form
6.314×10^5 A	631400.0 A	631.4 kA
	112103 Ω	
		16 mA
	9286 V	
		22 µF
1.264×10^{-3}		
	1200000000	
		4700 µF
	0.00822 V	
2.2×10^7 Ω		
		0.8 mA

3 18 000 Ω   = _____

_____ mA = 21.82 A

3564 Ω   = _____ kΩ

_____ A   = 1526 µA

960 µA   = _____ A

the equations. Cover what you want to know with your finger and see what the remaining quantity equals. For example, in Figure 1.22(b) I (current) is covered and the part of the triangle still visible indicates that current is equal to voltage divided by resistance.

The unit of resistance, the ohm, is very small and it is quite normal to use many thousands of ohms at a time. For this reason it is common to talk of kilo-ohms (kΩ) and mega-ohms (MΩ) meaning thousands and millions of ohms respectively.

Mathematically it is normal to express these in engineering standard form:

$$1 \text{ k}\Omega = 1000 \ \Omega = 1 \times 10^3 \ \Omega$$

$$1 \text{ M}\Omega = 1 \ 000 \ 000 \ \Omega = 1 \times 10^6 \ \Omega$$

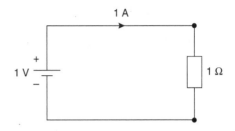

Figure 1.23   The simplest Ohm's law calculation

The simplest Ohm's law calculation is as follows. In Figure 1.23 the battery – or source – has a value of 1 V. The load across which the battery is connected is a resistor which has the unlikely value of 1 Ω. The current is given by

$$I = \frac{V}{R} = \frac{1 \text{ V}}{1 \ \Omega} = 1 \text{ A}$$

The voltage and resistance equations can be used to check this result:

$$V = I \times R = 1 \text{ A} \times 1 \ \Omega = 1 \text{ V}$$

$$R = \frac{V}{I} = \frac{1 \text{ V}}{1 \text{ A}} = 1 \ \Omega$$

This circuit is a little too simple to have much practical value but it does serve to illustrate the principle of Ohm's law. Figure 1.24 gives some more examples.

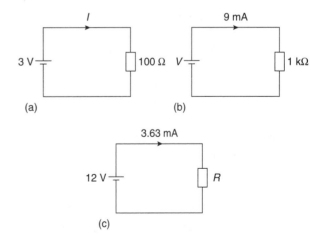

Figure 1.24

In Figure 1.24(a),

$$I = \frac{V}{R} = \frac{3 \text{ V}}{100 \ \Omega}$$

$$= 0.03 \text{ A} = 30 \times 10^{-3} \text{ A} = 30 \text{ mA}$$

In Figure 1.24(b),

$$V = I \times R$$

$$= 9 \text{ mA} \times 1 \text{ k}\Omega$$

$$= 9 \times 10^{-3} \text{ A} \times 1 \times 10^3 \text{ }\Omega$$

$$= 0.009 \text{ A} \times 1000 \text{ }\Omega$$

$$= 9 \text{ V}$$

In Figure 1.24(c),

$$R = \frac{V}{I} = \frac{12 \text{ V}}{3.63 \text{ mA}}$$

$$= \frac{12 \text{ V}}{0.00363 \text{ A}} = 3305 \text{ }\Omega = 3.3 \text{ k}\Omega$$

As you will probably know, it is only the simplest circuits that have only one resistor. More often there is a combination of resistors which can be resolved into the equivalent of one resistor. This is discussed further in the section on network theory (page 22).

1.3 Resistors

The manufactured version of resistance is the resistor. This is an electrical component which, when used as part of an electrical circuit, is intended to introduce a certain amount of resistance into the circuit. In many applications the purpose of the resistor is to prevent the amount of current exceeding a certain value.

Two symbols are used to designate a resistor; these are given in Figure 1.25. Common types of resistors include wire-wound resistors, carbon and metal film resistors and moulded carbon resistors.

Figure 1.25 Symbols used to designate a resistor in a circuit

Wire-wound resistor

Wire-wound resistors

Wire-wound resistors are made by using lengths of wire of which the exact resistance per centimetre is known. The wire is then wound round a former and covered with a coating such as vitreous enamel. The coating protects against moisture and also acts as an insulator.

Wire-wound resistors are typically used in applications where a high power dissipation is required. They suffer from the disadvantage that, unless special methods of construction are adopted, they have inductive properties which can affect their behaviour at high frequencies.

Carbon and metal film resistors

Carbon and metal film resistors are manufactured by depositing carbon onto a ceramic or metal substrate. A wide range of values can be produced with a good degree of accuracy. Tolerances of ±2% are common.

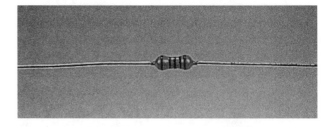

Carbon film resistor

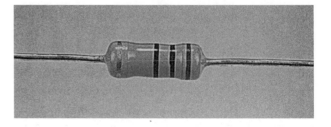

Metal film resistor

Carbon composition resistors

Carbon composition resistors are manufactured by mixing carbon granules in an adhesive binder. The amount of carbon is changed to alter the amount of resistance. The disadvantage is that their resistance values are not very accurate, with tolerances of around ± 10% being common.

Tolerance

Tolerance gives an indication of the possible maximum and minimum values by which a resistor may deviate from its specified value. Common tolerance values are 2%, 5%, 10% and 20%.

A 1000 Ω resistor which had a stated tolerance value of 10% could have an actual value of between

$$1000 - 10\% = 1000 - 100 = 900 \ \Omega$$

and

$$1000 + 10\% = 1000 + 100 = 1100 \ \Omega$$

Tolerance series

The mathematical basis of the tolerance series of preferred values is based on the root of 10 of that series. Thus the E6 20% series has six values between 1 and 6.8 as follows:

1.0, 1.5, 2.2, 3.3, 4.7, 6.8

The E12 series of 10% tolerance has twelve values which are calculated in the same manner. There are twelve values between 1 and 10:

1.0, 1.2, 1.5, 1.8, 2.2, 2.7, 3.3, 3.9, 4.7, 5.6, 6.8, 8.2

The E24 5% series has twenty-four values:

1.0, 1.1, 1.2, 1.3, 1.5, 1.6, 1.8, 2.0, 2.2, 2.4, 2.7, 3.0, 3.3, 3.6, 3.9, 4.3, 4.7, 5.1, 5.6, 6.2, 6.8, 7.5, 8.2, 9.1

Because a resistor may have any value within its tolerance above its coded value, manufacturers produce a range of values (preferred values) to cover all possible resistances. For example, in E24 there would be 1 Ω, 10 Ω, 100 Ω, 1 kΩ etc. or 1.1 Ω, 110 Ω, 1.1 kΩ and so on.

Power rating

The power rating is the maximum continuous power that can be dissipated by the resistor without risk of damage. The power can be calculated using the standard formula $P = I^2R$ watts.

The physical size of a resistor is a good guide to its power rating. The greater the size of the resistor the larger its rating. A typical power rating would be quoted as 0.25 W at 70 °C.

Stability

The stability expresses how accurately a resistor can maintain its value over a given length of time.

Code marking of resistors

Resistors are marked in a number of ways to enable you to determine what value and tolerance they have. The most common are explained below.

The colour code

A resistor has coloured bands painted on it towards one end. There can be three, four or five bands. Each colour represents a digit (see Table 1.1). The value of the resistor may be decoded from the bands.

Table 1.1

Colour	Digit
Black	0
Brown	1
Red	2
Orange	3
Yellow	4
Green	5
Blue	6
Violet	7
Grey	8
White	9

The colour code used for resistors is also very often used for wiring, e.g. a red wire would go to tag 2, a green wire to tag 5 etc.

Four-banded resistors With four-banded resistors the first two bands signify the digits of the resistor value and the third band the number of zeros to add (it is sometimes referred to as the multiplier). The fourth band gives details of the resistor's tolerance (Figure 1.26).

Three-banded resistors These are decoded in exactly the same way as four-banded resistors

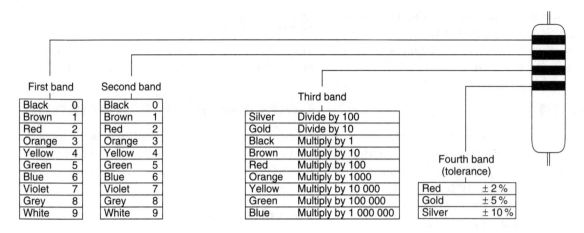

Figure 1.26   Four-banded resistors

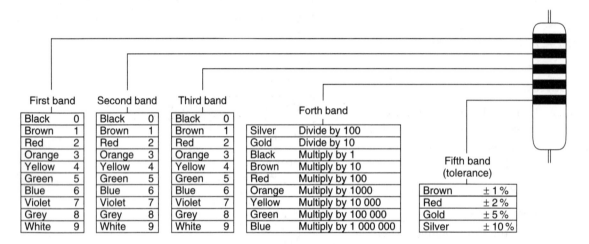

Figure 1.27   Five-banded resistors

Table 1.2

Value	Code mark
0.27 Ω	R27
3.3 Ω	3R3
10 Ω	10R
220 Ω	220R
1 kΩ	1K0
68 kΩ	68K
4.7 MΩ	4M7

except that the tolerance band is not present.
No fourth band signifies ±20% tolerance.

Five-banded resistors   You will see from Figure
1.27 that five-banded resistors are decoded in a
very similar manner to four-banded resistors,
although a greater accuracy can be expressed.

The printed code

A printed code is put on the side of a resistor and
is commonly used for wire-wound and other high
wattage resistors. It is also found on circuit
diagrams.

The code consists of letters and numbers:

R = × 1

K = × 1000

M = × 1 000 000

Examples of resistor markings using the printed
code are given in Table 1.2. Tolerances are added
by placing an extra letter at the end of the code,
the extra letter being as follows:

J   ±   5%

K   ±   10%

M   ±   20%

A 470 Ω resistor with a 10% tolerance would have
a printed code marking of

470R K

Exercise 2

Complete the following tables to familiarise yourself with the resistor colour codes.

1

Value	First band	Second band	Third band	Fourth band	Max/min value
18 Ω ± 10%					
220 Ω ± 5%					
56 kΩ ± 10%					
6.8 kΩ ± 5%					
470 kΩ ± 20%					
3.3 kΩ ± 5%					
1.2 kΩ ± 10%					

2

Value	First band	Second band	Third band	Fourth band	Max/min value
	Yellow	Violet	Orange	Gold	
	Red	Violet	Brown	Silver	
	Orange	White	Red	Silver	
	Blue	Grey	Silver	Gold	
	Grey	Red	Green	Silver	
	Orange	Orange	Brown	No band	
	White	Brown	Black	Gold	

Answers

1 Brown Grey Black Silver
   Red Red Brown Gold
   Green Blue Orange Silver
   Blue Grey Gold Gold
   Yellow Violet Yellow
   Orange Orange Red Gold
   Brown Red Red Silver

2 47 kΩ ± 5%   44.65 kΩ→ 49.35 kΩ
   270 Ω ± 10%   243 Ω→ 297 Ω
   3.9 kΩ ± 10%   3.51 kΩ→ 4.29 kΩ
   0.69 Ω ± 5%   0.655 Ω→ 0.724 Ω
   9.2 MΩ ± 10%   8.28 MΩ→ 10.12 MΩ
   330 Ω ± 20%   264 Ω→ 396 Ω
   91 Ω ± 5%   86.45 Ω→ 95.55 Ω

Variable resistors

A variable resistor is a type of resistor that allows the exact amount of resistance used to be adjusted.

In Figure 1.28 the resistance between the two ends of the track is, say, 1 kΩ. The moving contact, known as the wiper or slider, can be positioned to tap off any proportion of the 1 kΩ. If, for example, it was set half way the resistance between either track end and the slider would be 500 Ω.

Variable resistors are also known as potentiometers or 'pots' and are available in rotary or slider form. For low wattage purposes they are manufactured from carbon. Wire-wound

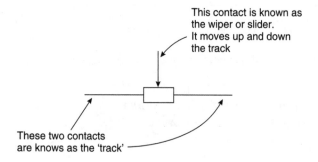

Figure 1.28   *A variable resistor*

construction is used where higher powers are handled. Common values of potentiometers are 1K, 4K7, 10K, 22K, 47K, 100K, 470K.

Log and lin

Variable resistors are specified not only by their value but also by the manner in which the resistance changes as the slider moves over the track. If the change in resistance between the slider and one end of the track is proportional to the amount that the slider is moved the potentiometer is said to have a linear movement.

A logarithmic potentiometer is manufactured so that the resistance between slider and track changes in a logarithmic manner as the slider is adjusted. 'Log' pots are used in volume control and other audio applications.

Preset variables

A preset potentiometer (Figure 1.29) is similar to a conventional variable resistor except that its setting is usually adjusted by a screwdriver. Once set it is not normally altered.

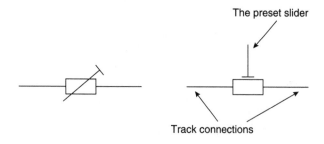

Figure 1.29   *Preset potentiometers*

When a preset variable is incorporated into a circuit it is sometimes referred to as a trimmer and can be used to finely adjust a voltage (see Figure 1.30).

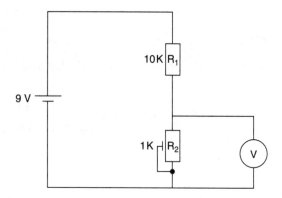

Figure 1.30   *Adjusting the preset potentiometer will give a 'fine control' of the voltage across it (i.e. it will 'trim' it)*

Practical connection of a variable/preset resistor

A variable resistor can be connected in a circuit in one of two ways, as shown in Figure 1.31. If a variable resistor is to be used as part of a potential divider network to set the voltage at a point in the circuit, it is good practice to incorporate a low value resistor between the track of the variable and the supply. This safety measure prevents the full supply being applied to the slider when it is wound fully home (see Figure 1.32).

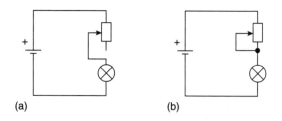

Figure 1.31   *Practical connection of a variable resistor*

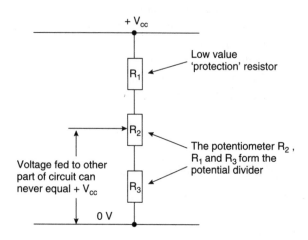

Figure 1.32

Preset resistor

The light-dependent resistor

With a light-dependent resistor (LDR) the value of the resistance varies between limits according to the amount of light that is incident upon it. It is not the same as a photo cell, which generates a voltage when light is incident upon it. Its symbol is given in Figure 1.33. The resistance of the resistor decreases as the intensity of light it is exposed to increases (see Figure 1.34).

One of the most common LDRs is the ORP12. In complete darkness it has a maximum resistance value of mega-ohms. This can decrease to as little as 80 Ω in bright light. This LDR finds wide application in circuits which are controlled by light, e.g. automatic outside lights, conveyor stop–start mechanisms in factories etc. (see Figure 1.35).

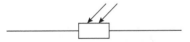

Figure 1.33   Symbol used to designate a light-dependent resistor in a circuit

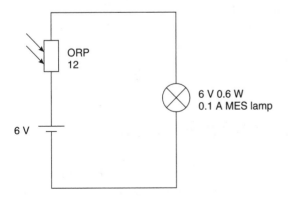

Figure 1.34   Covering and uncovering the LDR will cause the brightness of the lamp to alter

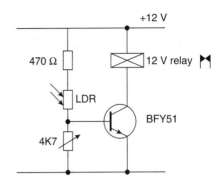

(a)

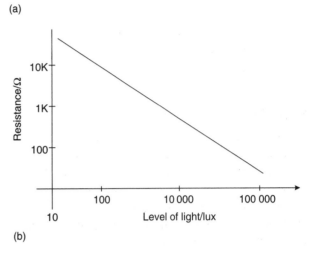

(b)

Figure 1.35   (a) Relay activated by ORP12; (b) graph showing the typical change of an ORP12's resistance to different levels of light

ORP12

The thermistor

Unlike a conventional resistor where it is important that value does not change with variations in temperature, the thermistor is manufactured so that it does exactly this. There are two types of thermistor. If the ohmic value increases as the temperature increases the thermistor is said to have a positive temperature coefficient. Alternatively, the temperature coefficient is said to be negative if the resistance of the thermistor decreases as the

Bead thermistor and disc thermistor

(a)   (b)

Figure 1.36   Symbol used for a thermistor with (a) a positive temperature coefficient and (b) a negative temperature coefficient

temperature increases. Figure 1.36 gives the symbols used for each of these resistors.

Thermistor types are quoted according to their ohmic value at a certain temperature. Typical examples would be:

1500 Ω (±20%) at 25 °C changing to 52 Ω at 125 °C

15 kΩ (±5%) at 25 °C changing to 320 Ω at 100 °C

Thermistors are used in heat- and temperature-sensing circuits, often in conjunction with an integrated circuit known as a comparator (see page 166).

Measuring a resistor

To measure the value of a resistor a meter set to the ohms range should be connected directly across the component as shown in Figure 1.37. It is important that your hands are not in contact with the resistor at the time of making the measurement as you will measure your own body resistance in parallel with the ohmic value of the component.

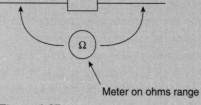

Meter on ohms range

Figure 1.37

When measuring the value of a resistor in a circuit check that the power supply is switched *off*. Failure to switch off is likely to damage the meter or give a false reading.

Checking the resistance in a circuit

When you wish to measure the value of a resistor that is already connected in a circuit you must remember that there may be a parallel path across the resistor that will cause the meter to give a reading different from that expected.

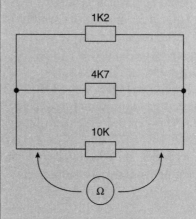

Figure 1.38   The meter reads the equivalent resistance of the 10K, 4K7 and 1K2 resistors in parallel, i.e. 873 Ω and not 10 kΩ

Consider the circuit shown in Figure 1.38. The 10K resistor is in a parallel arrangement with the 4K7 and the 1K2 resistors. The meter reads 873 Ω instead of the expected 10 kΩ as this is the overall equivalent resistance of the circuit.

Resistors in series

Finding the equivalent combination of resistors in series is a simple matter of adding the values of the resistors together, making sure that you are working in common units, i.e. always in ohms, kilo-ohms (kΩ) or mega-ohms (MΩ). In Figure 1.39, for example, between the points x and y the equivalent resistance is $R_1 + R_2 + R_3$. In general,

$$R_T = R_1 + R_2 + R_3 + \ldots + R_n$$

where n is the number of resistors.

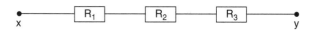

Figure 1.39

Guided examples

1 See Figure 1.40.

$$R_T = R_1 + R_2 + R_3$$
$$= 33\ \Omega + 100\ \Omega + 96\ \Omega$$
$$= 229\ \Omega$$

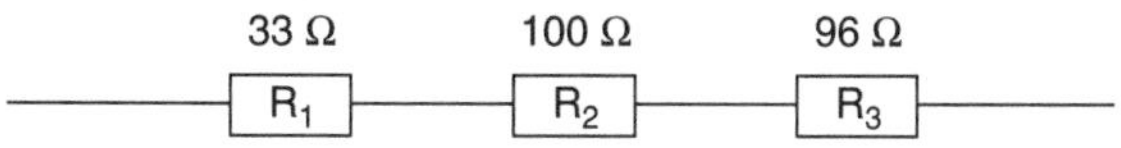

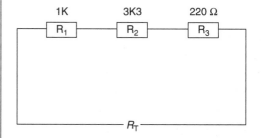

Figure 1.40

2 See Figure 1.41.

$$R_T = R_1 + R_2 + R_3$$
$$= 1\ k\Omega + 3.3\ k\Omega + 220\ \Omega$$
$$= 4.3\ k\Omega + 0.22\ k\Omega$$
$$= 4.52\ k\Omega = 4520\ \Omega$$

Figure 1.41

3 See Figure 1.42 (note how the circuit has been redrawn).

$$R_T = R_1 + R_2 + R_3$$
$$= 10\ k\Omega + 4.7\ k\Omega + 1\ M\Omega$$
$$= 14.7\ k\Omega + 1000\ k\Omega$$
$$= 1014.7\ k\Omega = 1.0147\ M\Omega$$

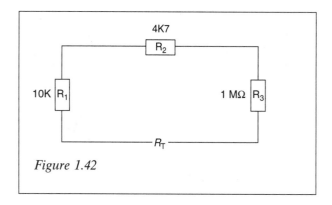

Figure 1.42

Practical 4

Resistors in series

Connect two resistors in a series arrangement as shown in Figure 1.43. Now connect the meter across the ends of the combination as shown and note the reading.

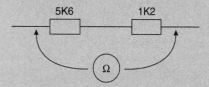

Figure 1.43

Theoretically, the answer is easily obtained by adding the two resistances together:

$$R_T = R_1 + R_2$$
$$= 5.6\ k\Omega + 1.2\ k\Omega$$
$$= 6.8\ k\Omega$$

Your meter reading should be within 20% of the theoretical answer, assuming that each resistor has a tolerance of 10%, i.e. your answer should be between 5.44 kΩ and 8.16 kΩ.

Practical use of resistors in series

Resistors can be used to 'lose' a voltage so that the supply voltage can be reduced to a lower value, for example 12 V can be reduced to 9 V. It is not the most satisfactory method as it wastes power but the problem could be tackled as in Figure 1.44.

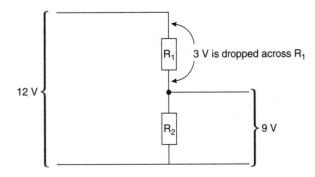

Figure 1.44

Resistors in parallel

Resistors can also be connected in parallel. Once again the combination of resistors can be resolved mathematically into the equivalent of one resistor. Unlike with resistors in series, where values are simply added together, there are two methods for solving a parallel circuit, the product over sum rule and the reciprocal rule.

> Where two resistors of equal value are in parallel with each other, and are not connected to any other component, the overall resistance is equal to half the value of one resistor. For example, two 1K resistors in parallel have an equivalent resistance of 500 Ω (see Figure 1.45).

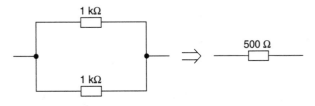

Figure 1.45

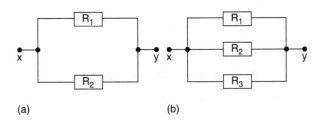

(a)   (b)

Figure 1.46

The product over sum rule can be used if there are only two resistors in parallel. It is simple and easy to use and states that the equivalent resistance between x and y in Figure 1.46(a) is given by

$$R_T = \frac{R_1 \times R_2}{R_1 + R_2} = \frac{\text{product}}{\text{sum}}$$

The reciprocal rule is used if there are more than two resistors in parallel. In Figure 1.46(b) the resistance between x and y is given by

$$\frac{1}{R_T} = \frac{1}{R_1} + \frac{1}{R_2} + \frac{1}{R_3}$$

$$\therefore R_T = \frac{1}{1/R_1 + 1/R_2 + 1/R_3}$$

Guided examples

1   See Figure 1.47.

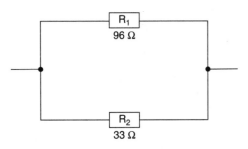

Figure 1.47

$$R_T = \frac{R_1 \times R_2}{R_1 + R_2} = \frac{96 \times 33}{96 + 33} = \frac{3168}{129}$$

$$\therefore R_T = 24.56 \ \Omega$$

Alternatively, using the reciprocal rule:

$$\frac{1}{R_T} = \frac{1}{R_1} + \frac{1}{R_2}$$

$$= \frac{1}{96} + \frac{1}{33}$$

$$= 0.0104 + 0.0303$$

$$= 0.0407$$

Now take the reciprocal of this by dividing it into 1 or using the $1/x$ key on your calculator:

$$R_T = 24.57 \ \Omega$$

which is almost the same!

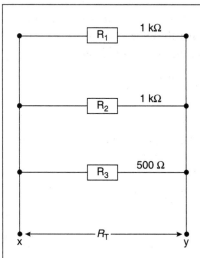

Figure 1.48

2 See Figure 1.48. Using the reciprocal rule the resistance between x and y is

$$\frac{1}{R_T} = \frac{1}{R_1} + \frac{1}{R_2} + \frac{1}{R_3}$$

$$= \frac{1}{1\text{ k}\Omega} + \frac{1}{1\text{ k}\Omega} + \frac{1}{500\ \Omega}$$

$$= \frac{1}{1000} + \frac{1}{1000} + \frac{1}{500}$$

$$= 1 \times 10^{-3} + 1 \times 10^{-3} + 2 \times 10^{-3}$$

$$= 4 \times 10^{-3}$$

$$\therefore R_T = \frac{1}{4 \times 10^{-3}}$$

$$= 0.25 \times 10^3$$

$$= 250\ \Omega$$

Alternative quick method

Did you spot that R_1 and R_2 were both 1 kΩ? Their equivalent resistance is therefore 500 Ω. The circuit can now be redrawn as in Figure 1.49. The overall equivalent resistance is 500 Ω in parallel with 500 Ω which is 250 Ω.

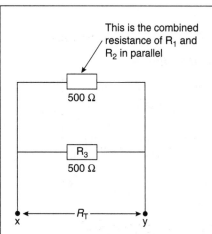

Figure 1.49

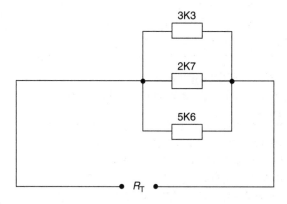

Figure 1.50

3 See Figure 1.50.

$$\frac{1}{R_T} = \frac{1}{R_1} + \frac{1}{R_2} + \frac{1}{R_3}$$

$$= \frac{1}{3.3} + \frac{1}{2.7} + \frac{1}{5.6}$$

$$= 0.303 + 0.3703 + 0.178$$

$$\therefore \frac{1}{R_T} = 0.852$$

$$\therefore R_T = \frac{1}{0.852} = 1.17\text{ k}\Omega$$

Practical 5

Resistors in parallel

Connect two resistors in a parallel arrangement as shown in Figure 1.51. Now connect the meter across the ends of the combination as shown and note the reading.

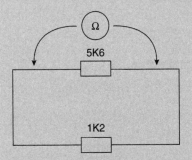

Figure 1.51

Theoretically, the answer is easily obtained by calculating the effective value of the two resistors together:

$$R_T = \frac{R_1 \times R_2}{R_1 + R_2}$$

$$= \frac{5.6 \times 1.2}{5.6 + 1.2} \, k\Omega$$

$$= 0.988 \, k\Omega = 988 \, \Omega$$

Your meter reading should be within 20% of the theoretical answer, assuming that each resistor has a tolerance of 10%, i.e. your answer should be between 790.4 Ω and 1185.6 Ω.

Resistors in series–parallel circuits

In Figure 1.52 resistors are placed in series and in parallel. R_1 is in series with R_2 which is in parallel with R_3. To solve a circuit such as this it is normal practice to tackle the parallel circuit first, resolving this into its equivalent resistance and then adding the result to the value of the series resistor. Examples of this procedure are given in the following Guided Examples.

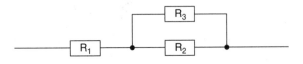

Figure 1.52

Guided examples

1　In Figure 1.53 the total resistance between x and y is given by

$$R_T = R_1 + \frac{R_2 \times R_3}{R_2 + R_3}$$

$$= 1 + \frac{5.6 \times 10}{5.6 + 10}$$

where we are working in kilo-ohms, so

$$R_T = 1 + \frac{56}{15.6}$$

$$= 1 + 3.59$$

$$\therefore R_T = 4.59 \, k\Omega$$

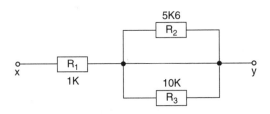

Figure 1.53

2　In Figure 1.54,

$$R_T = R_1 + R_2 \| R_3 + R_4$$

where $\|$ means 'in parallel with'; therefore

$$R_T = 10 + \frac{1}{1/5.6 + 1/10} + 0.56$$

where we are again working in kilo-ohms. So

$$R_T = 10 + \frac{1}{0.178 + 0.1} + 0.56$$

$$= 10 + 3.60 + 0.56$$

$$= 14.16 \, k\Omega$$

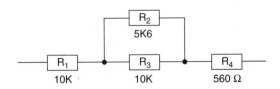

Figure 1.54

3 In Figure 1.55,

$$R_T = R_1 \| R_2 \| R_3 + R_4$$

$$= \frac{1}{1/10 + 1/2.7 + 1/6.8} + 220$$

$$= \frac{1}{0.1 + 0.37 + 0.147} + 220$$

$$= \frac{1}{0.617} + 220$$

$$= 1.62 + 220$$

$$= 221.62 \text{ k}\Omega$$

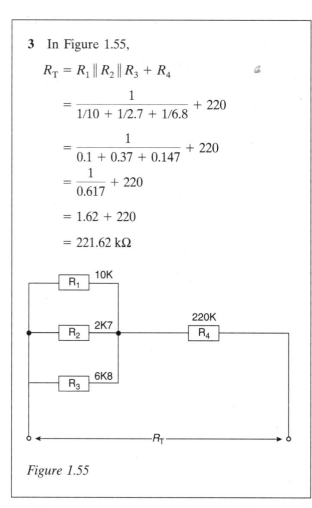

Figure 1.55

Practical 6

Resistors in series–parallel

In Practicals 4 and 5 you used series and parallel connections. The next circuit is a combination of the two and hence is known as the series–parallel connection.

Connect the circuit as shown in Figure 1.56 and use a meter to measure the voltages across each of the resistors, recording your answers in the table provided.

Now use the meter to measure the current via each of the resistors as shown in Figure 1.57. Enter the answers in the appropriate parts of the table.

Of course, once again it is possible to calculate the currents in the circuit and then compare practical results with theoretical answers. The calculations are shown below:

$$R_T = 6.8 + \frac{5.6 \times 1.2}{5.6 + 1.2}$$

working in kilo-ohms, so

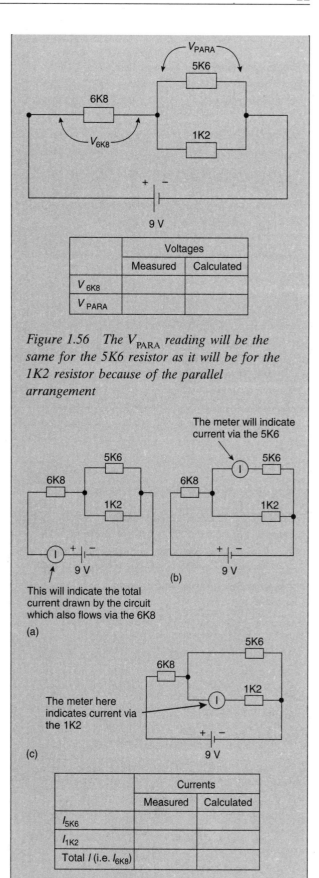

	Voltages	
	Measured	Calculated
V_{6K8}		
V_{PARA}		

Figure 1.56 The V_{PARA} reading will be the same for the 5K6 resistor as it will be for the 1K2 resistor because of the parallel arrangement

The meter will indicate current via the 5K6

This will indicate the total current drawn by the circuit which also flows via the 6K8

(a)

(b)

The meter here indicates current via the 1K2

(c)

	Currents	
	Measured	Calculated
I_{5K6}		
I_{1K2}		
Total I (i.e. I_{6K8})		

Figure 1.57 The meters will read (a) the total current drawn by the circuit, which is also the current via the 6K8 resistor; (b) the current via the 5K6 resistor; (c) the current via the 1K2 resistor

$$R_T = 6.8 + \frac{6.72}{6.8}$$

$$= 7.78 \text{ k}\Omega$$

$$I_T = \frac{V}{R_T} = \frac{9 \text{ V}}{7.78 \text{ k}\Omega} = 1.16 \text{ mA}$$

$$V_{6K8} = I \times R$$

$$= 1.16 \text{ mA} \times 6.8 \text{ k}\Omega$$

$$V_{6K8} = 7.89 \text{ V}$$

$$V_{5K6} \text{ or } V_{1K2} = \text{supply voltage} - V_{6K8}$$

$$= 9 - 7.89$$

$$= 1.11 \text{ V}$$

$$I_{5K6} = \frac{V}{R} = \frac{1.11 \text{ V}}{5.6 \text{ k}\Omega} = 0.198 \text{ V}$$

$$I_{1K2} = \frac{V}{R} = \frac{1.11 \text{ V}}{1.2 \text{ k}\Omega} = 0.925 \text{ V}$$

Open and short circuits

Resistance checks are one of the ways in which the location of a fault in a circuit can be narrowed down to a specific area. There are two extremes of incorrect resistance: the open circuit and the short circuit.

The open circuit

Points x and y in Figure 1.58 indicate a break in the circuit. The resistance between the two points is very large, in fact to all intents and purposes it is equal to infinity. No current can flow through this infinite resistance and so no voltage is present on the other side of it,

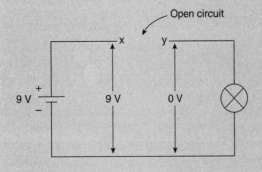

Figure 1.58 The lamp does not light as no current can pass through the infinite resistance of the open circuit

although a voltage can be measured at the point of open circuit.

The short circuit

The short circuit is the opposite of the open circuit and is another common fault. A short circuit occurs where two parts of a circuit touch each other. In Figure 1.59 the short is present at points P and Q. Because the points are in direct contact with each other the resistance between them is zero and maximum current will flow. The voltage across a short circuit is always zero.

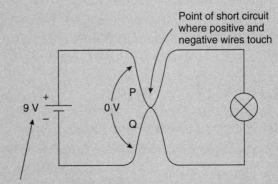

Figure 1.59 The 9 V will drop to 0 V the instant that the short circuit occurs. The lamp does not light as all the current passes through the short circuit which is the path of least resistance

1.4 **Network theory**

So far we have considered simple circuits which have series, parallel or series–parallel combinations of resistors and lamps. In every case they were solved by reducing the combination to one resistor whose value was equivalent to the value of all the individual resistors.

This method breaks down when circuits become more complicated. Consider, for example, the circuit depicted in Figure 1.60.

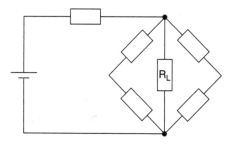

Figure 1.60

How would you go about finding the current through the middle resistor R_L using Ohm's law? Although it is possible to solve it by the above method, the calculation is very complex. A better method is to use one of the laws of network theory. These are Kirchhoff's laws, the superposition theorem, Thévenin's theorem and Norton's theorem.

Kirchhoff's laws

Kirchhoff's first law (or current law)

This first law states that:

> The algebraic sum of the currents at any node in a network is zero

This can be expressed mathematically as

$$\Sigma i = 0 \text{ at any node}$$

where the Greek letter sigma (Σ) means 'sum'.

Fine, but what does it mean?

Any point in a circuit where two or more currents meet is called a node. An easier way of saying this is: 'what flows in must flow out'.

Imagine a point P in a circuit where several current paths meet (Figure 1.61). If we decide that currents flowing towards P are positive and those flowing away from P are negative then the

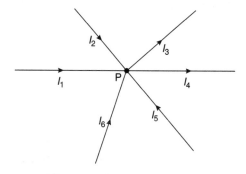

Figure 1.61

algebraic sum is, according to Kirchhoff,

$$I_1 + I_2 - I_3 - I_4 + I_5 + I_6 = 0$$

and so

$$I_1 + I_2 + I_5 + I_6 = I_3 + I_4$$

Kirchhoff's second law (or voltage law)

This second law states that:

> In any mesh (or closed loop) of a network the algebraic sum of the e.m.f.s applied within the mesh is equal to the algebraic sum of the voltage drops around the mesh.

We already know, from Ohm's law, that a voltage drop or potential difference is the product of resistance and the current that flows through that resistance ($V = IR$). From this we can express Kirchhoff's second law mathematically as

$$\Sigma E = \Sigma(IR) \text{ in any closed loop}$$

If we stop to think about this it's pretty obvious. Just looking at a simple series closed loop (Figure 1.62) we can use Ohm's law to verify the second law.

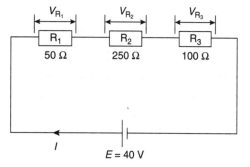

Figure 1.62

Ohm says:

$$I = \frac{E}{R_T}$$

Here R_T is the total series resistance:

$$R_T = R_1 + R_2 + R_3$$
$$= (50 + 250 + 100) \ \Omega$$

Therefore

$$R_T = 400 \ \Omega$$

So

$$I = \frac{40}{400} \text{ A}$$

Therefore

$$I = 100 \text{ mA}$$

Kirchhoff says:

$$E = V_{R_1} + V_{R_2} + V_{R_3}$$

Now $V = IR$, so

$$V_{R_1} = (100 \times 10^{-3}) \times 50 = 5 \text{ V}$$

$$V_{R_2} = (100 \times 10^{-3}) \times 250 = 25 \text{ V}$$

$$V_{R_3} = (100 \times 10^{-3}) \times 100 = 10 \text{ V}$$

So, according to Kirchhoff,

$$E = (5 + 25 + 10) \text{ V}$$

$$= 40 \text{ V, which is correct!}$$

This means that Kirchhoff's second law and Ohm's law appear not to contradict each other which is good news!

Now we shall learn how to apply Kirchhoff's laws to various networks to determine any unknown current or voltages.

First we divide the network into separate loops and allocate a current to each loop. **Next** we generate equations relating voltage drops to e.m.f.s within each loop. **Finally**, we solve these equations simultaneously to find each unknown in turn. Let's try a few examples, step by step.

Find the current flowing through each of

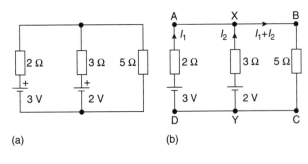

(a) (b)

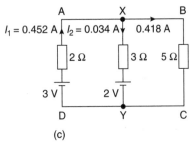

(c)

Figure 1.63 Note that in part (c) I_2 is shown flowing in its true direction

the resistors in the circuit shown in Figure 1.63(a).

First we need to label each node or corner and the current in each branch of the circuit. If it turns out that the actual current in the circuit is flowing in a different direction to the one we have picked, it will not matter. The magnitude of the current will be correct and a minus sign in the answer will tell us that our chosen direction is wrong (Figure 1.63(b)).

Let us suppose that the current is flowing in the conventional direction for each of the e.m.f. sources in our circuit, i.e. the circuit is labelled as shown in Figure 1.63(b). In this circuit we have three loops, ABCDA, AXYDA and XBCYX. We also have two unknown currents, I_1 and I_2, so we need to generate two simultaneous equations (one for each unknown).

Let us choose loops ABCDA and XBCYX and develop equations for each loop. The e.m.f. within the loop must be equal to the voltage drops around that loop: for the loop ABCDA,

$$3 = 2I_1 + 5(I_1 + I_2)$$

$$\therefore 3 = 7I_1 + 5I_2 \tag{1}$$

For loop XBCYX,

$$2 = 3I_2 + 5(I_1 + I_2)$$

$$\therefore 2 = 5I_1 + 8I_2 \tag{2}$$

Now we have to solve these equations simultaneously. Multiply Equation (1) by 8 to get

$$24 = 56I_1 + 40I_2 \tag{3}$$

Multiply Equation (2) by 5 to get

$$10 = 25I_1 + 40I_2 \tag{4}$$

Next, subtract (4) from (3) to give

$$14 = 31I_1$$

$$I_1 = 14/31 = 0.452 \text{ A}$$

Now we have a value for I_1 we can substitute it into Equation (1) to get I_2:

$$3 = 7(0.452) + 5I_2$$

$$3 = 3.17 + 5I_2$$

$$3 - 3.17 = 5I_2$$

$$I_2 = \frac{3 - 3.17}{5} \text{ A}$$

$$= -0.034 \text{ A}$$

This means that I_2 is flowing in the opposite direction to the one we chose initially. The current through the 5 Ω resistor is $I_1 + I_2 = 0.452 - 0.034 = 0.418$ A. Figure 1.63(c) illustrates the results.

Guided examples

1 Calculate the current flowing through each of the resistors in the circuit given in Figure 1.64(a).

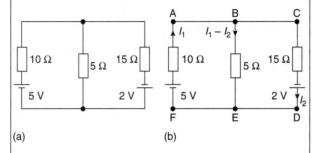

(a)   (b)

Figure 1.64

Once again we need to allocate loops and currents as shown in Figure 1.64(b).

Loop ABEFA

$$5 = 10I_1 + 5(I_1 - I_2)$$

$$\therefore\ 5 = 15I_1 - 5I_2 \tag{1}$$

Loop BCDEB

$$2 = -5(I_1 - I_2) + 15I_2$$

$$\therefore\ 2 = -5I_1 + 20I_2 \tag{2}$$

Multiply Equation (2) by 3 to get

$$6 = -15I_1 + 60I_2 \tag{3}$$

Add (1) to (3) to give

$$11 = 55I_2$$

$$\therefore\ I_2 = 11/55 = 0.2\ \text{A}$$

Substitute for I_2 in (1) to give

$$5 = 15I_1 - 1$$

$$\therefore\ I_1 = (5 + 1)/15 = 0.4\ \text{A}$$

Therefore, the current in the 5 Ω resistor is

$$0.4 - 0.2 = 0.2\ \text{A}$$

Just as a check calculate the voltage across each arm of the circuit using Ohm's law:

$$V_{AF} = 5 - 10(0.4) = 1\ \text{V}$$

$$V_{BE} = 5(0.2) = 1\ \text{V}$$

$$V_{CD} = 15(0.2) - 2 = 1\ \text{V}$$

As the resistors are in a parallel arrangement the voltage across each one should be the same, which is true.

2 Calculate the current in the 10 Ω resistor in the circuit shown in Figure 1.65(a).

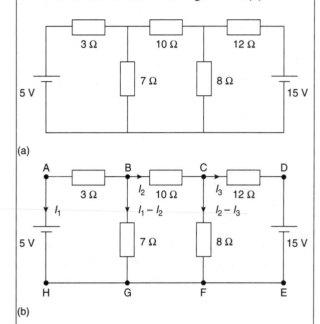

(a)

(b)

Figure 1.65

Label the loops and allocate currents as shown in Figure 1.65(b). This time we have three unknowns, I_1, I_2 and I_3, and so we need to generate three equations.

Loop ABGHA

$$5 = 3I_1 + 7(I_1 - I_2)$$

$$5 = 10I_1 - 7I_2$$

$$\therefore\ I_2 = 0.5 + 0.7I_2 \tag{1}$$

Loop BCFGB

$$0 = 10I_2 + 8(I_2 - I_3) - 7(I_1 - I_2)$$

$$\therefore\ 0 = 25I_2 - 7I_2 - 8I_2 \tag{2}$$

Loop CDEFC

$$-15 = 12I_3 - 8(I_2 - I_3)$$

$$-15 = 20I_3 - 8I_2$$

$$\therefore\ I_3 = -0.75 + 0.4I_2 \tag{3}$$

Now we substitute (1) and (3) in place of I_1 and I_3 in (2) to get

$$0 = -(0.5 + 0.7I_2) + 25I_2 - (-0.75 + 0.4I_2)$$

$$0 = -3.5 - 4.91I_2 + 25I_2 - 3.2I_2 + 6$$

$$16.9I_2 = -2.5$$

$$\therefore \quad I_2 = -0.15 \text{ A}$$

So 0.15 A is flowing through the 10 Ω resistor in the opposite direction to the direction which we marked on the circuit diagram.

Practical 7

Kirchhoff's laws

The object of this practical is for you to prove to yourself that Kirchhoff's laws hold true. You will build a circuit and use it to measure voltages and currents. You can then calculate the theoretical answers and compare them with the practical ones. Hopefully they will agree!

Set up the circuit as shown in Figure 1.66. Note that during the course of the practical it will be necessary to disconnect resistors to insert meters so do not make the wiring too permanent.

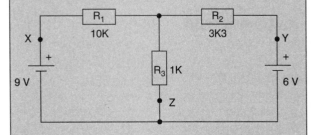

Figure 1.66

Use a meter set to the appropriate range to measure the voltage across each of the three resistors and record the readings in the results table.

Taking a reading of the current is slightly more complicated than measuring the voltage drops. A current meter has to be inserted in turn near each resistor to determine the current flowing through it.

Insert a meter (on mA range) between the 9 V source and resistor R_1 at point X to

measure I_2, the current drawn from the 9 V supply. You will need to set the meter to measure on a range that can display up to 1 mA. Note the reading on the meter and enter this in the appropriate part of the results table.

Now reconnect point X and insert the meter at Y in order to read the current drawn from the 6 V supply that flows via R_2, the 3K3 resistor. Once again enter this reading in the results table.

Finally, measure the current flowing through the load. Insert the meter at point Z to determine the current through the 1K load and again note the result.

A worked solution to the calculation part of this exercise is given below so you can check your answers. When comparing your calculated answers with your practical answers be prepared for some discrepancy – things never work exactly in practice!

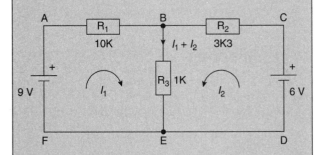

Figure 1.67

Consider Figure 1.67. Using $V = IR$ for loop ABEF,

$$9 = R_1I_1 + R_3(I_1 + I_2)$$

$$9 = 10I_1 + 1(I_1 + I_2)$$

$$9 = 11I_1 + I_2 \tag{1}$$

For loop CBED,

$$6 = R_2I_2 + R_3(I_1 + I_2)$$

$$6 = 3.3I_2 + 1(I_1 + I_2)$$

$$6 = 3.3I_2 + I_1 + I_2$$

$$6 = 4.3I_2 + I_1 \tag{2}$$

To solve (1) and (2), multiply (2) by 11 to give

$$66 = 47.3I_2 + 11I_1 \tag{3}$$

Subtract (1) from (3) to give

$66 = 47.3I_2 + 11I_1$

$9 = I_2 + 11I_1$

$\overline{57 = 46.3I_2 + 0}$

$\therefore I_2 = \dfrac{57}{46.3} = 1.23 \text{ mA}$

To find I_1, substitute I_2 into Equation (1):

$9 = 11I_1 + I_2$

$9 = 11I_1 + 1.23$

$9 - 1.23 = 11I_1$

$\therefore I_1 = \dfrac{7.77}{11} = 0.706 \text{ mA}$

To check, substitute the answers into Equation (2):

$6 = 4.3(1.23) + 0.706$

$6 = 5.289 + 0.706$

$\therefore 6 = 5.995$

which is near enough!

	Practical reading	Calculated answer
Voltage drop across R_1 (V_{R_1})		
Voltage drop across R_2 (V_{R_2})		
Voltage drop across R_3 (V_{R_3})		
Total voltage drops		

	Practical reading	Calculated answer
Current via R_1 (I_1)		
Current via R_2 (I_2)		
Current via R_3 (I_3)		

Superposition theorem

While we are considering networks with more than one e.m.f. it is worth looking at the superposition theorem. This theorem tells us that in any linear circuit an e.m.f. produces the same effect whether it acts alone or together with other e.m.f.s in the circuit.

Any resistive circuit is referred to as linear.

This means that, if we have a circuit with several e.m.f.s in it, we can analyse the circuit by looking at the currents due to each e.m.f. in turn, with all the others replaced by their internal resistance. It is easiest to consider this by working through an example.

Suppose we need to find the current through the 5 Ω resistor in the circuit shown in Figure 1.68. First, consider the 3 V battery acting alone (Figure 1.69). Now we have 5 Ω in parallel with 3 Ω giving an equivalent resistance of

$R_{e1} = 15/8 = 1.875 \text{ Ω}$

where subscript e1 stands for 'element 1'. R_{e1} is in series with the 2 Ω resistor giving a total circuit resistance of

$R_{T1} = 2 + 1.875 = 3.875 \text{ Ω}$

This gives a total circuit current of

$I_T = 3/3.875 = 0.774 \text{ A}$

Using this current we can find the voltage developed across the 5 Ω and 3 Ω resistors (in parallel):

$V_{Re1} = 0.774 \times 1.875 = 1.45 \text{ V}$

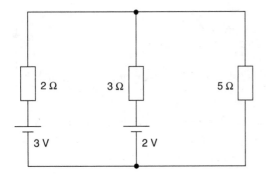

Figure 1.68

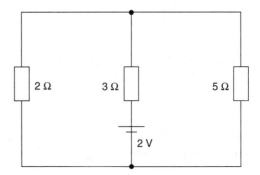

Figure 1.70

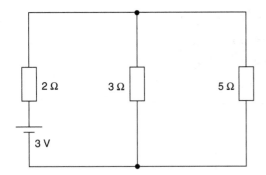

Figure 1.69

So the current through the 5 Ω resistor due to the 3 V e.m.f. is

$$\frac{V_{Re1}}{R} = \frac{1.45}{5} = 0.29 \text{ A}$$

Now we consider the 2 V battery acting alone (see Figure 1.70). The 2 Ω resistor is now in parallel with the 5 Ω resistor, giving an equivalent resistance of

$$R_{e2} = \frac{10}{7} = 1.43 \text{ Ω}$$

The total resistance in this circuit is

$$R_{T2} = 3 + 1.43 = 4.43 \text{ Ω}$$

The total current from the battery is

$$I_{T2} = \frac{2}{4.43} = 0.45 \text{ A}$$

The voltage developed across the 2 Ω and 5 Ω resistors in parallel is

$$V_{Re2} = 0.45 \times 1.43 = 0.64 \text{ V}$$

The current through the 5 Ω resistor due to the 2 V battery alone is given by

$$\frac{V_{Re2}}{5} = \frac{0.64}{5} = 0.13 \text{ A}$$

If we now add together the current from each battery in turn we will have the current through the

5 Ω resistor in the full circuit. The total current through the 5 Ω resistor is 0.29 + 0.13 = 0.42 A.

Now, let's look at the last example we did using Kirchhoff's laws (Guided Examples on page 25, Question 2) and see whether we obtain the same answers when we use the superposition theorem.

We need to find the current in the 10 Ω resistor (Figure 1.71). The answer we expect is approximately 0.15 A flowing to the left of our diagram. The reason why the answer is approximate is because we rounded all our numbers to two decimal places and at the end of a long calculation the answer may be out by a few hundredths.

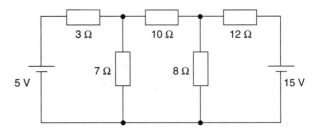

Figure 1.71

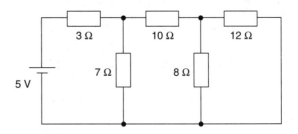

Figure 1.72

Consider the 5 V e.m.f. only (Figure 1.72). The 12 Ω and 8 Ω resistors are in parallel and so

$$R_{e1} = \frac{96}{20} = 4.8 \text{ Ω}$$

R_{e1} is in series with the 10 Ω resistor, giving a resistance of 14.8 Ω. The 14.8 Ω is in parallel with the 7 Ω resistor, giving

$$R_{e2} = \frac{103.6}{21.8} \approx 4.75 \ \Omega$$

This is in series with the 3 Ω resistor, giving us a total resistance for this first circuit of

$$R_{T1} = 4.75 + 3 = 7.75 \ \Omega$$

where T1 is short for 'total resistance 1'.

Now the total current for this circuit is

$$I_{T1} = \frac{5}{7.75} \approx 0.65 \ \text{A}$$

so the voltage drop across the 3 Ω resistor is $0.65 \times 3 = 1.95$ V. The voltage drop across the 7 Ω resistor is the total voltage drop minus the voltage drop across the 3 Ω resistor: $5 - 1.95 = 3.05$ V. This means that the current through the 7 Ω resistor is $3.05/7 \approx 0.44$ A. The current in the 10 Ω resistor is the total current less the current through the 7 Ω resistor so $I_{10\Omega} = 0.65 - 0.44 = 0.21$ flowing to the right of our diagram.

It is worth noting that in this example, so far, we have used Ohm's law, both of Kirchhoff's laws and the superposition theorem!

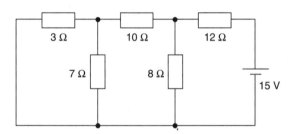

Figure 1.73

Now consider just the 15 V battery (Figure 1.73). The 3 Ω resistor in parallel with the 7 Ω resistor gives a resistance of 21/10 = 2.1 Ω. This in series with the 10 Ω resistor gives a resistance of 12.1 Ω in parallel with 8 Ω to give 96.8/20.1 ≈ 4.82 Ω. This in series with 12 Ω gives a total resistance of 16.82 Ω.

Now, we have a total current of $I_{T2} = 15/16.82 \approx 0.89$ A and so

$$V_{12\Omega} = 12 \times 0.89 = 10.68 \ \text{V}$$

and

$$V_{8\Omega} = 15 - 10.68 = 4.3 \ \text{V}$$

Therefore

$$I_{8\Omega} = \frac{4.32}{8} = 0.54 \ \text{A}$$

and

$$I_{10\Omega} = 0.89 - 0.54 = 0.35 \ \text{A}$$

flowing to the left of our diagram.

The total current through the 10 Ω resistor is $0.35 - 0.21 = 0.14$ A flowing left.

Allowing for the approximations made in both cases the answers obtained using Kirchhoff's laws and using the superposition theorem are the same.

Practical 8

Superposition theorem

The purpose of this practical is to compare results obtained practically with those obtained using the superposition theorem. We shall use the circuit given in Figure 1.74.

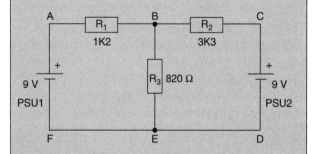

Figure 1.74

Set up the circuit as in Figure 1.75; note that only one power supply is being used.

Measure the voltage across each of the resistors in the circuit and enter the readings that you obtain in the appropriate results table.

To measure the current you will have to break the circuit at the three points marked X, Y and Z and insert your meter in series. Again, note the results that you get in the appropriate column of the results table.

Now set up the circuit shown in Figure 1.76. The circuit has been altered so that the first power supply has been replaced by a short circuit and the second power supply has been put back into the circuit.

Once again measure the voltages around the circuit and record the values. You will have to insert your meter to measure current at the points marked.

Now set up the circuit shown in Figure 1.77. The circuit has both power supplies connected simultaneously. Once again measure

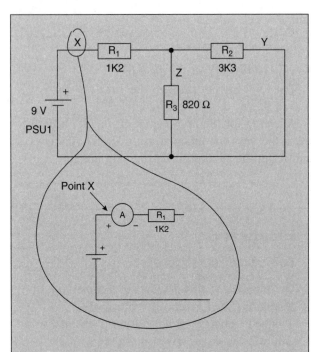

Figure 1.75   Second power supply has been removed and replaced by a short circuit

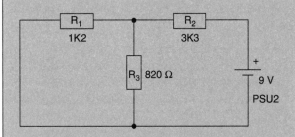

Figure 1.76   First power supply has been removed and replaced by a short circuit

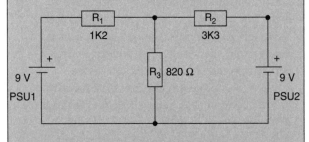

Figure 1.77

the voltages and currents and note the readings.

Use the method explained on page 00 to determine the theoretical answers. If you enter these in the appropriate places in the results tables you will be able to compare them with the ones that you obtained through building and testing the circuit.

To check your answers compare them with the calculations below.

Figure 1.78 shows the circuit with only the left-hand power supply included.

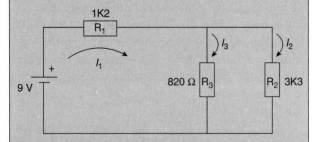

Figure 1.78

$$820\,\Omega\,\|3K3 = \frac{0.82 \times 3.3}{0.82 + 3.3} = \frac{2.706}{4.12}$$

$$= 657\,\Omega$$

Circuit current via R_1 is given by

$$I_{R_1} = \frac{9}{1K2 + 0.657} = 4.85\ \text{mA}$$

Circuit current via R_3 is given by

$$I_{R_3} = 4.85 \times \frac{3K3}{3K3 + 0.820} = 3.88\ \text{mA}$$

Circuit current via R_2 is given by

$$I_{R_2} = 4.85 \times \frac{0.820}{3K3 + 0.820} = 0.965\ \text{mA}$$

Therefore,

$$V_{R_1} = I_{R_1} \times R_1 = 5.82\ \text{V}$$

$$V_{R_2} = I_{R_2} \times R_2 = 0.965 \times 3K3 = 3.18\ \text{V}$$

$$V_{R_3} = I_{R_3} \times R_3 = 3.88 \times 0.82 = 3.18\ \text{V}$$

	Practical measured results			Calculated results		
	With PSU1 only	With PSU2 only	With both PSUs in circuit	With PSU1 only	With PSU2 only	With both PSUs in circuit
(Point X) Current via R_1						
(Point Y) Current via R_2						
(Point Z) Current via R_3						
Voltage across R_1						
Voltage across R_2						
Voltage across R_3						

Following on directly from the superposition theorem there are two other very useful theorems which allow us to represent networks by an equivalent voltage source and impedance (see page 87) or current source and impedance. Both theorems apply only to linear sources and components.

Thévenin's theorem

Thévenin's theorem states that the linear network behind a pair of terminals can be replaced by a constant-voltage generator. This generator has a voltage output equal to the voltage across its terminals when they are on open circuit. It also has an internal impedance equal to the impedance seen looking into the terminals when all the sources are removed and replaced by their internal impedances.

Norton's theorem

Norton's theorem states that we can replace the network behind a pair of terminals with a constant-current generator which has a current equal to the current we would get if the terminals were short circuited and an internal impedance equal to the impedance seen looking in at the terminals with all sources removed and replaced by their internal impedances.

Applying the theorems

If we look at a complex network (Figure 1.79) we can see how these theorems can make life simpler for us.

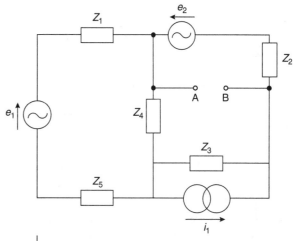

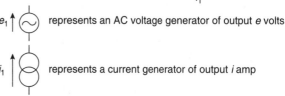

$e_1 \uparrow (\sim)$ represents an AC voltage generator of output e volts

$i_1 \uparrow (\otimes)$ represents a current generator of output i amp

Figure 1.79

Suppose you were asked to find the current flowing through a particular impedance Z_T connected across the terminals AB.

Without Thévenin's or Norton's theorem this would be very difficult. However, with them life is easier. We have a choice: we can produce a Thévenin equivalent circuit (called a constant-voltage equivalent circuit) or a Norton equivalent circuit (called a constant-current equivalent circuit).

Let the voltage equal V_{AB} when there is no impedance connected across AB (i.e. with AB an open circuit). Now take away all the sources and replace them with their internal impedances (see Figure 1.80).

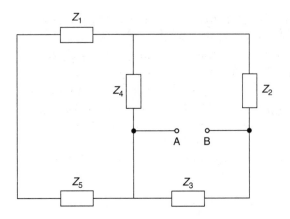

Figure 1.80

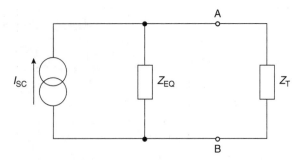

Figure 1.82

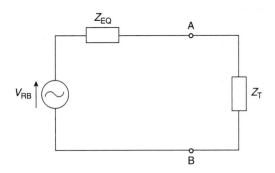

Figure 1.81

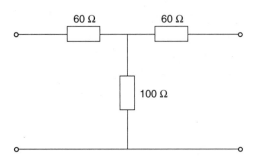

Figure 1.83

Looking into AB we can find the impedance by using Ohm's law. Let's call it Z_{EQ}.

We can draw the Thévenin equivalent circuit (Figure 1.81) and for an impedance of Z_T connected across AB we get a current given by

$$I = \frac{V_{AB}}{Z_{EQ} + Z_T} \text{ A}$$

Otherwise we can short circuit the terminals AB and calculate the current I_{SC} that would flow. Across the generator of I_{SC} we would connect the shunt impedance Z_{EQ} seen from the terminals, as before. This would give us the exact equivalent Norton version of the circuit (Figure 1.82) and the current flowing in Z_T would be given by

$$I = I_{SC} \frac{Z_{EQ}}{Z_{EQ} + Z_T} \text{ A}$$

Let's look at a typical problem. A source of 2 V e.m.f. and 40 Ω internal resistance is connected across a T-network, as shown in Figure 1.83. Calculate the resistance of the load impedance which will absorb maximum power and calculate that power.

Before we can apply our theorems to this problem we need to be aware of another theorem, the maximum power transfer theorem.

> The maximum power transfer theorem simply tells us that we transfer maximum power from a network to a load when the load impedance and the internal impedance of the network are equal in magnitude.

Now we know that, the problem is easy. First we find the Thévenin equivalent circuit and then we match the impedance. To sort out the equivalent circuit we are going to need to use Ohm's law.

Let's look at the initial situation given in Figure 1.84. We have 40 Ω in series with 60 Ω which combines to give 100 Ω as shown in Figure 1.85.

By examining this circuit we can see that half the source e.m.f. will be developed across the first

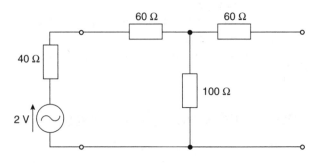

Figure 1.84

Gustav Robert Kirchhoff (1824–1887)

A German physicist, Kirchhoff was the first person to show that an electrical impulse moves at the speed of light. He is best known to us for his current and voltage laws but the bulk of his work was really in the field of spectroscopy. Together with Bunsen, Kirchhoff developed the first spectroscope and in 1857 when Bunsen developed the Bunsen burner they were able to lead the way, by spectroscopy, to the discovery of new elements including caesium and rubidium.

As a result of the developments from this work Kirchhoff was the first to suggest 'black body radiation'.

100 Ω and half across the second 100 Ω, giving an open-circuit voltage of 1 V.

Now we take away the source and replace it with its internal impedance as shown in Figure 1.86.

Finally, we draw the Thévenin equivalent circuit (Figure 1.87) and we know that for maximum power transfer we need to match the internal impedance of 110 Ω with the load.

Now we can calculate the power transferred to the load. This will be given by $W_L = V_L^2/Z_L$ watts.

$$\therefore\ W_L = (0.5)^2/110 = 2.27\ \text{mW}$$

Just out of interest we could find the power dissipated in the load if it were connected directly to the source (Figure 1.88). The difference between the two powers would be the loss caused by the T-network. In telecommunication systems this would be called the insertion loss of the network.

The power dissipated in the load now would be given by $I_L^2 Z_L$ which gives $(2/150)^2 \times 110 = 19.5\ \text{mW}$.

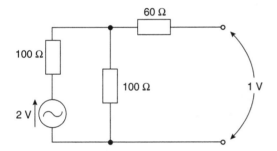

Figure 1.85

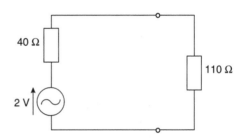

Figure 1.88

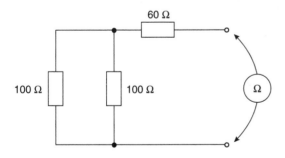

Figure 1.86

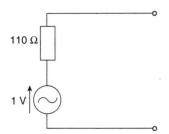

Figure 1.87

Multiple choice questions

1 The unit of electric charge is
  (a) the ampere
  (b) the volt
  (c) the joule
  (d) the coulomb.

2 In the circuit in Figure 1.89
  (a) L_2 will be brighter than L_1
  (b) both lamps will light with equal brightness
  (c) neither lamp will light
  (d) L_1 will be brighter than L_2.

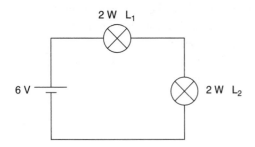

Figure 1.89

3 The circuit in Figure 1.90 illustrates the principle of
  (a) festoon lighting
  (b) series lighting
  (c) series–parallel lighting
  (d) series voltage distribution.

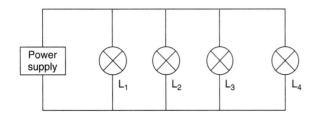

Figure 1.90

4 The current drawn by the circuit in Figure 1.91 will be
  (a) 3.45 A

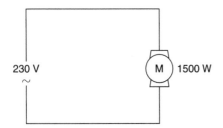

Figure 1.91

  (b) 6.52 A
  (c) 0.153 A
  (d) 1.53 A.

5 The circuit in Figure 1.92 has a resistance equivalent to
  (a) 7.05 kΩ
  (b) 12 kΩ
  (c) 3 kΩ
  (d) 14.1 kΩ.

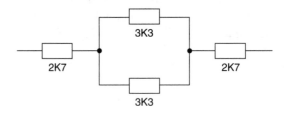

Figure 1.92

6 If the voltage across the 2K2 resistor in Figure 1.93 is 8 V the current through R_1 is
  (a) 22 mA
  (b) 3.64 mA
  (c) 3.22 mA
  (d) 0.42 mA.

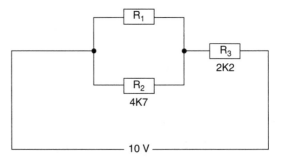

Figure 1.93

7 The physical size of a resistor is an indication of its
  (a) temperature coefficient
  (b) power rating
  (c) inductive properties
  (d) carbon former.

8 With the slider in Figure 1.94 set to its mid-point the voltage across AB will be
  (a) −3 V
  (b) 0 V
  (c) +3 V
  (d) −2.4 V.

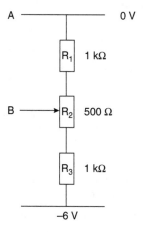

Figure 1.94

9 If $R_1 = R_2 = R_3$ in Figure 1.95 which of the following statements is true:
(a) The voltage across all resistors will be equal
(b) The voltage across R_1 will be less than that across R_3
(c) The voltage across R_1 will be double that across R_2
(d) The voltage in will equal the voltage out.

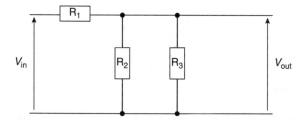

Figure 1.95

10 The potential difference across R_3 in Figure 1.96 is
(a) 0 V
(b) 5 V
(c) 6.02 V
(d) 3.97 V.

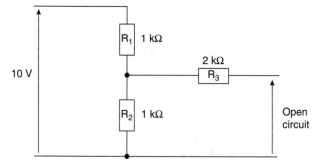

Figure 1.96

2

Capacitance

2.1 Electrostatics

Before we can study capacitance we must look briefly at electrostatics. This term applies to the properties and behaviour of electric charge in the steady state.

There are two polarities of charge which are called positive (the charge carried by a proton) and negative (the charge carried by an electron).

There is a force of attraction between these two polarities and, similar to magnetic poles, **like charges repel** and **unlike charges attract**. In many ways electrostatic effects are similar to electromagnetic effects. In the magnetic system we have a 'magnetic field' consisting of 'magnetic flux' produced by a 'magnetomotive force' (m.m.f.). In the electrostatic system we have an 'electric field' consisting of 'electrostatic flux' produced by an 'electromotive force' (e.m.f.).

Force between charged particles

Coulomb's law states that

> The force between two quantities of charge Q_1 and Q_2 placed a distance r apart is proportional to the product $Q_1 Q_2$ and inversely proportional to the distance r.

Both these facts are fairly obvious. The larger the two charges are, the more we would expect them to

attract each other, and the further apart we put them the weaker we would expect the attraction between them to be. Figure 2.1 shows the lines of electric flux between two charges. The strength of attraction (or repulsion) also depends on the medium (or material) between the two charges. This is because it is easier to set up electric flux in some materials than in others.

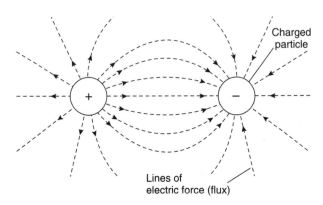

Figure 2.1   *The electric field between two charged particles*

Because of the work carried out by Coulomb the unit of electric charge is named after him.

Potential gradient

As we move along a line of flux the voltage difference between the point on the line and the point at which the line terminates decreases. This is the potential gradient and is defined as the voltage drop per unit length of electric path:

$$E = \frac{V}{d} \text{ volts per metre}$$

where d is the distance in metres between the electrodes.

This potential gradient is also known as electric force or electric field strength.

Electric field

If, instead of isolated charges, we look at the field between two charged plates parallel to each other we notice a slight 'bulging' of the field at the edges

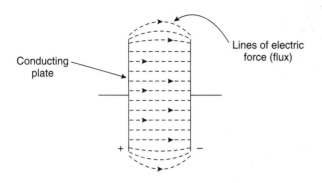

Figure 2.2   The electric field between two charged parallel plates

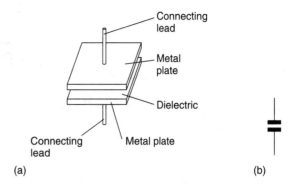

Figure 2.3   (a) Construction of a capacitor; (b) symbol for a capacitor

(Figure 2.2). This is called fringing and is due to the mutual repulsion between the lines of flux. For most of our purposes the fringing is so small that we can ignore it and assume that the flux lies perpendicular to the plates. This means that the potential gradient can be treated as uniform over the whole area.

Electric flux density

The symbol for electric flux is ψ (the Greek letter psi).

A positive charge of 1 C (coulomb) is said to emit one line of electric flux, which terminates at a negative charge of 1 C. If the charge on the electrodes (plates) is Q coulombs, the flux ψ between the plates is Q coulombs. The electric flux density is given by

$$D = \frac{Q}{a} \text{ coulombs per metre}$$

where a is the area in square metres between the plates perpendicular to the direction of the lines of flux.

2.2 Capacitance

Capacitance is the property of storing electrical energy.

A capacitor is a component designed specifically for storing electrical energy. Any two conductors separated by an insulating material or dielectric

have capacitance. Generally a capacitor is constructed of parallel plates separated by a thin layer of dielectric material (see Figure 2.3(a)).

When there is a difference in potential between the plates the capacitor is said to be charged and when there is no potential difference (p.d.) between the plates the capacitor is discharged.

When the switch S_1 in Figure 2.4 is closed, electrons will flow from plate A of the capacitor to the positive terminal of the battery. At the same time electrons flow from the negative terminal of the battery to plate B. As the charge builds up on the plates it tends to oppose this current (the charging current) until eventually the current ceases. At this point the p.d. between the plates is equal to the e.m.f. of the battery and the capacitor is fully charged.

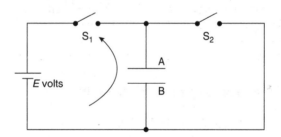

Figure 2.4   The arrow indicates the direction of electron flow when S_1 is closed and S_2 open

If we now open S_1 the capacitor will remain charged, in theory, forever. In practice the charge leaks away slowly through the dielectric. This is because, in reality, the resistance of the dielectric is less than infinite. Work has been done in charging the capacitor and setting up the electric field between the plates. An amount of energy, equal to that expended in doing this work, is now stored in the form of an electric field. This energy can be retrieved by discharging the capacitor.

If we now close switch S_2 electrons will flow from plate B to plate A (discharge current) until the p.d. between the plates is zero. This will

collapse the electric field and the energy stored will
be dissipated.

Relationship between capacitance and charge

If we increase the charge on the plates of a
parallel plate capacitor from Q_1 to Q_2 the electric
field strength between the plates is increased
(see Figure 2.5). If the field strength is increased
then the work required to move a small charge
between the plates is also increased. Since the p.d.
between the plates is equal to the work done in
moving a small charge between the plates, the p.d.
is also increased.

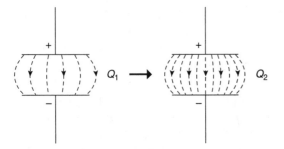

*Figure 2.5   The effect on the field lines of increasing
the charge of a parallel plate capacitor*

When we look at the ratio of p.d. to charge, for
any particular capacitor, we find that it is a
constant. So, Q/V is constant for a given capacitor.
This constant is the **capacitance** of the capacitor, i.e.

$$C = \frac{Q}{V}$$

Units of capacitance

The unit of capacitance is the farad (F). As we
can see from the equation for capacitance this
is derived from 'charge per volt' (1 F is the
capacitance of a capacitor that requires a p.d. of
1 V to maintain a charge of 1 C on that capacitor).

In practice the farad is a very large basic unit
and in electronics we usually deal with much
smaller values of capacitance. For this reason we
use the following sub-multiples of the unit:

microfarad (μF) = 10^{-6} farad

picofarad (pF) = 10^{-12} farad

nanofarad (nF) = 10^{-9} farad
(also called the kilopicofarad (kpF))

Now that we know the relationship between
capacitance, charge and p.d. any one can be found
if the other two are known:

$$C = \frac{Q}{V} \text{ farads} \quad V = \frac{Q}{C} \text{ volts}$$

$$Q = CV \text{ coulombs}$$

Energy stored in a capacitor

We have seen that, when a capacitor is charged,
work is done in moving the charge against the p.d.
established between the plates, and that this work is
stored as energy in the electric field between the
plates.

When a constant charging current of I amps
flows for a period of t seconds the p.d. developed
across the capacitor is given by

$$V = \frac{It}{C} \text{ volts}$$

since $Q = It$ coulombs.

If the current is constant then the p.d. will rise
from zero to V volts at a constant rate in t seconds.
This means that the average value of p.d. over the
period is $V/2$ volts. Now,

$$Q = It \text{ coulombs}$$

and

$$Q = CV \text{ coulombs}$$

Therefore,

$$I = \frac{CV}{t}$$

From these equations it can be seen that to store
the same quantity of charge a small capacitor
requires a large voltage whilst a large capacitor
requires a small voltage. Note that the charge held
by a capacitor is also proportional to the current
and the time that it flows for. The latter property is
extremely useful in circuits that only have to
operate for a set amount of time.

When a steady current of I amps flows for a
period of t seconds and the voltage remains
constant at V volts the energy is given by

$$\text{energy} = VIT \text{ joules (watts} \times \text{seconds)}$$

We can use this information to derive an expression
for the energy stored in a charged capacitor:

$$\text{energy stored} = \text{average voltage} \times \text{steady current} \times \text{period } t$$

$$= \frac{1}{2}V \times \frac{CV}{t} \times t \text{ joules}$$

energy stored $= \frac{1}{2} CV^2$ joules

Physical factors determining capacitance

When manufacturers produce capacitors they need to be able to determine the capacitance and the suitability of the capacitor for particular applications. Many materials are available and each offers advantages over others in some aspect of the capacitor's performance.

Plate area

For a simple parallel plate capacitor, the capacitance is proportional to the cross-sectional area of the electric field between the plates. If we increase the surface area a of the plates the cross-sectional area of the field increases. Therefore we conclude that capacitance is proportional to the surface area of the plates facing each other, i.e. $C \propto a$.

Dielectric thickness (distance between the plates)

The further apart the plates are placed the smaller the capacitance between them. Thus for large values of capacitance we need very thin layers of dielectric. So we can say that capacitance is inversely proportional to the distance d between the plates, i.e. $C \propto 1/d$.

Number of dielectric layers

In most cases the space available for electronic components is very limited. For this reason, instead

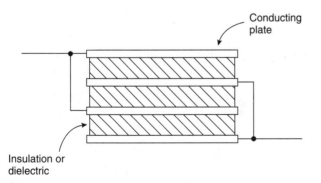

Figure 2.6   Rather than making a very large capacitor often a stack of smaller plates is used to increase the surface area

of using one pair of plates with a very large surface area, we often use a stack of smaller plates to give the overall surface area required (Figure 2.6).

The outside surfaces of the plates at either end of the stack play no part in determining the capacitance so the parameter we require is the number n of dielectric layers used. This is sometimes referred to as the number of plates minus one. Obviously, the greater the number of plates is, the greater the effective surface area and the greater the resultant capacitance. This means that capacitance is proportional to the number of dielectric layers, i.e. $C \propto n$.

Dielectric material

If we use different insulating materials between the plates we find that different values of capacitance are obtained. This is because it is easier to set up electric flux in some materials than in others. The ease with which electric flux can be established in a material is called the **permittivity** of the material. In order to quantify this for a material we find the material's relative permittivity (or dielectric constant) ϵ_r. This is found experimentally by comparing the capacitance of a capacitor using the material as a dielectric with the capacitance of the same capacitor using a vacuum (free space) as the dielectric. Air is considered to have a relative permittivity of 1, i.e. the same as free space. If C_1 is the capacitance with the material as the dielectric and C_2 is the capacitance with air as the dielectric, then $\epsilon_r = C_1/C_2$ for the material. As we might expect, the easier it is to set up flux in a material the greater the capacitance is when using that material.

So, capacitance is proportional to the relative permittivity of the dielectric, i.e. $C \propto \epsilon_r$.

Permittivity of free space

Now that we have the relationship between all these characteristics and capacitance we need a constant to equate them. This is called the permittivity of free space, ϵ_0.

The permittivity of free space is defined as the ratio of electric flux density to potential gradient in a vacuum:

$$\epsilon_0 = \frac{D}{E} = \frac{Q}{a} \div \frac{V}{d} = \frac{Qd}{Va}$$

and we know that

$$\frac{Q}{V} = C$$

so, by substitution,

$$\epsilon_0 = \frac{Cd}{a}$$

and from this

$$C = \frac{\epsilon_0 a}{d} \text{ farads}$$

The permittivity of free space has a constant value of $\epsilon_0 = 8.85 \times 10^{-12}$ F m^{-1}. The product of ϵ_0 and ϵ_r is called the **absolute permittivity** ϵ:

$$\epsilon = \epsilon_0 \epsilon_r$$

Formula for the capacitance of a capacitor

Now that we know how the dimensions and materials used are related to the capacitance of the finished component we can combine them in an equation:

$$C = \frac{\epsilon_0 \epsilon_r n a}{d}$$

where C is the capacitance in farads, ϵ_r is the relative permittivity, ϵ_0 is the permittivity of free space, n is the number of dielectric layers, a is the surface area of one side of one plate in square metres and d is the distance between the plates in metres.

2.3 Capacitors

After resistors it is probable that capacitors are the most widely used electronic component. They come in a vast range of values and in many shapes and sizes.

The fundamental property of a capacitor is that it stores electric charge. This charge is available even after the supply that has been used to put charge into the capacitor is removed. This is the reason that you may well have received a shock from a piece of equipment even after the supply has been taken away.

The function of a capacitor

Capacitors have many functions, the most common of which are as follows:

(a) acting as a block to DC whilst continuing to pass an AC signal;
(b) forming part of a filter circuit to remove unwanted voltage;
(c) acting as a device to smooth out variations of rectified DC in a power supply (this is another aspect of filtering);
(d) coupling an AC signal from one part of a circuit to another;
(e) storing charge to be used to trigger a device (a camera flash for example); and
(f) acting as a timer when used in conjunction with a suitable resistor.

The construction of a capacitor

There are a number of types of capacitor each of which is manufactured in a different way. The process used is determined by various factors including the value and the working voltage required.

Types of capacitors

Capacitors can be grouped into one of two categories: fixed or variable.

Fixed capacitors

Fixed capacitors come in so many shapes and sizes that it is impossible to give examples of all of them. However, they all use the principle of two parallel plates separated by an insulating dielectric. Because there are so many types available, fixed capacitors tend to be sub-classified by dielectric type.

Silvered mica capacitors

Typical range of values	1 pF to 0.1 μF
Tolerance	±0.25% to ±5%
Typical maximum working voltage	350 V (DC)

Mica capacitors are common because they have the advantage of having a compact size and a high

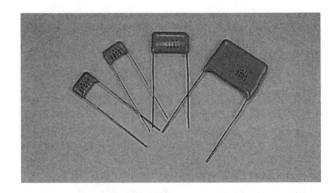

Silvered mica capacitor

working voltage. If the dielectric is coated with silver a greater stability can be obtained, although the cost of production is obviously increased.

Polyester capacitors

Typical range of values	10 nF to 2.2 µF
	(0.01 µF to 2.2 µF)
Tolerance	±20%
Typical maximum	
working voltage	400 V (DC)

Polyester capacitors are temperature sensitive. This makes them unsuitable for most timing applications. They are extensively used, however, for de-coupling and coupling.

Polyester capacitor

Polystyrene capacitors

Typical range of values	10 pF to 10 nF
Tolerance	±20%
Typical maximum	
working voltage	150 V (DC)

These capacitors have the advantage that they have a relatively close tolerance and can therefore be used when an accurate value is required. At a quick glance polystyrene capacitors can be mistaken for being electrolytic, but they are non-polarised.

Electrolytic capacitors

> If an electrolytic capacitor in a circuit begins to get hot it is a sure sign that it is either connected backwards or is operating above its working voltage.

Typical range of values	0.1–10 000 µF
Tolerance	±20% or even ±50%
Typical maximum	
working voltage	500 V (DC)

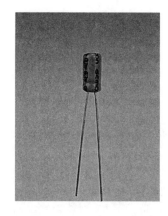

Electrolytic capacitor

Like the capacitors previously considered electrolytic capacitors (Figure 2.7) come in fixed values. They differ from the capacitors discussed earlier in that they are *polarised*. This means that they have to be connected the correct way round. Failure to do this will destroy the capacitor and can result in an explosion.

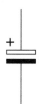

Figure 2.7   Symbol used for an electrolytic capacitor

Electrolytic capacitors are most commonly found as smoothing capacitors in the power supplies of equipment. For safety reasons they should always be discharged before any service work is undertaken. They also find wide application in coupling and de-coupling.

Tantalum capacitors

Typical range of values	0.1–100 µF
Tolerance	±20%
Typical maximum	
working voltage	30 V (DC)

Tantalum capacitors (Figure 2.8) are polarity sensitive. They have the advantage over a conventional electrolytic capacitor that they are physically very small. The range of working voltages available is restricted.

Tantalum bead capacitor

Figure 2.8   Symbol used for a tantalum capacitor

Variable air-spaced capacitor

Variable capacitors

For some applications, typically tuning, capacitors need to be variable. Unlike fixed capacitors there are only three main types of variable capacitor.

The air-spaced capacitor

Typical range of values   50–500 pF
Tolerance   ±30%
Typical maximum
working voltage   500 V (DC)

The air-spaced capacitor (Figure 2.9) was most commonly used for radio tuning prior to the advent of varicaps (see below). It still finds wide application in the aerial tuning units of transmitters. The working voltage is affected by the distance between the plates. Use of a capacitor with too low a working voltage will result in arcing or flash-over between the plates.

Figure 2.9   Symbol used for an air-spaced capacitor

The mica trimmer

Typical range of values   1–50 pF
Tolerance   ±10%
Typical maximum
working voltage   100 V (DC)

Figure 2.10   Symbol used for a mica trimmer

The mica trimmer (Figure 2.10) is also known as a compression trimmer. The distance between the mica plates is adjusted with a small screw. This alters the capacitance. Trimmers are used where a very fine adjustment of a capacitance value is needed. Typical applications include adjusting the frequency of a crystal and fine-tuning aerial circuits in car radios.

Trimmer capacitor

The varicap diode

Typical range of values   500–620 pF
Tolerance   ±10%
Typical maximum
working voltage   10 V (DC)

In appearance the varicap (Figure 2.11) (occasionally known as a varactor diode) is virtually indistinguishable from a normal diode. Note that the circuit symbol is also diode-like. Unlike all the other capacitors considered – which are passive – the varicap is an active component and therefore a reverse bias DC supply must be maintained across it. Manufacturers often publish a characteristic graph which gives the capacitance between anode and cathode for various voltages across the diode.

Figure 2.11   Symbol used for a varicap diode

Table 2.1   Capacitance value table

Picofarad (pF)	Nanofarad (nF)	Microfarad (mF)	Capacitance code (E1A)
10	0.010	0.00001	100
15	0.015	0.000015	150
22	0.022	0.000022	220
33	0.033	0.000033	330
39	0.039	0.000039	390
47	0.047	0.000047	470
68	0.068	0.000068	680
82	0.082	0.000082	820
100	0.10	0.0001	101
150	0.15	0.00014	151
220	0.22	0.00022	221
330	0.33	0.00033	331
470	0.47	0.00047	471
680	0.68	0.00068	681
820	0.82	0.00082	821
1000	1.0	0.001	102
1500	1.5	0.0015	152
2200	2.2	0.0022	222
3300	3.3	0.0033	332
3900	3.9	0.0039	392
4700	4.7	0.0047	472
6800	6.8	0.0068	682
10 000	10.0	0.01	103
15 000	15.0	0.015	153
22 000	22.0	0.022	223
33 000	33.0	0.033	333
47 000	47.0	0.047	473
68 000	68.0	0.068	683
82 000	82.0	0.082	823
100 000	100.0	0.1	104
150 000	150.0	0.15	154
220 000	220.0	0.22	224
330 000	330.0	0.33	334
470 000	470.0	0.47	474
680 000	680.0	0.68	684
820 000	820.0	0.82	824
1 000 000	1000.0	1.0	105
1 500 000	1500.0	1.5	155
2 200 000	2200.0	2.2	225
10 000 000	10 000.0	10.0	106

Tolerance codes

C	≡	±0.25 pF	J	≡	±5%
D	≡	±0.50 pF	K	≡	±10%
F	≡	±1%	M	≡	±20%
G	≡	±2%	Z	≡	+80% and −20%

Varicaps find wide application in the tuning of TVs and digital radios. They have replaced the air-spaced capacitor as the most common type of tuning component.

Practical markings of capacitors

Three methods are used to indicate the value of a capacitor: the printed code, the colour code and the printed value. The capacitor colour code is shown on the inside front cover.

A printed value is the easiest way for capacitors to be marked. The value of the component in microfarads is written onto the case of the capacitor. Note that most capacitors are also marked with the maximum working voltage of the component and its tolerance. The latter may be coded as a letter – see Table 2.1 for details.

Having looked at the theory and constructional features of capacitors we will now examine their behaviour in circuits. The first thing to determine is what happens to capacitance when we interconnect a number of capacitors.

Capacitors in series

When an e.m.f. of E volts is applied across the circuit shown in Figure 2.12, assuming that the capacitors are initially uncharged, electrons will flow from plate A to the positive terminal of the battery. This means that plate A will have acquired a positive charge. The lines of electric flux from plate A will terminate on plate B which must then acquire a negative charge equal in magnitude to the positive charge on plate A. Plate B obtains this charge by attracting electrons from plate C.

Plate C now has a positive charge equal to that on plate A. Flux from plate C will terminate on plate D and so on.

After a very short time this movement of charge (current) stops and each capacitor will be charged. In effect, one amount of charge Q has moved around the circuit and the change in charge on each capacitor is therefore the same. Since each capacitor started with no charge it follows that the charge on each is now the same.

The total charge Q_T in the circuit is therefore the same as the charge on each capacitor:

$$Q_T = Q_1 = Q_2 = Q_3 \text{ coulombs}$$

The p.d. between the plates on each capacitor must add up to the applied e.m.f. (Kirchhoff's second law – see page 23). So,

$$E = V_1 + V_2 + V_3 \text{ volts}$$

Since all the charges are equal (Q) we can say that

$$V_1 = \frac{Q}{C_1} \quad V_2 = \frac{Q}{C_2} \quad V_3 = \frac{Q}{C_3}$$

Therefore,

$$E = \frac{Q}{C_1} + \frac{Q}{C_2} + \frac{Q}{C_3} \text{ volts}$$

By dividing by Q we get

$$\frac{E}{Q} = \frac{1}{C_1} + \frac{1}{C_2} + \frac{1}{C_3}$$

The total effective capacitance of the circuit is given by

$$C_T = \frac{Q}{E} \text{ farads}$$

Therefore the total circuit capacitance is

$$\frac{1}{C_T} = \frac{1}{C_1} + \frac{1}{C_2} + \frac{1}{C_3} \text{ farads}$$

Note that the product over sum rule works for two capacitors in series.

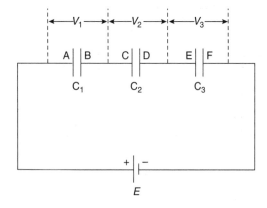

Figure 2.12

Guided examples

1 In Figure 2.13 the two capacitors are in series. The equivalent capacitance may be calculated using one of two methods:

Figure 2.13

$$C_T = \frac{C_1 \times C_2}{C_1 + C_2}$$

$$= \frac{1 \times 10}{1 + 10} = \frac{10}{11}$$

$$= 0.909 \ \mu F$$

Or

$$\frac{1}{C_T} = \frac{1}{C_1} + \frac{1}{C_2}$$

$$= \frac{1}{1} + \frac{1}{10}$$

$$= 1 + 0.1 = 1.1 \ \mu F$$

$$\therefore C_T = 0.909 \ \mu F$$

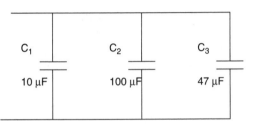

Figure 2.14

2 In this example, three capacitors are placed in a parallel arrangement in a circuit (Figure 2.14). Here it is best to use the reciprocal rule which is the same as for resistors in parallel:

$$\frac{1}{C_T} = \frac{1}{C_1} + \frac{1}{C_2} + \frac{1}{C_3}$$

$$= \frac{1}{10} + \frac{1}{100} + \frac{1}{47}$$

$$= 0.1 + 0.01 + 0.021$$

$$= 0.131$$

$$\therefore C_T = 7.634 \ \mu F$$

Capacitors in parallel

With the arrangement shown in Figure 2.15 the p.d. across each capacitor (*V* volts) is equal to the applied e.m.f. (*E* volts) (Kirchhoff's second law). Let the charge on C_1 be Q_1, the charge on C_2 be Q_2 and the charge on C_3 be Q_3 coulombs.

As each capacitor is charged up the electrons drawn from the battery split up at node X and the electrons from the opposite plates returning to the battery combine at terminal Y (Kirchhoff's first law) so that the total charge in the circuit is given by

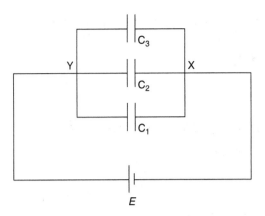

Figure 2.15

$$Q_T = Q_1 + Q_2 + Q_3 \text{ coulombs}$$

Also, we know that

$$Q_1 = VC_1 \quad Q_2 = VC_2 \quad Q_3 = VC_3$$

Therefore, by substitution,

$$Q_T = VC_1 + VC_2 + VC_3$$

$$Q_T = V(C_1 + C_2 + C_3)$$

Therefore

$$\frac{Q_T}{V} = C_1 + C_2 + C_3$$

The effective total capacitance of the circuit is

$$C_T = \frac{Q_T}{V}$$

and so, for a parallel circuit,

$$C_T = C_1 + C_2 + C_3 \text{ farads}$$

Note that, arithmetically, these results are opposite to those for a resistor circuit.

Guided example

In Figure 2.16 the three capacitors are in parallel. The overall equivalent capacitance value is

$$C_T = C_1 + C_2 + C_3$$

$$\therefore C_T = 1 + 0.1 + 10 = 11.1 \ \mu F$$

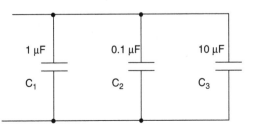

Figure 2.16

Capacitors in series–parallel

Combinations of capacitors may be connected in series–parallel arrangements as shown in Figure 2.17.

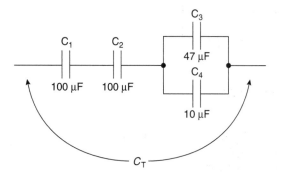

Figure 2.17

When solving this type of problem each group should be solved individually and then the resultant of the set of groups (in this case just two) calculated. In this example we first solve C_1 and C_2 using the product over sum rule:

$$\frac{C_1 \times C_2}{C_1 + C_2} = \frac{100 \times 100}{100 + 100}$$

$$= \frac{10^4}{200} = 50 \ \mu F$$

Then we solve C_3 and C_4:

$$C_3 + C_4 = 47 \ \mu F + 10 \ \mu F$$

$$= 57 \ \mu F$$

The circuit is now equivalent to that shown in Figure 2.18.

Figure 2.18

The overall equivalent capacitance is

$$\frac{50 \times 57}{50 + 57} = 26.63 \ \mu F$$

Michael Faraday (1791–1867)

Faraday was an English physicist and chemist. One of ten children, he started work as an apprentice bookbinder. Faraday later got work as an assistant/servant to Sir Humphry Davy. It was during this time that he showed himself to be one of the greatest scientists of all time. As a chemist he was the first to produce temperatures below zero Fahrenheit in the laboratory for his work on liquifying gases, and he also discovered benzene. As a physicist he developed the methods and terminology of electrolysis, and the laws he developed brought electrochemistry into the modern age.

Faraday was responsible for the discovery and explanation of a wealth of electromagnetic phenomena, and what endears him to most engineering students is the fact that, as an uneducated man, he explained it all without mathematics, which were not his strong point. Later, when men like Maxwell tackled the same problems from a mathematical point of view, they were able only to show that Faraday had been correct even without the mathematics.

It could reasonably be suggested that Faraday, more than any other person, is responsible for our 'electrified' world today, and of course the unit of capacitance is derived from his name.

Multiple choice questions

1 A capacitor of 10 µF has a terminal potential difference of 6 V. The charge stored is
  (a) 60 C
  (b) 60 µC
  (c) 1.66 µC
  (d) 0.6 C.

2 The distance between the plates of a capacitor is doubled. The value of the capacitance will be
  (a) doubled
  (b) halved
  (c) quadrupled
  (d) quartered.

3 The value of capacitance is
  (a) proportional to the area of the plates
  (b) inversely proportional to the area of the plates
  (c) exponentially proportional to the area of the plates
  (d) equal to the area of the plates.

4 A capacitor commonly used for tuning purposes could be
  (a) electrolytic
  (b) tantalum
  (c) low tolerance
  (d) air-spaced.

5 Which of the following formulae are correct for determining the voltage across a capacitor?
  (a) $V = QC$
  (b) $V = \dfrac{Q}{C}$
  (c) $V = CIt$
  (d) $V = \dfrac{\epsilon_0 \epsilon_r A}{d}$

6 The overall equivalent capacitance of the circuit in Figure 2.19 is
  (a) 9.99 nF
  (b) 9.99 µF
  (c) 5 µF
  (d) 20 µF.

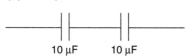

Figure 2.19

7 The equivalent capacitance of the circuit in Figure 2.20 is

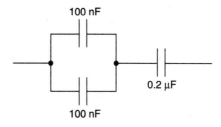

Figure 2.20

  (a) 100 nF
  (b) 3 µF
  (c) 100.2 µF
  (d) 50.2 µF.

8 The voltage across C_1 in Figure 2.21 is
  (a) 50 V
  (b) 66.6 V
  (c) 33.3 V
  (d) 100 V.

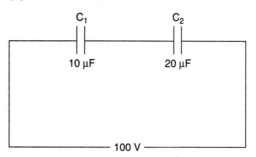

Figure 2.21

9 An electrolytic capacitor will have a typical value of
  (a) 1000 µF, 1 V
  (b) 1000 nF, 100 V
  (c) 1000 pF, 100 V
  (d) 1000 µF, 35 V.

10 If the capacitor in Figure 2.22 is charged to a value of 50 V the energy stored will be
  (a) 15 mC
  (b) 756 µC
  (c) 23.84 mC
  (d) 2.75 µC.

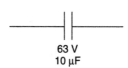

Figure 2.22

3.1 Magnetic fields and electric currents

The motor principle 49

One of the most important areas of electrical engineering is the effects and applications of combined electrical and magnetic properties. From observation and experimentation with electromagnetics the pioneers of our industry developed much of the groundwork of modern technology.

We know from earlier work that whenever an electric current flows through a conductor a magnetic field is set up around the conductor. This is a radial field and, like all magnetic fields, it has a direction. The field direction can easily be found using Maxwell's corkscrew rule.

> Maxwell's corkscrew rule states that, if a right-handed corkscrew is driven into the end of the conductor in the direction of the current, the direction of rotation of the corkscrew is in the direction of the magnetic field (see Figure 3.1).

Note that when we mark current direction on the *cross-section* of a conductor we still use an arrow in the following way:

⊙ the point of the arrow shows the current flowing towards you

⊕ the flight of the arrow shows the current flowing away from you

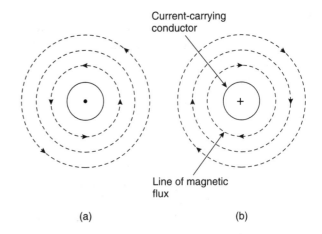

Figure 3.1 Field direction around a conductor carrying current (a) towards you and (b) away from you

Maxwell's corkscrew rule is alternatively stated as the right-hand grip rule:

> If a conductor were gripped in the right hand with the thumb extended in the direction of the current the fingers would be curled in the direction of the magnetic field (see Figure 3.2).

(This is really a slightly modified version of the rule for solenoid polarity.)

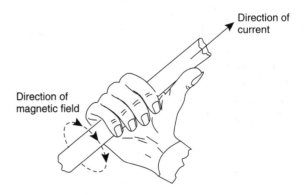

Figure 3.2 The right-hand grip rule

Now, the field around a conductor will behave like any other magnet and attract or repel other

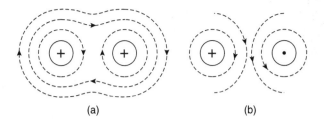

Figure 3.3

magnets depending upon the polarity of their fields.

Consider two conductors close together and running parallel to each other. If they were both carrying current in the same direction they would have a field pattern around them as shown in Figure 3.3(a) and there would be a force of attraction between them. If we reversed the current in one conductor there would be a force of repulsion, as shown in Figure 3.3(b).

We can see why this occurs by looking at the gap between the two conductors. When the currents are flowing in the same direction the fields tend to cancel each other out, creating no field between the conductors. When one current is reversed we get a concentration of flux all going the same way between the conductors and therefore there is a force of repulsion between adjacent flux lines. If one of the conductors could move it would, which leads to the motor principle.

Before we can utilise this principle we need to look at the force acting on the conductor and try to determine its direction of action and its strength or magnitude.

The motor principle

If we put our current-carrying conductor in the magnetic field of a permanent magnet, there will be an interaction between the two fields which again will tend to cause motion of the conductor.

It is important to note that if the conductor is lying parallel to the field of the permanent magnet then there is no force acting upon it.

To keep the idea (and the maths!) simple we assume an even (or uniform) field acting at right angles to the conductor (see Figure 3.4).

We can see that on one side of the conductor the flux from the permanent magnet is acting in the same direction as the flux around the conductor. This will produce a strong magnetic effect on this side. At the same time, the field on the other side of the conductor is acting in opposition to the permanent magnet's flux, thus weakening the field. The result of this is to produce a force acting on the conductor as shown in Figure 3.5.

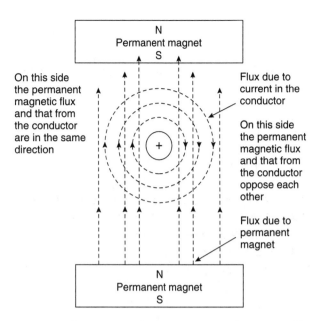

Figure 3.4 Magnetic flux lines of a conductor and a permanent magnet producing a uniform field acting at right angles to the conductor

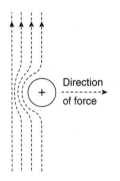

Figure 3.5 The direction of the force acting on a current-carrying conductor in a magnetic field

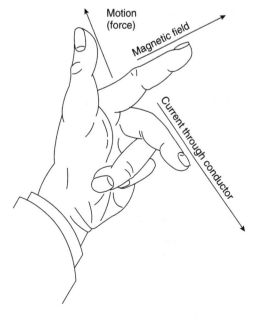

Figure 3.6 Fleming's left-hand rule

The direction of force

The direction in which this force acts depends on the direction of the current and the direction of the flux due to the permanent magnet.

The direction of the force can easily be predicted by using our hands again!

> Fleming's left-hand rule states that if the thumb and first two fingers of the left hand are placed mutually at right angles, and if the index finger points in the direction of the magnetic field from the permanent magnet and the second finger points in the direction of current flow through the conductor, then the thumb will point in the direction of the force acting on the conductor. As an aid to memory: First finger indicates Field, seCond finger indicates Current and thuMb indicates Motion (Figure 3.6).

Remembering that, by convention, magnetic fields point from north to south, check Fleming's left-hand rule on the examples given in Figure 3.7.

If we know the direction of any two of our variables (current, field or force) the direction of the third can be found.

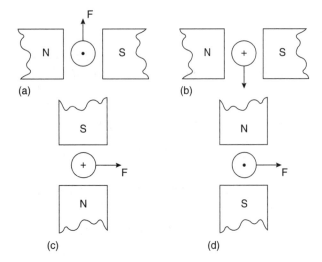

Figure 3.7

Magnitude of the force

Now that we have sorted out the direction in which the force acts we need to know how large the force is.

From the way in which the force is developed we can see that, the larger the current is, the larger the force will be ($F \propto I$).

Also, the stronger the magnetic field, i.e. the greater the flux density B, the stronger the force will be ($F \propto B$).

Lastly, it follows that the larger the length over which the interaction between the two fields occurs the greater the force will be ($F \propto l$).

From this we obtain an expression for the force, in newtons, acting on a current-carrying conductor at right angles to a uniform magnetic field:

$$F = BIl \text{ newtons}$$

where B is the flux density in teslas, I is the current in amps and l is the length of the conductor perpendicular to the field in metres.

An aside

It is interesting to note that the idea of a force acting on two parallel conductors gives rise to the definition of the ampere, our basic unit.

Ampere's law tells us that for two parallel conductors placed d metres apart and carrying currents of I_1 and I_2 amperes the force per unit length is

$$F = 2 \times 10^{-7} d I_1 I_2 \text{ newtons per metre}$$

By making I_1 and I_2 equal to 1 A and d equal to 1 m we obtain the following definition:

> 1 A is that current which, when maintained constant in each of two rectilinear, infinitely long, parallel conductors of negligible cross-section, situated in a vacuum and separated by 1 m, would produce a force equal to 2×10^{-7} newtons per metre length.

Guided examples

1   A wire 25 cm long is placed at right angles to a uniform magnetic field of flux density 2 T. When a direct current of 2.5 A is passed through the wire what will be the magnitude of the force acting on the wire?

$$F = BIl$$

$$\therefore \ F = 2 \times 2.5 \times 25 \times 10^{-2}$$

$$= 1.25 \text{ N}$$

2 When a direct current of 5 A is passed through a wire placed perpendicular to a uniform field of flux density 0.6 T a force of 2 N acts upon the wire. What length of wire is in the field?

$$F = BIl$$

$$\therefore l = \frac{F}{BI} \text{ metres}$$

$$= \frac{2}{0.6 \times 5} \text{ m}$$

$$= 0.666 \text{ m} = 66.6 \text{ cm}$$

3 In what direction does the force act on the wire shown in Figure 3.8?

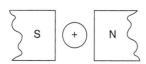

Figure 3.8

Fleming's left-hand rule indicates that the force will act vertically.

4 The wire in Question 1 is now bent back on itself in a loop as shown in Figure 3.9(a). Determine the size and direction of the force acting on each limb of the loop.

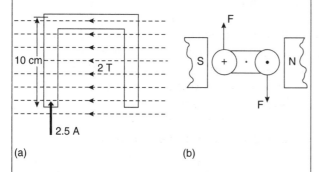

(a)   (b)

Figure 3.9

The effective length of wire at right angles to the field is 10 cm on each limb and no force acts on the 5 cm of loop parallel to the permanent magnet's flux. The force per arm is $F = BIl$ (N), so

$$F = 2 \times 2.5 \times 10 \times 10^{-2}$$

$$= 0.5 \text{ N per arm}$$

By applying Fleming's left-hand rule we see that the force on each arm will tend to cause rotation about a pivot in the centre of the 5 cm limb (Figure 3.9(b)). This is, of course, the basis of a DC motor.

Exercise

1 Using Fleming's left-hand rule with Figure 3.10 determine the direction of the force in part (a), the flux in part (b) and the current in part (c).

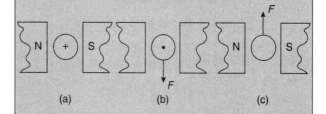

(a)   (b)   (c)

Figure 3.10

2 If the tendency for rotation of the loop is as shown in Figure 3.11, which is the north pole of the permanent magnets?

[Left-hand side]

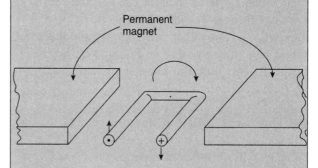

Figure 3.11

3 A wire of 30 cm length carrying a DC current of 3 A is placed perpendicular to a uniform magnetic field such that the entire length is in the field. If the force exerted on the wire is 0.8 N calculate the flux density of the field. [0.88 T]

4 Find the force acting on the wire shown in Figure 3.12 given that the flux density of the permanent magnetic field is 1.5 T.

[0.3 N]

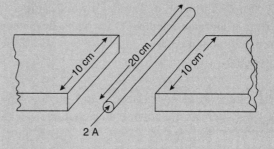

Figure 3.12

3.2 **The generator principle of electromagnetic induction**

Whenever a conductor passes through, or 'cuts', a line of magnetic flux a small voltage is developed in the conductor. This voltage is called an **induced e.m.f.**. This *always* occurs when magnetic flux is cut by a conductor. Even kicking a tin can down the road would cause an induced e.m.f. in the can as it passed through the earth's magnetic field! Of course, in this rather extreme example the e.m.f. would be extremely small and impractical to use.

Clearly it is useful to know the polarity and magnitude of an induced e.m.f.

The fact that electromagnetic induction occurs was discovered in 1831 by one of electrical engineering's most famous scientists: Michael Faraday. After a series of experiments Faraday expressed his results in the form of a law.

> When the magnetic flux linking a conductor changes, an e.m.f. is induced in the conductor such that the magnitude of the e.m.f. is proportional to the rate of change of flux linkage.

Practically speaking, moving a conductor in a stationary magnetic field will cause an e.m.f. to be induced in the conductor.

This is only one of the many important laws and discoveries which Faraday made before his death in 1867. Hot on the heels of Faraday's work came a law from a German scientist, Lenz, again developed from experimental data.

> The direction of an induced e.m.f. is always such as to oppose the change producing it.

Armed with these two laws we are in a position to look in more detail at electromagnetic induction.

E.m.f. induced by conductor movement

If we think of a conductor moving through a uniform magnetic field at right angles to the flux, we can apply the two laws to examine the resultant e.m.f. induced (the result would be the same if the conductor were stationary and the magnet were moved) (see Figure 3.13).

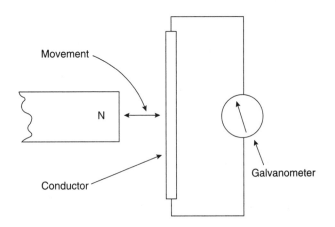

Figure 3.13

As the magnet is moved towards the conductor the galvanometer needle is deflected to one side. As the magnet is moved away the direction of needle deflection changes (the voltage changes polarity). Also, if the speed of movement of the magnet is increased the amount of deflection is increased (a larger voltage is induced). This, of course, supports Faraday's law.

Magnitude of induced e.m.f.

If we let the amount by which the flux linking with the conductor changes be $d\Phi$ and the time taken for this change be dt, then the rate of change is $d\Phi/dt$. From Faraday's law we get

$$E = \frac{d\Phi}{dt}$$

and from Lenz's law this becomes

$$E = -\frac{d\Phi}{dt} \text{ volts}$$

When we move a conductor of length l metres, at right angles, through a uniform field of flux density B tesla at a velocity of v metres per second (Figure 3.14) then, in one second, we will move through an area of field equal to $l \times v$ metres squared.

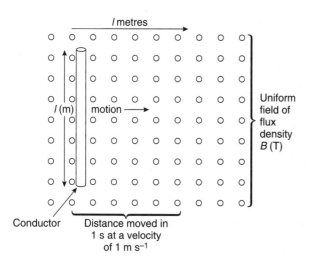

Figure 3.14

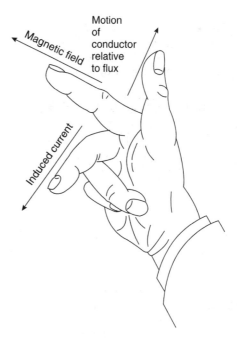

Figure 3.15 *Fleming's right-hand rule*

Since the flux density is B webers per square metre we have a rate of change of flux linkage, and hence an induced e.m.f. of

$$E = -Blv \text{ volts}$$

Note that the minus sign results from Lenz's law.

Direction of induced e.m.f.

The direction of induced e.m.f. can be determined from Lenz's law since the current which results from the induced e.m.f. sets up a magnetic field around the conductor which tries to oppose the motion causing it. In terms of this resulting current the direction is easily found by using our hands, yet again!

> Fleming's right-hand rule states that if the thumb and first two fingers of the right hand are placed mutually at right angles, and if the index finger points in the direction of the magnetic flux and the thumb points in the direction of motion of the conductor through the flux, then the second finger points in the direction of the induced current (Figure 3.15).

Practical 1

The purpose of this practical is to appreciate the generator principle of electromagnetic induction.

In Figure 3.16 it is essential that the magnet used is substantial. The meter should

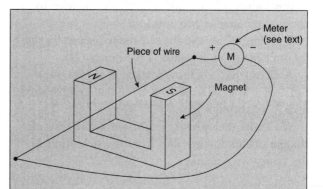

Figure 3.16

ideally be an extremely sensitve centre-zero type. The type of wire could typically be 7 or 16 stranded.

Set up the circuit as above and move the wire in and out of the magnetic field slowly watching the galvanometer at the same time. The meter will deflect as the conductor is moved within the magnetic field.

If the conductor is now moved away from the influence of the magnetic field the meter will indicate zero, showing that no voltage has been induced.

Finally, as a matter of interest, the same effect can be achieved by keeping the conductor still and moving the magnet backwards and forwards. However, with the weight of magnets this wears the arm out considerably!

Inductance

We have seen that the magnitude of an induced e.m.f. is proportional to the length of conductor within the field linking it. One way of increasing the length in the field is to wind a long conductor into a coil. We call such a coil an inductor.

If we have an inductor of N turns in a changing magnetic field it is equivalent to having N conductors in that field. Now the induced e.m.f. is given by

$$E = -N \frac{d\Phi}{dt} \text{ volts}$$

(assuming all the turns link with all the flux).

Self-inductance

We say that a circuit has self-inductance if, as current changes in that circuit, the magnetic flux produced causes an e.m.f. to be induced back into the circuit.

We know from Lenz's law that the direction of this induced e.m.f. will be such that it tries to oppose the change producing it.

The symbol we use for self-inductance is L and the unit of self-inductance is the henry (H).

A circuit has a self-inductance of 1 H if an e.m.f. of 1 V is induced in it by a change of current of 1 A s⁻¹ through it.

We know that what is important is the **rate of change** of flux linkage and from the definition of the henry we get that

$$e = -L \frac{di}{dt} \text{ volts}$$

where L is the self-inductance in henrys. Now we have

$$e = -L \frac{di}{dt} = -N \frac{d\Phi}{dt}$$

So

$$L = N \frac{d\Phi}{di} \text{ henrys}$$

or

$$\text{self-inductance} = \frac{\text{change in flux linkage}}{\text{change in current}}$$

Coil construction

By winding a long conductor into a coil we concentrate a lot of flux in a small space. If the centre (or core) of the coil is a magnetic material such as ferrite then all the available flux will be concentrated in the core rather than the surrounding air. This results in maximum flux linkage with the coil.

If the change in flux $d\Phi = \Phi$ and the change in current $di = I$ then

$$L = \frac{N \times \Phi}{I} \text{ henrys} \tag{1}$$

but

$$\frac{\text{m.m.f.}}{\text{reluctance}} = \frac{NI}{S} \text{ webers} \tag{2}$$

where m.m.f. is the magnetomotive force (NI) and reluctance is the opposition to the setting up of flux.

So, by substituting (2) in (1),

$$L = \frac{N}{I} \times \frac{NI}{S} = \frac{N^2}{S} \text{ henrys}$$

This shows how the self-inductance varies with the square of the number of turns, the type of core material and the size of the coil.

The direction of the flux around the coil can be found by applying the 'grip rule' again (Figure 3.17).

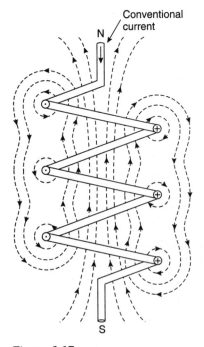

Figure 3.17

Energy stored in an inductor

When a current passes through an inductor a magnetic field is set up around the inductor. To set up the field we must expend some energy. We know that this energy is stored in the field because when the current is turned off we get the energy back in the form of the induced e.m.f. which tries to maintain the current.

If the inductance was pure, i.e. if it had no resistance, we would get back exactly the same amount of energy that we put in. In practice, of course, the inductor is made of wire which has resistance so some energy is lost in the form of heat.

The energy used when a source of V volts supplies a current of I amps for t seconds is given by

energy = VIt joules

If V were applied to a pure inductor the current would increase linearly to some value I after t seconds and the average over that time would be $\frac{1}{2}I$ amps.

We know that

$$e = -L\frac{dI}{dt}$$

and so if I rose from zero in t seconds the average induced e.m.f. would be LI/t. Also,

average power = $L\dfrac{I}{t} \times \dfrac{1}{2}I$

energy stored in an inductor

= power × time = $\dfrac{1}{2}LI^2$

Mutual inductance

We know that *any* conductor cut by magnetic flux will have an e.m.f. induced in it. Supposing we used the flux around one inductor to cut the turns of a second inductor. The e.m.f. induced in the second inductor would be the result of what we call mutual inductance.

In order to make sure that all the flux from the first coil cuts all the turns of the second coil (i.e. we get maximum mutual inductive coupling) we can wind both inductors onto the same, high permeability, core. This arrangement is called a transformer (Figure 3.18) and is discussed further on page 57.

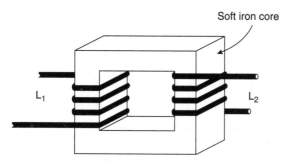

Figure 3.18   A transformer

Like self-inductance the unit of mutual inductance is the henry. A circuit is said to have a mutual inductance M of 1 H when an e.m.f. of 1 V is induced in one circuit as a result of current changing at a rate of $1\ A\ s^{-1}$ in the other.

The unit of inductance

Although inductances are measured in henrys (given the symbol H), it is quite normal to have sub-units measured in millihenrys and microhenrys. Like resistors, preferred values are manufactured (the E6 series) although it is quite common for technicians to wind their own.

Inductances are also classified by a 'Q' factor. The higher the Q the better the quality of the coil, although low Q coils are useful in some applications, e.g. when a broad bandwidth is required.

Inductors

An inductor is the term given to a component which is manufactured to provide inductance. It normally consists of a coil of wire which is wound around a material known as a former. Inductors are sometimes called chokes.

The function of an inductor

The most common uses of inductors are as follows:

(a) filtering a power supply to remove variations of DC and leave a smoothed level DC output;
(b) filtering a power supply line to remove noise;
(c) tuning a circuit in conjunction with either a series or a parallel capacitor;
(d) acting with another inductor to provide feedback in an oscillator circuit.

The construction of an inductor

Inductors tend to be classified by the type of former that they use.

Air-cored inductors   Air-cored inductors (Figure 3.19) are wound on a plastic tube (which has no electrical properties) or are free-standing and supported by the rigidity of the wire which makes up the coil.

Air-cored inductors are used in a wide variety of radio applications for tuning purposes and matching aerial impedances. In transmitters they tend to be

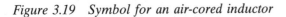

Figure 3.19   Symbol for an air-cored inductor

physically quite large to prevent the high voltages present from arcing between turns. Smaller self-supporting air-cored inductors are used in VHF radios (i.e. at frequencies from 80 MHz upwards).

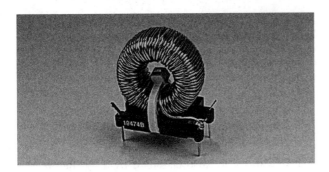

High current toroidal inductor

Ferrite-cored inductors   This type of inductor (Figure 3.20) is wound on a piece of ferrite (such as the ferrite rod aerial) or on a hollow tube which contains iron dust. They are used for frequencies below 80 MHz and are one of the most common forms of inductors encountered. The presence of the dust core increases the amount of inductance present.

Figure 3.20   Symbol for a ferrite-cored inductor

Some ferrite inductors are manufactured with movable cores which are referred to as slugs. Moving the position of the slug changes the value of the inductance present and can be a method of altering the frequency of a resonant circuit.

Where inductors are used for audio applications and for mains smoothing a laminated iron core is commonly used.

Practical markings of inductors

The value of the inductor can be printed on the outside of the component. An alternative method is to use the standard colour code with the colours giving the value of the choke in millihenrys.

DC resistance of an inductor

As an inductor is merely a coil of wire wound around a former, the DC resistance of the inductor is very small. A value of 150 Ω is a typical figure,

although the actual resistance does depend on what type of inductor is being considered. In general, the greater the value of inductance (i.e. in henrys) the larger the DC resistance.

Self-capacitance of an inductor

As each turn of the inductor is insulated from the next turn, capacitance between turns is present. The principle of this is illustrated in Figure 3.21.

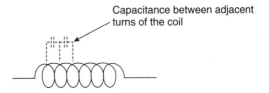

Figure 3.21   Self-capacitance of an inductor

The presence of this capacitance along with the inductance of the choke can form a resonant circuit (see page 99) on its own. This can lead to problems of self-resonance and steps are taken to prevent this by adopting special methods of winding.

Connecting inductors

Inductors can be connected, like other components, in series or parallel. There is another factor, however, which has to be borne in mind – whether or not the inductors have any mutual inductance between them (i.e. does the changing voltage in one affect the other). If there is mutual inductance between them they are said to be mutually coupled. To complicate matters further the coupling may be aiding or opposing.

Inductors in series   Assuming there is no mutual coupling between the inductors the formula for inductors in series is the same as for resistors in series:

$$L_T = L_1 + L_2 + \ldots$$

If mutual inductance is present, however, this has to be taken into account and the formula becomes

$$L_T = L_1 + L_2 \pm 2M$$

where $\pm M$ is the amount of coupling (+ if the series arrangement aids coupling; – if the series arrangement opposes coupling) (Figure 3.22).

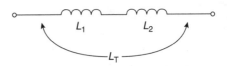

Figure 3.22   Inductors in series

Inductors in parallel Again, assuming no mutual coupling between inductors the formula for inductors in parallel is the same as for resistors in parallel:

$$L_T = \frac{L_1 \times L_2}{L_1 + L_2}$$

Where mutual inductance is present the formula is modified to

$$L_T = \frac{1}{\dfrac{1}{L_1 + M} + \dfrac{1}{L_2 + M}}$$

if the parallel arrangement aids coupling and

$$L_T = \frac{1}{\dfrac{1}{L_1 - M} + \dfrac{1}{L_2 - M}}$$

if the parallel arrangement opposes coupling (Figure 3.23).

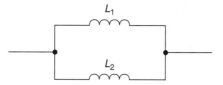

Figure 3.23   Inductors in parallel

> It is almost impossible to measure the value of an inductor in a circuit, although a continuity test will give an indication of whether a coil has gone open circuit or not. One of the most accurate, if not practical, methods is to disconnect the choke from the circuit and connect it to an inductance bridge.

The transformer principle

With the arrangement shown in Figure 3.18 earlier, L_1 is called the **primary** and L_2 is called the **secondary**.

When a current is passed through the primary a magnetic field is set up around it and the lines of flux from this field cut the turns of the secondary. If the current in the primary is alternating the field will be continually changing and a correspondingly changing e.m.f. will be induced in the secondary.

To consider transformer behaviour it is convenient first to assume no losses, although, in fact, all transformers suffer from loss due to both the electrical components and the magnetic components.

Miniature mains transformer

The ideal transformer

An ideal transformer has the following properties:

(a) zero winding resistance,
(b) infinite primary and secondary inductance,
(c) perfect coupling,
(d) zero capacitance between turns.

For simplicity we can assume that all voltages and currents are sinusoidal.

No-load conditions

If we assume that there are no losses in our ideal transformer then *all* the flux produced by the primary links with *all* the turns of the secondary. So we can say that the e.m.f. induced in each turn is the same for the primary and secondary windings.

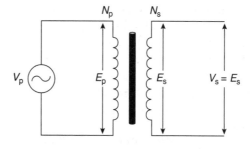

Figure 3.24

In Figure 3.24 let N_p be the number of turns on the primary and N_s be the number of turns on the secondary. The e.m.f. induced in the primary is

$$E_p = N_p \times \text{e.m.f. induced per turn} \qquad (1)$$

and the e.m.f. induced in the secondary is

$$E_s = N_s \times \text{e.m.f. induced per turn} \qquad (2)$$

Dividing (1) by (2) we get

$$\frac{E_p}{E_s} = \frac{N_p}{N_s}$$

(the e.m.f. per turn cancels). Thus,

> voltage ratio = turns ratio

If the secondary voltage is less than the primary voltage the transformer is known as step-down. If the reverse applies it is called step-up.

On-load condition

Connecting a load to the transformer will cause current to flow both in the primary (I_p) and in the secondary (I_s) windings, as shown in Figure 3.25.

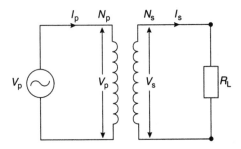

Figure 3.25   The transformer with a load causes current to flow in both the primary and the secondary

Mathematically, this current is linked to the number of turns (turns ratio) and the primary voltage:

$$\frac{V_p}{V_s} = \frac{I_s}{I_p} = \frac{N_p}{N_s}$$

From this we note a very important principle:

> If the voltage is stepped down the current is stepped up.

The reverse also applies.

> Stepping up the voltage steps down the current.

Guided examples

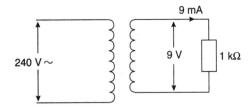

Figure 3.26

1   In the transformer in Figure 3.26 the primary current can be found from

$$\frac{V_p}{V_s} = \frac{I_s}{I_p}$$

$$\frac{240}{9} = \frac{9\,\text{mA}}{I_p}$$

$$\therefore 26.66 = \frac{9\,\text{mA}}{I_p}$$

$$\therefore \quad I_p = \frac{9\,\text{mA}}{26.66} = 337.58\,\mu\text{A}$$

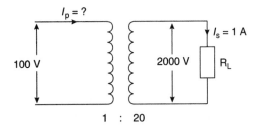

Figure 3.27

2   The turns ratio for the transformer in Figure 3.27 is stated as 1:20, i.e. for every turn on the primary there are 20 on the secondary. The transformer is therefore a step-up transformer. Using

$$\frac{I_s}{I_p} = \frac{N_p}{N_s}$$

to find I_p,

$$\frac{1\,\text{A}}{I_p} = \frac{1}{20}$$

$$\therefore \frac{1\,\text{A}}{I_p} = 0.05$$

$$\therefore \quad I_p = \frac{1}{0.05} - 20\,\text{A}$$

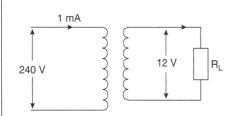

Figure 3.28

3 Tabulate the value of the resistive load R_L in the circuit in Figure 3.28.

First, find I_s from

$$\frac{V_p}{V_s} = \frac{I_s}{I_p}$$

$$\frac{240}{12} = \frac{I_s}{I_p}$$

$$20 = \frac{I_s}{1 \text{ mA}}$$

$$\therefore I_s = 20 \times 1 \text{ mA} = 20 \text{ mA}$$

$$R_L = \frac{V_s}{I_s} = \frac{12 \text{ V}}{20 \text{ mA}} = 600 \ \Omega$$

Relays

A relay (see Figure 3.29) is a device that can be categorised as electromechanical – i.e. it has moving parts (which is the 'mechanical' bit) which are driven by the presence of an electric current.

The relay is widely used when two circuits of dissimilar voltage levels need to be interfaced with each other. A typical example is the use of a low voltage sensing circuit to turn a much higher

Figure 3.29   Symbol for a relay

High current relay

Miniature relay

Reed relay

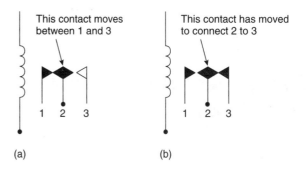

(a)   (b)

Figure 3.30   (a) De-energised relay; (b) energised relay

voltage on and off, for instance an automatic sensor to switch the mains on and off in an automatic porch light.

The principle of operation

The relay uses the principle that when a current flows through a conductor a magnetic field is built up around the conductor (i.e. Faraday's law).

In Figure 3.30 a coil has a set of three contacts positioned close to it and within the effect of its magnetic field. Contact 2 is pivoted (it can move) and is also spring loaded. When no current flows through the coil the relay is said to be de-energised and the contacts are positioned as shown in Figure 3.30(a), i.e. there is a connection between contacts 1 and 2.

When a current is passed through the coil the magnetic field produced around the coil causes the pivoted contact (2) to be drawn to contact 3.

The circuit between 1 and 2 is thus broken and a circuit is made between 2 and 3 as shown in Figure 3.30(b). As the coil may only need a very small voltage to cause it to operate and as the contacts are isolated from the coil, the relay's usefulness is readily apparent. When the current through the coil is removed the relay de-energises and the spring tensioning of the contacts breaks the circuit between 2 and 3. The pivoted contact 2 now returns to its 'at rest' position, re-making the circuit between contacts 1 and 2.

From Figure 3.30 it can be seen that even the simple relay that we are considering has a total of five contacts: three which make and break the circuit and two which supply the coil. It is not surprising that a more complicated relay can have more than twenty contacts, which can make things confusing when wiring!

3.3 **DC transients**

Charge and discharge of capacitors	**60**
Growth of current in an L–R circuit	**64**

Charge and discharge of capacitors

To understand the way in which voltage, charge and current vary in capacitive circuits it is easiest to begin with an ideal case. Let us assume we have a pure capacitor in a circuit with no other resistance. We will also assume that the battery has no internal resistance. This is theory – if only real life could be that simple!

Pure capacitive circuit

In the circuit in Figure 3.31 we will assume that the capacitor C is uncharged. When switch S_1 is closed (with S_2 open) there will be a current i and C will charge. The voltage across C (V_C) will then be equal to the applied voltage E. The current will cease and the charge stored will be

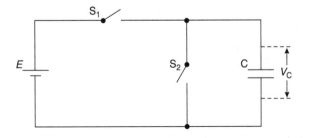

Figure 3.31

$$Q = CV_C \text{ coulombs}$$

An electrostatic field will have been established between the plates.

As this is a pure capacitor it will charge instantly, and for an infinitely short time an infinite current will have flowed since we have no resistance to limit it.

If we now open switch S_1 the charge will remain on C and V_C will remain constant.

However, when S_2 is closed the capacitor will discharge as there is a short circuit across it. The electrostatic field through the dielectric will collapse, the returned energy ($\frac{1}{2}CV_C^2$) will drive an infinite current back through the circuit in the opposite direction to the charging current and V_C will instantly fall to zero.

This sequence of events is illustrated in Figure 3.32.

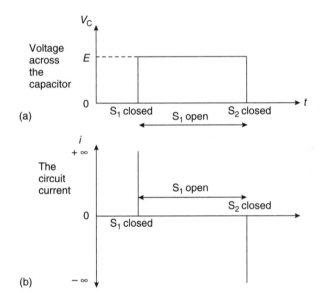

Figure 3.32   Voltage and current around the pure capacitive circuit given in Figure 3.31

Charge and discharge of a capacitor via a resistance

Unfortunately, in real circuits there is always some resistance. Although this can be a physical component or inherent resistance we can make life as simple for ourselves as possible by lumping all the circuit resistance together and representing it as a single resistor. This arrangement is a little more complicated to deal with than the pure capacitor we have just looked at.

In Figure 3.33, when we close the switch S we know, from Kirchhoff, that the voltage across R (V_R) and the voltage across C (V_C) add up to the supply voltage:

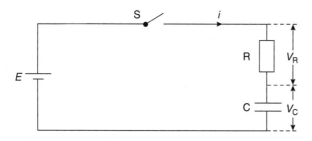

Figure 3.33   Current i charges C via R

$$V_R + V_C = E = V_{max} \text{ volts}$$

If C is initially discharged then $V_C = 0$ V so, at the instant we switch on, $V_R = E = V_{max}$ volts.

For the series circuit shown, Ohm's law tells us that the instantaneous current $i = V_R/R$ amps and so the initial current $I_{max} = E/R$ amps.

Now as C starts to charge V_C rises and, since $V_R = E - V_C$, we see that V_R starts to fall. Because $i = V_R/R$, i also falls.

When C is fully charged $V_C = V_{max}$ and therefore V_R and i must equal zero.

Decay of charging current

The growth of V_C and the decay of i both follow exponential laws. This means that the initial rate of change is very high and the rate of change falls away, with time, to zero (Figure 3.34).

When we apply an e.m.f. to a series C–R circuit the charging current decays exponentially. Mathematically we can find the value of the charging current at any instant from an equation which uses 'natural' logarithms or 'logs to the base e'. The equation for instantaneous charging current is

$$i = \frac{V}{R} \, e^{-t/CR} \text{ amps}$$

Therefore $i = I_{max} e^{-t/CR}$ amps where i is the instantaneous value of the current after t seconds, I_{max} is the initial value of the charging current

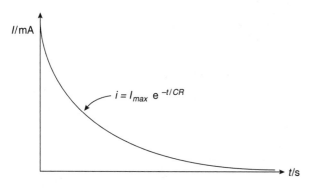

Figure 3.34   The level of circuit current i drops as the capacitor charges

(in amps), R is the total series resistance (in ohms), C is the total capacitance (in farads), t is the time elapsed from switch closure (in seconds) and e is the exponential constant (this is the base of Naperian or natural logarithms and we take its value to be 2.718).

Growth of charge and voltage

We know from Ohm's law that the voltage developed across a resistor R is given by $V_R = iR$ volts.

We also have an expression for i, the instantaneous current. So, if we substitute for i we obtain

$$V_R = \frac{V_{max}R}{R} \, e^{-t/CR}$$

Therefore

$$V_R = V_{max} \, e^{-t/CR} \tag{1}$$

But, $E = V_C + V_R$ and therefore $V_C = E - V_R$. Now, if we substitute for V_R from Equation (1) we get

$$V_C = V_{max} - V_{max} e^{-t/CR}$$

If we take V_{max} out as a factor we get an expression for the instantaneous value of voltage across a capacitor during charging:

$$V_C = V_{max}(1 - e^{-t/CR}) \tag{2}$$

The instantaneous value of charge (q) is

$$q = CV_C$$

Thus $q = CV_{max}(1 - e^{-t/CR})$ coulombs; therefore

$$q = Q(1 - e^{-t/CR}) \tag{3}$$

where Q is the final value of charge on the fully charged capacitor.

Equations (2) and (3) give us the value of V_C or q at any time (t seconds) after the start of charging. A graph of the growth of q or V_C is again exponential (see Figure 3.35).

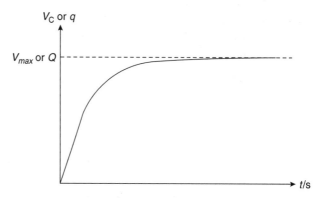

Figure 3.35 Growth of charge/voltage in a capacitor

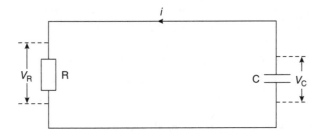

Figure 3.36   *As C discharges current i passes via R and develops a voltage V_R across it*

Discharge of an R–C circuit

After the capacitor has been fully charged we could replace the battery with a short circuit and let the capacitor C discharge through the resistor R (Figure 3.36).

The discharge current i will be equal to V_C/R amps. At the instant we start the discharge $V_C = V_{max}$ volts and so the initial discharge current $I_0 = V_{max}/R$ amps.

When V_C has fallen to zero the current ceases and the capacitor is fully discharged. The initial charge on the capacitor is $Q = CV_{max}$ and if the capacitor continued to discharge at its initial rate it would discharge in Q/I_{max} seconds.

$$\frac{Q}{I_0} = \frac{V_{max}C}{V_{max}/R} = CR \text{ seconds}$$

We shall return to this expression in the section on time constants.

The real equation for the charge on a capacitor at any instant during discharge is

$$q = Q\,e^{-t/CR} \text{ coulombs}$$

where Q is the initial charge (in coulombs), q is the charge (in coulombs) left after t seconds of discharge, C is the total series capacitance (in farads) and R is the total series resistance (in ohms).

Now,

$$V_C = \frac{q}{C} \text{ volts}$$

Therefore,

$$V_C = \frac{Q\,e^{-t/CR}}{C} \text{ volts}$$

or

$$V_C = V_{max}\,e^{-t/CR} \text{ volts}$$

where V_{max} is the initial p.d. across the capacitor.
Also,

$$i = -\frac{V_C}{R}$$

Thus,

$$i = -I_{max}\,e^{-t/CR} \text{ amps}$$

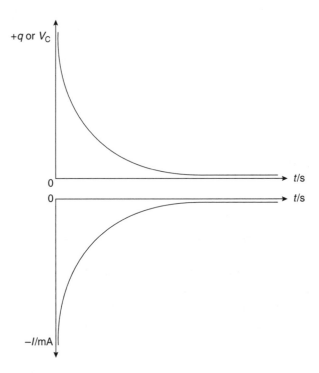

Figure 3.37   *(a) The voltage of a capacitor falls exponentially as it discharges; (b) the current passed when a capacitor discharges is exponential and in the opposite direction to the charge current*

where I_{max} is the initial discharge current. The minus sign is simply to show that the current is in the opposite direction to our original charging current.

The graphs of discharge current and voltage are, of course, exponential (Figure 3.37).

Practical 2

Capacitor charge and discharge

The purpose of this practical is to construct a useful alarm circuit which, in conjunction with an oscilloscope, can also be used for observing how a capacitor charges and discharges. The circuit is based on the famous integrated circuit timer, the NE555. You will meet other versions of this versatile circuit throughout the course of this book.

Connect up the circuit as shown in Figure 3.38. The output of the circuit can be connected direct to a piezo sounder or via a capacitor (e.g. 0.1 μF) to a conventional loudspeaker. Assuming you have built the circuit correctly you should be able to hear a low frequency tone.

By connecting the oscilloscope between the top of the timing capacitor C_1 and 0 V it is possible to monitor the changing voltage

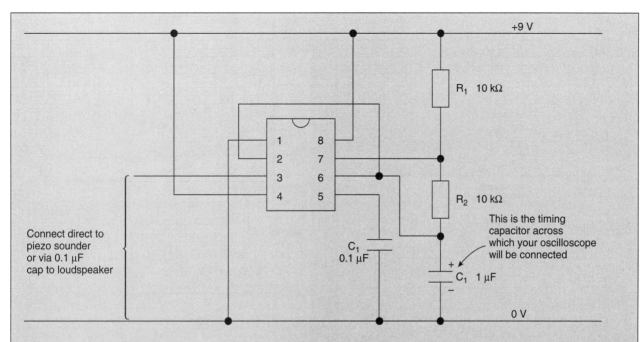

Figure 3.38   The NE555 timer

across this capacitor as it charges via the resistor timing chain (R_1 and R_2) and discharges via the 555 integrated circuit.

Note that C_1 is an electrolytic capacitor and has to be connected with the correct polarity.

It is also possible, of course, to look at the output of the 555 which is applied to the sounder or loudspeaker. This will be a rectangular waveform. Its total duration may be used to calculate the frequency of the output (as described on page 70).

The results which you should obtain are given in Figure 3.39.

Note how the pattern of the voltage across the capacitor follows an exponential shape in both charge and discharge as explained on page 61.

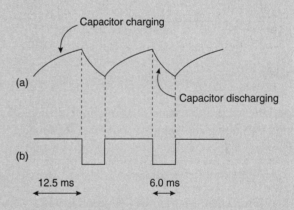

Figure 3.39   (a) Voltage across C_1; (b) output of IC_1 at pin 3

The time constant of C–R circuits

The time constant of a C–R circuit is the time taken for the charge on a capacitor to rise from zero to its maximum value, assuming the initial rate of charge remains constant.

Suppose that when fully charged $Q = CV$ coulombs and the constant charging current is $I = V/R$ coulombs per second. Since $t = Q/I$ seconds the time required to charge the capacitor at a constant current of V/R amps is

$t = CV \div V/R$ seconds

Therefore the time constant τ is

$$\tau = CR \text{ seconds}$$

where C is the capacitance in farads and R is the resistance in ohms.

In fact, the time constant comes, not from a constant current, but from a constant rate of change of current. In practice, however, the charging current does not decay linearly. After a period of CR seconds the capacitor will only have charged to 63.2% of its maximum value (see Figure 3.40).

If we look at the change in charge over one time

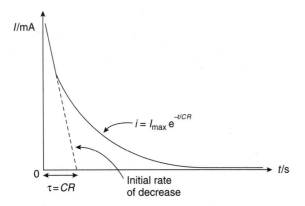

Figure 3.40

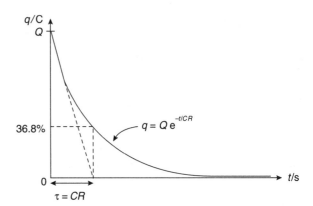

Figure 3.42

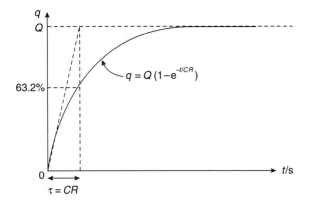

Figure 3.41

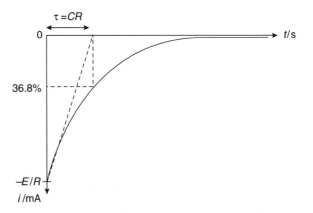

Figure 3.43

constant we see the same relationship. This is easily done by finding the value of q at $t = CR$ seconds (Figure 3.41):

$$q = Q(1 - e^{-t/CR}) \text{ coulombs}$$

Therefore, when a period of CR seconds has elapsed,

$$q = Q(1 - e^{-CR/CR}) \text{ coulombs}$$

$$= Q(1 - e^{-1})$$

$$= Q(1 - 1/e)$$

Therefore,

$$q = Q(1 - 1/2.718)$$

$$= Q(1 - 0.368)$$

$$= Q(0.632)$$

So,

$$q = 63.2\% \ Q \text{ coulombs}$$

Exactly the same theory applies to discharge except that it must be remembered that after CR seconds q will be only 36.8% of its original value, since it will have fallen from Q by 63.2% (see Figures 3.42 and 3.43).

For most practical purposes we normally say that a capacitor will fully charge or discharge in 5CR seconds.

Just as it takes time to charge a capacitor via a resistor, there is also time involved in changing the current through an inductive–resistive circuit. Again the rates of change follow exponential laws.

Growth of current in an L–R circuit

We have seen that, in reality, as well as self-inductance L, an inductor has some resistance and this is usually represented as a series (loss) resistor (R in Figure 3.44).

If L was negligible the current would rise instantaneously to a value of V/R amps.

But with L in circuit, as soon as the current starts to increase there is an induced e.m.f. and its direction is such as to oppose the growth of current (Lenz's law) and so slow the growth. This means that the rate of growth depends on the circuit inductance.

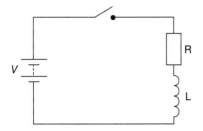

Figure 3.44

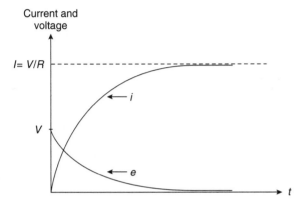

Figure 3.45   The current rises rapidly at first and then levels off; e is the voltage across the inductor L

When we first connect the circuit the current starts to rise rapidly (Figure 3.45). The resultant e.m.f. of self-inductance is large and the rate of change of current decreases. Eventually the current reaches its maximum value V/R, the rate of change is zero and so the induced e.m.f. is also zero.

If we say that the current at any instant is i amps and the induced e.m.f. at the same instant is e volts, then

$$V = e - iR$$

We can see from the graph that as i gets larger e gets smaller and since e is proportional to $\mathrm{d}i/\mathrm{d}t$ it follows that the rate of change of current decreases as shown in the graph.

Time constant for current growth in L–R circuits

Just as in a C–R circuit there is a time taken for the current to reach its maximum value in L–R circuits. In theory the time taken is infinite but, for all practical purposes, the maximum value is reached in a fraction of a second dependent on the values of R and L.

We define the time constant as follows.

The time constant is the time taken for the current to reach its maximum value if the initial rate of change were maintained constant.

In fact, because the growth is exponential, the current will rise to 63.2% of its final steady-state value in one time constant period.

The time constant is $\tau = L/R$ seconds where L is the inductance in henrys and R is the resistance in ohms (Figure 3.46).

In exactly the same way as we did for the growth and decay of charge in capacitive circuits we can express the exponential curve mathematically.

The instantaneous current is given by

$$i = I(1 - e^{-Rt/L}) \text{ amps}$$

The induced e.m.f. at any instant t is given by

$$e = Ve^{-Rt/L} \text{ volts}$$

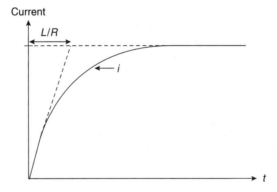

Figure 3.46

Decay of current in an L–R circuit

Once the current has reached its maximum value the rate of change is zero and so the magnetic field around the coil is constant. No change of flux linkage means no induced e.m.f. in the inductor.

If, at this point, we take away the source and replace it by a short circuit (Figure 3.47) the current will tend to fall to zero. This cannot happen instantaneously because as soon as the current starts to fall the magnetic field starts to collapse.

Figure 3.47

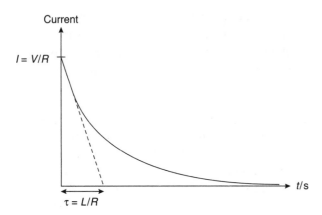

Figure 3.48

The resulting change of flux linkage induces an e.m.f. which opposes the change (good old Lenz's law again).

The presence of the induced e.m.f. slows the rate at which the current falls and we get the now familiar exponential decay. The time constant is still defined in terms of the time taken to decay to zero if the initial rate of decay were maintained. In one time constant period the current will fall to 36.8% of its original value, i.e. it drops by 63.2%. The time taken for this to happen is given by $\tau = L/R$ seconds.

Once again we can express the curve mathematically using the exponential function $i = Ie^{-Rt/L}$ (see Figure 3.48).

James Clerk Maxwell (1831–1879)

Maxwell was born to wealthy Scottish parents and showed himself to be a keen mathematician from an early age. He graduated in mathematics from Cambridge and was appointed professor at Aberdeen in 1856. Like many great scientists Maxwell worked on several different areas of interest but probably his greatest achievement was to put into mathematical form the words and ideas of Faraday concerning the nature of magnetic fields. Working on the concept of lines of force Maxwell developed a set of mathematical equations which linked electrical effects and magnetic effects and showed them to be inseparable.

A generation after Maxwell's death Albert Einstein came along and produced theories which upset almost all classical physics but Maxwell's equations remained as valid as they are today.

Multiple choice questions

1 The conductor in Figure 3.49 is moved up and down so that it cuts the magnetic field lines. If a galvanometer is connected across the ends of the conductor
  (a) the needle will move to a constant positive value
  (b) the needle will alternate between positive and negative

  (c) the needle will move to a constant negative value
  (d) the needle will generate a voltage that will move the conductor.

2 The energy stored around the inductor in Figure 3.50 will be
  (a) 47 μJ
  (b) 2.21 μJ
  (c) 470 J
  (d) 2.35 μJ.

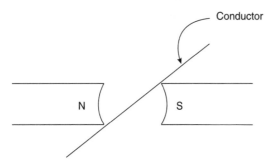

Figure 3.49

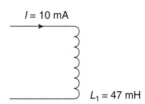

Figure 3.50

3 A common use of an inductor is
  (a) as a power dissipator
  (b) as a series choke
  (c) as a resistive load
  (d) as a variable tuning component.

4 In Figure 3.51 the current in the primary is
  500 mA. The value of the secondary current is
  (a) 5 A
  (b) 24 mA
  (c) 5 mA
  (d) 42 mA.

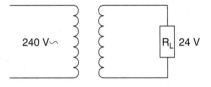

Figure 3.51

5 The output voltage of a transformer is
  determined by
  (a) the turns ratio
  (b) the eddy current losses
  (c) the power developed in the windings
  (d) the impedance of the load.

6 A relay often has a diode connected across it
  because it
  (a) protects against back e.m.f. across the
     relay contacts
  (b) provides an indication of when the relay is
     energised
  (c) speeds up the operation of the coil
  (d) short circuits the relay coil when current
     is interrupted.

7 The transformer in Figure 3.52 is
  (a) step-up
  (b) step-down
  (c) off load
  (d) open circuit in the primary.

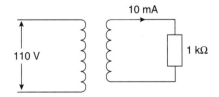

Figure 3.52

8 A typical inductor would have a resistance of
  (a) 0.5 Ω
  (b) 1 kΩ
  (c) 100 Ω
  (d) 500 Ω.

9 In the circuit in Figure 3.53 S_1 is closed. The
  capacitor C_1 will be fully charged after
  (a) 2 ms
  (b) 5 ms
  (c) 5 μs
  (d) 1 ms.

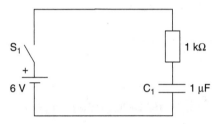

Figure 3.53

10 The relay in Figure 3.54 has to operate after
  5 s. The value of the capacitor should be
  (a) 500 μF
  (b) 50 μF
  (c) 100 μF
  (d) 1000 μF.

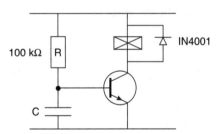

Figure 3.54

4

AC circuits

4.1 AC waveforms and their representation

Up to now we have looked at direct current (DC), i.e. a current which passes in one direction all the time. The e.m.f. which produces DC has a fixed polarity, e.g. that produced by a battery. This means that one terminal is always positive with respect to the other, and since conventional current passes from positive to negative its direction is also fixed.

If we plot a graph of a DC voltage or current against time we can see that, even though it may vary in level, the voltage or current always stays in the same quadrant. That is, it is always positive or always negative even if it is not of a constant value.

All the currents or voltages shown in Figure 4.1 are direct because their direction, or polarity, is constant.

When we look at the way power companies generate and distribute electricity we see that they use currents which repeatedly change direction. The current alternately flows in opposite directions. This type of current is called an alternating current (AC).

Once again, the voltage source which produces this type of current must also be changing polarity repeatedly.

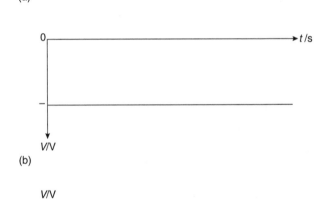

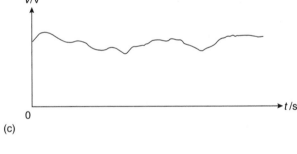

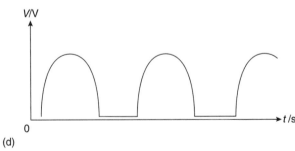

Figure 4.1   (a) Steady positive DC; (b) steady negative DC; (c) varying DC; (d) pulses of DC

It is also the case that, in electronics, most of the signals which we use are AC. So we shall now look at the nature of this current further.

The sinewave

To investigate the simplest way of generating an AC voltage waveform we look at the case of a basic generator where a single loop of wire is rotated in a magnetic field (Figure 4.2).

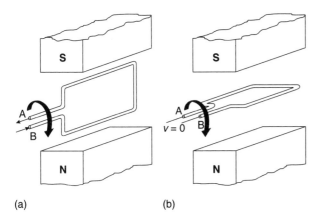

(a)   (b)

Figure 4.2   A single loop alternator: (a) V_{out} maximum; (b) V_{out} minimum

We know from our investigations into electromagnetic induction that an e.m.f. will be induced in the loop, the maximum value occurring when the conductor is at right angles to the permanent magnetic field. What we have not yet thought about in detail is how the induced voltage changes as the loop is rotated.

Figure 4.3 illustrates that as the loop is turned through 90° from its original position to a point where it is at right angles to the permanent magnetic field, the voltage available across the ends of the coil (AB) rises from zero to a positive maximum.

If rotation of the loop is continued through a further 90° it will come to rest 180° from its starting point. Throughout this rotation the voltage across the ends of the coil will decline back to zero in the manner shown.

Rotating the loop a further 180° in the same direction will produce the negative portion of voltage. The loop has now travelled through a complete turn and is back in its original position.

The shape of the waveform over one revolution – or cycle – is known as a sinewave and the voltage that is produced is *alternating* as it has both positive and negative values.

The horizontal axis of the graph of the voltage produced can be calibrated in one of two units. It took 360° (or 2π radians for the mathematically minded) to produce the complete voltage waveform and it is therefore logical to calibrate the scale in degrees or radians as we have in Figure 4.3. However, the rotation of the loop would have taken a certain length of time to complete: 1 s for example, or 1 ms. Thus we could also calibrate the horizontal axis in increments of time.

> It is quite possible for our AC voltage to be superimposed on a DC level as Figure 4.4 shows.

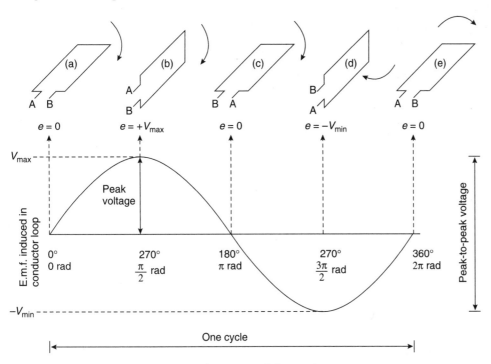

Figure 4.3   One complete cycle of a sinusoidal waveform

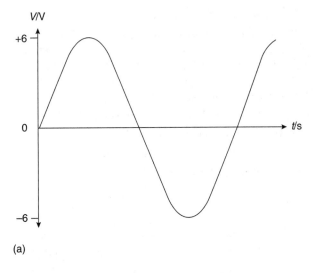

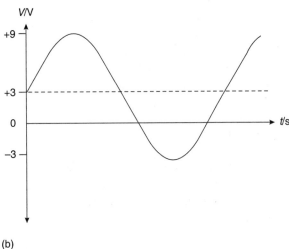

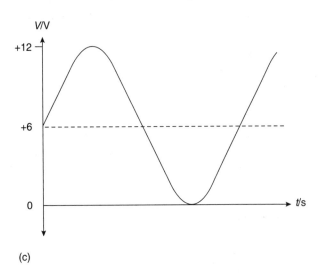

Figure 4.4 (a) Pure AC sinewave, 12 V pk–pk;
(b) AC 12 V pk–pk sinewave with a 3 V DC level;
(c) unidirectional, same AC sinewave but with a 6 V
DC level (no change of polarity occurs)

Sinewave terminology

Unlike a steady DC voltage the value of an AC voltage constantly varies. For this reason when we talk of an AC voltage we have to specify exactly which part of the waveform we mean.

The most commonly used terms are cycle, periodic time, frequency, wavelength, amplitude, peak value, peak to peak value, RMS and average. These are illustrated in Figure 4.5 and will now be explained in more detail.

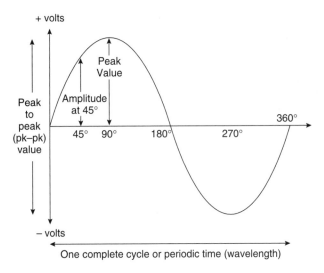

Figure 4.5   Sinewave terminology

Cycle

Cycle is the term given for the period from any point on a waveform to the same point on the following waveform. One complete sinewave takes 360° and this is one cycle.

Periodic time

The periodic time is the duration of one cycle expressed in seconds.

Frequency

Frequency is defined as the number of cycles that occur in 1 s. The unit used to be 'cycles per second' but it has now been changed to hertz (Hz).

If one waveform is at a higher frequency compared with another it will complete more cycles in the same length of time (see Figure 4.6).

Frequency and periodic time are related; if one is known the other can easily be calculated:

$$\text{frequency} = \frac{1}{\text{periodic time}} \text{ Hz}$$

$$\text{periodic time} = \frac{1}{\text{frequency}} \text{ s}$$

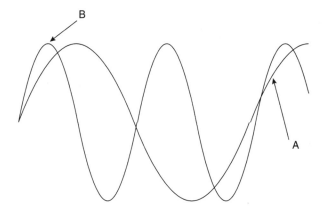

Figure 4.6   Waveform B completes two cycles in the time that waveform A completes one. Waveform B therefore has twice the frequency of waveform A

Guided examples

1 If a waveform has a periodic time of 20 ms, what is its frequency?

$$\text{frequency} = \frac{1}{\text{periodic time}} \text{ Hz}$$

$$= \frac{1}{20 \text{ ms}}$$

$$= 50 \text{ Hz}$$

2 A waveform has a frequency of 2500 Hz. What is its periodic time?

$$\text{periodic time} = \frac{1}{\text{frequency}} \text{ s}$$

$$= \frac{1}{2500}$$

$$= 0.0004 \text{ s}$$

$$= 0.4 \text{ ms}$$

Wavelength

The wavelength is the length, in metres, of one cycle. Wavelength is given the symbol λ (the Greek letter lambda). Generally we are interested in wavelength when we deal with transmitted waveforms such as sound or radio waves.

$$\lambda = v/f \text{ metres}$$

where f is the frequency in hertz and v is the velocity of propagation in metres per second. The velocity of propagation is the velocity at which the wave travels through a medium. Usually we take a constant value for sound waves through air and radio waves through a vacuum, i.e.

sound $v = 331 \text{ m s}^{-1}$

radio waves $v = 3 \times 10^8 \text{ m s}^{-1}$

You may have noticed that the velocity of radio waves is the same as the speed at which light travels. This is because both light and radio waves are examples of electromagnetic radiation and they differ from each other only in their wavelength.

Amplitude and peak values

The term amplitude refers to the 'height' of the waveform measured at a specific time. For electronics engineers, amplitude is usually measured in volts or amps. However, it could equally well be measured in air pressure units (for sound waves) or metres (for waves in water) etc.

When we want to measure amplitude there are several relevant ways we might want to express it, depending on our point of interest.

Peak to peak (pk–pk)   The peak to peak amplitude is the distance from the top to the bottom of the waveform.

Peak (or maximum value)   For a pure AC waveform the peak value is the distance from zero to the maximum displacement in either direction, i.e. it is half the pk–pk value (see Figure 4.7).

RMS (or effective value)   RMS value stands for the 'root mean squared' value. The way to think of this is that it is the value of DC which would produce the same heating effect as the AC waveform.

This is by far the most important way of expressing an AC voltage. Unless otherwise stated we always give the RMS value of an AC waveform. For example, we all know that the UK mains supply is 230 V. This is the RMS value, and most of our test instruments are calibrated to indicate RMS values when we measure AC.

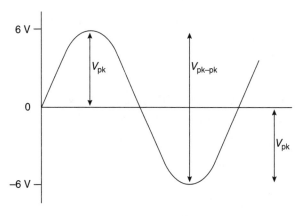

Figure 4.7   Peak (pk) and peak to peak (pk–pk) values. V_{pk} (or V_{max}) = 6 V; $V_{pk–pk}$ = 12 V

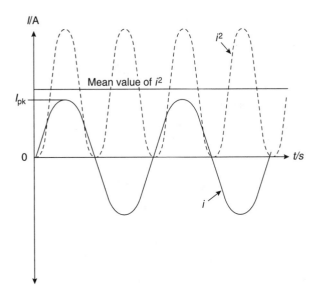

Figure 4.8   If we square all the instantaneous values i of I we get all positive values

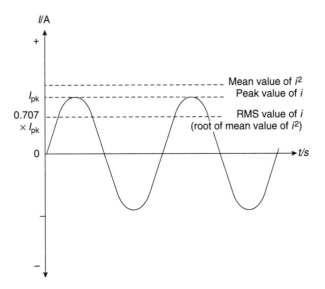

Figure 4.9   RMS value of i

We know that in a DC circuit a resistor of value R ohms drawing a current of I amps will dissipate a power of I^2R watts. If we consider an alternating current through the same resistor then, *providing that I is the RMS value*, the shape of the AC waveform is irrelevant and the equation for power is still correct.

If we square all the instantaneous values of I we get all positive values (Figure 4.8). Now we find the average or *mean* of all these *squared* values. Having found the mean we need to find the effective value, which will be the square root of this mean – hence the **root mean square** value.

The power dissipated in a resistor R is given by

(the mean value of i^2) × R watts

So the effective value of i will be given by

$\sqrt{}$ (mean value of i^2) amps

For a sinewave i^2 has a maximum value of I_{pk}^2. The mean value of i^2 is $I_{pk}^2/2$. Thus for a sinewave the RMS value is $\sqrt{(I_{pk}^2/2)}$. This is $I_{pk}/\sqrt{2}$ which equals $1/\sqrt{2} \times I_{pk}$, and $1/\sqrt{2} \approx 0.707$. So we get:

For a sinewave the RMS value is given by 0.707 × the peak, i.e.

$V_{RMS} = 0.707 \times V_{pk}$

$I_{RMS} = 0.707 \times I_{pk}$

See Figure 4.9. By transposition,

$V_{pk} = 1.414 V_{RMS}$

The UK mains is quoted as 230 V RMS. Therefore $V_{pk} = 230 \times 1.414 = 325.22$ V. That is quite important to know because it means we must allow for a voltage swing of $2V_{pk}$ (or V_{pk-pk}) ≈ 650 V.

Average value   Providing a sinewave rises by a positive amount and falls negative by the same amount the average value of a complete cycle must be 0 V. The average of one half cycle is used mainly when dealing with calculations concerned with rectification. The average value would need to be calculated using integration, or a similar technique, for each different waveform, but for a sinewave the average value is easily found:

$$V_{av} = 0.637 V_{max} \text{ and } I_{av} = 0.637 I_{max}$$

Remember that this figure, 0.637 $(2/\pi)$, only applies to sinewaves.

Instantaneous value   The instantaneous value is the value of voltage or current at any instant in time. If we imagine the AC waveform starting at $t = 0$ s and at some instant later we take a 'snapshot' of the value of the variable, then this will be an instantaneous value.

Before we can determine instantaneous values we need to consider again the production of a sinewave from a rotating loop. This time, however, the loop will be regarded as a single line.

In Figure 4.10 let the length of the line OP represent the maximum value of an AC voltage and let it rotate at a constant speed anticlockwise.

The sinewave is a plot of the instantaneous values of QP (the perpendicular height from P) and

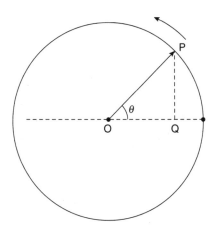

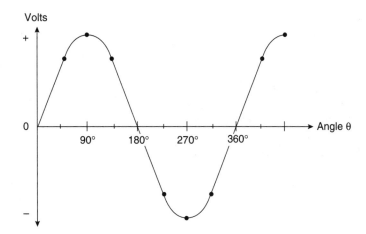

Figure 4.10

since OP represents a maximum voltage the plot is of the instantaneous voltage v.

Using Pythagoras's theorem, the line QP = OP $\sin \theta$. So, for a sinewave the instantaneous voltage v is

$$v = V_{max} \sin \theta \text{ volts}$$

This means that the value of the voltage at any instant can be found by inserting V_{max} and the value of θ at that instant.

Angular velocity

In our calculations we shall often need to state v or i as a function of time, rather than as a function of θ. It would be convenient if we could replace the angle θ on the x axis with something directly related to time.

We first express θ in radians instead of degrees. A radian is the angle at the centre of a circle which is subtended by an arc at the circumference which is equal in length to the radius of the circle. It's easier to draw than to say! See Figure 4.12.

Guided examples

1 A sinewave is expressed as

$v = V_{max} \sin \theta$ volts

If the peak value is 2 V what will be the instantaneous value 45° into the cycle?

$v = 2 \sin 45°$

$\quad = 2 \times 0.707$

$\therefore v = 1.414 \text{ V}$

2 Use the expression $v = V_{max} \sin \theta$ to determine the amplitude 180° into the cycle of the sinewave given in Figure 4.11.

$v = V_{max} \sin \theta$

$v = 5 \sin 180°$

$v = 5 \times 0$

$v = 0 \text{ V}$

This is confirmed by examining the figure,

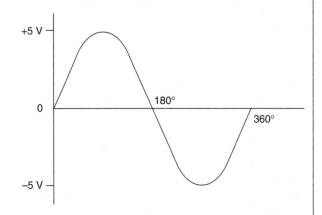

Figure 4.11

as 180° is the point where the graph crosses through 0 V.

NB: Although we have expressed voltage as a sinewave it is quite possible to write current in the same way:

$i = I_{max} \sin \theta$

Exercise

The first part of some of the following
questions has been completed as an example.

1 Determine the periodic time for
frequencies of
(a) 50 Hz,   (b) 20 Hz,   (c) 200 Hz.

(a) $T = \dfrac{1}{f}$

$ = \dfrac{1}{50}$

$ = 20$ ms

 [(b) 50 ms,   (c) 5 ms]

2 Determine the frequencies for periodic
times of
(a) 4 ms,   (b) 50 ms,   (c) 500 μs.

(a) Since $T = 1/f$, then $f = 1/T$ and so

$f = \dfrac{1}{T}$

$ = \dfrac{1}{4 \times 10^{-3}}$

$ = 250$ Hz

 [(b) 20 Hz,   (c) 2000 Hz]

3 An alternating current completes five
cycles in 8 ms. Determine its frequency.

 [625 Hz]

4 Calculate the RMS values of sinusoidal
currents and voltages of maximum values
(a) 20 A,   (b) 60 V,   (c) 5 mA.

(a) Since

 RMS value = 0.707 × maximum value

then

$I_{RMS} = 0.707 \times I_{max}$

$\phantom{I_{RMS}} = 0.707 \times 20$

$\phantom{I_{RMS}} = 14.14$ A

 [(b) 42.42 V,   (c) 3.535 mA]

5 Determine the peak and mean values for
(a) 240 V RMS supply,
(b) 500 V RMS supply.

(a) $V_{RMS} = 0.707 \times V_{max}$

But

$ V_{max} = V_{pk}$

Therefore

$V_{pk} = \dfrac{V_{RMS}}{0.707}$

$\phantom{V_{pk}} = \dfrac{240}{0.707}$

$\phantom{V_{pk}} = 339$ V

Now

$ V_{av} = 0.637 \times V_{max}$

$\phantom{xx V_{av}} = 0.637 \times 339$

$\phantom{xx V_{av}} = 216$ V

 [(b) 707 V, 450 V]

6 A supply voltage has a mean value of
150 V. Determine its maximum and RMS
values.

 [235 V, 166 V]

7 Draw two cycles of a sinewave to scale
with a peak value of 10 A at a frequency
of 50 Hz.

8 Briefly describe what is meant by the
terms RMS and average value in relation
to a sinewave.

9 A sinusoidal current has a peak value of
30 A and a frequency of 70 Hz. At time
$t = 0$ s, the current is zero. Express the
instantaneous current i in the form
$i = I_{max} \sin(\omega t)$.

 [$i = 30 \sin(314t)$]

10 An alternating voltage is given by
$v = 452 \sin(314t)$. Determine
(a) the RMS voltage, (b) the frequency,
(c) the instantaneous value of voltage
when $t = 4$ ms.

 [(a) 319 V,   (b) 50 Hz,   (c) 430 V]

11 Find the peak value, the RMS value, the
periodic time and the frequency of each of
the following:

(a) $v = 90 \sin(400\pi t)$ volts
(b) $i = 50 \sin(100\pi t)$ amps
(c) $e = 200 \sin(628.4t)$ volts

[(a) 90 V, 63 V, 5 ms, 200 Hz;
(b) 50 A, 35 A, 0.02 s, 50 Hz;
(c) 200 V, 141.4 V, 0.01 s, 100 Hz]

Sinewave terminology

In a DC circuit, current flows constantly in one direction.

In an AC circuit, current flows alternately in one direction and then in the opposite direction.

Frequency is the number of cycles per second and is expressed in hertz.

Amplitude is the peak or maximum value of a repeating waveform that varies with time.

Peak to peak value is the sum of the positive and negative peak values, regardless of the waveform.

Periodic time (T) is the time taken in seconds to complete one cycle:

$$T = \frac{1}{f}$$

where f is the frequency in hertz.

Phase is the fractional difference in time or phase angle between two waves whose frequencies are equal.

Angular velocity (ω) is the product of the frequency of a sinusoidal quantity and the factor 2π:

$$\omega = 2\pi f \text{ rad s}^{-1}$$

Instantaneous values are the values of a varying quantity at particular instants in time:

$e = E \sin\theta$ or $v = V \sin\theta$

$e = E \sin(\omega t)$ or $v = V \sin(\omega t)$

$i = I \sin\theta$

$i = I \sin(\omega t)$

(The symbols to denote instantaneous values are lower case letters. Upper case letters denote peak values.)

Average value (mean value) is the value taken over one half cycle of a sinewave.

average value = $0.637E$

average value = $0.637I$

RMS value (effective value) is that value of AC current or voltage that will do the same work as the same value of DC.

RMS value = $0.707E$

RMS value = $0.707I$

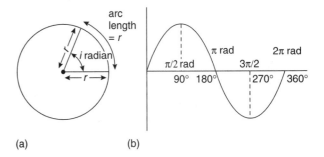

(a)   (b)

Figure 4.12   Definition of a radian

The circumference of a circle is given by $2\pi r$ so there must be 2π radians in one revolution (360°).

360° = 2π radians

Therefore

1° = $\pi/180$ radians

Therefore

1 radian = $180°/\pi$ = 57.3°

If the rotating radius goes completely around the circle once (one cycle) in 1 s, the frequency f of the plotted waveform is 1 Hz.

The radius will have moved through 2π radians so the angular velocity is $2\pi r$ radians per second. $2\pi f$ is abbreviated to the symbol ω (omega).

We can now rewrite the general formula for a sinewave and change the θ part to $2\pi f$. As we are interested in an instantaneous value after a certain time the expression becomes

$$v = V_{max} \sin(\omega t) \text{ volts}$$

where V_{max} is the peak voltage, $\omega = 2\pi f$ and t is the time in seconds. Don't forget that ωt is measured in radians and not degrees.

Similarly, the instantaneous (sinewave) current is expressed as

$$i = I_{max} \sin(\omega t) \text{ amps}$$

Guided examples

1 A sinewave is expressed as

$$v = V_{max} \sin(\omega t)$$

If its frequency is 1 kHz and its peak voltage is 8 V calculate the instantaneous value after 0.25 ms. (Don't forget to put your calculator into radian mode!)

Using

$$
\begin{aligned}
v &= V_{max} \sin(\omega t) \\
&= 8 \times \sin(2\pi f t) \\
&= 8 \times \sin(2\pi \times 1 \times 10^3 \times 0.25 \times 10^{-3}) \\
&= 8 \times \sin(\pi/2) \\
&= 8 \times \sin(1.57 \text{ rad}) \\
&= 8 \times 0.999 \\
&= 7.99 \text{ V}
\end{aligned}
$$

The answer can be checked graphically as shown in Figure 4.13 (f = 1 kHz; therefore periodic time = $1/(1 \times 10^3)$ = 1 ms).

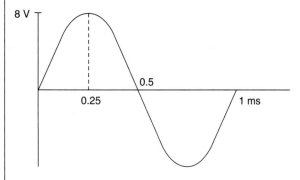

Figure 4.13

2 A sinusoidal current is given by

$$i = 25 \sin(314t) \text{ amps}$$

Determine (a) the peak value, (b) the angular velocity, (c) the frequency and periodic time and (d) the instantaneous current 12 ms into the cycle.

(a) Peak value I_{max} = 25 A.

(b) Angular velocity $\omega = 2\pi f$ = 314 rad s^{-1}.

(c) $\omega = 2\pi f$. Therefore $f = \omega/2\pi = 314/2\pi$ = 50 Hz.

$t = 1/f = 1/50$ = 20 ms.

(d) When t = 12 ms, $i = 25 \sin(314 \times 12 \times 10^{-3})$ = −14.7 A.

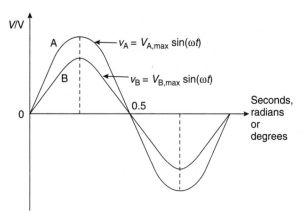

Figure 4.14

Phase difference

Two alternating quantities with the same frequency are said to be **in phase** if they pass through the same point of their cycle at the same time.

If they pass through the same point at different times they are **out of phase**. The quantity that passes the point first is said to 'lead' and the one which arrives afterwards is said to 'lag'. Figure 4.14 shows two sinusoidal voltages of the same frequency but having different peak values. You can see that the peak and zero points of each sinewave occur at the same time – they are aligned time wise. A better way of expressing this is to say that they are in phase.

Mathematically we can say that, for waveform A,

$$v_A = V_{A,max} \sin(\omega t)$$

and for waveform B,

$$v_B = V_{B,max} \sin(\omega t)$$

The important point to note is that $\sin(\omega t)$ occurs in both equations as there is no time difference between the two waveforms.

Leading and lagging

Two sinewaves A and B are represented in Figure 4.15. In this case each waveform has the same peak

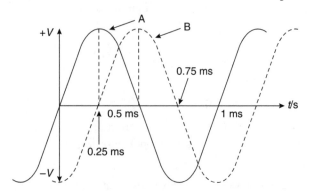

Figure 4.15   Waveform A leads waveform B as A reaches its peak value before B

value. They are both of the same frequency as each has the same periodic time. However, waveform A is at its peak value after 0.25 ms, whereas waveform B reaches its peak value after 0.5 ms. We can thus say that A leads B by a time of 0.25 ms. In terms of angle (one cycle = 360° or 2π rad) A leads B by 90° (or $\pi/2$ rad). Incidentally, the reverse can also be said, i.e. B lags A by 90° or $\pi/2$ rad.

Mathematically our sinewave expression for A now changes slightly to take account of this:

$$v_A = V_{A,max} \sin(\omega t + 90°)$$

or, using radians,

$$v_A = V_{A,max} \sin(\omega t + \pi/2)$$

which says that A leads B by $\pi/2$ rad.

If, as in Figure 4.16, A reaches its positive peak as B falls to its negative peak the two waveforms are phase displaced by 180°. The net result of this is that the overall voltage present is zero as the two waveforms cancel. Waveforms A and B are said to be in anti-phase.

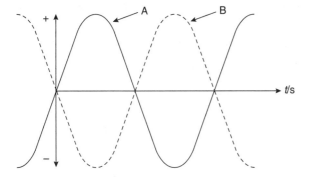

Figure 4.16   Waveforms A and B are in anti-phase. A attains its maximum positive value as B attains its maximum negative value

Phasor representation of AC

We now know that an AC voltage has more than one quantity to be considered at any time. We can talk in terms of amplitude, frequency and phase.

The actual process of drawing sinewaves each time we want to show AC voltages is very time consuming and we need an easier method of representing them. This is done by using *phasors* which, by means of a straight line, give all the information about a sinewave at some point in its cycle.

In Figure 4.17(a) the loop of wire in which an AC voltage is induced is shown part of the way through its 360° rotation. In Figure 4.17(b) the loop is represented by a rotating line OA. The length of OA is the maximum voltage that can ever be obtained (i.e. the peak value) and the angle θ is the

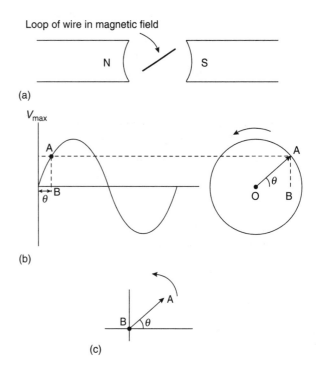

Figure 4.17   Phasor representation of a sinewave

same as the angle through which the loop has rotated in an anticlockwise direction from the horizontal.

The size of the voltage induced in the loop at this point is given by the line AB and, as expected, this corresponds directly to the instantaneous height of the sinewave. The angle θ is the point at which the amplitude is measured.

The phasor representation of the sinewave is shown in Figure 4.17(c) where the length of the line AB is the amplitude and the angle is θ degrees.

Guided example

Represent the sinewave in Figure 4.18 by means of a phasor at $\pi/4$ rad into its cycle.

We shall arrive at the phasor in two ways. First, the value $\pi/4$ rad is directly equivalent

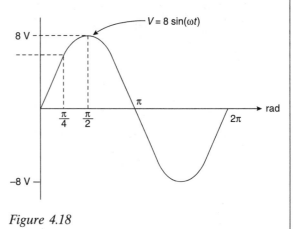

Figure 4.18

to 45°. Figure 4.18 shows that at this point the value of the sinewave is approximately 5.5 V. The phasor will therefore have a length equal to this. The angle of the phasor from the reference is $\pi/4$ rad or 45°.

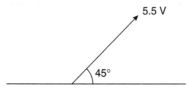

5.5 V

45°

Alternatively, and much more quickly, we can tackle the problem mathematically:

$$v = V_{max} \sin(\omega t)$$
$$\therefore V = 8 \times \sin(\pi/4)$$
$$= 8 \times 0.707$$
$$= 5.65 \text{ V}$$

5.65 V

$\theta = \dfrac{\pi}{4}$ rad = 45°

Indicating an AC voltage using a phasor

Now we have proved that it is easier to use phasor representation than to draw the equivalent sinewave, we can use mathematical terminology to describe an AC voltage expressed in phasor form. The answer to the Guided Example above could be written

5.65 V   45°

The voltage   The phase angle

Phasor representation of two voltages in phase

We now consider again two AC voltages in phase but with different peak values. The phasors that

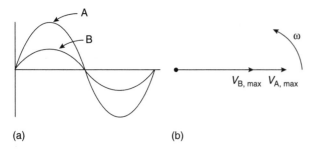

A

B

ω

$V_{B, max}$ $V_{A, max}$

(a)   (b)

Figure 4.19   Two in-phase AC voltages represented in phasor form. ω is the angular velocity

represent them must be on the same line but one will be bigger than the other. In Figure 4.19(a) voltage A has a larger peak value than B. Consequently the two phasors to represent these voltages appear as in Figure 4.19(b).

Mathematically we can say that

$$v_A = V_{A,max} \sin(\omega t)$$

and

$$v_B = V_{B,max} \sin(\omega t)$$

where the ωs are equal.

Phasor representation of a lagging AC voltage

The two voltages A and B in Figure 4.20(a) are such that B lags A by an angle of ϕ degrees. Note that the two phasors that represent this (Figure 4.20(b)) are of different lengths ($V_{A,max}$ is longer than $V_{B,max}$) depicting the difference in peak values. They are separated by the same angle ϕ.

Writing the general expression for a sinewave for waveforms A and B illustrates the difference in angle:

$$v_A = V_{A,max} \sin(\omega t)$$
$$v_B = V_{B,max} \sin(\omega t - \phi)$$

which shows that B lags A by ϕ degrees.

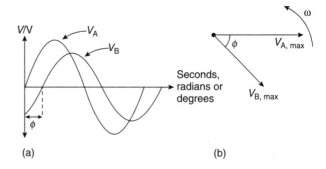

V/V

V_A

V_B

Seconds, radians or degrees

ϕ

ω

ϕ

$V_{A, max}$

$V_{B, max}$

(a)   (b)

Figure 4.20   Waveform B lags waveform A by ϕ degrees

Phasor representation of a leading voltage

In Figure 4.21 the phase of the two voltages has reversed and V_B now leads V_A by an angle of ϕ degrees. The position of the phasors will alter as shown in Figure 4.21(b).

In sinewave terminology this can be expressed as

$$v_A = V_{A,max} \sin(\omega t)$$
$$v_B = V_{B,max} \sin(\omega t + \phi)$$

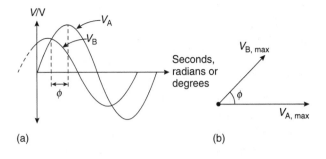

(a)   (b)

Figure 4.21   Waveform B leads waveform A by φ degrees

Adding AC waveforms

If two or more AC voltage sources are connected in series we can only add their peak values together to obtain the overall voltage if both have the same frequency and are in phase.

If the waveforms differ in frequency and/or phase we have to use one of three methods: the graphical solution, the phasor solution or the mathematical solution.

Graphical solution

The graphical solution is best illustrated with an example. Three branch currents in an AC circuit are represented as follows:

$i_1 = 20 \sin(314t)$ mA

$i_2 = 10 \sin(314t - \pi/3)$ mA

$i_3 = 5 \sin(314t + \pi/6)$ mA

This is shown in Figure 4.22. To determine the total current supplied, add the individual values. At 90° $i_1 = 20$ mA, $i_2 = 5$ mA, $i_3 = 5$ mA. Therefore total current $i_T = 30$ mA.

Phasor solution

The phasor solution is another type of graphical solution but is much easier than adding sinewaves. The phasors representing each of the AC waveforms to be added are drawn on the same phasor diagram (see Figure 4.23(a)).

To obtain the sum of the two voltages we go through a process known as 'completing the parallelogram'. This is the term given to the process of extending the phasors and obtaining the diagonal. Figure 4.23(a) is modified to give Figure 4.23(b). The resultant of the two voltages is the length of the diagonal at the angle shown.

Mathematical solution

The mathematical solution uses trigonometry to find the phasor sum of AC quantities. When

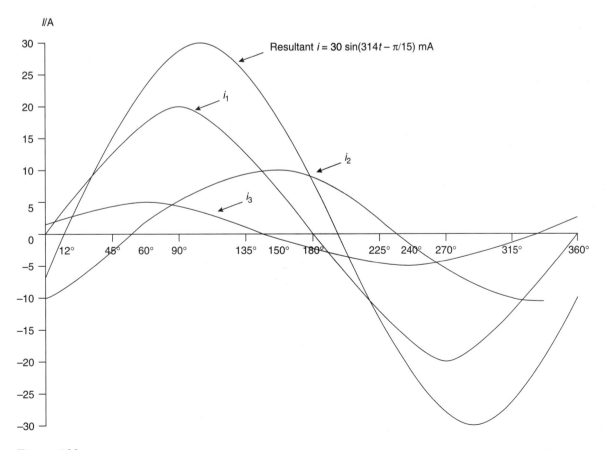

Figure 4.22

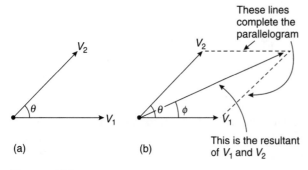

Figure 4.23

we look at a phasor diagram we can see that each phasor can be resolved into two components – a vertical component and a horizontal component.

If we resolve each phasor we end up with a series of vertical components which can be added together and a series of horizontal components which can be added together. The two sums of these components are at right angles to each other so we can find their resultant by using Pythagoras's theorem.

Let's consider the same three currents as those used with the graphical solution: $i_1 = 20 \sin(314t)$ mA, $i_2 = 10 \sin(314t - \pi/3)$ mA and $i_3 = 5 \sin(314t + \pi/6)$ mA.

First we find the vertical component (see Figure 4.26):

$$i_1 = 0$$

$$i_2 = -10 \sin 60° = -8.66 \text{ mA}$$

$$i_3 = +5 \sin 30° = +2.5 \text{ mA}$$

The resultant vertical component is –6.16 mA.
Next we find the horizontal component:

$$i_1 = +20 \text{ mA}$$

$$i_2 = +10 \cos 60° = +5 \text{ mA}$$

$$i_3 = +5 \cos 30° = +4.33 \text{ mA}$$

The resultant horizontal component is +29.33 mA.

Now all we have to do is apply Pythagoras's theorem and we can find the resultant of all three currents:

$$I_{\text{resultant}} = \sqrt{(6.16)^2 + (29.33)^2}$$

$$= 29.95 \text{ mA}$$

$$(\approx 30 \text{ mA})$$

Guided example

Two AC voltages are to be added. The first is $V_1 = 30$ V $\angle 60°$ and the second is $V_2 = 40$ V $\angle 5°$ (see Figure 4.24).

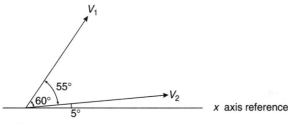

Figure 4.24

In Figure 4.25 these are drawn to scale and the parallelogram is completed. The length and angle of the resultant can be measured with appropriate drawing instruments.

If you try this you will find that the resultant is 62.5 V at an angle of 23°.

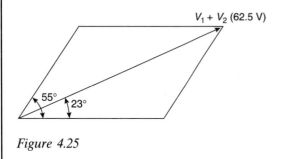

Figure 4.25

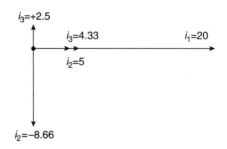

Figure 4.26

Figure 4.28   (a) Fundamental f_A; (b) second harmonic with half the amplitude of the fundamental; (c) third harmonic with one-third of the amplitude of the fundamental; (d) fourth harmonic with one-quarter the amplitude of the fundamental; (e) resultant of parts (a)–(d) – note that already the waveform is tending towards a 'sawtooth' waveform; (f) a fundamental plus an infinite number of odd harmonics will produce a 'square wave'

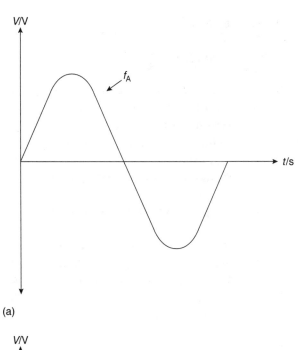

(a)

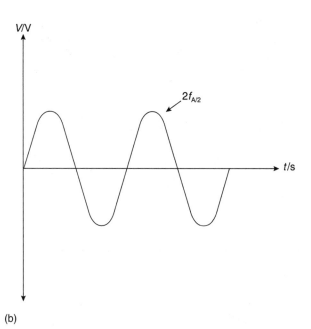

(b)

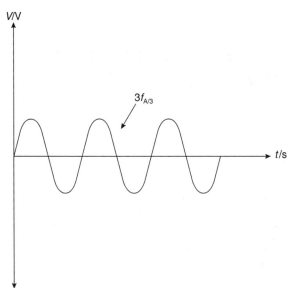

(c)

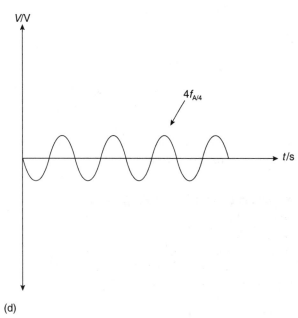

(d)

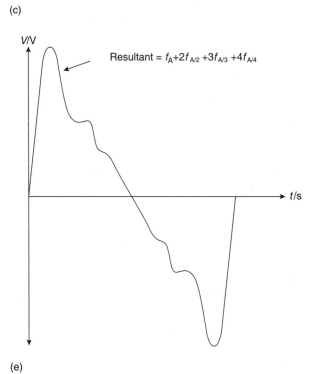

(e)

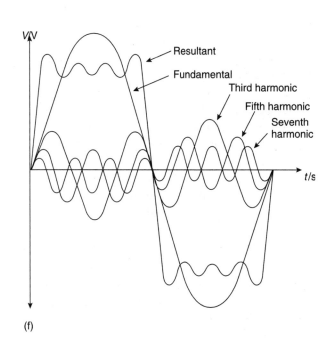

(f)

lagging by

$$\phi = \tan^{-1}(6.16/29.33)$$

$$= \tan^{-1} 0.21$$

$$= 11.85° (\approx 12°)$$

This is illustrated in Figure 4.27.

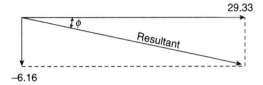

Figure 4.27

Now we can express the total current mathematically:

$$12° = 12 \times \pi/180 = \pi/15 \text{ rad}$$

Therefore

$$i = 30 \sin(314t - \pi/15) \text{ mA}$$

Now that we know how to represent AC quantities and how to calculate their combined effect, we need to examine the effects of our passive electronic components on the relationships between AC voltage, current and resistance.

Fourier's theorem

Jean Baptiste Joseph Fourier (1768–1830) discovered that all periodic functions can be expressed as a sum of sinusoidal components. Basically, this means that *any* complex waveform consists of a given number of sinewaves of given frequency, amplitude and phase.

One sinewave is at the same frequency as the complex wave and is called the **fundamental**. Added to this are the given harmonics.

A **harmonic** is a sinusoid at a frequency which is a multiple of the fundamental. That is, if the fundamental has a frequency of f hertz the second harmonic will be at $2f$ hertz, the third at $3f$ hertz etc. These are grouped as 'odd harmonics' (first, third, fifth etc.) and 'even harmonics' (second, fourth etc.)

Consider a 'sawtooth' waveform. This can be built from a fundamental plus the second harmonic in phase at half the amplitude, plus the third at a third of the amplitude and so on.

Similarly a 'square wave' may be shown to consist of a fundamental plus an infinite number of odd harmonics.

Both these forms can be seen appearing in the last two parts of Figure 4.28 (page 81).

4.2 Series AC circuits

Pure resistance in an AC circuit

In the case of a pure resistance we know, from Ohm's law, that the p.d. developed across it is directly proportional to the current through it. This applies to the instantaneous values if we are considering AC.

NB: By the term pure we mean that the circuit is considered to have no losses.

Thus V and I will be in phase with each other and Ohm's law applies. The phasor diagram will have both V and I shown in phase along the same line (Figure 4.29(b)).

The instantaneous voltage is given by $v = \hat{V} \sin(\omega t)$ volts and the instantaneous current is given by $i = \hat{I} \sin(\omega t)$ amps (see Figure 4.29(c)).

As power is given by $W = I \times V$ watts the instantaneous power is given by

$$v \times i = \{\hat{V} \sin(\omega t)\} \times \{\hat{I} \sin(\omega t)\}$$

$$= \hat{V}\hat{I} \sin^2(\omega t) \text{ watts}$$

Pure inductance and inductive reactance

We already know that when a voltage is applied to an inductor a back e.m.f. is induced which opposes the voltage that produces it. The current through the inductor lags the applied voltage by 90° ($\pi/2$ rad) and opposition is offered to the flow of charge (see Figure 4.30).

Mathematically we can express this using the general sinewave formulae:

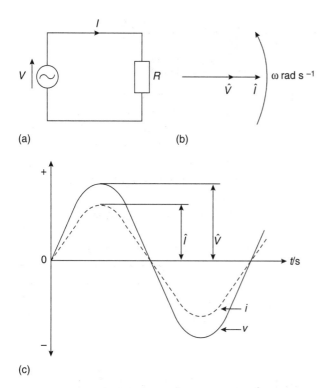

(a)   (b)

(c)

Figure 4.29 Resistance in an AC circuit: $\hat{V} = V_{max}$ or V_{pk}; $\hat{I} = I_{max}$ or I_{pk}; v, instantaneous voltage; i, instantaneous current

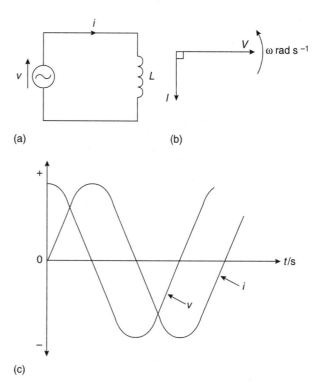

(a)   (b)

(c)

Figure 4.30 Inductance in an AC circuit. Current I lags the voltage V by 90°

$$v = V_{max} \sin(\omega t)$$

$$i = I_{max} \sin(\omega t - \pi/2)$$

As the frequency of the applied AC voltage is increased the current decreases. The opposition offered to the current is frequency dependent. For this reason we don't call it resistance but refer to it as **inductive reactance**.

Figure 4.31

Inductive reactance is the opposition offered to AC via an inductor. It is given the symbol X_L and is calculated from

$$X_L = 2\pi f L$$

$$= \omega L$$

where $\omega = 2\pi f$.

If a graph is plotted of inductive reactance against frequency in a pure inductive circuit a straight line will be obtained as the relationship is linear (see Figure 4.31).

The unit of reactance is the ohm and the current can still be calculated using Ohm's law. Therefore

$$I = \frac{V}{X_L}$$

Guided example

In Figure 4.32 the voltage applied to the circuit can be rewritten as

$$\begin{aligned} v &= V_{max} \sin(\omega t) \\ &= 50 \sin(2\pi \times 1 \times 10^3 t) \\ &= 50 \sin(6.28 \times 1 \times 10^3 t) \\ &= 50 \sin(6.28 \times 10^3 t) \end{aligned}$$

$$\begin{aligned} X_L &= 2\pi f L \\ &= 2\pi \times 1 \times 10^3 \times 0.1 \times 10^{-3} \\ &= 0.628 \ \Omega \end{aligned}$$

The peak current is

$$I = \frac{V}{X_L} = \frac{50}{0.628} = 79.62 \text{ A}$$

The current 0.3 ms into the cycle is calculated by first finding the instantaneous voltage:

$$\begin{aligned} v &= V \sin(\omega \times 0.3 \text{ ms}) \\ &= 50 \sin(2\pi f \times 0.3 \times 10^{-3}) \\ &= 50 \sin(6.28 \times 1 \times 10^3 \times 0.3 \times 10^{-3}) \\ &= 50 \sin 1.884 \end{aligned}$$

Remember to work in radians on your calculator! So

$$v = 47.57 \text{ V}$$

Therefore current

$$I = \frac{V}{X_L} = \frac{47.57}{0.628} = 75.75 \text{ A}$$

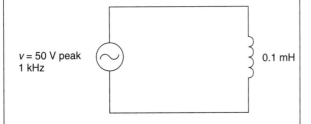

$v = 50$ V peak
1 kHz

0.1 mH

Figure 4.32

Practical 1

Inductive reactance

The purpose of this practical is to show how the reactance of an inductor varies with the frequency of the applied voltage. You can calculate the theoretical answers and see how they compare with your practical results.

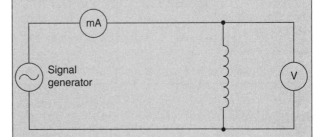

Figure 4.33

Connect up the circuit shown in Figure 4.33. You must make sure that the meters you use are capable of reading up to a frequency of at least 16 kHz and preferably 20 kHz. The standard analogue AVO 8 is quite sufficient but you need to check the specification of digital meters.

Set the output of the signal generator to provide an output of 4 V on the meter across the inductor. Set the frequency to 2 kHz. Note the current that is indicated on the meter. Repeat this for each of the frequencies given in the results table, making sure that each time you adjust the frequency the voltage across the inductor is kept at 4 V.

Function generator with digital display

Using the formula $X_L = V/I$ calculate the inductive reactance from your practical answers for each of the frequencies.

Use the conventional inductive reactance formula $X_L = 2\pi fL$ to calculate the theoretical reactance and enter your answers in the table.

Frequency (kHz)	2	4	6	8	10	12	14	16
Volts (V)								
Current (mA)								
$X_L = V/I \; \Omega$								
$X_L = 2\pi fL \; \Omega$								

Capacitance and capacitive reactance

When a voltage is applied to a capacitor the capacitor will take a finite length of time to charge. The current that charges the capacitor will flow first and then the voltage that results will be built up across the plates of the capacitor. From this it follows that in a circuit of pure capacitance the current leads the voltage. It does so by an angle of 90° (see Figure 4.34).

Mathematically, this can be expressed as follows:

$$v = V_{max} \sin(\omega t)$$

$$i = I_{max} \sin(\omega t + \pi/2)$$

As the frequency of the applied AC is increased the current increases, although the relationship is not linear but inversely proportional. This implies that the opposition offered to current changes with frequency.

The opposition to AC via a capacitor is known as capacitive reactance. It is given the symbol X_C and calculated from

$$X_C = \frac{1}{2\pi fC} = \frac{1}{\omega C}$$

where $\omega = 2\pi f$.

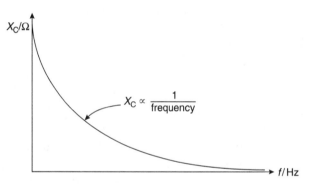

Figure 4.35   Capacitive reactance plotted against frequency

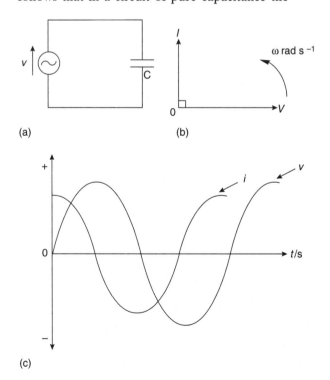

Figure 4.34   Capacitance in an AC circuit. Current I leads the voltage V by 90°

CIVIL
This word has been used for many years by students of electronics to help them remember what leads or lags what in inductive and capacitive circuits. It works as follows:

In a Capacitor current (*I*) comes before (or leads) Voltage

C I V I L

Voltage comes before current (*I*) in an inductor (*L*)

Practical 2

Capacitive reactance

The purpose of this practical is to show how the reactance of a capacitor varies with the frequency of the applied voltage. You can calculate the theoretical answers and see how they compare with your practical results.

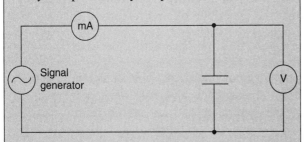

Figure 4.36

Connect up the circuit shown in Figure 4.36. You must make sure that the meters you use are capable of reading up to a frequency of at least 16 kHz and preferably 20 kHz. The standard analogue AVO 8 is quite sufficient but you need to check the specification of digital meters.

Set the output of the signal generator to provide an output of 4 V on the meter across the capacitor. Set the frequency to 2 kHz. Note the current that is indicated on the meter. Repeat this for each of the frequencies given in the results table, making sure that each time you adjust the frequency the voltage across the capacitor is kept at 4 V.

Using the formula $X_C = V/I$ calculate the capacitive reactance from your practical answers for each of the frequencies.

Use the conventional capacitive reactance formula $X_C = 1/2\pi fC$ to calculate the theoretical reactance and enter your answers in the appropriate part of the table.

Frequency (kHz)	2	4	6	8	10	12	14	16
Volts (V)								
Current (mA)								
$X_C = V/I\ \Omega$								
$X_C = 1/2\pi fC\ \Omega$								

From the results table it is possible to plot two graphs:

(a) the practical reactance of the capacitor obtained by using the formula $X_C = V/I$;
(b) the theoretical reactance obtained by calculation using $X_C = 1/2\pi fC$.

From extension of the graph you should see that the higher the frequency is the less the reactance of the capacitor until, at a frequency of infinite hertz, the reactance is zero.

Guided example

Calculate the capacitive reactance of the capacitor and the peak current for Figure 4.37.

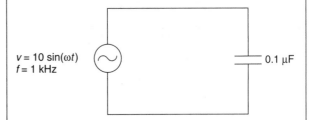

Figure 4.37

$$X_C = \frac{1}{2\pi fC}$$

$$= \frac{1}{2 \times \pi \times 1 \times 10^3 \times 0.1 \times 10^{-6}}$$

$$= 1.59\ \text{k}\Omega$$

The peak current is given by

$$I = \frac{V_{peak}}{X_C} = \frac{10}{1.59 \times 10^3} = 6.28\ \text{mA}$$

If a graph is plotted of capacitive reactance against frequency it will take the form of Figure 4.35.

As with inductive reactance the unit of capacitive reactance is the ohm and Ohm's law can be used to calculate the current. Therefore

$$I = \frac{V}{X_C}$$

Components in an AC circuit

Pure resistance

$$I = \frac{V}{R}$$

Resistance does not vary with frequency. Current and voltage are in phase.

Pure inductance

$$I = \frac{V}{X_L}$$

where $X = 2\pi fL$.

Inductive reactance increases with frequency. Voltage leads current by 90°.

Pure capacitance

$$I = \frac{V}{X_C}$$

where $X_C = 1/2\pi fC$.

Capacitive reactance decreases with frequency. Current leads voltage by 90°.

Power in a reactive circuit
No power is dissipated in a purely reactive component.

All the theory we have looked at so far assumes *pure* inductance or capacitance but in reality there is always a loss resistance in any coil or capacitor. In an inductor there is the resistance of the wire and the capacitance between the turns. In a capacitor there is the leakage resistance of the dielectric, and in some types of capacitor construction there is inductance due to the rolling, or coiling, of the plate area. This loss resistance will dissipate power (I^2R).

As usual, life is not as straightforward as we might like, so we need to look at the combined effects of both reactive and resistive components. Let us first consider series connections.

Resistance and inductance in series

In any series circuit (Figure 4.38) the current is common to all components. Thus we use the current as the reference phasor and show all other

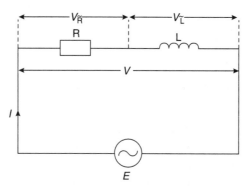

Figure 4.38   Resistance and inductance in series

quantities relative to it. We know that the voltage developed across a resistor is in phase with the current and that the voltage across an inductor leads the current by 90° (see Figure 4.39).

The sum of the voltage across the resistor (V_R) and the voltage across the inductor (V_L) gives the total voltage across the circuit, which must equal the applied e.m.f. (Kirchhoff's law): $E = V_{\text{supply}}$ volts. A straightforward addition cannot be used because of the phase difference. As Figure 4.39 shows, the resultant is the vector sum.

The opposition to current is a combination of resistance and inductive reactance and is called the circuit **impedance**. The symbol for impedance is Z and the unit of measurement is the ohm:

$Z = V/I$ ohms

From Figure 4.39 we can see that a right-angled triangle is formed which can be solved using Pythagoras's theorem:

$$V_{\text{supply}}^2 = V_R^2 + V_L^2$$

$$V_{\text{supply}}^2 = (IR)^2 + (IX_L)^2$$

Now, the total voltage equals $V_{\text{supply}} = IZ$, so

$$(IZ)^2 = I^2R^2 + I^2X_L^2$$

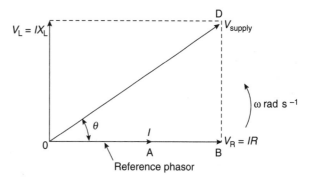

Figure 4.39

Dividing by I gives

$$Z^2 = R^2 + X_L^2$$

$$\therefore \text{ circuit impedance } Z = \sqrt{(R^2 + X_L^2)}$$

From the phasor diagram (Figure 4.39) we see that V leads I by some angle θ. This is what we expect for an inductive circuit. If we look again at the phasor diagram we see that this angle can easily be found:

$$\tan \theta = \frac{DB}{OB}$$

$$= \frac{V_L}{V_R}$$

$$= \frac{IX_L}{IR}$$

$$= \frac{I\omega L}{IR}$$

$$\therefore \tan \theta = \frac{\omega L}{R}$$

$$\therefore \quad \theta = \tan^{-1} \frac{\omega L}{R}$$

NB: $\tan^{-1}$ = arctan; $\tan^{-1}$ is read as 'the angle whose tangent is'.

To express the impedance phasor fully we must quote its magnitude and direction. So

$$Z = \sqrt{(R^2 + \omega^2 L^2)} \ \tan^{-1}(\omega L/R) \text{ ohms}$$

Guided examples

1 A resistor and an inductor are connected to an AC supply as shown in Figure 4.40. The value of the resistor is 30 Ω. The inductor has a reactance of 18 Ω. What is

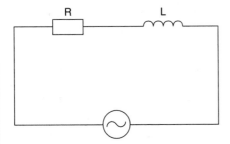

Figure 4.40

the total opposition offered to the current by the circuit?

For the words 'total opposition offered to the current' read impedance. The resistance and inductive reactance are separated by 90° as the phasor diagram in Figure 4.41 shows.

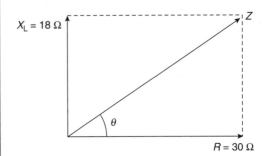

Figure 4.41

The circuit impedance Z is given by

$$Z = \sqrt{(30^2 + 18^2)}$$
$$= \sqrt{(900 + 324)}$$
$$= \sqrt{(1224)}$$
$$= 35 \ \Omega$$

The angle of impedance is given by

$$\theta = \tan^{-1}\left(\frac{X_L}{R}\right)$$
$$= \tan^{-1}\left(\frac{18}{30}\right)$$
$$= 31°$$

$$\therefore \text{ impedance} = 35 \ \Omega \ \angle \ 31°$$

2 For the circuit in Figure 4.42 calculate the impedance and use this to find the peak current.

As we have to find the impedance we first need to find X_L:

$$X_L = \omega L = 2\pi f L$$

Since $v = 10 \sin(628t)$, ω must be 628.

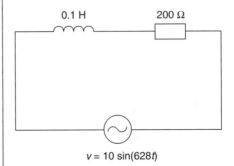

$v = 10 \sin(628t)$

Figure 4.42

Therefore

$$X_L = \omega L = 628 \times 0.1 = 62.8 \ \Omega$$

So

$$Z = \sqrt{(X_L^2 + R^2)}$$
$$= \sqrt{(62.8^2 + 200^2)}$$
$$= \sqrt{(3944 + 40\,000)}$$
$$= \sqrt{(43\,944)}$$
$$= 209 \ \Omega$$

The angle of impedance is given by

$$\theta = \tan^{-1}\left(\frac{X_L}{R}\right)$$
$$= \tan^{-1}\left(\frac{62.8}{200}\right)$$
$$= 17°$$
$$\therefore Z = 209 \ \Omega \ \angle \ 17°$$

For the peak current,

$$I = \frac{V_{peak}}{Z} = \frac{10}{209} = 0.048 \ A = 48 \ mA$$

3   Find the impedance of the circuit shown in Figure 4.43.

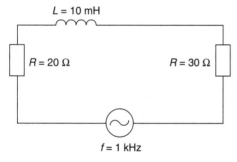

Figure 4.43

$$X_L = 2\pi fL$$
$$= 2 \times \pi \times 1 \times 10^3 \times 10 \times 10^{-3}$$
$$= 20 \times \pi$$
$$= 62.8$$
$$R = 30 + 20$$
$$= 50$$
$$\therefore Z = \sqrt{(62.8^2 + 50^2)}$$
$$= 80.3 \ \Omega$$

The angle of impedance is given by

$$\tan^{-1}\left(\frac{X_L}{R}\right) = \tan^{-1}\left(\frac{62.8}{50}\right) = 51.5°$$
$$\therefore Z = 80.3 \ \Omega \ \angle \ 51.5°$$

4   Find the reactance and the current when an inductor of 12 H is connected across a 110 V, 50 Hz supply.
    Given $L = 12$ H, $V = 110$ V and $f = 50$ Hz,

$$X_L = 2\pi fL$$
$$= 2 \times \pi \times 50 \times 12$$
$$= 3768 \ \Omega$$
$$I = V/X$$
$$= 110/3768$$
$$= 0.0292 \ A$$
$$= 29.2 \ mA$$

5   An inductor of 50 mH inductance and 6 Ω resistance is connected across a 60 V, 60 Hz supply. Calculate the current in the circuit.

$$X_L = 2\pi fL$$
$$= 2 \times \pi \times 60 \times 50 \times 10^{-3}$$
$$= 18.8 \ \Omega$$
$$Z = \sqrt{(X_L^2 + R^2)}$$
$$= \sqrt{(18.8^2 + 6^2)}$$
$$= 19.8 \ \Omega$$
$$I = V/Z$$
$$= 60/19.8$$
$$= 3.03 \ A$$

Resistance and capacitance in series

We are still considering a series circuit (Figure 4.44) so once again current is common to all components in the circuit and is the reference phasor for our phasor diagram.

From Figure 4.45 we can readily see that the voltage lags the current. The total circuit voltage is the phasor sum of the voltage across the resistor and the voltage across the capacitor (Kirchhoff again!). From the figure we can apply Pythagoras's theorem and our knowledge of Ohm's law to find the circuit impedance.

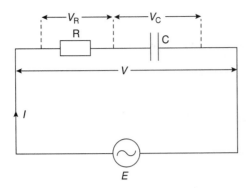

Figure 4.44   Resistance and capacitance in series

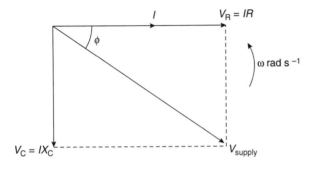

Figure 4.45

$$V^2_{\text{supply}} = V^2_R + V^2_L$$

$$V^2_{\text{supply}} = (IR)^2 + (IX_C)^2$$

Now, total voltage $V_{\text{supply}} = IZ$, and so

$$(IZ)^2 = (IR)^2 + (IX_C)^2$$

Note that IX_C could be written as $I \times 1/\omega C = I/\omega C$; the result will be the same! Dividing by I gives

$$Z^2 = R^2 + X^2_C$$

$\therefore$ circuit impedance $Z = \sqrt{(R^2 + X^2_C)}$

From the phasor diagram I leads V. The angle can be calculated as

$$\tan \phi = \frac{V_C}{V_R}$$

$$= \frac{I \times X_C}{I \times R}$$

$$= \frac{I \times 1/\omega C}{I \times R}$$

$$= \frac{I/\omega C}{IR} = \frac{1}{\omega CR}$$

So the phase angle of the circuit impedance is given by

$$\phi = \tan^{-1}(1/\omega CR)$$

Guided examples

1   Determine the impedance of the circuit in Figure 4.46.

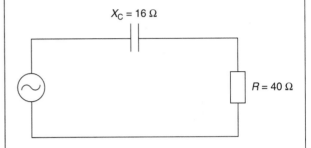

Figure 4.46

$$
\begin{aligned}
Z &= \sqrt{(R^2 + X^2_C)} \\
&= \sqrt{(40^2 + 16^2)} \\
&= \sqrt{(1600 + 256)} \\
&= \sqrt{(1856)} \\
&= 43.1 \ \Omega
\end{aligned}
$$

The phase angle is given by

$$\tan^{-1}\left(\frac{X_C}{R}\right) = \tan^{-1}\left(\frac{16}{40}\right)$$

$$= \tan^{-1} 0.4$$

$$= 21.8°$$

Therefore

$$Z = 43.1 \ \Omega \ \angle -21.8°$$

Note the minus sign to denote a lag.

2   For the circuit in Figure 4.47 calculate the impedance and the peak current that is drawn from the supply.

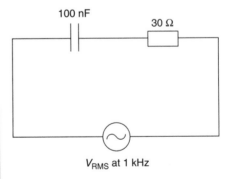

Figure 4.47

The supply voltage is given in RMS form. We express this in peak form:

$$V_{\text{peak}} = \frac{V_{\text{RMS}}}{0.707} = \frac{50}{0.707} = 70.72 \text{ V}$$

Therefore we can write

$$v = V_{\text{max}} \sin(\omega t)$$

as

$$v = 70.72 \times \sin\{(2 \times \pi \times 1 \times 10^3)t\}$$

$$= 70.72 \sin(6283t)$$

$$\therefore \omega = 2\pi f = 6283$$

So,

$$X_C = \frac{1}{\omega_C} = \frac{1}{6283 \times 100 \text{ nF}} = 1591.6 \text{ }\Omega$$

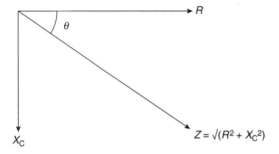

Figure 4.48

From Figure 4.48

$$Z = \sqrt{(R^2 + X_C^2)}$$

$$= \sqrt{(30^2 + 1592^2)}$$

$$= \sqrt{(2\ 530\ 000)} = 1592 \text{ }\Omega$$

Now,

$$\tan^{-1}\left(\frac{X_C}{R}\right) = \tan^{-1}\left(\frac{1592}{30}\right)$$

$$= 89°$$

Therefore

$$Z = 1592 \text{ }\Omega \angle{-89°}$$

The peak current is given by

$$I = \frac{V_{\text{peak}}}{Z}$$

$$= \frac{70.72}{1592}$$

$$= 44.42 \text{ mA}$$

3 Calculate the impedance of the circuit in Figure 4.49.

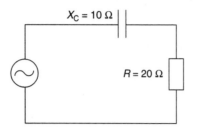

Figure 4.49

$$Z = \sqrt{(R^2 + X_C^2)}$$

$$= \sqrt{(20^2 + 10^2)}$$

$$= \sqrt{(400 + 100)}$$

$$= \sqrt{(500)}$$

$$= 22.36 \text{ }\Omega$$

$$\tan^{-1}\left(\frac{X_C}{R}\right) = 26.56°$$

4 Calculate the current in the circuit in Figure 4.50.

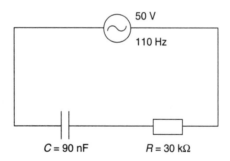

Figure 4.50

$$X_C = 2\pi f C$$

$$= 2 \times \pi \times 110 \times 90 \times 10^{-9}$$

$$= 6.2 \times 10^{-5}$$

$$Z = \sqrt{(R^2 + X_C^2)}$$

$$= \sqrt{(30000^2 + 0.000062^2)}$$

$$= \sqrt{(30000^2)}$$

$$= 30\ 000$$

$$I = \frac{V}{Z}$$

$$= \frac{50}{30\ 000}$$

$$= 0.002 \text{ A}$$

Power dissipated in a purely inductive or capacitive circuit

Power in a DC circuit or an AC circuit of pure resistance can be found using the standard formulae.

A problem arises if we attempt to apply this to a circuit that contains capacitance or inductance, as the voltage and current are never at the same value simultaneously.

It can be proved that the power waveform of a pure circuit is as shown in Figure 4.51.

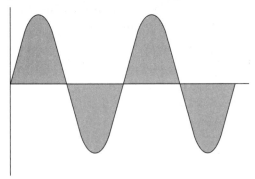

Figure 4.51   Power in a circuit of pure inductance or pure capacitance

From Figure 4.51 you can see that the average power dissipated is zero as the positive half cycles are cancelled out by the negative ones. At this stage it can be accepted without proof that purely reactive components do not dissipate any power at all. The energy is fed to the component during one part of the cycle, stored in the component as a magnetic or electrostatic field and then returned to the source in the other part of the cycle.

A function generator in use in a steel works in Holland

Power in a non-pure AC circuit

Up to now we have used one of three formulae to calculate power in a DC circuit. These are as follows:

$$P = I^2R$$

$$P = \frac{V^2}{R}$$

$$P = IV$$

In an AC circuit of *pure resistance* any of the above will hold true as the voltage and the current will be in phase, which is the same as in a DC circuit.

In an AC circuit of pure capacitance or inductance, as I and V are 90° opposed, no power will be dissipated and all power delivered to the circuit in one quarter cycle will be returned to the source in the next quarter cycle.

However, when we look at an AC circuit that has impure inductance or impure capacitance the situation is more complicated.

In Figure 4.52 there are meters to record the value of the supply voltage and the current that is drawn from the supply. The current, however, is determined by the circuit impedance as this is the overall opposition to the flow of AC. We can therefore say that at face value the power apparently drawn from the supply is $I \times V$ watts.

> apparent power = $I \times V$

Apparent power is the product of the RMS voltage and the RMS current in an AC circuit and is usually quoted in volt amps and not in watts.

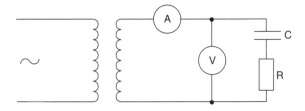

Figure 4.52   The product IV gives the apparent power in the circuit

True power

Considering the problem a little more deeply, we now have to think of the phase relationship between the voltage and the current. Figure 4.53 shows the voltage leading on the current as we are

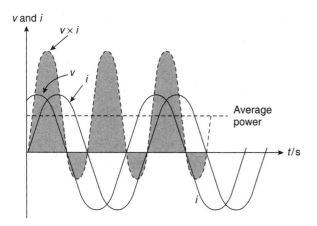

Figure 4.53   Power in an AC circuit of inductance and resistance

dealing with an inductive circuit. The instantaneous values of the two are different at any one time.

The true power in the circuit is the power developed in the resistive element and this will be dependent on the value of this resistance and the component of the total voltage that is developed across it. For this reason the power developed in the resistance will be less than the total power (i.e. the apparent power) and we can therefore say that **true power is always less than apparent power**.

True power is calculated by determining the size of the voltage and current in the resistive element of the circuit and multiplying them together. This is easily done by returning once more to a phasor diagram.

The voltages associated with the circuit in Figure 4.54 are represented in Figure 4.55(a). The voltage across R (V_R) can be found by breaking

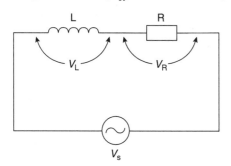

Figure 4.54

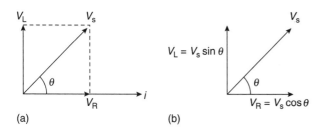

Figure 4.55

down the triangle into its quadrature components, which gives Figure 4.55(b). So, the voltage across the resistor is $V \cos \theta$ where θ is the phase angle. To obtain the power dissipated in the resistance all we have to do is multiply $V \cos \theta$ by I (as power = IV watts), which gives

true power = $VI \cos \theta$

Power triangle

We have already established that the average power dissipated in a pure capacitor or inductor is zero.

In a resistor the power W dissipated is $I^2_{RMS} R$ watts.

In a circuit containing R, L and C the power dissipated is $I^2 R$. Now,

$$W = I^2 R$$

$$I = \frac{V}{Z}$$

$$\therefore W = \frac{V}{Z} IR$$

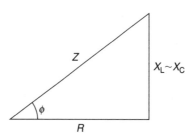

Figure 4.56

From the impedance triangle (Figure 4.56)

$$\frac{R}{Z} = \cos \phi$$

$$\therefore W = VI \cos \phi$$

The product of V and I is called the 'volt amps' (VA) of the circuit. We know it is larger than the real power W (except in a resistive circuit, where it is the same). The circuit VA is the apparent power S and the ratio of W to S is the power factor:

$$\text{power factor} = \frac{W \text{ (watts)}}{S \text{ (volt amps)}}$$

As we already know, the power factor for a resistive circuit is unity, for a reactive circuit it is zero and for a sinusoid it is $\cos \phi$.

A phasor can be broken down into its quadrature components and if we do that for the current we get components of $I \cos \phi$ and $I \sin \phi$

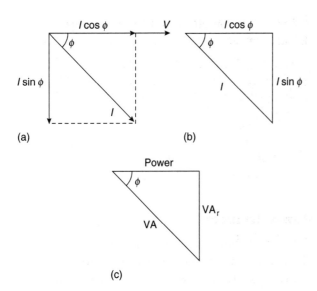

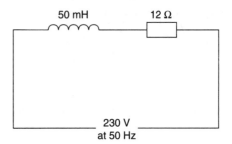

Figure 4.57

(Figure 4.57(a)). If we multiply each arm of the resultant triangle (Figure 4.57(b)) by V we obtain the power triangle (Figure 4.57(c)), where

$VI \cos \phi$ = true power

$VI \sin \phi$ = wattless or reactive power (VA_r)

VI = apparent power (VA)

Power factor

The term $\cos \theta$ is known as the circuit power factor and can also be found from

$$\text{power factor} = \frac{\text{true power}}{\text{apparent power}}$$

The value of the power factor must always be between +1 and −1 and is important as it ultimately determines how much current exists in the AC circuit. It is quite possible for large currents to be drawn with only a small amount of useful work being done – not a situation to be encouraged!

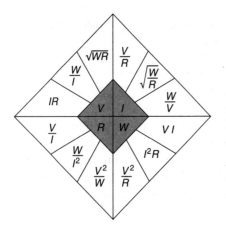

The handy diamond: each quadrant gives the power and Ohm's law formula for the element you choose

Guided examples

1 For the circuit in Figure 4.58 determine (a) the current, (b) the phase angle, (c) the apparent power, (d) the true power and (e) the power factor.

Figure 4.58

(a) To determine the current, find the circuit impedance:

$$X_L = \omega L = 2\pi f L$$
$$= 2 \times \pi \times 50 \times 50 \times 10^{-3} = 15.7\ \Omega$$
$$Z = \sqrt{(X_L^2 + R^2)}$$
$$= \sqrt{(15.7^2 + 12^2)} = \sqrt{(390)}$$
$$\therefore Z = 19.76\ \Omega$$
$$I = \frac{V}{Z} = \frac{230}{19.76} = 11.64\ A$$

(b) The phase angle is given by

$$\theta = \tan^{-1}\left(\frac{X_L}{R}\right)$$
$$= \tan^{-1}\left(\frac{15.7}{12}\right) = 52.6°$$

(c) The apparent power is

$$IV = 11.64 \times 230 = 2677\ W$$

(d) The true power is

$$IV \cos \theta = 11.64 \times 230 \times \cos 52.6°$$
$$= 11.64 \times 230 \times 0.607$$
$$= 1626\ W$$

(e) The power factor is

$$\frac{\text{true power}}{\text{apparent power}} = \frac{1626}{2677} = 0.607$$

or

$$\text{power factor} = \cos \theta$$
$$= \cos 52.6° = 0.607$$

2 For the circuit shown in Figure 4.59 determine (a) the current drawn, (b) the apparent power and (c) the true power.

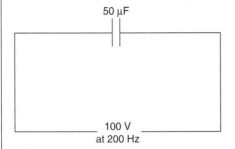

Figure 4.59

(a) The current drawn is

$$I = \frac{V}{Z}$$

Now,

$$Z = \sqrt{(X_C^2 + R^2)}$$

but $R = 0\ \Omega$ as the circuit is pure. So, $X_C = Z$.

$$X_C = \frac{1}{2\pi fC} = \frac{1}{\omega C}$$

$$= \frac{1}{2 \times \pi \times 200 \times 50 \times 10^{-6}}$$

$$= 15.92\ \Omega$$

$$\therefore I = \frac{V}{X_C} = \frac{100}{15.92} = 6.28\ \text{A}$$

(b) The apparent power is

$$IV = 6.28 \times 100$$

$$= 628\ \text{VA}$$

(c) The true power is given by $IV \cos \theta$. $\theta = 90°$ as the circuit is pure capacitance, so

$$IV \cos \theta = 6.28 \times 100 \times \cos 90°$$

$$= 6.28 \times 100 \times 0$$

$$= 0\ \text{W}$$

This is the answer we expect as no power is developed in a pure reactance.

Power factor in a circuit of pure inductance

When a circuit is purely inductive the current lags the voltage by 90°. The power developed in the inductance (the true power) is

$VI \cos 90°$

Now, $\cos 90° = 0$ and so

true power $= VI \times 0 = 0\ \text{W}$

Power factor in a circuit of pure capacitance

In a circuit of pure capacitance the current leads the voltage by 90° and the circuit's true power is again

$VI \cos 90°$

Again, $\cos 90° = 0$ and so

true power $VI \times 0 = 0\ \text{W}$

Just what we'd expect!

4.3 Parallel AC circuits

So far we have only considered series combinations of resistors, inductors and capacitors. When we look at parallel circuits the first thing to notice is that the reference phasor changes. The quantity common to all components in parallel with each other is voltage.

Resistors and inductors

As shown in Figure 4.60, the voltage phasor is the reference. The current in the resistor is in phase with the voltage and the inductor current lags the voltage by 90° (remember CIVIL) (Figure 4.60(b)).

Now we have constructed the phasor diagram we can start applying Pythagoras!

When we are dealing with phasors we have two parts: the magnitude (or size) and the direction (or phase angle). To show that we are expressing

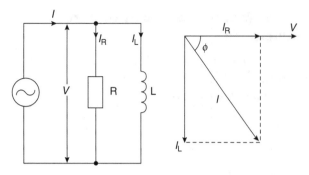

Figure 4.60 Resistors and inductors in parallel

just the magnitude we put the quantity in 'goal posts'.

So, the magnitude of the current is given by

$$|I| = \sqrt{(I_R{}^2 + I_L{}^2)}$$

and by substitution from Ohm's law,

$$|I| = \sqrt{\left(\frac{V^2}{R^2} + \frac{V^2}{\omega^2 L^2}\right)}$$

$$= V\sqrt{\left(\frac{1}{R^2} + \frac{1}{\omega^2 L^2}\right)}$$

But $I = V/Z$ and so

$$\frac{1}{Z} = \sqrt{\left(\frac{1}{R^2} + \frac{1}{\omega^2 L^2}\right)}$$

The common denominator is $\omega^2 L^2 R^2$ which, taken out of the root sign, gives ωLR. Taking the reciprocal gives

$$|Z| = \frac{\omega LR}{\sqrt{(R^2 + \omega^2 L^2)}} \text{ ohms}$$

The reciprocal of impedance is called **admittance**. This has the symbol Y and its unit of measurement is the siemen which has the unit symbol S. Also,

conductance $(G) = 1/R$ siemens

susceptance $(B) = 1/X$ siemens

admittance $(Y) = 1/Z$ siemens

So from $1/Z = \sqrt{(1/R^2 + 1/\omega^2 L^2)}$ ohms we get $Y = \sqrt{(G^2 + B^2)}$ siemens.

Our phasor diagram shows that V leads I (or I lags V) by ϕ, so with a bit of trigonometry we get

$$\tan \phi = \frac{I_L}{I_R}$$

$$= \frac{V/\omega L}{V/R}$$

$$= \frac{R}{\omega L}$$

$$\therefore \phi = \tan^{-1}\left(\frac{R}{\omega L}\right)$$

Thus the full expression for the phasor Z is

$$Z = \frac{\omega LR}{\sqrt{(R^2 + \omega^2 L^2)}} \ \tan^{-1}\left(\frac{R}{\omega L}\right) \text{ ohms}$$

No power is dissipated in the inductive branch of the circuit so all the power is dissipated in the resistive arm:

$$W = \frac{V^2}{R} \text{ watts}$$

The power factor is VI_R/VI, but $I_R = I \cos \phi$ and so the power factor is $(VI \cos \phi)/VI = \cos \phi$.

Resistors and capacitors

Applying Pythagoras's theorem to Figure 4.61(b):

$$|I| = \sqrt{\left(\frac{V^2}{R^2} + V^2\omega^2 C^2\right)}$$

$$= V\sqrt{\left(\frac{1}{R^2} + \omega^2 C^2\right)} \text{ amps}$$

$$\therefore \left|\frac{V}{I}\right| = \frac{1}{\sqrt{\{(1/R^2) + \omega^2 C^2\}}}$$

$$\therefore |Z| = \frac{R}{\sqrt{(1 + \omega^2 R^2 C^2)}}$$

Once again, we can find ϕ from the phasor diagram:

$$\tan \phi = \frac{V\omega C}{V/R} = \omega CR$$

$$\therefore \phi = \tan^{-1}(\omega CR)$$

Therefore,

$$Z = \frac{R}{\sqrt{(1 + \omega^2 R^2 C^2)}} \ \tan^{-1}(\omega CR) \text{ ohms}$$

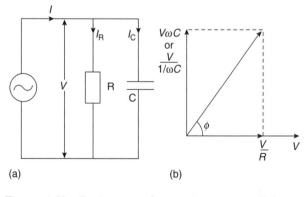

Figure 4.61 Resistors and capacitors in parallel

We have established now that no power is dissipated in the capacitive arm, so all the dissipated power is in the resistive arm: $W = V^2/R$ watts. Now,

$$\text{power factor} = \frac{VI_R}{VI}$$

but $I_R = I \cos \phi$ and so the power factor is $(VI \cos \phi)/VI = \cos \phi$; no surprise there!

We have looked at all the combinations of two components in AC circuits but we have not considered the effects of having all three of our passive components connected at once. This is what we shall do next.

The impedance of circuits containing inductors, capacitors and resistors

Let's look first of all at the series circuit because this is the simplest (see Figure 4.62).

All we need to do is resolve the phasors acting at 180° to each other, which is achieved by simple subtraction, and then apply Pythagoras's theorem.

In Figure 4.63 we assume $X_L > X_C$ and so

$$|V| = \sqrt{\{(IR)^2 + (IX_L - IX_C)^2\}}$$
$$= I\sqrt{\{R^2 + (X_L - X_C)^2\}}$$

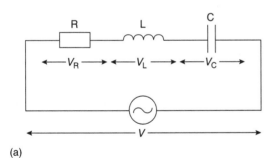

(a)

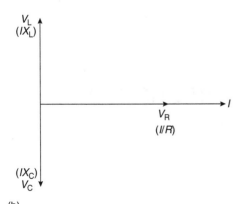

(b)

Figure 4.62   Resistors, inductors and capacitors in series

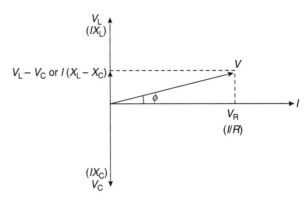

Figure 4.63

$$\therefore \frac{|V|}{|I|} = |Z| = \sqrt{\{R^2 + (X_L - X_C)^2\}}$$

The phase angle is

$$\phi = \tan^{-1}\left(\frac{X_L - X_C}{R}\right)$$

As a general case the equation is in terms of the difference between X_L and X_C since we don't know which may be the larger of the two:

$$Z = \sqrt{\{R^2 + (X_L \sim X_C)^2\}} \tan^{-1}\left(\frac{X_L \sim X_C}{R}\right)$$

Resistors, inductors and capacitors in parallel

First we can look at all three positive components connected in parallel with each other (Figure 4.64(a)), although this is not quite the case that occurs in practice.

Once again the assumption is that X_L is greater than X_C. This, of course, need not be the case.

$$|I| = \sqrt{\{(I_R)^2 + (I_C - I_L)^2\}}$$
$$= \sqrt{\left\{\left(\frac{V}{R}\right)^2 + \left(\frac{V}{X_C} - \frac{V}{X_L}\right)^2\right\}}$$
$$= V\sqrt{\left\{\left(\frac{1}{R}\right)^2 + \left(\frac{1}{X_C} - \frac{1}{X_L}\right)^2\right\}}$$

$$\therefore \frac{V}{I} = Z = \frac{1}{\sqrt{[(1/R)^2 + \{(1/X_C) - (1/X_L)\}^2]}}$$

or

$$|Z| = \frac{1}{\sqrt{\{(1/R)^2 + (\omega C - 1/\omega L)^2\}}}$$

The phase angle is

$$\phi = \tan^{-1}\left(\frac{I_C - I_L}{I_R}\right)$$

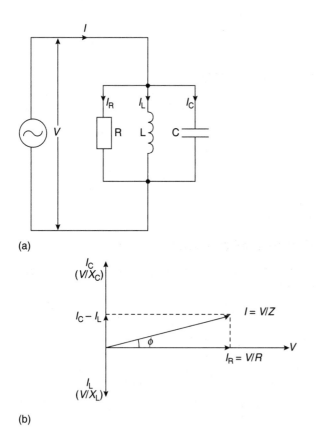

(a)

(b)

Figure 4.64   Resistors, inductors and capacitors in parallel

$$= \tan^{-1}\left\{\frac{(V/X_C) - (V/X_L)}{V/R}\right\}$$

$$= \tan^{-1}\left\{\frac{(1/X_C) - (1/X_L)}{1/R}\right\}$$

$$= \tan^{-1}[R\{\omega C - (1/\omega L)\}]$$

Thus, if $X_L > X_C$ ϕ is negative and if $X_L < X_C$ ϕ is positive.

The normal parallel combination takes into account the resistance of the coil. In practice, pure inductance does not occur and so the resistance of the coil will show itself as a resistive component in the inductive arm of the circuit. The capacitor can, in practice, be regarded as pure. Thus a practical parallel circuit appears as shown in Figure 4.65.

The situation is just a little more complicated now. The current in the capacitor leads the voltage by 90°, so we get the situation shown in Figure 4.66.

When we add this to the phasor diagram we get Figure 4.67.

We cannot just apply Pythagoras's theorem to this. We could resolve the vectors into their vertical and horizontal components but this is a lengthy process. Generally, this type of AC problem is examined using complex algebra, but we do not need this until later.

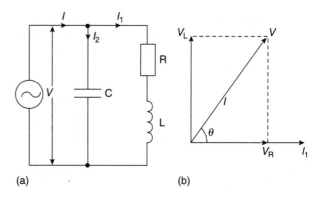

Figure 4.65

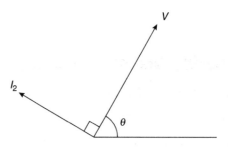

Figure 4.66

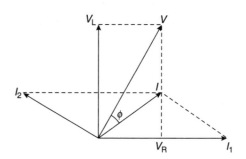

Figure 4.67

So far we have taken each example as having X_L greater than X_C and we have seen that equally we could have had X_L less than X_C. But what about the special case when $X_L = X_C$? The special condition under which this occurs is called **resonance**.

4.4 Resonance

An AC circuit which contains both resistive and reactive components is said to be at resonance when **the total current drawn from the source is in phase with the applied voltage**.

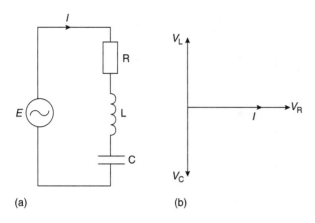

Figure 4.68

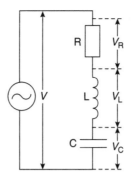

Figure 4.69

Series resonance

Looking at Figure 4.68,

$$E = V_L + V_C + V_R$$

For E to be in phase with I, $|V_C|$ must equal $|V_L|$. This means that X_C must equal X_L so that they cancel each other and the circuit is purely resistive at resonance.

The frequency at which this occurs is the resonant frequency f_0.

$$|X_L| = |X_C|$$

$$\therefore 2\pi f_0 L = \frac{1}{2\pi f_0 C}$$

and so by transposition

> resonant frequency $f_0 = \dfrac{1}{2\pi\sqrt{(LC)}}$ Hz

We know that $|Z| = \sqrt{\{R^2 + (X_L \sim X_C)\}}$ and at resonance $X_L \sim X_C = 0$, so

$$|Z| = \sqrt{R^2}$$

$$\therefore Z = R \angle 0°$$

at resonance. The current and voltage are in phase.

Q factor

The Q factor of a coil is a measure of its 'quality'. This is given by the ratio of its resonance to its effective resistance ($\omega L/R$).

The Q factor of a capacitor is the ratio of its reactance to its resistance, $Q = 1/(\omega CR)$.

Q factor of a series circuit

For a simple series circuit (Figure 4.69) at resonance, $Q = (1/R)\sqrt{(L/C)}$.

At f_0, $X_L = X_C$ and $Z = R$. If V is sinusoidal, $V_R = IR$, $V_L = I\omega L$ and $V_C = I/\omega C$. At f_0, $I = V/R$, so substituting for V_L and V_C we get

$$V_L = \frac{V\omega_0 L}{R} \quad \text{and} \quad V_C = \frac{V}{\omega_0 CR}$$

But $\omega_0 = 1/\sqrt{(LC)}$ and so, at f_0,

$$V_C = V_L = V\left(\frac{1}{R}\right)\sqrt{\left(\frac{L}{C}\right)} = VQ$$

This means that the voltage across C or L is Q times greater than the applied voltage. For this reason Q is called the **voltage magnification** of the circuit. For a series resonant circuit,

$$Q = \frac{Q_L \times Q_C}{Q_L + Q_C}$$

Q is proportional to the **selectivity** of the circuit and is sometimes given as

$$Q = \frac{f_0}{f_2 - f_1} = \frac{f_0}{\text{bandwidth}}$$

where f_0 is the resonant frequency and f_2 and f_1 are the upper and lower half-power frequencies.

Response of a series resonant circuit

At resonance the impedance of the series circuit has fallen to a minimum of just R, the resistance in the circuit. This may be just the resistance of the wire in the coil.

As we move away from the resonant frequency so the impedance increases. If we go above resonance X_L is getting larger; if we go below resonance X_C is increasing (Figure 4.70).

This property of resonant circuits allows us to use them for applications where we require frequency-selective circuits, such as tuned amplifiers and oscillators and even some types of filter.

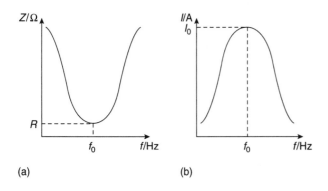

(a)   (b)

Figure 4.70   Variation of (a) impedance and (b) current close to the resonant frequency

Bandwidth

For a series circuit we can define bandwidth as the range of frequency over which the circuit current is equal to or greater than 0.707 $(1/\sqrt{2})$ of its value at resonance (Figure 4.71).

An alternative definition is that it is the range of frequency over which the power dissipated in the circuit falls to half its value at resonance.

Using a logarithmic unit called the decibel, a half-power reduction is equivalent to a fall of 3 dB, and so the half-power points are often referred to as the 3 dB points.

The current in the circuit is given by

$$I = \frac{V}{\sqrt{\{R^2 + (\omega L + 1/\omega C)^2\}}} \tan^{-1}\left(\frac{\omega L - 1/\omega C}{R}\right)$$

There will be two frequencies at which $R^2 = (\omega L + 1/\omega C)^2$. At these frequencies, $I = V/(\sqrt{2} R) \tan^{-1}(\pm 1)$. Therefore

$$I = 0.707 V/R \pm 45°$$

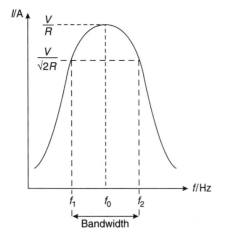

Figure 4.71   Bandwidth is defined as the range of frequency over which the circuit current is equal to or greater than 0.707 $(1/\sqrt{2})$ of its value at resonance

If the resonant frequency is f_0 the bandwidth is f_0/Q. This means that the better the components, i.e. the smaller their resistance, the higher the Q of the circuit and the narrower the bandwidth.

Impedance at half-power points

At –3 dB points $(\omega L \sim \omega C)^2 = R^2$ and so, for a series circuit,

$$|Z| = \sqrt{\{R^2 + (\omega L \sim \omega C)^2\}}$$

$$\therefore Z = \sqrt{(R^2 + R^2)}$$

So, at half-power points,

$$Z = \sqrt{2} R \text{ ohms}$$

Practical 3

Series resonance

The purpose of this practical is to show how the impedance of a series tuned circuit changes with alteration of applied frequency. After you have done the practical work you can calculate the theoretical resonant frequency and compare it with the one obtained in practice.

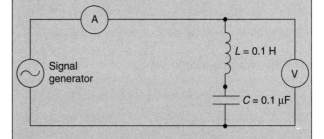

Figure 4.72

Connect up the circuit in Figure 4.72. Once again, as in some of the other practicals the meters that you use must be capable of reading up to 20 kHz. Do not forget that this practical is using an AC source (i.e. the signal generator) so both of the meters need to be set to AC ranges. The generator ideally should have a low operational impedance (say 5 Ω).

Adjust the current meter to a range which will allow it to read up to 10 mA and the voltmeter to a range which allows it to easily display 2 V. Set the output of the signal generator to a frequency of 500 Hz and adjust the output level until the voltmeter registers 2 V. Record the current meter reading in the results table.

Frequency

Volts

Current

Impedance

Now reset the signal generator to a frequency of 1 kHz making sure that the voltmeter still registers 2 V. If it does not, adjust the output level of the signal generator appropriately. Once again note the current.

Gradually increase the frequency of the generator watching carefully for the current in the circuit to increase to a maximum. When this happens set the signal generator to frequencies within the 500 Hz steps for more accurate readings.

Using the formula

$$f_0 = \frac{1}{2\pi\sqrt{(LC)}}$$

calculate the theoretical resonant frequency of the circuit.

From the results table plot a graph of impedance against frequency using the x axis for frequency and the y axis for impedance.

The point of minimum impedance (see page 99) is the actual resonant frequency of the circuit. It is at this point that the maximum current is being drawn from the source. This is why the circuit is sometimes known as an acceptor circuit.

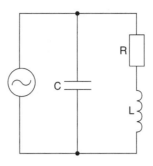

Figure 4.73

$$\therefore \quad \omega_0 = \sqrt{\left(\frac{1}{LC} - \frac{R^2}{L^2}\right)}$$

and

$$f_0 = \frac{1}{2\pi}\sqrt{\left(\frac{1}{LC} - \frac{R^2}{L^2}\right)}$$

In the absence of R,

$$f_0 = \frac{1}{2\pi}\sqrt{\left(\frac{1}{LC}\right)} \text{ Hz}$$

At resonance,

$$\frac{1}{Z} = \frac{R}{R^2 + \omega_0^2 L^2}$$

At f_0,

$$C = \frac{L}{R^2 + \omega_0^2 L^2}$$

$$\therefore R^2 + \omega_0^2 L^2 = \frac{L}{C}$$

$$\therefore \quad \frac{1}{Z} = \frac{R}{L/C}$$

$$Z = \frac{L}{CR} \text{ ohms}$$

This gives the **dynamic impedance** Z_D which behaves as a pure resistance (see Figure 4.74).

Parallel resonance

Resonance will occur in the circuit given in Figure 4.73 at a frequency when

$$C = \frac{L}{R^2 + \omega^2 L^2}$$

since this will mean V and I are in phase. At this frequency

$$R^2 + \omega^2 L^2 = \frac{L}{C}$$

$$\therefore \quad \omega^2 L^2 = \frac{L}{C} - R^2$$

$$\therefore \quad \omega^2 = \frac{1}{LC} - \frac{R^2}{L^2}$$

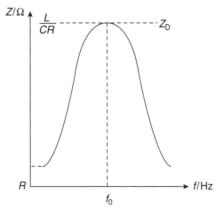

Figure 4.74   Dynamic impedance

Q factor of a parallel circuit

As with the series circuit,

$$Q_L = \frac{\omega L}{R}$$

$$Q_C = \frac{1}{\omega CR}$$

$$Q = \frac{f_0}{f_2 - f_1}$$

For a parallel circuit, $I_L = I_C = QI$. Since $E = IL/CR$ at f_0,

$$
\begin{aligned}
I_0 &= E\omega_0 C \\
&= (IL/CR)(\omega_0 C) \\
&= I(\omega_0 L/R) \\
\therefore\ I_0 &= QI
\end{aligned}
$$

Impedance at half-power points

Because Z is a maximum at resonance and the 3 dB points are at 0.707 of the peak, Z at the half-power points is

$$Z_{\text{half-power}} = Z_D \times 0.707 \text{ or } Z_D/\sqrt{2}$$

Circulating current

Theoretically, no current flows *through* the circuit in Figure 4.75 at resonance because I_L and I_C are in anti-phase.

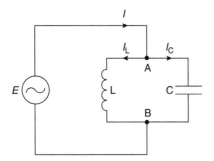

Figure 4.75

However, in practice the branch current may be very large. This occurrence is explained because $I_L = -I_C$. This means that when the current in the inductive arm is at a maximum, flowing from A to B, the current in the capacitive arm is at a maximum flowing from B to A.

In this way the current flows *around* the circuit and is referred to as a **circulating current**.

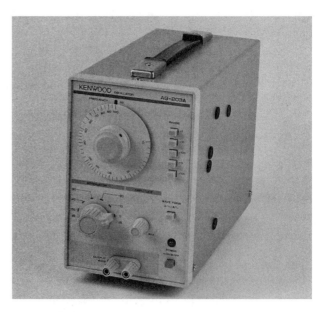

RC oscillator

The value of this current is given by

$$I_L = I_C = \frac{I}{\omega L} = V\omega C$$

But $\omega_0 = 1/(\sqrt{LC})$ and so

$$I_{\text{circ}} = \frac{VC}{\sqrt{LC}} = V\sqrt{\left(\frac{C}{L}\right)} \text{ amps}$$

Joseph Henry (1797–1878)

Henry was an American physicist who, like Faraday, was from a poor background and had no formal education. Through a series of coincidences Henry became aware of the experimental findings of Oersted and like Faraday he was enthusiastic in pursuing the work. It is arguable whether Henry, in fact, discovered electromagnetic induction before Faraday but in any event Faraday was the first to publish. Henry went on to do a great deal of developmental work on induction and the design of inductors and electromagnets. His work was honoured after his death by naming the unit of inductance after him.

Multiple choice questions

1 The instantaneous value of the sinewave in Figure 4.76 $3\pi/2$ rad into its cycle is
   (a) 6 V
   (b) 4.24 V
   (c) 0 V
   (d) –6 V.

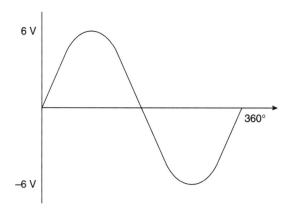

Figure 4.76

2 A sinewave is represented by the expression $v = 10 \sin(6284t)$. The frequency of the sinewave is
   (a) 1000 Hz
   (b) 6284 Hz
   (c) 62.84 kHz
   (d) 10 Hz.

3 Waveform A in Figure 4.77 is denoted by the expression $v = V_{A,max} \sin(\omega t)$. The expression to denote waveform B time related to waveform A is
   (a) $v_B = V_{B,max} \sin(\omega t + \pi)$
   (b) $v_B = V_{B,max} \sin(\omega t - \pi/2)$
   (c) $V_B = V_A V_B \sin(\omega t)$
   (d) $V_A = V_B \sin(\omega t)$.

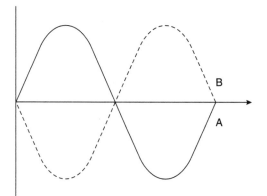

Figure 4.77

4 A square wave consists of
   (a) a sinewave plus a number of even harmonics
   (b) a sinewave plus an infinite number of even harmonics
   (c) a sinewave plus a number of odd harmonics
   (d) a sinewave plus an infinite number of odd harmonics.

5 Waveform B in Figure 4.78 is
   (a) the first harmonic of waveform A
   (b) the second harmonic of waveform A
   (c) the third harmonic of waveform A
   (d) the fourth harmonic of waveform A.

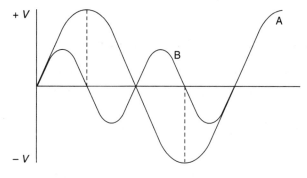

Figure 4.78

6 The average value of a sinusoidal voltage is 15.69 V. Which of the diagrams in Figure 4.79 represents the voltage?

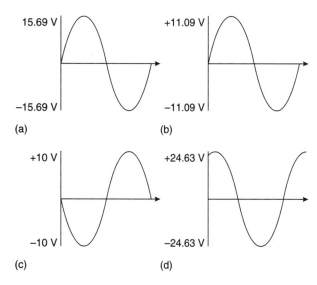

Figure 4.79

7 The frequency of an AC waveform is 1.5 kHz.
The periodic time is
(a) 1.5 µs
(b) 66 ms
(c) 666 µs
(d) 1.5 ms.

8 Which of the diagrams in Figure 4.80 illustrates
an AC waveform?

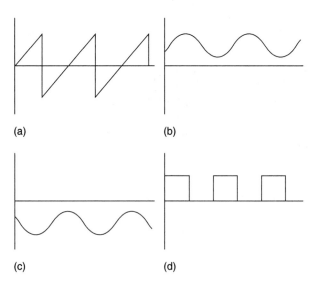

(a)   (b)

(c)   (d)

Figure 4.80

9 The power developed in the resistor R in
Figure 4.81 is
(a) 20 W
(b) 1.0 W
(c) 2 W
(d) 1.25 W.

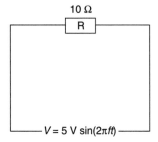

Figure 4.81

10 Two AC voltages are represented by the phasor
diagram in Figure 4.82. Which of the following
statements is true?
(a) V_2 leads V_1
(b) V_1 leads V_2
(c) V_1 lags V_2
(d) V_1 and V_2 are in phase.

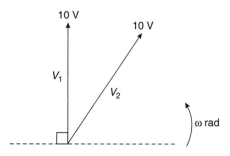

Figure 4.82

5

Semiconductors, diodes and transistors

5.1 Semiconductors

We are all familiar with the terms insulator and conductor. If you were asked to define them you would quite correctly say something along the lines that one is the opposite of the other. You could then give examples: for instance, an insulator does not pass an electric current and therefore has a high resistance, whereas a conductor is a material that readily allows electrons to flow and therefore has a low resistance.

In fact, we have given examples of the two extremes:

| Insulator | Conductor |
| High resistance | Low resistance |

Between these materials there is a group which are neither good conductors nor good insulators. These materials are called semiconductors.

The two most commonly used semiconductors in the electronics industry are silicon (Si) and germanium (Ge). As silicon is the most common material from which semiconductor components are made we will refer to this in the following descriptions.

During manufacture of the semiconductor the silicon has its chemical composition altered by the introduction of another substance such as gallium. The original silicon is no longer pure and is often known as doped silicon. This doping changes the atomic structure of the silicon.

N-type and p-type semiconductors

If the result of this addition (doping) produces silicon that has extra electrons it is said to be n-type. (The n stands for negative as extra electrons introduce a negative charge.)

If the doping leaves the silicon short of an electron(s) it assumes a positive charge and is therefore known as p-type (Figure 5.1).

On their own p-type or n-type semiconductors will act as resistors, passing a current in either direction and developing a voltage across them. When a piece of p-type and a piece of n-type are formed together at a junction the silicon behaves in a different manner.

The p–n junction

In Figure 5.2 a piece of silicon has been doped with p- and n-type impurities. When a p–n junction is present in this form the silicon behaves differently from when it is on its own. The ability of the whole

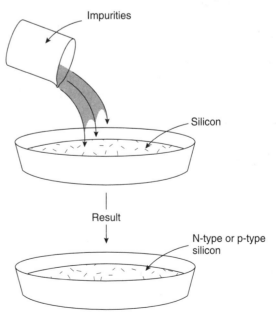

Figure 5.1 Making n- or p-type silicon

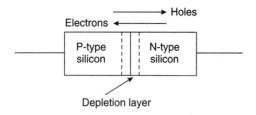

Figure 5.2   *A 'depletion layer' is formed at the p–n junction as p and n carriers move across the junction*

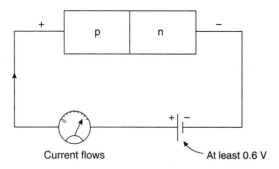

Figure 5.3   *Forward bias p–n junction*

silicon block to conduct a current will now be dependent on the magnitude and polarity of the voltage that is applied across it. This voltage has to overcome the potential barrier of the depletion layer.

In Figure 5.3 the p–n block of silicon has a voltage across it from a battery. Provided that the battery exceeds a certain voltage (approximately 0.6 V) current will flow and thus the resistance from p to n must be low. Under these conditions the junction is said to be forward bias.

In Figure 5.4 the polarity of the battery has been reversed so that the positive 0.6 V from the battery is now connected to the n-type silicon whilst the negative terminal of the battery is connected to the p-type material. Under these conditions no appreciable current will flow and therefore the resistance from p to n is high. The junction is said to be reverse bias.

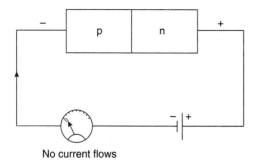

Figure 5.4   *Reverse bias p–n junction*

5.2 Diodes

What we have just described is known as diode action and from now on we will refer to the p–n junction as a diode.

> In summary, the diode conducts current in one direction only (from p to n) but this will only happen if it is forward bias.

The connections of a diode

The connections (electrodes) to a diode are known as the anode and the cathode, the anode being the p 'side' and the cathode being the n 'side' (Figure 5.5).

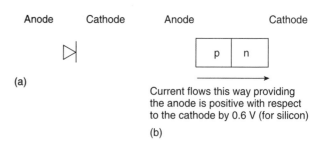

Current flows this way providing the anode is positive with respect to the cathode by 0.6 V (for silicon)

(b)

Figure 5.5   *(a) A diode; (b) a p–n junction equivalent of the diode*

Practical diodes

Diodes are available in many shapes and sizes. Whilst they are all made using p–n junctions and perform the same job by acting as a 'one-way valve' of electric current, they can be manufactured to do other tasks, e.g. to give off light (the light-emitting diode (LED)), to act as a variable capacitor by using the change of capacitance that occurs when the

IN4000 series diode

reverse bias voltage is altered (the varicap), or to respond to light (the photodiode).

Polarity markings

By convention diodes have only one electrode marked – the cathode. Sometimes this is done with a silver, red or black line, sometimes with a dot. You can see examples of this from the diodes in the picture.

IN5400 series diode

If you find a component that you suspect to be a diode it is possible to discover which electrode is which by a simple test (see Practical 1).

Practical 1

Testing a diode

Take any diode – or a component that you suspect to be a diode – and connect it in either of the two circuits shown in Figure 5.6.

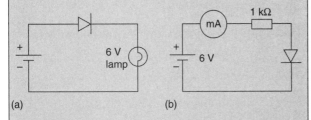

(a)   (b)

Figure 5.6

In the simple circuit of Figure 5.6(a) note the polarity of the battery. When the diode is connected so that the lamp lights the cathode of the diode is nearest to the negative of the battery. Reverse the diode and the lamp will not light.

Figure 5.6(b) shows how the anode and cathode of a diode can be determined by using a current meter. As the resistance of the diode is lowest in the direction of current flow it follows that the cathode is once again connected to the negative of the battery. Reversing the diode connections will give no current flow and the meter will read 0 mA.

It is also possible to determine the electrodes of a diode by using a multimeter switched to the resistance range.

Practical 2

Measuring the forward and reverse resistances of a diode

As you have already seen, the diode has the property that it has a low resistance in one direction (from anode to cathode) and a high resistance in the other (from cathode to anode).

The purpose of this practical is to get you used to measuring diodes on a meter and to know what readings to expect.

Analogue meters

One of the peculiarities of the analogue meter is that when it is switched to a resistance range the polarity of its leads reverses so that the negative lead becomes positive and the positive lead negative. Whilst this does not matter when using the meter to measure resistance it has major implications if semiconductors are to be checked.

Digital meters

Digital meters differ from analogue meters and normally provide a special range which is solely for checking semiconductors. The readout on the meter is not the resistance of the diode's p–n junction, as it is on the analogue meter, but the actual voltage drop across the junction. For a silicon diode this will be about 0.6 V and for a germanium diode 0.2 V.

When the diode is reversed, the meter usually indicates overload, which means that no current is flowing via the diode and the voltage across it is the battery voltage of the meter.

In the next two examples the same diode is checked twice, once using an analogue meter and once using a digital meter.

Using the analogue meter

Connect up the diode as in the circuit shown in Figure 5.7 taking care to couple the meter with the correct polarity. Note that if you do not make a proper connection to the diode and just hold the meter leads across it, the resistance of your body could adversely affect the reading of the meter.

The reading on the meter will be the forward resistance of the diode's junction.

Analogue meter

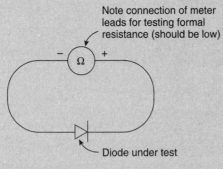

Note connection of meter leads for testing formal resistance (should be low)

Diode under test

Figure 5.7

It should be low, say 15 Ω or thereabouts. Your result will be affected by the ohms scale that is selected on the meter (because of the different voltage batteries that are switched in internally), e.g. if you now turn to the ohms ×100 scale the reading changes to approximately 1000 Ω (if using an AVO 8 meter).

Alter the connections to the diode so that it is now as shown in Figure 5.8. The meter pointer will not move. This does not mean that there is zero resistance – i.e. a short circuit – across the diode (!) but that there is a very large resistance. On an ohms ×1 scale the reading is greater than 2000 Ω. Switching

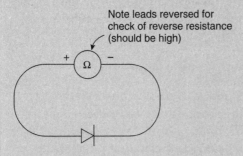

Note leads reversed for check of reverse resistance (should be high)

Figure 5.8

to a higher ohms range will have no effect on the reading of the meter.

Using the digital meter

Notice how the diode is inserted into the sockets marked with a diode symbol. If the diode is placed in line with the symbol by the socket the display will show a reading of the forward voltage drop. This will differ from diode to diode but should be around 0.6 V for silicon diodes and 0.2 V for germanium diodes.

Change the connections of the diode around in the socket. The meter now shows a reading which is an indication of a high resistance. This is normally the maximum value that the display can show.

Digital meter

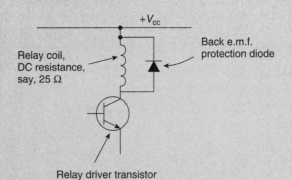

$+V_{cc}$

Relay coil, DC resistance, say, 25 Ω

Back e.m.f. protection diode

Relay driver transistor

Figure 5.9

Remember that when measuring a diode in circuit a component in parallel with the diode will often cause an unexpected reading. Consider the circuit arrangement in Figure 5.9.

In this circuit the diode is incorporated across the relay coil as a protection device for the transistor which is driving the relay. As the DC resistance of the coil is very low (say, for example, 25 Ω) and the coil is connected in parallel with the diode, if a meter is placed across the diode to measure either its forward or reverse resistance it will show the same reading either way. This will not be the diode's resistance but that of the coil, i.e. 25 Ω.

The table contains several diode types. For each of the diodes measure the forward and reverse resistances using digital and analogue meters. Note the difference in readings obtained with each type of meter.

Diode type	Forward resistance		Reverse resistance	
	Digital meter	*Analogue meter*	*Digital meter*	*Analogue meter*
1N4148				
1N4002				
OA91				
1N4005				
1N5400				

Practical 3

Plotting the characteristics of a diode

This practical is designed to enable you to discover how the current through a diode changes for different voltages across the diode.

Plotting the forward characteristic

The circuit in Figure 5.10 consists of a single diode with a resistor in series to limit the current to a safe value. When you have set it up, switch on the power supply (ensuring that it is at minimum output setting) and gently increase its output until the voltmeter across the diode reads 0.1 V. Note the reading on the current meter and increase the output of the power supply until the voltage across the diode reads 0.2 V. Once again note the current that is flowing.

Repeat this for the voltages given in the following table.

Voltage (V)	0.1	0.2	0.3	0.4	0.5	0.6	0.7
Current							

Plotting the reverse characteristic

Switch off the power supply and rearrange the circuit to obtain that shown in Figure 5.11. You will have to select a lower current range on the ammeter and a higher voltage range (at least 100 V) on the voltmeter. Switch on

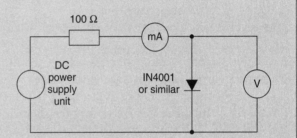

Figure 5.10

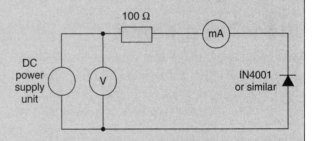

Figure 5.11

the power supply and adjust its outputs to give a reading of 15 V on the meter indicating the voltage across the diode. Note the current flowing at this voltage. Now increase the output of the power supply in the steps indicated in the results table up to a value of 30 V, each time recording the reading on the ammeter.

Voltage (V)	5	10	20	25	30	50	100
Current							

The characteristics of a diode

The word characteristic often appears in electronics. It is generally used where a component's behaviour is investigated for various values of voltage and current and the results that are obtained are plotted as a graph.

The characteristic is useful because it allows us to predict how a component will behave before we put it into a circuit. A suitable method of plotting the characteristic of a diode is shown in Practical 3.

Typically, when the characteristic of a diode is plotted its shape will be as shown in Figure 5.12. Note the two quadrants. The forward bias quadrant clearly shows how current only flows in the forward direction (i.e. from anode to cathode) once the voltage across the diode has exceeded 0.6 V. Before this voltage is reached the amount of current that is passed is minimal. This is because the diode is 'off' and therefore has a high resistance.

The reverse bias quadrant shows that even when a large voltage is placed across the diode, so that the cathode is more positive than the anode, it will still not pass current. Its resistance is therefore high. If the reverse bias voltage is increased beyond a certain level (the peak inverse rating) the diode will break down and cease to show diode-like properties.

Choosing a diode

When looking up diodes in a component supplier's catalogue you will find a bewildering range from which to make your selection. Signal diodes and

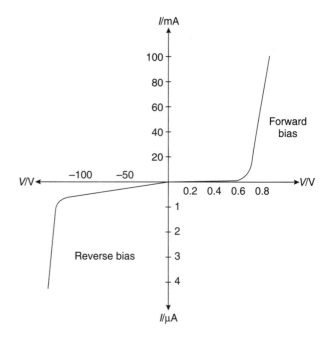

Figure 5.12   The diode characteristic

rectifier diodes both perform the same function except that the former operate with much lower forward currents and maximum peak inverse voltages.

The Zener diode

The Zener diode owes its name to C. Zener who did the experimental work and suggested a theory in 1934 to explain the breakdown effects of dielectrics.

We have already seen what happens to a conventional diode when we put too much reverse bias across the p–n junction, i.e. breakdown. The

Peak inverse voltage   Maximum forward current

Signal Diodes								
Type No. and Manufacturer		**Price Each**	**Construction**	**Case Style**	**PIV V**	**Max I_F (average)**	**Max reverse current I_R (μA @ V)**	**Application**
BAR28	ST	45p	Schottky barrier	D035	70V	15mA	<200nA @ 50V	Low forward voltage (V_F = 410mV at 1mA), suitable replacement for germanium, very fast >10GHz
BAX13		7p	Si diffused whiskerless	D035★	50V	75mA	<200nA @ 50V	Fast logic
BAX16		9p	Si diffused whiskerless	D035★	150V	200mA	<100nA @ 150V	General purpose
BY206		34p	Si double diffused	D014	350V	400mA	<2μA @ 300V	Top level detector and scan rectifier and for h.f. power supplies. Soft recovery
OA47		36p	Ge gold bonded	D07	25V	110mA	<100μA @ 25V	High speed switch
OA90		24p	Ge point contact	D07	30V	10mA	<1.1mA @ 30V	High frequency detector
OA91		24p	Ge point contact	D07	115V	50mA	<275μA @ 100V	General purpose
OA95	SEM	29p	Ge point contact	D07	115V	50mA	<250μA @ 100V	General purpose
1N914		5p	Si whiskerless	D035	100V	75mA	<25nA @ 20V	Fast logic
1N916		6p	Si whiskerless	D035	100V	75mA	<25hA @ 20V	Low capacitance 1N914
1N4148		5p	Si whiskerless	D035	100V	75mA	<25nA @ 20V	Fast logic

Diode type   Cost   Look at this in conjunction with a case layout chart

Reading a supplier's catalogue

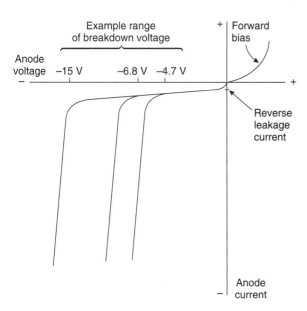

Figure 5.13   The Zener characteristic

Photodiode

Figure 5.14   Symbol used for a photodiode

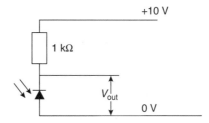

Figure 5.15 V_{out} will change according to the level of light on the diode

resulting high current destroys the diode. However, Zener diodes are designed to work in the breakdown region without being destroyed.

By heavily doping the diodes in a closely controlled way breakdown will occur at voltages less than –5 V. This breakdown is due to the Zener effect. Breakdown at higher voltages can be obtained by modifying the doping, although breakdown then becomes a combination of the Zener and avalanche effects. The details of these effects are of more interest to a physicist than to us; we are more interested in how we can use them.

A whole range of Zener diodes are manufactured with various values of breakdown voltage (see Figure 5.13). Once breakdown occurs the voltage across the diode is maintained constant – we cannot develop voltage across what in effect is a short circuit. This means that we can use a Zener diode as a voltage reference device.

Zener diodes are always operated in the reverse bias mode and always with a series resistor to limit the breakdown current. Without the resistor the diode would be destroyed by self-heating.

The photodiode

The photodiode (Figure 5.14) is different from the others discussed in that it is usually operated in reverse bias. When light shines on the transparent window in the diode case the reverse resistance decreases. It is often used in security systems and conveyor belt counting mechanisms. The advantage of the photodiode over the light-dependent resistor is that it is much more sensitive and has a faster response time. In Figure 5.15 V_{out} will change according to the level of light incident on the diode (NB: The +10 V is not a critical value).

The light-emitting diode

The light-emitting diode (LED) differs from a normal diode in that, when a current of sufficient magnitude flows through it, light is emitted. The advantage of the LED over a conventional lamp is that it will not burn out or require replacing, provided it is treated correctly.

LEDs come in a variety of shapes and sizes. Prices vary according to how often the type of LED is used. Colours other than red can be more expensive and also use different bias voltages and currents. LEDs that transmit in the infrared range are also available and are extensively used in remote control and security applications.

As a comparison, the LED has an output power of around 1 mW compared with a standard battery torch which has about ten times that amount.

An LED will not emit light unless it has the correct currents and voltages set up around it. As these differ for different types of LED it is necessary to check the manufacturer's data book or the component supplier's catalogue.

The data given in Table 5.1 are for a standard 0.2 inch LED. The table gives typical figures for forward current and forward voltage drop. Other figures, often maximum values, are also given. The values in the table can be used to calculate the

(a)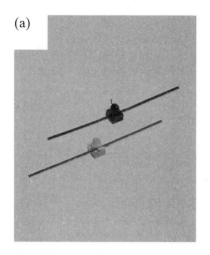

(b)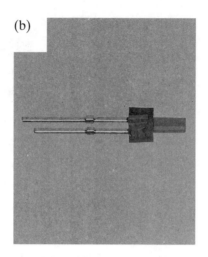

(c)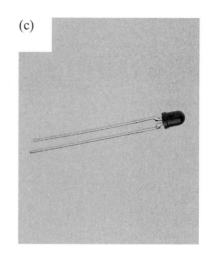

(a) AlGaAs red LED; (b) 2 mm flat top LED; (c) low current diffused LED

value of the resistor that must be placed in series with the LED when incorporating it in a circuit.

Calculating the series resistance required for an LED

The value of the resistor required for an LED can be calculated using Ohm's law by taking values of forward current and forward voltage drop from Table 5.1.

For Figure 5.16 the formula we require is

$$R_{\text{limiting}} = \frac{V_{\text{supply}} - V_{\text{f}}}{I_{\text{f}}}$$

Using the figures from the component supplier's data quoted in Table 5.1 and assuming a 9 V supply rail gives

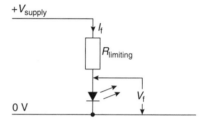

Figure 5.16

$$R_{\text{limiting}} = \frac{(9 - 2)\,\text{V}}{10\,\text{mA}} = \frac{7\,\text{V}}{10\,\text{mA}} = 700\,\Omega$$

(We use the nearest preferred value, i.e. 680 Ω.)

Table 5.1   Technical specification of an LED (quoted at 25 °C)

	Red	Green	Yellow	Red (wide angle)	Units
I_{F} max	30	30	30	40	mA
I_{F} typ	10	10	10	10	mA
V_{R} max	3	3	3	3	V
P_{D} max	100	115	115	115	mW
Derate power	1.3	1.6	1.5	1.5	mW/°C
V_{F} at I_{F} typ	2	2	2	2	V
Intensity at I_{F} typ	5	5	5	4	mcd
Viewing angle	30	30	30	80	deg
Peak wavelength	635	565	585	635	nm

NB: I_{F} max, *maximum forward current*; I_{F} typ, *typical forward current*; V_{R} max, *maximum reverse voltage before the diode is damaged*; V_{F} at I_{F} typ, *typical forward voltage for I_{F} typ (10 mA in this case)*.

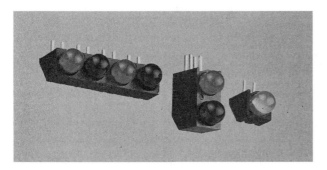

Single, dual and quad low current LEDs

Unlike conventional diodes LEDs are easy to destroy if a relatively small reverse voltage is applied across them. For the standard LED this is no more than about 3 V.

Additionally, it is worth noting that if an LED is run without a series resistor the diode will be destroyed.

Testing an LED

There are two methods of testing LEDs. The easiest is to use a digital meter with an LED test position which actually lights the diode if it is working satisfactorily. An alternative is to connect the LED into a test circuit as shown in Figure 5.17.

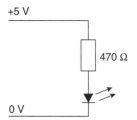

Figure 5.17   Typical LED test circuit

Where an expensive LED is being used it is normal to connect a diode across it for protection purposes (see Figure 5.18).

The seven-segment display

A seven-segment display is a collection of LEDs arranged in a pattern so that when the appropriate sections of the pattern are forward bias figures will be formed (Figure 5.19). As a seven-segment display is just a collection of single LEDs grouped together, each segment usually has to have a limiting resistor connected in series with it. The exception is when the series resistor is contained

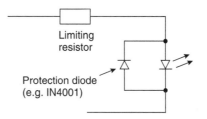

Figure 5.18   Protecting LEDs with a reverse diode. Where an expensive LED is used it is normal to connect a diode across it as shown for protection purposes

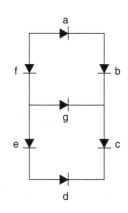

Figure 5.19   A seven-segment display

within the integrated circuit that is driving the display. The same rules apply for calculating the value of the series resistor as for individual LEDs.

Common anode or common cathode? Seven-segment displays come in two forms (sometimes called packages), common anode or common cathode. It is important to know what type of package you have as it determines the type of integrated circuit that is used to drive it.

The common-anode display is one in which all the anodes are connected to a single line which is fed out as one pin of the seven-segment display. The principle is illustrated in Figure 5.20.

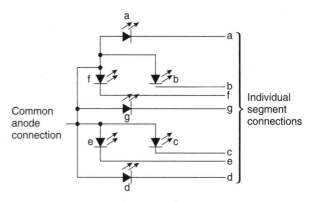

Figure 5.20   Common-anode seven-segment display

The common-cathode display is the opposite; the cathodes are all joined together whilst the anodes are fed to individual pins at the back of the display. The equivalent circuit is shown in Figure 5.21.

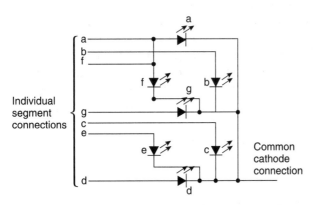

Figure 5.21   Common-cathode seven-segment display

5.3 Bipolar transistors

Transistors revolutionised electronics when, in the 1950s, their small size heralded the start of the era of portable consumer goods. There are two types of transistor, the bipolar and the unipolar. Each operates in a different manner and has different applications.

The two sorts of bipolar transistor are the n–p–n and the p–n–p (see Figure 5.22). As n–p–n transistors are the most commonly used we shall discuss the operation of the device based around this type.

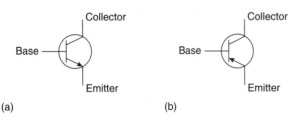

(a)   (b)

Figure 5.22   (a) N–p–n transistor; (b) p–n–p transistor

The transistor has three electrodes which are known as the base, emitter and collector. Between each of these electrodes there are p–n junctions just as in the diodes that we have already discussed. It is therefore possible, in theory, to separate the transistor into its individual p–n junctions as shown in Figure 5.23.

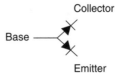

Figure 5.23   The diode analogy of a transistor

The three main functions of the transistor are

(a) to amplify AC or DC signals,
(b) to act as a switch,
(c) to act as an electronically controlled variable resistor.

Making a transistor conduct

The diode analogy of the transistor in Figure 5.23 shows that the transistor will only conduct if the p–n junctions are biased correctly. In Figure 5.24(a) the transistor's collector–emitter junction is connected to battery 2. The base–emitter junction is biased via battery 1. The resistor is in the circuit to limit the current and prevent the transistor destroying itself.

The voltage between the base and the emitter *forward biases* the p–n junction and, provided that the collector is positive enough compared with the emitter potential, will cause it to conduct. A typical value for the forward biasing of the transistor is about 0.6 V although some books refer to 0.7 V. In practice we will not use a separate battery. It is much more economical to use a resistor dropped from the positive supply rail as in Figure 5.24(b).

Once a transistor is forward biased, current can flow through the junctions in the directions marked in Figure 5.24(b). Compared with the action of a diode the following important statements can be made.

(a) If the transistor base–emitter junction is reverse bias no current flows via the collector or base. The resistance from collector to emitter is therefore high.
(b) When the transistor's base–emitter junction is forward bias, base and collector current flows.

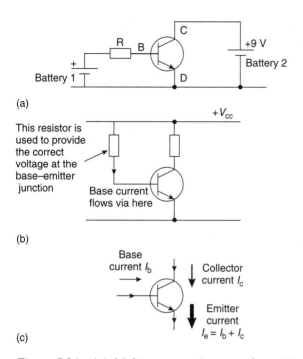

(a)

This resistor is used to provide the correct voltage at the base–emitter junction

Base current flows via here

(b)

Base current I_b

Collector current I_c

Emitter current $I_e = I_b + I_c$

(c)

Figure 5.24 (a) Making a transistor conduct; (c) direction of currents drawn by a forward bias transistor (note different sizes of the arrows)

The resistance between collector and emitter is therefore low.

From Figure 5.24(c) you can see the direction of the current paths in the transistor. Current enters in two directions – via the collector and via the base.

A very important point to note is the difference in the size of these currents, and we have attempted to stress this point by the thickness of the arrows indicating the currents. The current I_b that flows via the base is very much less than the collector current I_c. The emitter current I_e is the sum of the base and the collector currents. Mathematically,

$$I_e = I_b + I_c$$

As a useful rule of thumb:

$$100\% \ (I_e) = 2\% \ (I_b) + 98\% \ (I_c)$$

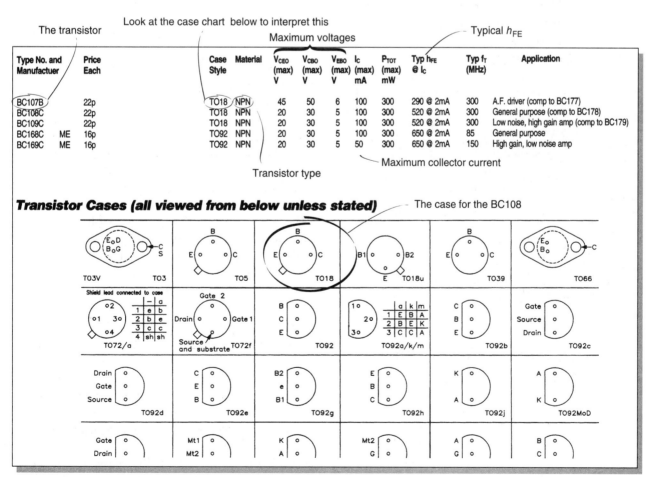

The transistor

Look at the case chart below to interpret this

Maximum voltages

Typical h_{FE}

Type No. and Manufactuer	Price Each		Case Style	Material	V_{CEO} (max) V	V_{CBO} (max) V	V_{EBO} (max) V	Ic (max) mA	P_{TOT} (max) mW	Typ h_{FE} @ I_c	Typ f_T (MHz)	Application
BC107B	22p		TO18	NPN	45	50	6	100	300	290 @ 2mA	300	A.F. driver (comp to BC177)
BC108C	22p		TO18	NPN	20	30	5	100	300	520 @ 2mA	300	General purpose (comp to BC178)
BC109C	22p		TO18	NPN	20	30	5	100	300	520 @ 2mA	300	Low noise, high gain amp (comp to BC179)
BC168C	ME	16p	TO92	NPN	20	30	5	100	300	650 @ 2mA	85	General purpose
BC169C	ME	16p	TO92	NPN	20	30	5	50	300	650 @ 2mA	150	High gain, low noise amp

Transistor type

Maximum collector current

Transistor Cases (all viewed from below unless stated)

The case for the BC108

TO3V   TO3   TO5   TO18   TO18u   TO39   TO66

TO72/a   TO72f   TO92   TO92a/k/m   TO92b   TO92c

TO92d   TO92e   TO92g   TO92h   TO92j   TO92MoD

Reading a supplier's catalogue

Identification of transistor electrodes

Transistors have three legs or electrodes and are made in all shapes and sizes. This makes it quite difficult to identify individual electrodes from memory. However, manufacturers have standardised on a system of case styles. Now it is simply a matter of identifying the transistor type and then looking up its associated appropriate pinout.

Practical 4

The transistor as an amplifier

This practical should enable you to prove to yourself that a transistor amplifies. You can also use it to calculate current gain.

Connect up the circuit shown in Figure 5.25. The two lamps are exactly the same. Check that you have got the transistor electrodes around the correct way and then switch on.

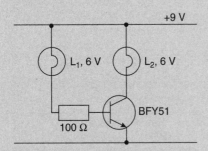

Figure 5.25

The lamp L_2 connected in the collector of the transistor should light. This proves that the transistor is forward biased and drawing collector current. The lamp L_1 connected in the base of the transistor remains unlit even though there *must* be current flowing through it for the transistor to operate.

It therefore follows that the collector current I_c is very much greater than the base current I_b, i.e. it has been amplified.

The current gain of the transistor

As the transistor is an amplifier it is an active device. That is, it provides gain because the output is larger than the input. The measurement of gain in any device is 'what comes out' divided by 'what goes in'. As we have seen, the output is the collector current and the input is the base current. Therefore,

$$\text{current gain} = \frac{\text{output current}}{\text{input current}}$$

$$= \frac{\text{collector current}}{\text{base current}}$$

$$= \frac{I_c}{I_b}$$

Current gain is given the symbol h_{FE}. Note that it has no unit as it is the ratio of two currents.

Guided example

The transistor in Figure 5.26 has a collector current of 2 mA. If the base current is 20 μA the current gain is

$$\frac{I_c}{I_b} = \frac{2\,\text{mA}}{20\,\mu\text{A}} = 100$$

Incidentally, the emitter current of the transistor can also be calculated using the standard formula $I_e = I_b + I_c$. I_c is 2 mA + 20 μA = 2.002 mA.

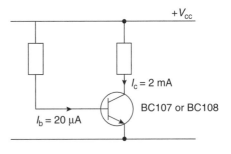

Figure 5.26

At this point it is important to clarify that we are talking about the DC conditions of a transistor. That is, no signal voltage that we wish to amplify has yet been applied. Another way of expressing this is to say that the transistor is in its *quiescent state* (the use of upper case letters in the abbreviation h_{FE} signifies this).

The current gain of a transistor is easily found by looking in a component supplier's catalogue. For each type of transistor a typical current gain h_{FE} is given for a typical value of collector current. Alternatively, h_{FE} may be calculated by measuring the currents through a transistor once it is forward bias.

Transistor characteristics

We have already talked of the characteristics of a diode and how, in graphical form, they can be used

Practical 5

Measurement of h_{FE}

The circuit that is given in Figure 5.25 can be modified and used to determine h_{FE}. Insert current meters at the appropriate points so that the circuit now appears as in Figure 5.27. Read the meters and divide the value of I_c by I_b.

Using a BC108 transistor a typical result would be $I_b = 30$ μA and $I_c = 4$ mA. Therefore,

$$h_{FE} = \frac{4\,\text{mA}}{30\,\mu\text{A}} = 133$$

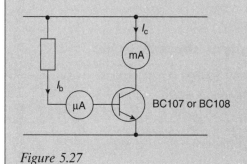

Figure 5.27

to predict how a diode will behave. The same is true for a transistor although, unlike the diode, it is possible to plot more than one graph as there are three currents in the transistor at any one time.

The input characteristic

The input characteristic is shown in Figure 5.28. It provides an indication of the amount of base current that will flow for different values of voltage across the base–emitter junction. As it deals with the response of a p–n junction it is similar to the forward characteristic of a diode. The transistor only draws base current when the knee voltage

of the characteristic is exceeded. The gradient of this graph can be calculated from the change in base–emitter voltage divided by the corresponding base current change:

$$\text{gradient} = \frac{\Delta V_{be}}{\Delta I_b}$$

As this is effectively an Ohm's law calculation and both of the axes are to do with what happens at the input to the transistor, it follows that the calculation gives the **input resistance of the transistor**. This is given the abbreviation h_{ie}. It is important because it is used in equivalent circuit calculations which we discuss later.

The transfer characteristic

The transfer characteristic is found by plotting values of base current against corresponding values of collector current; a typical example is shown in Figure 5.29. The values required to plot this graph are easily found by using the circuit in Figure 5.27 and substituting a variable resistor in the base. The resistor can then be adjusted to allow different values of base current to flow. Note that the voltage between collector and emitter is kept at a constant value.

The graph in Figure 5.29 can be used as a method of finding the current gain of the transistor when amplifying a signal, as

$$h_{fe} = \frac{\Delta I_c}{\Delta I_b}$$

Notice how lower case letters are now used to label h_{fe} to signify signal amplification.

Transistor output characteristic

Of the three characteristics the transistor output characteristic appears to be the most complicated;

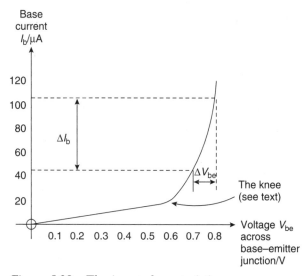

Figure 5.28   The input characteristic

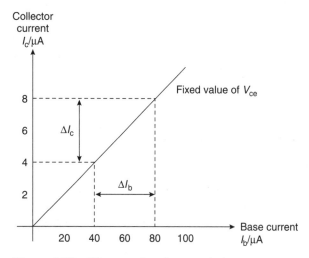

Figure 5.29   The transfer characteristic

an example is shown in Figure 5.30. This characteristic portrays the relationship between collector–emitter voltage V_{ce} and collector current I_c for various values of base current I_b. The maximum collector–emitter voltage can never exceed the supply voltage, 10 V.

From Figure 5.30 we can tell that if the voltage V_{ce} between the collector and the emitter of the transistor is, say, 7 V and the base current I_b is 60 µA the value of the collector current will be 12.9 mA.

Alternatively, we may want to look at the behaviour of the transistor when the voltage between the collector and the emitter is 3 V and the base current is 20 µA. We can predict that the collector current I_c will be 4 mA.

What do we use characteristics for?

What do we use characteristics for is a question frequently asked by students! Of the three graphs considered (Figures 5.28–5.30) the final one, the output characteristic, is the most common. It is used in the design of amplifiers and enables us to predict how an amplifier will perform once we apply a signal to it, i.e. how the amplifier will behave when we alter it from its *quiescent state* to its *dynamic state*.

Amongst other things the output characteristic can help us work out

(a) the maximum input signal that the amplifier can handle without risk of damage to the transistor and without distortion occurring;
(b) the size of the output signal and hence the power output level;
(c) the dynamic voltage gain of the amplifier;
(d) how to calculate the values of bias components that are needed to enable us to design and build an amplifier;

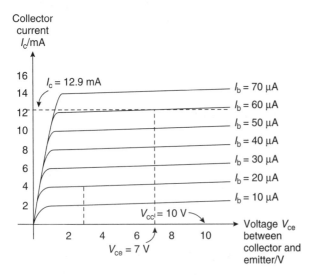

Figure 5.30 The output characteristic

(e) the amount by which the transistor amplifies the input base current, i.e. the current gain h_{fe} of the transistor.

You can now see that the output characteristic is a very useful graph indeed!

Practical 6

Plotting transistor characteristics

This practical is designed to enable you to plot the characteristics of a BC108 n–p–n transistor. We then go on to use the graphs obtained to design a simple amplifier.

The output characteristic

The circuit in Figure 5.31 can be used to obtain readings for the output characteristic. The output characteristic shows how, with a fixed value of base current, collector current alters as the value of collector voltage is changed.

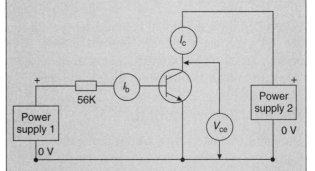

Figure 5.31

Adjust the output of power supply 1 until the meter reading the base current I_b registers 10 µA. This level of current should remain constant regardless of changes in the collector

I_b (µA)	\multicolumn{9}{c}{V_{ce} (V)}
	1	2	3	4	5	6	7	8	9
10									
20									
35									
40									
50									
70									

current I_c. Now adjust the output of power supply 2 to give various values of collector voltage as detailed in the results table.

At each value of collector voltage note the corresponding value of collector current and enter it in the table (in mA).

When you have completed the readings for a base current of 10 μA reset power supply 1 to provide a base current of 20 μA and repeat the operation (and so on for the values of base current given in the table). Now plot a graph of V_{ce} (on the x axis) against I_c (on the y axis).

Input characteristic

The circuit in Figure 5.32 can be used to obtain readings for the input characteristic. The input characteristic shows the relationship between base–emitter voltage V_{be} and base current I_b. It is obtained with the collector–emitter voltage held constant.

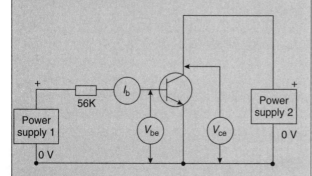

Figure 5.32

Adjust power supply 2 to give a collector voltage of 3 V. Adjust the output of power supply 1 to give the values of base current detailed in the results table and at each setting record the corresponding base–emitter voltage. Plot a graph of V_{be} (on the x axis) against I_b (on the y axis).

The transfer characteristic

The circuit in Figure 5.33 can be used to obtain readings for the transfer characteristic. The transfer characteristic shows the relationship between input and output currents of the transistor for a set value of collector–emitter voltage. The slope or gradient of the graph gives the DC current gain of the transistor at that value of collector–emitter voltage.

Set the output of power supply 2 to give

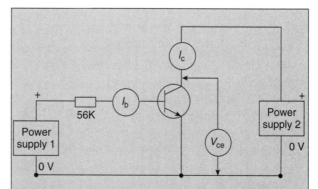

Figure 5.33

I_b (μA)	V_{be} (V)
10	
20	
35	
40	
50	
70	

a collector–emitter voltage of 3 V. Now adjust the output of power supply 1 to provide the values of base current detailed in the results table. This can be repeated for a collector–emitter voltage of 6 V. Plot a graph of I_b (on the x axis) against I_c (on the y axis).

| I_b (μA) | I_c (mA) | |
	$V_{ce} = 3$ V	$V_{ce} = 6$ V
10		
20		
35		
40		
50		
70		

The transistor as a switch

From the characteristics that we have discussed we can see that no current can flow via the collector of a transistor if the base–emitter bias is not at the necessary level to turn the transistor on.

The actual value of bias will determine the amount of current flow. At one extreme, if the bias is 0 V the transistor will not conduct (sometimes called 'cut-off'), collector current will be 0 mA and

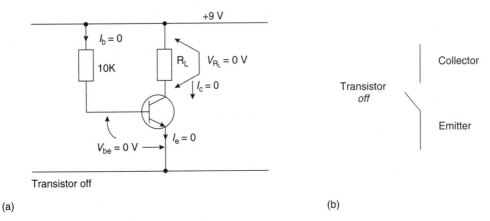

Figure 5.34   (a) Note that no collector current flows, i.e. the collector–emitter resistance is high; (b) switch analogy

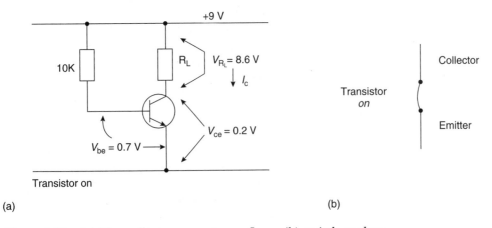

Figure 5.35   (a) The collector current now flows; (b) switch analogy

0 V will be dropped across the load resistor R_L. This is shown in Figure 5.34. The voltage between the collector and the emitter is therefore V_{cc}.

As no current flows via the collector–emitter junction the resistance between these two points is extremely high and can be regarded as an open switch.

If we now consider the opposite condition where the base–emitter voltage is of a level that causes the transistor to draw the maximum amount of collector current, a large current will flow via the load resistor. (This is sometimes referred to as saturating the transistor.) Theoretically, under these conditions the whole of the supply could be developed across the load resistor, but in practice about 0.2 V will remain between the collector and the emitter of the transistor. This is illustrated in Figure 5.35.

Using the same principle as before, under this condition the resistance between the collector and the emitter must be low as a relatively large current flows.

If the bias is adjusted somewhere between 0 V and saturation level the resistance of the collector–emitter junction will also change, i.e. the transistor can behave as a voltage-dependent resistor.

Practical 7

The transistor as a switch

In this practical the ability of a transistor to operate as a switch will be investigated. You should be able to prove that when the transistor is not conducting the resistance between its collector and its emitter is high and it can therefore be regarded as an open switch, but when it is conducting the resistance between the collector and the emitter is low and the collector current flows via this route.

In Figure 5.36 an ORP12 light-dependent resistor (LDR) is used to switch on and off a 60 mA lamp. Under light conditions the only current drawn by the circuit is that which flows via the 10K resistor and the LDR itself.

When the LDR is held under darkened conditions its resistance increases and the voltage across it – and hence at the base of the transistor – rises. As this voltage biases the base–emitter junction of the BFY51 the

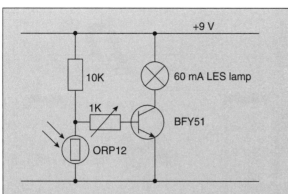

Figure 5.36

transistor now draws base current and the resultant collector current that flows operates the lamp.

Sometimes LEDs are also driven by transistors and a suitable circuit is shown in Figure 5.37. The current drawn by the LED is much greater than the base current of the transistor and if it was connected in this part of the circuit it would fail to light.

Note that it is common practice to drive a relay via a transistor.

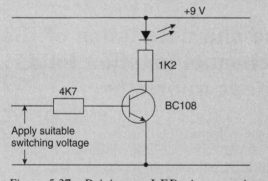

Figure 5.37 Driving an LED via a transistor

5.4 Field effect transistors

So far, we have dealt with the bipolar (i.e. n–p–n/p–n–p) transistor. During the course of the discussion we have established the following.

(a) The conventional transistor requires a forward bias voltage of 0.6 V between base and emitter for it to conduct. At the same time the collector must be held positive with respect to the emitter.
(b) The bipolar transistor is a current-operated device. That is, it takes a base current and amplifies it, the output current being available at the collector. We obtain a voltage out of the circuit by passing the collector current through a resistor and tapping the voltage across it.
(c) As the transistor is current operated it draws current from the supply. Its input resistance is therefore relatively low, although its exact value depends on the configuration in which the transistor is connected.

Field effect transistors (FETs) are referred to as unipolar transistors. Their method of operating differs from the conventional transistor and they consist of a semiconductor whose charge-carrying capacity is determined by the input voltage.

Types of field effect transistor

There are two types of FET:

(a) the junction FET (JFET) (Figure 5.38);
(b) the metal–oxide–semiconductor FET (MOSFET), sometimes called the insulated gate FET (IGFET).

The electrodes have been labelled for the symbols in Figure 5.38. Instead of the base, emitter and collector these are known as the gate, source and drain. Table 5.2 gives some data on various FETs.

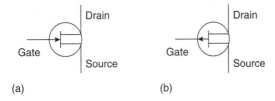

(a)   (b)

Figure 5.38 (a) JFET (n channel); (b) JFET (p channel)

Construction of the junction field effect transistor

Figure 5.39 shows that the JFET is made from p and n material; the precise construction determines whether an n- or a p-channel JFET is produced.

Making a junction field effect transistor conduct

Figure 5.40 shows typical potentials that are required around the electrodes of an n-channel JFET to make it conduct. Note that the gate voltage is negative with respect to the source. Assuming that the voltage between the drain and the source is above a critical value known as the pinch-off voltage, when the gate potential approaches 0 V maximum drain current will flow.

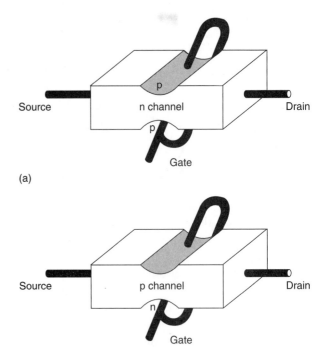

Figure 5.39 (a) Construction of an n-channel JFET; (b) construction of a p-channel JFET

The characteristics of the n-channel junction field effect transistor

Figure 5.40 illustrates in a simplistic manner the way the n-channel JFET behaves. However, to get the full picture we can plot, as with the bipolar transistor, a set of graphs or characteristics that reflect the way that the JFET will behave as potentials around its electrodes are altered.

Table 5.2   N-channel FET data

Type number and manufacturer	Case style	P_{TOT} (max) (mW)	V_{DS} (max) (V)	V_{DG} (max) (V)	V_{GS} (max) (V)	I_{GSS} (max) (nA)	Y_{FS} (typical) (µS) (V_{GS} = 0 V)	Maximum input capacitance (pF)	I_{DSS} (max) (mA)	Application
BF244A	TO92d	300	30	30	30	7	4500	4	25	DC, low and high frequency amps
MPF102 NSC	TO92c	310	25	25	25	2	1600 @ 100 MHz	7	20	RF amps
2N3819 SLX	TO92d	200	25	25	25	2	400	8	20	General purpose
2N5459 ME	TO92c	310	25	25	25	0.1	4500	7	16	General purpose
J109 SLX	TO92c	360	25	25	25	3	17 000	85	40	JFET
J112 SLX	TO92	360	35	35	35	1	6000	12	5	JFET
2N7000 SLX	TO92d	400	60	60	±40	10	200 000	30	1	Fetlington (Darlington FET), 200 mA

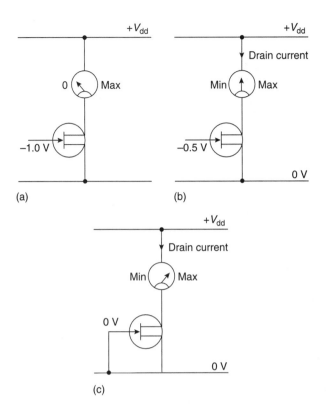

(a)

(b)

(c)

Figure 5.40

A typical output characteristic is shown in Figure 5.41 and you will immediately notice the similarity in shape to the bipolar characteristics that we have already looked at. The voltages and currents marked on the scales, however, are quite different.

The output characteristic in common-source mode

The graph in Figure 5.41 reflects how the drain current will vary for different values of the voltage V_{ds} between the drain and the source, with V_{gs} held at various steady values.

Interpretation of this characteristic shows us that, for example, if the drain–source voltage is 10 V and the gate–source potential is –1.0 V then the drain current is expected to be 5 mA. Alteration of the gate–source voltage will change the amount of drain current flowing. For example, if V_{gs} is changed to –0.5 V and V_{ds} is held constant the drain current increases to 6.5 mA.

In other words, the magnitude of the output current of the FET can be controlled by a small change in V_{gs}.

From this you can see that in the same way that we use a bipolar transistor's characteristics to see how it will behave we can also use those of a JFET for the same purpose.

However, the parameters that we have used before to describe how the conventional transistor operates (i.e. h_{fe} etc.) are not used and are replaced by the following.

Transfer characteristic and 'gm'

We have already stated that FETs are voltage operated and the level of drain current is controlled by the voltage between the gate and the source. Although this is shown by the output characteristic it can be more clearly illustrated by drawing the transfer characteristic alongside the output characteristic.

The transfer characteristic can be derived from the output characteristic by selecting a fixed value of drain–source voltage and plotting the values of drain current for the various levels of gate–source potential.

The ratio of change of drain current to change of gate–source voltage (with a constant V_{ds}) gives rise to the 'gm' parameter. That is,

$$gm = \frac{\Delta I_d}{\Delta V_{gs}}$$

This parameter is known as the **mutual conductance** of an FET. It is a measure of how a small change in voltage between the gate and the source will vary the drain current that flows. It can be looked upon in much the same way as we used h_{FE} when we considered the bipolar transistor.

From Figure 5.43 we can deduce that for a fixed V_{ds} of 12 V and a change of gate–source voltage from –4 V to –1.0 V the drain current will change from 4.2 mA to 10.2 mA.

The gm can therefore be calculated:

$$gm = \frac{\Delta I_d}{\Delta V_{gs}} = \frac{6\,mA}{3\,V} = 2\,mS$$

Typical values of gm quoted by manufacturers for JFETs range from 1 mS to 8 mS.

Note how the formula for gm is the reciprocal of resistance and the unit used is therefore that of conductance, the siemen or millisiemen.

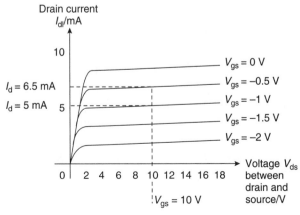

Figure 5.41   The output characteristic of a JFET

Practical 8

Plotting the output characteristic of an n-channel JFET

You can plot an output characteristic for an n-channel JFET using the circuit in Figure 5.42. Using RV_1 set the gate–source voltage to –2 V and then adjust RV_2 so that the value of the voltage between the drain and the source is 2 V. Note the drain current in the results table. Repeat the sequence by adjusting RV_1 and RV_2 to obtain the values of V_{gs} and V_{ds} given in the results table.

V_{gs} (V)	V_{ds} (V)								
	2	4	6	8	10	12	14	16	18
–2									
–1.5									
–1.0									
–0.5									
0									

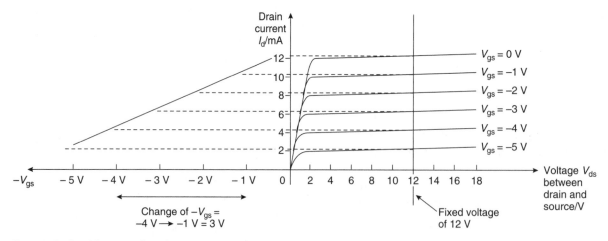

Figure 5.42

Figure 5.43 The transfer characteristic of a JFET

gm is an important figure as it partly determines the voltage gain of the circuit and also gives us an idea of the effectiveness of the FET. This will be dealt with when we examine the FET as an amplifier of a signal voltage.

The pinch-off voltage

The JFET operates with the gate negative with respect to the source and it is the size of this negative voltage that controls the conduction of the FET.

As the gate voltage approaches 0 V maximum drain current will begin to flow provided that the drain–source potential is above a critical level. This is known as the 'pinch-off voltage' and is widely quoted alongside the resulting drain current (Figure 5.44). The latter is usually given the symbol I_{dss} which stands for the value of drain current in common-source mode when the gate is short circuit to the source.

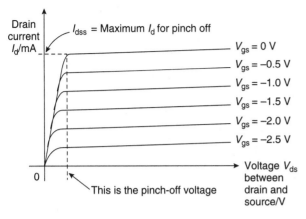

Figure 5.44

Input impedance

The input impedance of an FET (i.e. the impedance between gate and source) is very high as the input is in fact applied to a reverse bias diode junction. This high impedance (MΩ) means that the FET will not draw input current, and it is therefore a voltage-operated semiconductor.

The input impedance can be found by measuring the change in gate current that occurs when the gate–source voltage is varied. As the gate current is minimal it thus follows that the impedance value is very high.

To measure input impedance the voltage between the drain and the source must be held at a constant value. The value of input impedance is then calculated by using the formula

$$Z_{in} = \frac{\Delta V_{gs}}{\Delta I_g} \; \Omega$$

A figure of 10 MΩ is not unusual for the input impedance.

Output impedance

The output impedance of an FET can be found by using the output characteristic (Figure 5.45). With the gate–source voltage held constant a change is made in drain–source voltage and the corresponding alteration of drain current is measured. The output impedance can then be calculated using the formula

$$Z_{out} = \frac{\Delta V_{gs}}{\Delta I_d}$$

For the example given in Figure 5.45,

$$\frac{\Delta V_{gs}}{\Delta I_d} = \frac{(12-4)\ \text{V}}{(4.2-3.8)\ \text{mA}} = \frac{8}{0.4} = 20\ \text{k}\Omega$$

The field effect transistor as a variable resistor

We have seen that a very small voltage on the gate of an FET controls the amount of drain current that flows. Put differently, the resistance of the FET

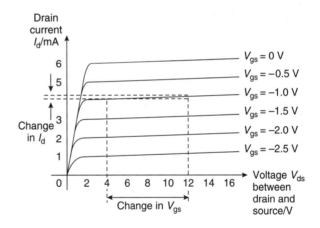

Figure 5.45

N Channel Field Effect Transistors										
Type No. and Manufacturer	Price Each	Case Style	P_TOT (max) mW	V_DS (max) V	V_DG (max) V	V_GS (max) V	I_GSS (max) nA	Y_FS (typical) µS (V_GS = 0V)	Max Input Capacitance (pF)	I_DSS (max) mA	Application
BF244A	48p		TO92d	300	30	30	30	7	4500	4	25	DC, low and high frequency amps
MPF102 NSC	55p	TO92c	310	25	25	25	2	1600 @ 100MHz 7	20	R.F. amps
2N3819 SLX	45p	TO92d	200	25	25	25	2	4000	8	20	General purpose
2N5459 ME	60p	TO92c	310	25	25	25	0.1	4500	7	16	General purpose
J109 SLX	80p	TO92c	360	25	25	25	3	17,000	85	40	JFET
J112 SLX	42p	TO92	360	35	35	35	1	6000	12	5	JFET
2N7000 SLX	32p	TO92d	400	60	60	±40	10	200,000	30	1	Fetlington (Darlington FET), 200mA continuous drain current, on-state resistance 2.4Ω (typical)

Case style (see page 115) — Maximum voltages — gm or Y_FS — Maximum drain current

Abbreviation for the manufacturer — Type of FET

Reading a supplier's catalogue

between drain and source must change as the gate potential is altered. Between the drain and source the FET can therefore be regarded as a voltage-controlled variable resistor.

In practice the FET is used quite widely in this form, particularly where a signal voltage has to be controlled. Automatic gain control in televisions and radios is a typical application where fluctuations of signal strength at the aerial are compensated for by reducing or increasing the amount of signal processed through the set's amplifiers (Figure 5.47).

Another common application that uses this principle is the Dolby noise reduction system used in recording.

The field effect transistor as a switch

As we have just mentioned, the resistance of the FET from drain to source is dependent on the gate–source voltage. Maximum drain current flows when the FET is fully on as the resistance from drain to source is minimal.

In this situation the FET can also be seen as a switch which, as it is closed, has minimal resistance.

At the other extreme, when the gate–source voltage is insufficient to bias the FET into drawing drain current, the opposite applies, i.e. the resistance from drain to source is extremely high. Under these conditions the FET can be viewed as an open circuit from drain to source or, to put it another way, an open circuit switch.

The FET configured as a switch is available in integrated circuit form. The 4051 can switch any one of eight lines to one output depending on the state of the control pins.

Practical 9

Using a JFET as an electronically controlled variable resistor

This practical is designed to prove that a JFET can be used as an electronically controlled variable resistor.

The principle is shown in Figure 5.46(a) and the actual circuit is given in Figure 5.46(b). R_1 and the JFET form a potential divider. The resistance of the JFET is set by the bias on its gate, which is controlled by RV_1.

Using Ohm's law we can say that when the resistance of the FET is the same as R_1 the voltage out will be half of the voltage in. Adjust RV_1 to set up this situation.

Now change the bias on the gate of the JFET, monitoring both the input and output signals on the oscilloscope. You will clearly see the peak to peak value of the output change as the gate bias is altered.

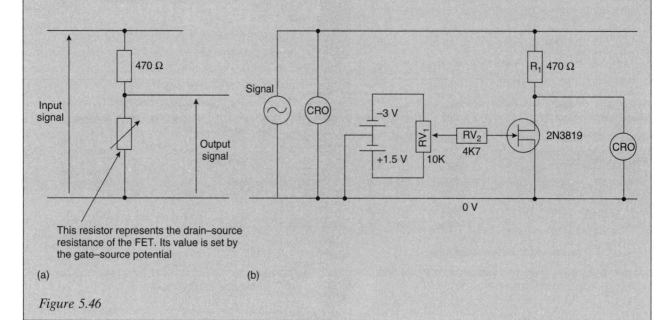

(a)   (b)

Figure 5.46

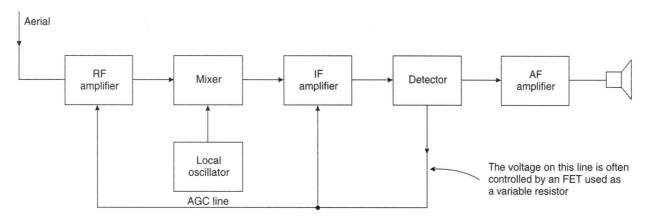

Figure 5.47   *A simple superheterodyne radio receiver*

Cassette deck with Dolby noise reduction

Georg Simon Ohm (1787–1854)

Ohm was a German physicist, the son of a master mechanic. Although he taught in High School, it was Ohm's ambition to teach in the University of Bavaria. After he formulated and publicised his law in Germany he not only failed to get a job in the University but even had to resign from the High School. This was because his idea met so much opposition and criticism from his fellow scientists.

After a few years his work became widely known outside Germany and was eventually recognised for its importance to science. With the help of King Ludwig I of Bavaria, Ohm finally got his appointment as Professor at the University in Munich in 1849. After his death the unit of electrical resistance was called the ohm in his honour.

Multiple choice questions

1 Which of the diagrams in Figure 5.48 is correct?

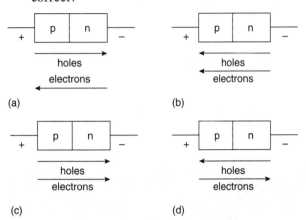

Figure 5.48

2 In Figure 5.49 the condition of the lamps will be
  (a) L_1 on, L_2 off, L_3 off
  (b) L_1 off, L_2 on, L_3 on
  (c) L_1 on, L_2 on, L_3 off
  (d) L_1 off, L_2 off, L_3 off.

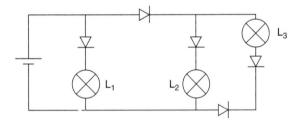

Figure 5.49

3 The conditions needed to bias a silicon diode on are
  (a) cathode positive with respect to anode by at least 0.2 V
  (b) cathode negative with respect to anode by at least 0.2 V
  (c) cathode positive with respect to anode by at least 0.6 V
  (d) cathode negative with respect to anode by at least 0.6 V.

4 A semiconductor is said to be forward bias when
  (a) leakage current flows from anode to cathode
  (b) the resistance is low from anode to cathode
  (c) reverse current flows from anode to cathode
  (d) current flows from anode to cathode.

5 The approximate voltage at point x in Figure 5.50 will be
  (a) –0.6 V
  (b) –0.2 V
  (c) +0.2 V
  (d) +0.6 V.

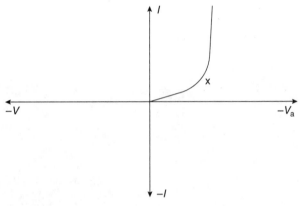

Figure 5.50

6 A diode biased into points PQ on the characteristic shown in Figure 5.51 could be used for
  (a) full-wave rectification
  (b) Zener stabilisation
  (c) half-wave rectification
  (d) reverse blocking.

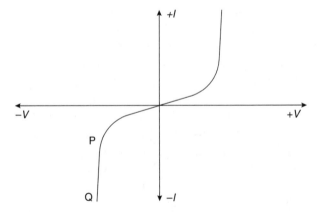

Figure 5.51

7 The value of R in Figure 5.52 is
  (a) 2.36 kΩ
  (b) 1.64 kΩ
  (c) 360 Ω
  (d) 2 kΩ.

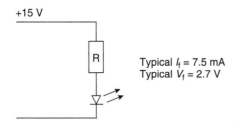

+15 V

R

Typical I_f = 7.5 mA
Typical V_f = 2.7 V

Figure 5.52

8 The resistance between points A and B in
Figure 5.53 when point A is positive with
respect to point B is found to be greater than 1
MΩ. The likely fault is
(a) D_2 is open circuit
(b) D_3 is short circuit
(c) D_2 is short circuit
(d) D_3 is open circuit.

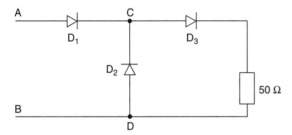

Figure 5.53

9 Which of the following readings would be likely
to indicate a faulty diode?
(a) 10 Ω forward reading, 300 Ω reverse
reading
(b) 300 Ω forward reading, 70 Ω reverse
reading
(c) 1 kΩ forward reading, 1 MΩ reverse
reading
(d) 30 Ω forward reading, 1 MΩ reverse
reading.

10 If D_1 in Figures 5.54 became a short circuit the
potential difference of R_3 would be
(a) 5 V
(b) 0 V
(c) 3.33 V
(d) 6.66 V.

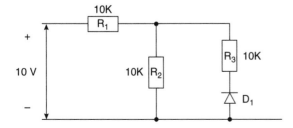

Figure 5.54

11 Which of the diagrams in Figure 5.55 indicates
the correct polarities for the transistor to
conduct?

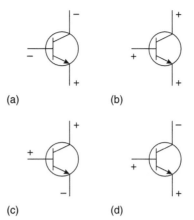

Figure 5.55

12 The emitter current of the transistor in Figure
5.56 will be
(a) 3225 μA
(b) 2000 μA
(c) 80 mA
(d) 105 μA.

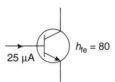

Figure 5.56

13 The values of the resistors R_1 and R_2 in Figure
5.57 are
(a) R_1 = 225 kΩ, R_2 = 2.22 kΩ
(b) R_1 = 420 kΩ, R_2 = 2.25 kΩ
(c) R_1 = 450 kΩ, R_2 = 4.5 kΩ
(d) R_1 = 409 kΩ, R_2 = 450 kΩ.

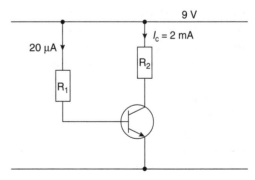

Figure 5.57

14 The transistor in Figure 5.58 is used as a switch.

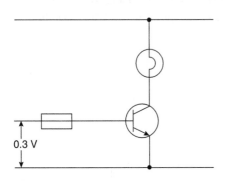

Figure 5.58

The resistance between the collector and the emitter will be approximately

(a) 1 kΩ
(b) 1 Ω
(c) 50 Ω
(d) 10 kΩ.

15 Which of the diagrams in Figure 5.59 is the symbol for one type of FET?

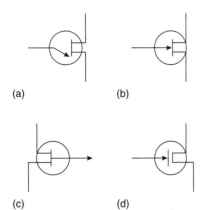

Figure 5.59

16 The FET is
(a) a high impedance current amplifier
(b) a low impedance voltage amplifier
(c) a low impedance current amplifier
(d) a high impedance voltage amplifier.

17 For an n-channel JFET to conduct
(a) the source should be positive with respect to the drain
(b) the gate must be held negative with respect to the source
(c) the gate should be held positive with respect to the source
(d) all potentials must exceed pinch-off level.

18 The letters in Figure 5.60 represent
(a) A: I_d, B: $-V_{gs}$, C: I_d
(b) A: I_d, B: V_{dd}, C: $-V_{gs}$
(c) A: I_d, B: V_{dg}, C: V_{gs}
(d) A: I_d, B: V_{ds}, C: $-V_{gs}$.

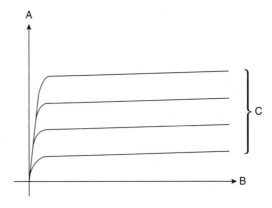

Figure 5.60

19 The gm of an FET is an indication of
(a) its voltage amplification
(b) its current amplification
(c) the load resistor's value
(d) the FET's output impedance.

20 FETs are used in preference to bipolar transistors where
(a) low voltage supplies are required
(b) the load must draw high current
(c) a low impedance is required
(d) a high impedance is required.

6

Power supplies

At the heart of nearly every piece of equipment is a power supply. This is acknowledged by saying that the circuit is active (i.e. requires a voltage for it to operate) as opposed to passive where no supply is required. An example of the latter would be a circuit that changes a DC voltage from one level to a lower one. The circuit could just consist of resistors and is therefore passive.

The purpose of a power supply is to convert a power source into a suitable type and level of voltage so that it can be used in circuitry. Typical examples of conversions include 230 V AC to 5 V DC, 110 V AC to 12 V DC etc.

Power supplies can increase or decrease voltages and generally are assumed to convert the power source into DC, although this does not always have to be the case.

Assuming that our power supply is to convert an AC 230 V supply into a lower DC voltage and is not going to provide a stabilised output (see page 135) it will consist of three blocks as shown in Figure 6.1. The fourth block marked 'Load' is used to represent any circuit or device that is connected to the output of the supply.

The transformer is required to change the high AC input voltage to a lower value. When building a power supply it is important to make sure that the transformer is capable of carrying the current that the circuit will have to provide. Its low voltage AC output is applied to the rectifier circuit.

The rectifier changes the AC voltage to DC and gives a pulsing output. The pulsing is smoothed into a steady voltage by the filter circuit and this voltage can be applied to the load or fed to a further circuit which will provide stabilisation.

6.1 Rectification

Rectification falls into two categories: half-wave and full-wave.

Half-wave rectification

Half-wave rectification is the simplest and, as the circuit in Figure 6.2 shows, uses only one diode.

Remembering that the diode conducts when the anode is positive with respect to the cathode, the diode will turn on for the duration of the input's positive half cycle only (A to B). When the input is in its negative half cycle (portion B to C) the diode will turn off and no current can flow. The output of the circuit is therefore positive pulses of voltage. As there is no negative voltage present the original AC has been changed to DC.

Figure 6.2   Half-wave rectification

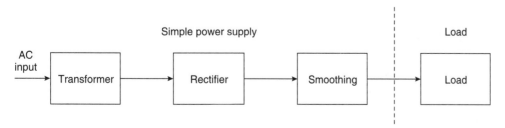

Figure 6.1   The component parts of a power supply

As a pulsing DC voltage the output of the half-wave rectifier circuit finds practically no use other than in battery chargers. If it is to be used to supply a steady voltage it will require filtering.

Practical 1

Connect up the circuit as shown in Figure 6.3. Apply an AC input from a signal generator of 2 V peak to peak at 100 Hz. Use a two-channel oscilloscope to monitor both the inputs and outputs simultaneously. Check the peak value of the output pulse and compare it with the peak value of the input. It will be smaller because of the voltage dropped across the diode.

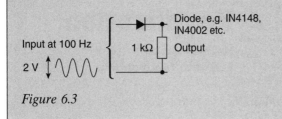

Figure 6.3

Full-wave rectification

The full-wave rectifier overcomes the disadvantages of the half-wave rectifier and is the most widely used method for converting AC to DC. Unlike the half-wave rectifier the circuit converts negative half cycles of input into positive half cycles of output so that the output consists of a series of positive pulses at twice the rate of the input frequency.

Full-wave rectification comes in a number of forms and can be achieved using either two or four diodes.

The bridge rectifier

Consider the circuit in Figure 6.4 operating during the first half cycle of input (points A to B) when point X is positive and point Y is negative. D_1 is biased on, enabling current to flow through it to the load R. This current returns along the negative

Bridge rectifier

rail to the network of diodes and, via D_3 which is also biased on, back to the source. During this time both D_4 and D_2 are non-conducting as they are held reverse biased by the polarity of the input.

During the negative half cycle of input (points B to C) the state of the diodes reverses. As point X is now negative with respect to point Y, D_1 is biased off. D_4 and D_2 will be forward biased and conduction therefore occurs via D_4, the load R, D_2 and back to the source.

As can be seen from the diagram the output is still not a smooth DC but is considerably better than that obtained from a half-wave rectifier. For more practical uses filtering is still necessary. The bridge rectifier's output consists of DC pulses at twice the frequency of the input.

Full-wave rectification using a centre-tapped transformer

An alternative method of full-wave rectification uses only two diodes. The disadvantage is that it requires a centre-tapped transformer and these can be expensive.

The circuit is shown in Figure 6.5. It utilises the principle that if a transformer secondary is centre tapped and held at 0 V the polarity of its windings will reverse at the same rate as the polarity of the input.

Thus, during the positive half cycle of input, if point A is assumed to be positive D_1 will become forward biased and current will be able to flow via the load back to earth via the centre tap. During

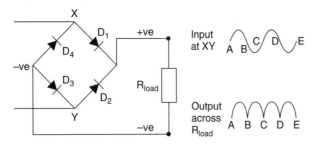

Figure 6.4   The bridge rectifier

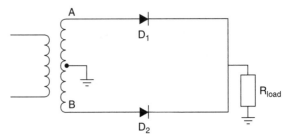

Figure 6.5

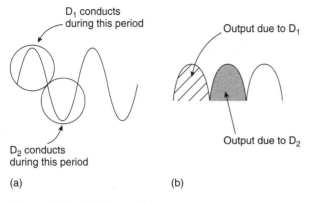

Figure 6.6 conducts during this period — D₁ conducts during this period; D₂ conducts during this period; Output due to D₁; Output due to D₂

Figure 6.6   (a) Input; (b) output

this time point B is negative which holds D_2 off. In the opposite half cycle point B will be positive and point A negative. D_1 will now be held off and D_2 will be forward biased. Current can therefore also flow via the load during this half cycle. This is shown in Figure 6.6. The output is therefore the same as for a bridge rectifier but only two diodes are used.

6.2 Smoothing

Action of the capacitor   **133**

Regardless of whether full- or half-wave rectification is used, the pulsing DC obtained has to be converted into a constant value. This is easily achieved by including a capacitor across the output of the rectifier. This is shown in Figure 6.8.

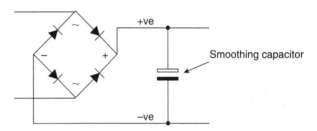

Figure 6.8

Without the capacitor, or if one of incorrect value is used, the voltage output will still contain some varying DC superimposed on a fixed DC level. This is known as **ripple voltage** and is a sign of a poorly designed power supply.

Action of the capacitor

At the instant of switch-on the capacitor charges to the peak of the rectifier output voltage. As this decreases back to zero the capacitor retains the majority of its charge and so the voltage across it stays reasonably constant. The 'lumpy' DC is thus evened out and hence the process is known as smoothing. This is illustrated in Figure 6.9.

As the capacitor charges to the peak value of the output its voltage rating should be approximately three times that of the RMS value required at the output. The actual value of capacitance used depends on the voltage and the current that the supply is to provide.

Electrolytic capacitors are normally used for smoothing purposes. This is because the large value of capacitance needed is virtually impossible to get in physically small packages.

Practical 2

Testing the bridge rectifier package

The bridge rectifier consists of four individual diodes. In practice these usually come in one single encapsulated package with four legs. Each leg is marked with the appropriate sign to enable easy identification of its connection.

View the bridge as four individual diodes and test each in turn (see Figure 6.7). Note that readings do not have to be exact.

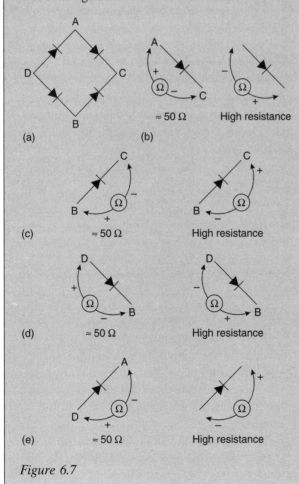

Figure 6.7

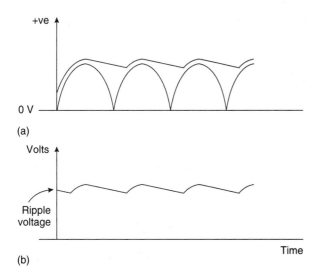

(a)

(b)

Figure 6.9   (a) The capacitor charges up and then only partially discharges as the rectified waveform drops to 0 V; (b) DC voltage with a ripple

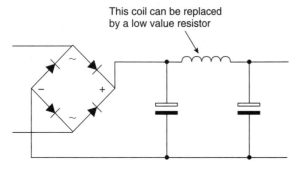

Figure 6.10   Use of a low pass filter to smooth DC

Further smoothing is usually added in the form of a low pass (ripple) filter, the complete circuit being as in Figure 6.10.

On or off load

The voltages so far discussed are for an 'off-load' supply. This means that the power supply unit has nothing connected to it and is therefore not providing any current to a load. When the load is connected (i.e. put 'on load') you expect the output to fall slightly as current is drawn and voltage is dropped across the component parts.

Fusing the supply

At the very instant of switch-on before the smoothing capacitor has had a chance to charge it appears for an instant as a short circuit. This results in a surge of current which can cause fuses to rupture.

To prevent this it is common to incorporate an anti-surge fuse in the positive rail, as shown in Figure 6.11(a). Fuses are also sometimes placed

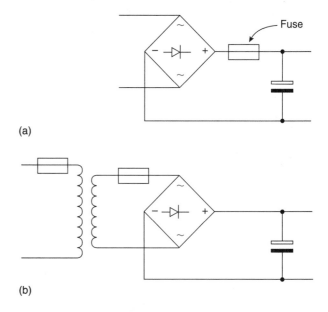

(a)

(b)

Figure 6.11

either side of the transformer as shown in Figure 6.11(b).

Practical 3

This practical is to show the actual voltages obtained at various places in a power supply and the effect of adding the smoothing capacitor to the output of a bridge rectifier. Any mains to low voltage transformer (i.e. a step-down) will do.

Connect the circuit as shown in Figure 6.12. Use a multimeter set to the appropriate range to obtain voltages at the two points shown on the circuit. Enter these readings into the results table.

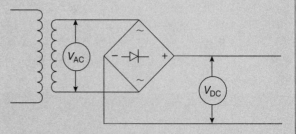

Figure 6.12

If we assume a transformer with a 9 V secondary you should have found that the voltage output is approximately 9 V (RMS). After the bridge rectifier the voltage read by the meter is the average (*not* 0.637) of the lumpy DC.

Now connect the smoothing capacitor in parallel as shown in Figure 6.13. Once again

	With C not in circuit	With C in circuit
Output voltage V_{AC} of transformer		
Output voltage V_{DC} of rectifier		

measure the DC voltage across the output of the bridge. Notice how it has increased. This is because the capacitor has charged to the peak of the rectified voltage. It will now be approximately $9 \times 1.414 = 12.72$ V.

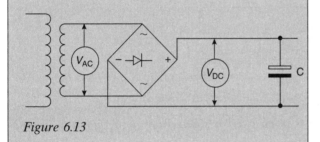

Figure 6.13

Obtaining a negative or split supply

When a circuit requires a negative voltage, slightly different connections of the bridge and its associated smoothing capacitor are needed. These are shown in Figure 6.14.

6.3 Regulated power supplies

With most modern electronic circuits we need a power supply which not only gives the correct output voltage but also keeps that voltage constant over a range of operating conditions. This is achieved by adding a **stabiliser** or **regulator** to our basic DC power supply, as shown in Figure 6.15.

There are two main effects against which we need to stabilise:

(a) changes in the amount of current drawn from the supply (load variation);
(b) changes in the voltage at the input to the supply, e.g. the mains.

We can treat all stabilisers, or regulators, as being of two basic types: series regulators and shunt regulators. The type is determined by where we place the controlling element, i.e. in series with the load (Figure 6.16) or in parallel with it (Figure 6.17).

Shunt regulators

The simplest regulator for us to start with is a shunt regulator using the properties of a Zener diode in reverse bias mode (see Figure 6.18).

D_1 provides half-wave rectification, C_1 is the smoothing capacitor, and R_1 and C_2 form the ripple filter. The part of the circuit we are interested in is the series resistor R_2 and the Zener diode Z_D shunting the load.

In this circuit the control element is the Zener diode operating at its breakdown voltage. This means that the voltage across the Zener, and therefore the load, remains constant across a range of load current.

The circuit works on the principle of shared current. The idea is to keep the sum of I_Z and I_L

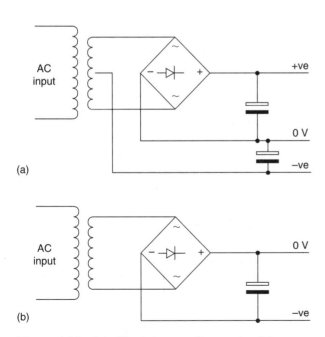

Figure 6.14   (a) Obtaining a split supply; (b) obtaining a negative supply

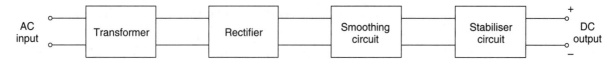

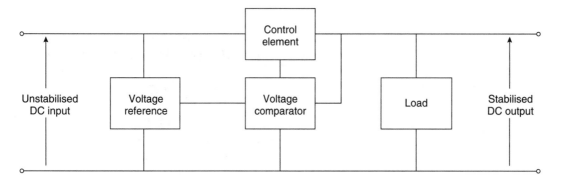

Figure 6.15   Stabilised power supply

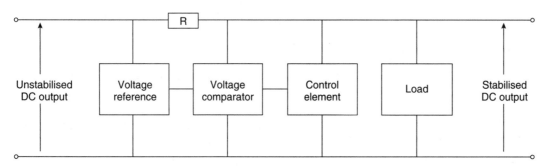

Figure 6.16   Series regulated supply. The control element is in series from input to output

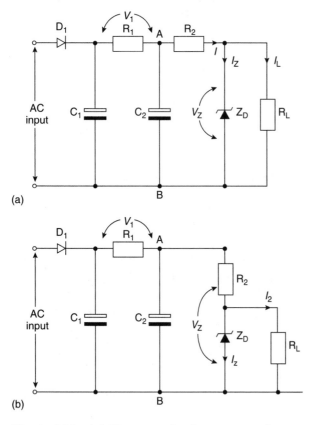

Figure 6.17   Shunt regulated supply. The control element is in parallel, or shunt, from input/output to ground

Figure 6.18   (a) Shunt regulated power supply;
(b) an alternative method of drawing the circuit

constant. If I_L increases by a few milliamps then I_Z decreases by the same amount. The series dropper R_1 passes the full current which remains constant:

$$I = I_L + I_Z \text{ amps}$$

The voltage dropped across R_1 (V_1) is equal to the difference between the unregulated DC (V_{AB}) and the Zener voltage:

$$V_1 = V_{AB} - V_Z \text{ volts}$$

As shown in Figure 6.19 the output will remain constant until the load current is so great that the Zener can no longer remain in breakdown. For good regulation we normally set the unregulated supply voltage to about three times the Zener diode breakdown voltage.

The main disadvantage of this type of regulator is that under no-load conditions ($I_L = 0$) the Zener diode must pass the full load current. This is inefficient since it means maximum current from the supply regardless of the load demand. It also means that we must choose a Zener capable of withstanding the full load current.

One solution to this disadvantage is to use a series regulator.

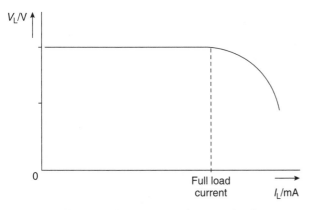

Figure 6.19   Regulation curve for simple shunt regulator

Series regulators

The circuit in Figure 6.20 uses a transistor connected in common-collector mode (emitter-follower) with the output taken at the emitter. The base of Tr_1 is held at a constant voltage by the reverse-biased Zener diode. The emitter 'follows' the base and so it also stays constant, at about 0.6 or 0.7 V below the base (silicon forward volt-drop), and this is the output voltage.

The circuit is able to provide reasonably large load currents since the emitter-follower also gives current gain. Notice that here the Zener is acting only as a voltage reference and so draws

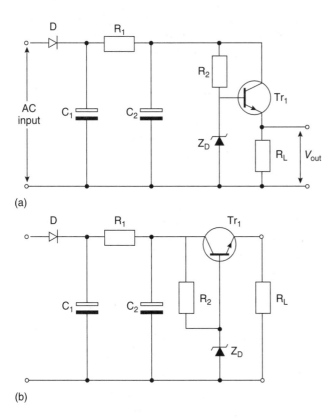

(a)

(b)

Figure 6.20   (a) Series regulator; (b) a more conventional representation

much less current than the Zener used in the shunt stabiliser. To ensure stability we design the circuit so that the Zener current is about five times Tr_1 base current.

Like all electronic circuits, this simple series regulator has disadvantages as well.

(a) For large currents, power Zeners and transistors are required, which adds to the cost.
(b) The sensitivity is limited. This means that the output voltage varies slightly before the control takes effect.

The solution to both these problems can be found using a two-transistor circuit.

Practical 4

Build the circuit shown in Figure 6.21. By placing load resistors of different values across the output and using a meter to measure the voltage across them you can draw a regulation graph. The point at which regulation ceases is where the load voltage is no longer constant. In each case the load current can be easily calculated. The table (incomplete) shows how a typical circuit will behave, and the sketch shows a typical graph.

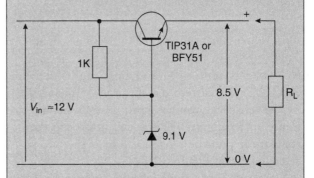

Figure 6.21

R_L	V_{out}	$I_{load} = V_{out}/R_L$
10K	8V5	0.85 mA
5K6	8V5	1.52 mA
1K	8V5	8.5 mA
560 Ω		
270 Ω		

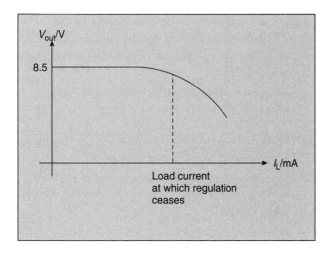

Two emitter-follower regulator

The two emitter-follower regulator will help to reduce the first problem if large currents are needed.

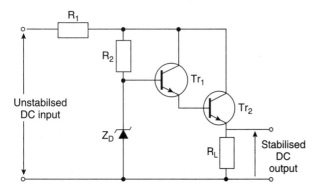

Figure 6.22   Two-transistor series regulator

In the circuit in Figure 6.22 we use a second emitter-follower (Tr_2) to give more current gain. Now load currents of several amps can be delivered and the Zener current remains a few milliamps.

The sensitivity can be improved by using a transistor to amplify the output voltage and then compare it with the reference. This is the arrangement in Figure 6.23.

Here the Zener diode is acting only as a reference device and so has a small current through

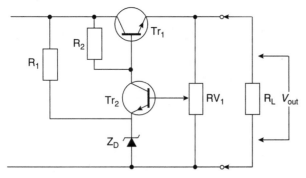

Figure 6.23   Series regulator with improved sensitivity

it. Tr_2 has its emitter fixed by the Zener and the output voltage is applied to its base via the slider of RV_1. Now, if any change occurs in the output voltage the change is amplified and applied to the base of Tr_1 which is the series control element. For example, consider that the output voltage rises slightly. The base of Tr_2 goes more positive with respect to the emitter, thus increasing the forward bias. As a result Tr_2 conduction increases. This draws a larger collector current via R_1, developing a larger voltage drop across R_2, and so the collector voltage at Tr_2 falls.

This means that the base voltage of Tr_1 falls and Tr_1 conducts less. The resistance (collector–emitter) of Tr_1 therefore increases and more voltage is dropped across it. The output voltage therefore falls to its original level. The setting of RV_1 enables the value of V_{out} to be altered.

We explain the operation as a set of sequential steps but, in practice, the control is continuous and so the variation in output does not occur.

Practical 5

You can use the circuit in Figure 6.24 wherever you need a low current DC supply. By placing resistors of various values (e.g. 500 Ω, 1K, 4K7) across the output terminals (Figure 6.25) and using current/voltage meters you can monitor the regulation that the circuit provides.

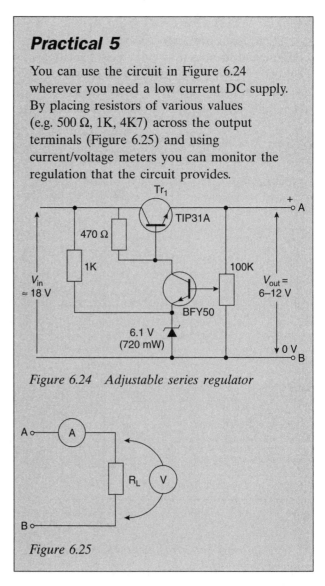

Figure 6.24   Adjustable series regulator

Figure 6.25

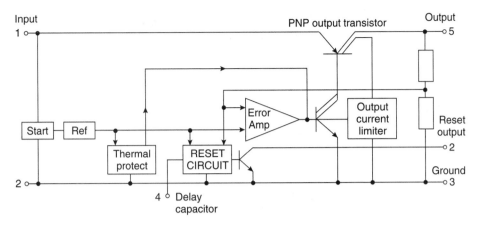

Figure 6.26 The internal circuitry of the L387A. Imagine the amount of discrete components needed to build the equivalent!

Integrated circuit regulators

Integrated circuit (IC) regulators come in two forms: variable or fixed. Both types have the advantage that they require few additional components connected around them. Figure 6.26 shows a typical IC. The majority have in-built circuitry which protects against excess heat or short circuits which makes them ideal for experimenters as they are very difficult to destroy.

IC regulators are identified by their type number (Figure 6.27). For the most common regulators that give a fixed voltage output the type number consists of four digits, the first two indicating whether the output voltage is positive or negative. Other regulators have three digits which may be preceded or followed by letters.

Connecting the 78 or 79 series regulator is very simple as the circuit in Figure 6.28 shows. From Table 6.1 you can see that the input voltage must be at least 8 V for the output to be 5 V.

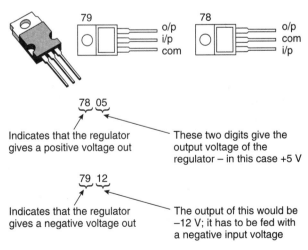

Figure 6.27 1 A fixed voltage regulators – 78/79 series

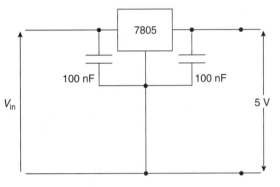

Figure 6.28 Connection of a series regulator. The two 100 nF capacitors are needed for noise suppression. They should be connected as close as possible to the IC

Practical 6

Build the circuit in Figure 6.29 and measure the input (V_{AB}) and output (V_{CD}) voltages. V_{CD} should be 12 V. Connect resistors of different values across terminals CD. The voltage should remain at 12 V until too much current is drawn.

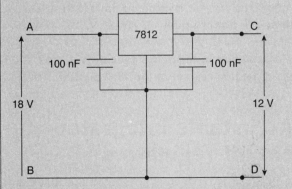

Figure 6.29 18 V is the minimum specified input voltage. It will work with a value greater than this

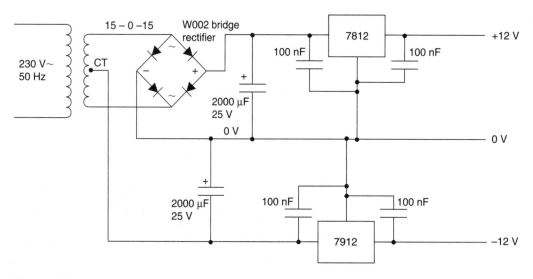

Figure 6.30

Table 6.1   Example of manufacturers' data for a regulator

		Manufacturer	Package	V_{in} absolute maximum (V DC)	V_{in} required to maintain regulation (V DC)	Line regulation (T = + 25 °C)* (typical)	Load regulation (T = + 25 °C)* (typical)	Output noise voltage (T = +25 °C) (10 Hz ≤ f ≤ 100 kHz)*
5 V	**2A** L78S05CV	SGS	TO220	35	8	100 mV (max) $(7{\leq}V_I{\leq}25)$ V DC	100 mV (max) $(20\ \text{mA}{\leq}I_o \leq 1.5\ \text{A})$	40 µV
12 V	L78S12CV	SGS	TO220	35	15	240 mV (max) $(14.5{\leq}V_I{\leq}30)$ V DC	240 mV (max) $(20\ \text{mA} \leq I_o \leq 1.5\ \text{A})$	75 µV
15 V	L78S15CV	SGS	TO220	35	18	300 mV (max) $(17.5{\geq}V_I{\geq}30)$ V DC	300 mV (max) $(20\ \text{mA} \leq I_o \leq 1.5\ \text{A})$	90 µV
24 V	L78S24CV	SGS	TO220	40	27	480 mV (max) $27{\leq}V_I{\leq}38)$ V DC	360 mV (max) $(20\ \text{mA} \leq I_o \leq 1.5\ \text{A})$	170 µV

A 'split' supply

In the use of operational amplifiers – and some other circuitry – it is common practice to use a three-rail power supply of, say, +9 V, 0 V, –9 V or +12 V, 0 V, –12 V.

The circuit in Figure 6.30 will provide +12 V, 0 V, –12 V and makes use of the 7812 and the 7912.

Adjustable integrated circuit regulators

Adjustable IC regulators give an output that can be set to any specific voltage within the limits of the chip itself. The selection of an adjustable regulator is a little more complicated than for a fixed regulator as there are many different types

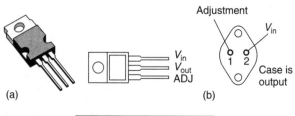

IC	Maximum I_L
LM317L	100 mA
LM317M	500 mA
LM317T	1.5 A

Figure 6.31   Variable voltage regulators – the LM317: (a) and (b) are alternative case styles

available. One of the most common is the LM317 series shown in Figure 6.31. These provide an output which is determined by the values of resistors connected around the IC. The 317 series have a letter following the digits which indicates the current that the regulator can supply.

Manufacturers' or component suppliers' data sheets can tell you all you need to know about a regulator and usually give a circuit diagram showing how to connect it. In the example in Table 6.1 you will see that the IC we are looking at is an L78S24CV which can provide up to 24 V at a maximum current of 2 A. The maximum input voltage that can be applied is 40 V and the minimum that is needed in order that the chip can provide the required output is 27 V.

Practical 7

The circuit in Figure 6.32 is particularly useful as it will power many of the projects throughout this book. If a higher load current needs to be allowed for then the LM338K can be substituted in place of the LM317K. This regulator will provide up to 5 A. Do not forget the heat sink!

When building a supply always remember that the transformer that is used must be capable of handling the load current plus 10%. This extra percentage is to cover any losses that occur in the transformer itself.

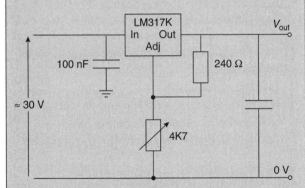

Figure 6.32   By changing the setting of the 4K7 potentiometer the output voltage can be varied between 3 V and 25 V. The IC should be mounted on a heat sink

Stabilisation factor

The extent to which a constant voltage-regulated supply stabilises against output voltage variation is given by the stabilisation factor S where

$$S = \frac{V_\mathrm{o}}{V_\mathrm{i}}$$

$$= \frac{\text{change in output voltage}}{\text{change in supply voltage}}$$

This is measured with a constant load current.

Typically S varies between 0.005 and 0.0002 (5 mV/V and 0.2 mV/V) depending on the complexity of the regulator.

A display of semiconductor devices

John Ambrose Flemming (1849–1945)

An English electrical engineer, Flemming graduated from University College London (UCL) in 1870 and went to Cambridge where he worked for Clerk Maxwell.

In 1885 he was appointed Professor of Electrical Engineering at UCL where he also worked as a consultant to Edison, the American company that was developing electric lighting.

Flemming worked with Marconi in the 1890s and he was the man who discovered and developed the idea of rectification using a thermionic valve. This was the first type of valve and led to the development of triodes, pentodes etc. which allowed the electronics industry to come into being.

Multiple choice questions

1 Which of the diagrams in Figure 6.34 is the output waveform for Figure 6.33?

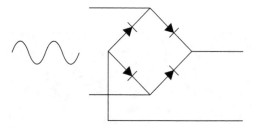

Figure 6.33

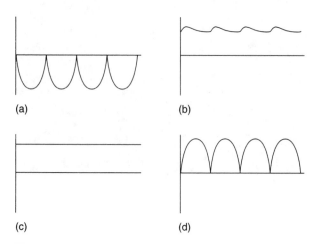

(a)   (b)

(c)   (d)

Figure 6.34

2 Which of the diagrams in Figure 6.36 is the output waveform for the circuit in Figure 6.35?

Figure 6.35

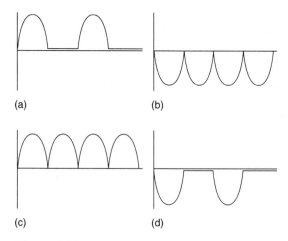

(a)   (b)

(c)   (d)

Figure 6.36

3 The voltage across AB in Figure 6.37 will be approximately
  (a) 9 V RMS
  (b) +9 V
  (c) 5.7 V
  (d) 12.7 V.

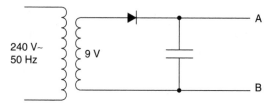

Figure 6.37

4 With reference to Figure 6.38 (opposite) the introduction of a 1 kΩ load across CD should result in
  (a) a higher output voltage
  (b) no change in output voltage
  (c) less current via L_1
  (d) greater voltage across C_1

5 The frequency of the ripple voltage across AB in Figure 6.38 will be
  (a) 110 Hz
  (b) 100 Hz
  (c) 50 Hz
  (d) 25 Hz.

6 The purpose of the component marked X in Figure 6.38 is
  (a) to act as a fuse
  (b) to provide a constant output voltage
  (c) to open circuit under load
  (d) to dissipate heat from the transformer.

7 The purpose of Tr_1 in Figure 6.39 is
  (a) to act as a variable resistor
  (b) to shunt excess load current

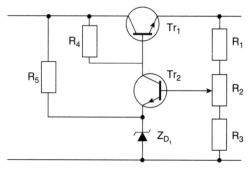

Figure 6.39

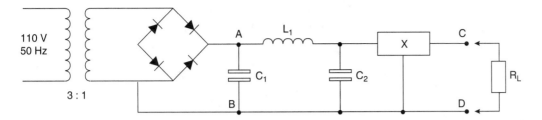

Figure 6.38

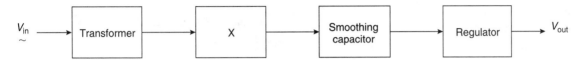

Figure 6.40

    (c)   to change the input current

    (d)   to change the voltage cross Z_{D_1}.

8 With reference to Figure 6.39 the likely effect of R_5 going open circuit would be

    (a) Tr_1 going short circuit

    (b)   the output voltage becoming equal to the input

    (c) Tr_2 going open circuit

    (d)   no output voltage.

9 The purpose of the box marked X in Figure 6.40 (above) is

    (a)   to change AC input voltage to a lower AC voltage

    (b)   to provide a level DC output voltage

    (c)   to change AC voltage to DC voltage

    (d)   to remove 50 Hz ripple.

10 The main difference between shunt and series regulation is that

    (a)   current is retained in the mains transformer

    (b)   all output current flows via the shunt impedance

    (c)   the series regulator has a parallel resistance

    (d)   excess current is shunted in parallel with the load.

7

Amplifiers

7.1 Transistor amplifiers

Designing an amplifier

We are going to start our amplifier design by
looking at the circuit that finds the most use.
It is known as the common-emitter configuration.
To start with we are going to set up the quiescent
DC conditions and we shall then consider the
amplifier with an input signal applied. This is
normally referred to as putting the amplifier under
dynamic conditions.

Setting up the quiescent conditions

Figure 7.1 shows the circuit diagram of a very
simple transistor amplifier. There are only two
resistors, the one in the collector (R_L) and the one
in the base (R_b). This type of circuit is said to be
resistance loaded as the collector is connected to a
resistor which forms its load.

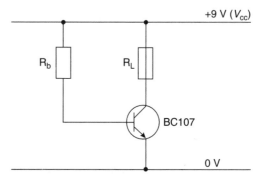

Figure 7.1   Simple base biasing

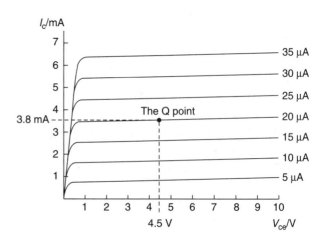

*Figure 7.2   Using the output characteristics for
circuit design*

The supply rail (often called V_{cc}) is +9 V and the
other rail is at 0 V. The transistor is a BC107; we
have already plotted the output characteristic for
this in the practical on page 118. It is reproduced in
Figure 7.2 as we shall need to mark values and
points on it.

Although all electronics engineers use the term V_{cc} to mean supply voltage, not everyone knows what it stands for. V_{cc} means the voltage at the collector and collector. Sounds confusing?

We start our amplifier design by looking at the output characteristic and identifying the middle values of the three parameters. This is necessary so that the value of collector voltage under quiescent conditions is half the supply voltage. (The reason for this is fully explained when we consider the amplifier with an input signal applied.)

From the characteristic in Figure 7.2,

(a) the 'middle' value of base current is 20 μA,
(b) the middle value of V_{ce} is 4.5 V.

By extrapolating on the graph we can see that the value of collector current (I_c) that will flow is 3.8 mA. We have marked this current on Figure 7.2 along with the base current and collector–emitter voltage. Where all these values intersect is usually referred to as the Q (quiescent) point of the amplifier. We now have enough information to calculate the value of the two resistors.

Calculating the base bias resistance R_b

We know that the voltage between the base and the emitter of a forward biased transistor is 0.6 V. The voltage across the base resistor is therefore (Figure 7.3)

$$V_{R_b} = V_{cc} - 0.6 \text{ V}$$
$$= 9 - 0.6$$
$$= 8.4 \text{ V}$$

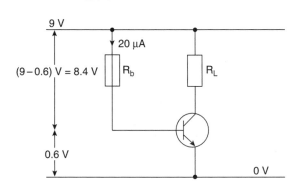

Figure 7.3

From the characteristic we have taken the base current to be 20 μA. The value of R_b can now be calculated as

$$R_b = \frac{8.4 \text{ V}}{20 \text{ μV}} = 420 \text{ k}\Omega$$

Calculating the collector load resistance R_L

We can now use the characteristic to help us calculate the collector load. This is usually found by measuring the value of the quiescent collector current when the transistor has half the supply voltage between collector and emitter (Figure 7.4)

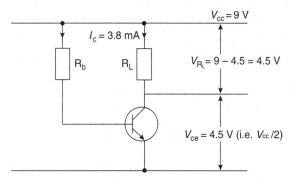

Figure 7.4

and using Ohm's law to calculate the corresponding value of resistance. From the characteristic,

$$V_{ce} = \frac{1}{2} V_{cc} = \frac{9}{2} = 4.5 \text{ V}$$

The value of the collector current at this voltage is 3.8 mA. Therefore the collector load resistance R_L is given by

$$R_L = \frac{V_{R_L}}{I_c}$$

$$= \frac{4.5 \text{ V}}{3.8 \text{ mA}} = 1.8 \text{ k}\Omega$$

We have now calculated the amplifier components and set the amplifier up for its DC quiescent conditions.

The disadvantages of simple base bias

The bias arrangement we have used is very simple but it has a number of disadvantages.

(a) The components are all calculated assuming that the characteristic of the transistor has been plotted. If, at any time, the transistor has to be changed it is highly unlikely that the replacement will be exactly the same as the original. This will alter the operating conditions of the circuit and cause distortion.

(b) If the V_{cc} rail alters in value the base current will change significantly. This will cause a corresponding change in collector current which will shift the operating point (Q) of the circuit.

(c) If the temperature of the transistor increases, the quiescent collector current will rise and once again the Q point will move and distortion will result.

On the plus side, the few components limit the amount of spurious noise in the circuit.

Potential divider biasing

The disadvantages outlined above can easily be overcome by using a potential divider to derive the base bias, as shown in Figure 7.5.

The current that flows via R_1 and R_2 has to be considerably larger than the quiescent base current that is drawn by the transistor. For convenience a factor of 10 is usually used. Thus $10I_b$ flows via R_1, $1I_b$ enters the base of the transistor and the remaining $9I_b$ flows via R_2. As the ratio of the current through R_1 to I_b is now 10:1 the effect of a change in the current through R_1 will cause I_b to alter by ten times less. In other words, a degree of **bias stabilisation** has been achieved.

The same argument applies if the transistor is changed for one with a different characteristic.

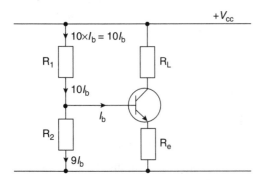

Figure 7.5   Stabilised potential divider biasing

The emitter resistor

Stabilised bias is also aided by the addition of a resistor between the emitter of the transistor and the ground rail (Figure 7.6). The purpose of this resistor is to prevent excess collector–emitter current from flowing if the transistor increases in temperature. If extra I_c flows, I_e will also increase as the equation $I_e = I_c + I_b$ always holds true.

The extra I_e will cause the voltage across the emitter resistor to increase, which reduces the effective base–emitter voltage of the transistor, biasing it back so that it conducts less and draws less collector current.

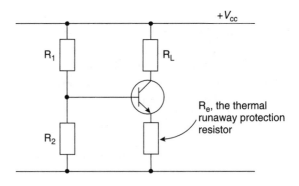

Figure 7.6

The emitter resistor therefore minimises the effects of temperature change and is sometimes called **thermal runaway protection**.

Guided example

Under normal conditions, let $I_e = 1$ mA (Figure 7.7). With respect to 0 V, $V_b = 1.6$ V and $V_{R_e} = 1$ V.

$$V_{be} = V_b - V_{R_e}$$
$$= 1.6 - 1.0 = 0.6 \text{ V}$$

If I_e rises from 1 mA to 1.2 mA V_{R_e} now rises from 1 V to

$$V_{R_e} = I_e \times R_e$$
$$= 1.2 \text{ mA} \times 1 \text{ k}\Omega$$
$$= 1.2 \text{ V}$$

The effect of this on V_{be} is

$$V_{be} = V_b - V_{R_e}$$
$$= 1.6 - 1.2 = 0.4 \text{ V}$$

Therefore V_{be} has *fallen* by 0.2 V, reducing the forward bias of Tr_1 and its conduction.

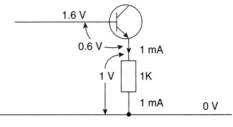

Figure 7.7

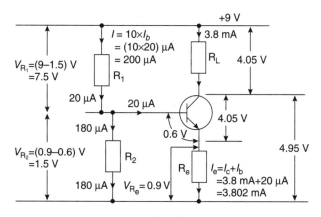

Figure 7.8

When calculating the emitter resistance it is quite usual to ignore the base current and say that the emitter current is almost equal to the collector current. This is because I_c is usually at least 60 times bigger than I_b. If we do this our value of R_e becomes

$$\frac{0.9 \text{ V}}{3.8 \text{ mA}} = 237 \ \Omega$$

– not much difference (and with a preferred value it wouldn't matter at all!).

Calculating the bias components with potential divider biasing

Figure 7.8 shows all the calculations for components and how the various potentials are determined. A fuller explanation is given in the following sections.

Once again we have used values taken from the characteristic drawn in Figure 7.2. If you look back you will see that the Q point for an I_b of 20 μA gives an I_c of 3.8 mA if we consider the collector–emitter voltage to be at half supply or thereabouts.

Calculating the emitter resistance R_e

To enable us to calculate the emitter resistance an assumption has to be made. This assumption is that we would normally expect the voltage across the emitter resistor to be 10% of the supply.

The characteristic in Figure 7.2 shows that the supply voltage is 9 V. Therefore

$$V_{R_e} = 10\% \times 9 \text{ V} = 0.9 \text{ V}$$

The current through this resistor is I_e:

$$I_e = I_b + I_c$$

$$= 20 \text{ μA} + 3.8 \text{ mA}$$

$$= 3.802 \text{ mA}$$

The value of R_e is

$$R_e = \frac{V_{R_e}}{I_e} = \frac{0.9 \text{ V}}{3.802 \text{ mA}} = 236 \ \Omega$$

Calculating the potential divider resistances R_1 and R_2

We know that the base–emitter voltage is 0.6 V and the voltage across the emitter resistor is 0.9 V. The potential across R_2 can be found as

$$V_{R_2} = V_{be} + V_{R_e}$$

$$= 0.6 + 0.9 = 1.5 \text{ V}$$

From this the voltage across R_1 is

$$V_{R_1} = V_{cc} + V_{R_e}$$

$$= 9 - 1.5 = 7.5 \text{ V}$$

As the current through R_1 and R_2 is ten times the quiescent base current it can be found as follows:

$$I_{R_1} = 10 \times I_b$$

$$= 10 \times 20 = 200 \text{ μA}$$

$$I_{R_2} = 10 \times I_b - I_b$$

$$= 200 - 20 = 180 \text{ μA}$$

Therefore the values of R_1 and R_2 can be calculated as

$$R_1 = \frac{V_{R_1}}{I_{R_1}} = \frac{7.5 \text{ V}}{200 \text{ μA}} = 37.5 \text{ k}\Omega$$

$$R_2 = \frac{V_{R_2}}{I_{R_2}} = \frac{1.5 \text{ V}}{180 \text{ μA}} = 8.33 \text{ k}\Omega$$

Calculating the value of the collector load resistance

As 0.9 V is dropped across R_e the remaining voltage that can now be developed across R_L is half of the remaining supply:

$$V_{R_L} = \frac{9 - 0.9}{2} = 4.05 \text{ V}$$

The current via R_L is $I_c = 3.8$ mA. Therefore

$$R_L = \frac{4.05 \text{ V}}{3.8 \text{ mA}} = 1.06 \text{ k}\Omega$$

Guided example

The output characteristic of a transistor is shown in Figure 7.9. We are going to use it to design a common-emitter transistor amplifier that uses potential divider biasing.

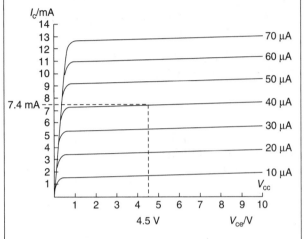

Figure 7.9

We start by marking the middle values of base current and V_{ce} on the characteristic. Next we draw the circuit diagram and mark on it any voltages and currents that we readily know (Figure 7.10).

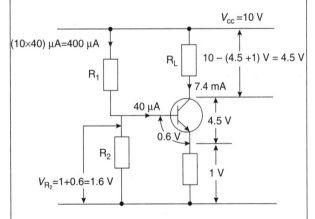

Figure 7.10

We can now calculate the values of the bias resistors as follows:

$$R_e = \frac{V_{R_e}}{I_e} = \frac{10\% \times V_{cc}}{I_c}$$

$$= \frac{1\ V}{7.4\ mA} = 135\ \Omega$$

$$R_1 = \frac{V_{R_1}}{I_{R_1}} = \frac{(10 - 1.6)\ V}{(10 \times 40)\ \mu A}$$

$$= \frac{8.4\ V}{400\ \mu A} = 21\ k\Omega$$

$$R_2 = \frac{V_{R_2}}{I_{R_2}} = \frac{V_{R_e} + V_{be}}{10I_b - I_b} = \frac{(1 + 0.6)\ V}{(400 - 40)\ \mu A}$$

$$= \frac{1.6\ V}{360\ \mu A} = 4.44\ k\Omega$$

$$R_L = \frac{V_{R_L}}{I_c} = \frac{(10 - 5.5)\ V}{I_c}$$

$$= \frac{4.5\ V}{7.4\ mA} = 608\ \Omega$$

We can also calculate the current gain by using the characteristic

$$\text{current gain} = h_{FE} = \frac{I_c}{I_b}$$

$$= \frac{7.4\ mA}{40\ \mu A} = 185$$

The characteristics and component values have so far been used to calculate the DC performance of the amplifier. We have not yet applied an AC signal to the input and analysed what happens under dynamic conditions.

Application of an input signal

The load line

We are once again going to use the output characteristic that we originally plotted on page 144 (Figure 7.2) and the simple base bias circuit. Before we begin to analyse how the circuit will behave with an input signal, we shall draw a 'load line' on the characteristic. The purpose of this is to enable us to predict how the transistor will respond to changes of voltage and current when a signal voltage is applied.

As the load line is a straight line we only need two points to plot it.

Point 1 of the load line This is the maximum voltage the transistor can ever have between its collector and emitter. This is obviously the supply voltage:

$$V_{ce}(\text{max}) = V_{cc} = 9\ V$$

Point 2 of the load line This is the maximum collector current that could ever possibly flow. This will occur if all the supply voltage is dropped across the collector resistor, i.e.

$$I_c(\max) = \frac{V_{cc} - V_{R_e}}{R_L}$$

$V_{R_e} = 0$ V as there is no R_e! Therefore

$$I_c(\max) = \frac{9\text{ V}}{1.18\text{ k}\Omega} = 7.63\text{ mA}$$

The load line can now be drawn and is shown in Figure 7.11. The circuit that we are going to use in the design is given in Figure 7.12 and you will see that this is merely simple base bias.

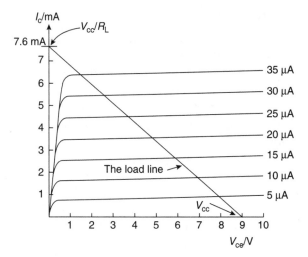

Figure 7.11   Plotting a load line

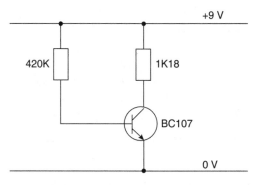

Figure 7.12   The values obtained using this circuit are used to determine the load line in Figure 7.11

Applying an input signal (amplifier under dynamic conditions)

In Figure 7.13 a signal has been applied to the base of the amplifier circuit. This signal could originate from any number of sources but typical examples include a cassette head or a microphone of appropriate impedance. For the purposes of investigation in the laboratory it is likely to be a signal generator.

Note that we have now included a capacitor C_1 between the signal source and the base of the

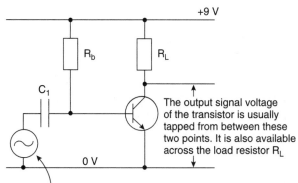

Figure 7.13

transistor. This is required to prevent the DC voltage at the base of the transistor being applied to the signal source. That is, the capacitor acts as signal coupling and a DC block. We shall deal with calculating its value on page 156.

The input signal is applied via the capacitor and develops across the base and the emitter of the transistor. Here it causes the base current to rise and fall from its quiescent value as the peak to peak value of the signal increases and decreases. For example, our characteristic shows the middle value of the quiescent (or standing) base current to be 20 μA. If the input signal causes this base current to rise and fall by 10 μA the overall base current will be sinusoidal, rising to 30 μA and falling to 10 μA around the quiescent current of 20 μA. The collector current will change proportionally and be multiplied by the h_{FE} (the current gain) of the transistor.

We can get the full picture by superimposing this on the output characteristic as in Figure 7.14 which

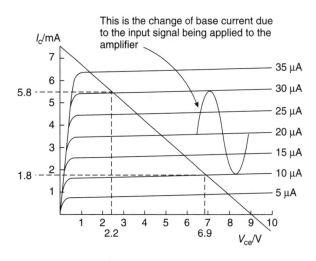

Figure 7.14   The change in I_c due to the change in I_b

Practical 1

Building a simple amplifier

We have calculated the values of the components for a simple base bias amplifier based on the BC107 (see page 144) and we shall now build the circuit in Figure 7.15.

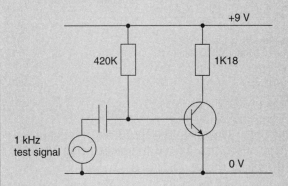

Figure 7.15

For testing purposes it is normal practice to apply a test signal of 1 kHz. The maximum peak to peak value that can be applied without distortion at the output will depend on the transistor itself, but 20 mV peak to peak is quite often used.

Connect the oscilloscope as shown in Figure 7.16. Channel 1 is used to monitor the input signal and channel 2 the output signal. To find the exact peak to peak value of input signal required it is best to compare input and output signals on the oscilloscope and check that there is no distortion to the output signal. If there is, reduce the peak to peak value of the input.

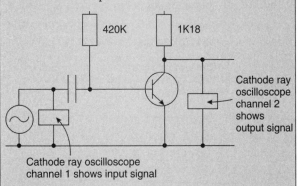

Figure 7.16

Checking that the circuit operates

Examine the two traces of the oscilloscope. Channel 2 should have a larger peak to peak value than channel 1. The voltage gain A_v of the amplifier is given by

$$A_v = \frac{\text{peak to peak value of output}}{\text{peak to peak value of input}}$$

In the circuit that we have built the output is 2 V peak to peak for an input signal of 20 mV peak to peak. The voltage gain of the amplifier is

$$A_v = \frac{2\ \text{V}}{20\ \text{mV}} = \frac{2}{0.02} = 100$$

Voltage checks

When you have built the circuit measure the voltages before applying the input signal. The most common error of construction is to position the transistor in the circuit incorrectly. If this is so, the case of the transistor (i.e. the collector) will not be at half the supply (4.5 V).

With no signal applied to the amplifier use a meter to measure the voltage between the base and the emitter. It should be 0.6 V. The voltage between the collector and the 0 V rail should be approximately half the supply.

If you increase the peak to peak value of the input you will reach a point where the output waveform begins to distort. Remember, the maximum signal that you can obtain from any amplifier is limited by the supply voltage.

shows how the collector current will rise and fall as the base current changes. It also shows, of course, what will happen to the collector–emitter voltage of the transistor.

From Figure 7.14 the collector current will fall to 1.8 mA and rise to 5.8 mA, i.e. the total change in I_c is 4 mA.

The collector–emitter voltage will fall to 2.2 V and rise to 6.9 V, i.e. the total change in V_{ce} is 4.7 V.

An amplifier using potential divider bias under dynamic conditions

We have already seen that the base bias circuit is used because the bias arrangements make it less susceptible to change of supply, transistor type etc.

In the circuit in Figure 7.17 the only extra component that affects it as an amplifier is the emitter resistor. From a DC aspect this resistor

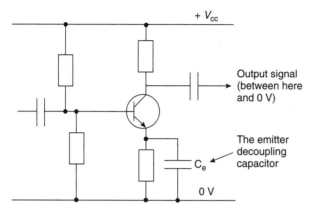

Figure 7.17

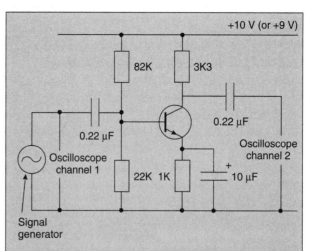

Figure 7.19

raises the potential of the emitter. However, by connecting a suitable capacitor across it, for an AC signal the emitter is still at ground potential. This capacitor is known as the emitter decoupling capacitor.

If the emitter decoupling capacitor is not connected in parallel with the emitter resistor the gain of the amplifier will be considerably reduced as negative feedback has been introduced. The circuit gain will be modified to (approximately) R_L/R_e.

Practical 2

Simple amplifier using potential divider biasing

In this practical you will build a small signal amplifier which can be used to handle signals such as those from a cassette head.

Build the circuit in Figure 7.18 taking care that the capacitors are inserted correctly and that the transistor electrodes are in the correct position. Incorrect positioning is one of the most common mistakes that is made when using transistors.

When you have constructed the amplifier couple it to the supply and signal generator ready for testing, as in Figure 7.19.

Initial tests

Set the signal generator to a frequency of 1 kHz with a peak to peak output voltage of 20 mV. Monitor this on channel 1 of the oscilloscope. Couple the other channel of the oscilloscope to the output and display the waveform obtained. This should be considerably larger than the input waveform. Note that its phase is 180° displaced from the input. This is to be expected for the common-emitter configuration.

From the oscilloscope it is possible to calculate the gain of the circuit at an input frequency of 1 kHz:

$$\text{gain} = \frac{V_{\text{out}}}{V_{\text{in}}}$$

Voltage and current readings

Place a current meter in series with the supply to determine the current drawn by the

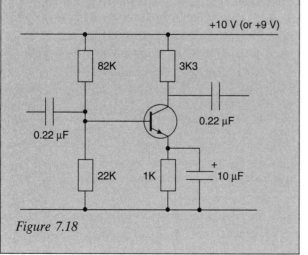

Figure 7.18

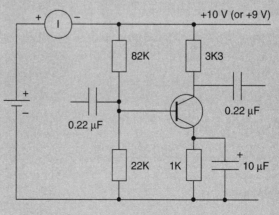

Figure 7.20

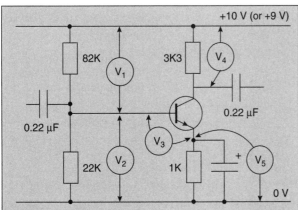

Figure 7.21

amplifier. A common error is to put the meter in parallel with the supply which not only gives an incorrect reading but often blows the fuse of the meter as well! Figure 7.20 should help you.

Use your meter to obtain voltage readings from the circuit at the points V_1–V_5 in Figure 7.21.

Phase change across a transistor

In a transistor the collector current is directly controlled by the base current. The level of base current is determined by the size of the input signal

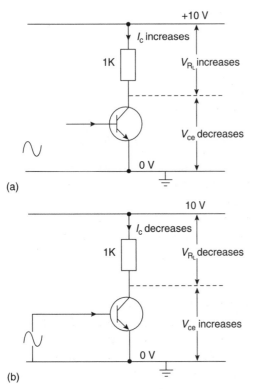

(a)

(b)

Figure 7.22   Phase change across a transistor: (a) as I_b goes positive (increases) V_{ce} decreases; (b) as I_b goes negative (decreases) V_{ce} increases

voltage. As the signal increases to its peak value, so does the base current. Similarly, as the input signal voltage decreases to its minimum value there will be a corresponding fall in base current.

As the collector current directly follows base current, so does the voltage across the load resistor through which I flows. As the individual voltages in the circuit must equal the supply the corresponding potential between collector and emitter must fall.

Let us look at this statement in association with the circuits in Figure 7.22. It is normal practice to lift the output of a transistor circuit between 0 V and collector as it is then referenced to 0 V which is usually earth potential. Thus, as the base input voltage rises this voltage will fall, and 180° phase change has occurred. (Incidentally, there is nothing to stop us lifting the output of the circuit from across the load resistor but it will no longer, of course, be referenced to 0 V.)

Clipping and bottoming distortion

The amplifier circuits that we have looked at so far have all been biased so that under quiescent conditions the potential of the collector with respect to ground is half the supply voltage.

This is not just coincidence. The reason is to allow the maximum possible output signal to be obtained without risk of distortion. Figure 7.23 illustrates this. As the collector–emitter voltage swings around 4.5 V the output signal can rise to a maximum value of +9 V or fall to a minimum value of 0 V.

If we increase the size of the input signal to a level where it causes a larger base current to flow the collector current will attempt to follow it but will be limited by the load resistor. This, in turn, increases the collector voltage to its maximum or minimum level. This is known as clipping or bottoming the output signal. The principle is shown in Figure 7.24.

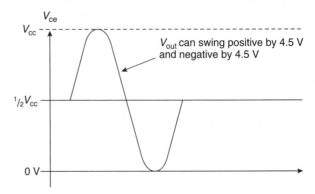

Figure 7.23   The maximum output signal is V_{cc} (i.e. 9 V peak to peak). This is produced by the maximum permissible base current

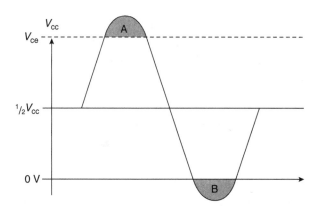

Figure 7.24 *Portion A of the output is clipped giving V_{out} a squared top. Portion B of the output is lost when the signal cannot drop below 0 V, which therefore squares off the output*

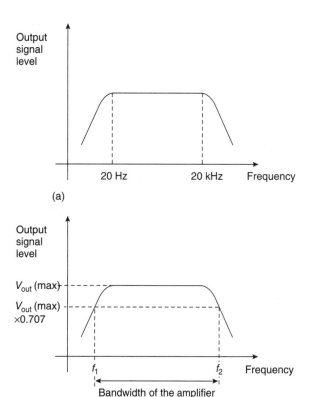

Figure 7.25

Distortion like this is usually called **overdriving**. Most of us have seen it if, when making an audio recording, we allow the level indication meter or LED bargraph to drive into the red. It sounds horrible too!

Summary

If the input current rises to too high a level the voltage across the load resistor will rise to the supply level and hence the output voltage will fall. No further output voltage can be obtained. The reverse also applies.

The frequency response of an amplifier

Whilst it is common practice to classify amplifiers by their power output this is meaningless if their frequency range is not stated.

The amplifier circuits that we have looked at so far have resistive loads and are for wideband applications, i.e. they are designed to operate over a large frequency range with no specific limits at either end. The perfect amplifier would operate with a frequency range, or bandwidth, of 0 Hz to infinite hertz which, of course, is impossible to obtain.

Calculating bandwidth

In practice we design circuits for a specific purpose. A perfect audio amplifier will provide a flat response over the audio range. This means that all frequencies within the bandwidth of 20 Hz to 20 kHz should receive an equal amount of amplification. The graphical picture of this is called

the response curve – a typical curve is given in Figure 7.25(a).

The bandwidth is calculated by obtaining the maximum output voltage, calculating 0.707 of this, marking it on the graph and then extrapolating points as shown in Figure 7.25(b).

Practical 3

The frequency response

To plot the frequency response of the amplifier (and hence obtain its bandwidth) it is necessary to measure its peak to peak output at a number of frequencies whilst the input is held at a constant value.

Keeping the amplifier connected as in Figure 7.19 and ensuring that the input from the signal generator is held constant at 20 mV peak to peak, adjust the frequency of the input to 100 Hz. Record the value of the output in the appropriate place in the table. Now re-adjust the signal generator to 200 Hz and re-read the value of the output. Enter this in the table and continue the procedure for the frequencies shown.

When you have completed the table the response curve can be drawn. It is common practice to use special graph paper for this which has a logarithmic scale on the x axis and a normal linear scale on the y axis. This is because the span of frequencies is so large that it would be impossible to accommodate them on normal paper and the human ear responds logarithmically to sound.

Obtaining the bandwidth

As explained, the bandwidth can be calculated by marking on the response curve the –3 dB or half-power points. Multiply the maximum output value by 0.707. Mark the answer obtained on the voltage output scale and draw a line parallel to the frequency axis so that it intersects the response curve at two points.

From the intersections drop two lines down to intersect the frequency axis. The points of intersection give the bandwidth limits and the bandwidth is the range of frequencies between the two.

The principle is illustrated in Figure 7.26 to guide you.

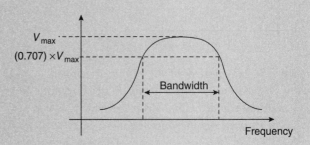

Figure 7.26

Frequency	200 Hz	500 Hz	1 kHz	2 kHz	3 kHz	4 kHz	5 kHz	6 kHz	7 kHz	8 kHz
V_{out}										
Frequency	9 kHz	10 kHz	20 kHz	30 kHz	40 kHz	50 kHz	60 kHz	70 kHz	80 kHz	90 kHz
V_{out}										
Frequency	100 kHz	200 kHz	300 kHz	400 kHz	500 kHz	600 kHz	700 kHz	800 kHz	900 kHz	1 MHz
V_{out}										

Selective amplifiers

If an amplifier is selective its response is no longer wideband, i.e. the frequency range over which it operates is limited. Typical amplifiers include those used in television and radio receivers at radio and intermediate frequencies and, at audio frequency, amplifiers to provide bass boost. As they are frequency selective they are said to be tuned. They can be identified in circuit diagrams by the use of resonant circuits or non-resistive loads in the collector.

A typical circuit and its response curve is shown in Figure 7.27.

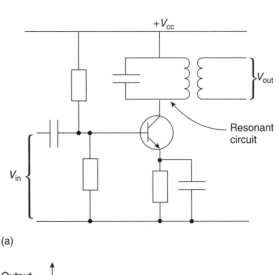

(a)

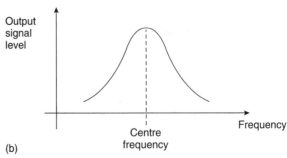

(b)

Figure 7.27   (a) The frequency component $(1/2\pi \sqrt{(LC)})$ of the resonant circuit determines the frequency and bandwidth of the amplifier; (b) typical response curve for part (a)

Components that determine the frequency response of a wideband amplifier

We have already mentioned that a resistance-loaded amplifier should have an infinite bandwidth. In practice this will never happen because of capacitance. This is present in two forms:

(a) the coupling and decoupling capacitors;
(b) stray capacitance.

Low frequency drop-off

From Chapter 4 we know that the opposition offered by a capacitor to an AC signal is known as its reactance. The reactance is inversely proportional to frequency so that when the frequency is very low the reactance is very high and vice versa. We consider again our circuit (shown in Figure 7.28) with capacitors C_1 and C_3 in series with the input and output signals.

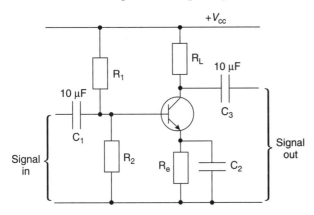

Figure 7.28   Capacitors C_1 and C_3 cause drop off in gain at low frequencies

Let us now suppose that the input signal to the amplifier is at a low frequency – say 10 Hz. The reactance of the coupling capacitors will be

$$X_C = \frac{1}{2\pi fC}$$

$$= \frac{1}{2\pi \times 10\text{ Hz} \times 10 \times 10^{-6}}$$

$$= \frac{1}{2\pi \times 10^{-4}}$$

$$= 1.592\text{ k}\Omega$$

The signal into the amplifier is therefore effectively passing through a reactance of almost 1.6 kΩ and will suffer severe attenuation. The output level of

the amplifier will therefore drop as less input signal is applied.

If we consider the opposite end of the scale where the input signal to the amplifier is relatively high – say 20 kHz – the reactance of the coupling capacitors is now

$$X_C = \frac{1}{2\pi fC}$$

$$= \frac{1}{2\pi \times 20 \times 10^3 \times 10 \times 10^{-6}}$$

$$= 0.796\ \Omega$$

Thus as signal frequency increases the coupling capacitors do not affect the signal's passage at all as their reactance becomes minimal and we need not consider them.

High frequency drop-off

One effect that exists between all points at different potential is capacitance. This is not from physical components that we have soldered in the circuit but is stray. It is shown in Figure 7.29 as dotted lines.

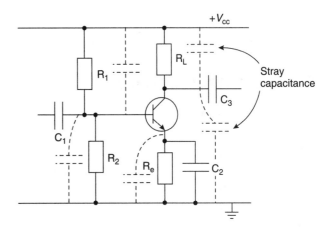

Figure 7.29

> Stray capacitance exists between all points at different potential.

You can see that this capacitance is parallel to earth and as soon as its reactance is low enough it will act as a low impedance path for the signal.

Using the same frequency values as before and nominating a value of 10 pF, the reactance of this capacitance at 10 Hz will be

$$X_C = \frac{1}{2\pi fC}$$

$$= \frac{1}{2 \times \pi \times 10 \ \times 10 \times 10^{-12}}$$

$$= \frac{1}{2\pi \times 10^{-8}}$$

$$= 0.159 \times 10^8 = 15.9 \ \text{M}\Omega$$

This is so large that no signal will be shunted via it to earth. However, if the frequency of the signal handled by the amplifier is 20 kHz the reactance of the stray capacitance will reduce to

$$X_C = \frac{1}{2\pi f C}$$

$$= \frac{1}{2 \times \pi \times 20 \ \times 10^3 \times 10 \times 10^{-12}}$$

$$= \frac{1}{40\pi \times 10^{-8}}$$

$$= 0.0796 \times 10^7 = 796 \ \text{k}\Omega$$

At this value the stray capacitance provides a relatively low impedance path to earth. The signal will see this as the path of least resistance and not be processed to the output of the amplifier (Figure 7.30).

It should be noted that at very high frequency the stray capacitance plays a significant part and circuit design has to take this into consideration.

Calculating coupling capacitance

The rule that is normally used for calculating a coupling capacitance is that the reactance of the capacitor should have a value of 10% of the input impedance of the amplifier at the lowest operating frequency that the amplifier is designed to handle. If these conditions are met the amount of signal lost across the capacitor will be minimal.

So, for example, if the amplifier is to handle a minimum frequency of 100 Hz and its input

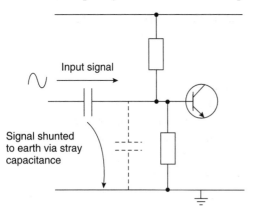

Figure 7.30   Stray capacitance shunts input signal to earth

impedance is 1 kΩ the value of the capacitor can be found from

$$10\% \ \text{of} \ 1 \ \text{k}\Omega = 10\% \times 1000 \ \Omega = 100 \ \Omega$$

Therefore X_C must be 100 Ω at 100 Hz.

$$X_C = \frac{1}{2\pi f C}$$

$$\therefore C = \frac{1}{2\pi f X_C}$$

$$= \frac{1}{2\pi \times 100 \ \text{Hz} \times 100 \ \Omega}$$

$$= 0.159 \times 10^{-4}$$

$$= 15.9 \ \mu\text{F}$$

Calculating the emitter decoupling capacitance

The value of the emitter decoupling capacitor is calculated in much the same way except that at the lowest operating frequency the reactance of the capacitor should not exceed a value of 10% of the emitter resistance.

For example, if the emitter resistance is 560 Ω and the lowest frequency is still 100 Hz the value of the decoupling capacitance will be

$$10\% \ \text{of} \ 560 \ \Omega = 56 \ \Omega$$

Therefore X_C must be 56 Ω at 100 Hz. Therefore

$$C = \frac{1}{2\pi f X_C}$$

$$= \frac{1}{2\pi \times 100 \ \text{Hz} \times 56 \ \Omega}$$

$$= 0.284 \times 10^{-4}$$

$$= 28.4 \ \mu\text{F}$$

Classes of bias

Class A

The amplifier circuits that we have looked at so far should give faithful reproduction if we use them correctly. That is, if we apply a sinewave at the input a larger sinewave appears at the output. This is known as class A biasing (Figure 7.31(a)). Sometimes it is known as 360° of output signal for 360° of input signal.

The disadvantage of class A bias is that even when no input signal is applied and the amplifier is in its quiescent state collector current is drawn from the supply. This can easily be seen by

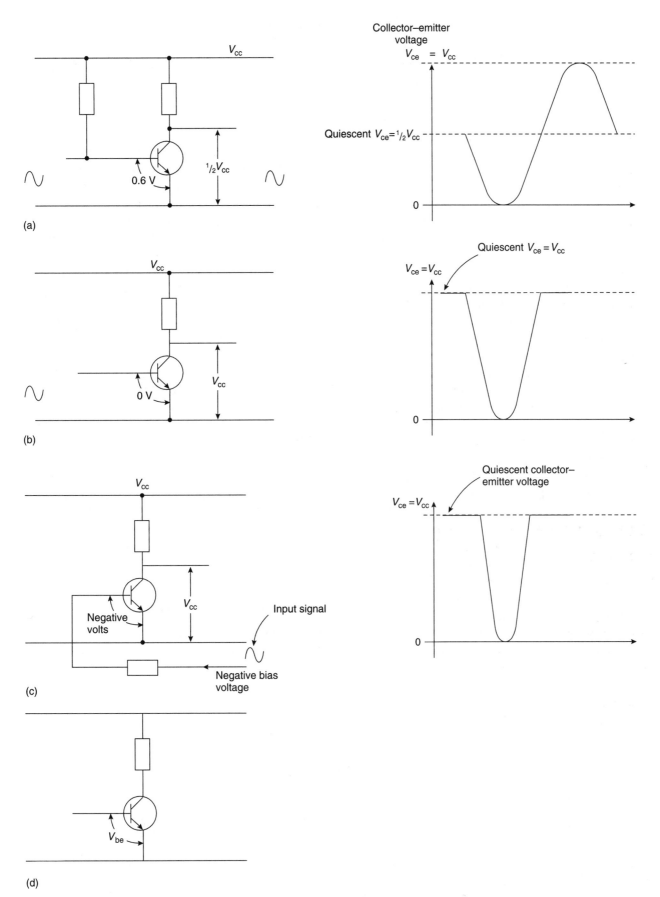

Figure 7.31   (a) Class A bias: V_{out} rises to $+V_{cc}$ and falls to 0 V symmetrical about 4.5 V; the peak to peak value is 9 V. (b) Class B bias: V_{out} can fall to 0 V but never rises above V_{cc}; the output is therefore only half a cycle, the peak value being V_{cc}. (c) Class C bias: V_{out} can still fall to 0 V but the half cycle is narrower than for class B as the current flows for less than half a cycle. (d) Class AB bias: the value of V_{be} lies between 0 and 0.4 V (approximately)

reference to the characteristic we looked at earlier in Figure 7.2 on page 144. Additionally, a circuit in class A bias is only 50% efficient at a maximum.

Put simply, if we bias in class A the circuit will run the supply battery down even when no signal requiring amplification is present, and 50% of the supply is wasted!

Class B

An alternative approach to circuit design is to bias the transistor so that when the input signal is absent no collector current is drawn. This means that the transistor is off and the voltage between the base and the emitter of the transistor is 0 V. When the signal to be amplified is applied at the input, part of it turns the transistor on, collector current then flows and an output voltage is developed.

At first glance this appears to have addressed the problems of class A, especially when we learn that the efficiency of a class B amplifier is up to 78%. There are disadvantages, however.

As the transistor is off, the quiescent collector voltage is V_{cc}. The output can therefore only consist of half cycles as the voltage can drop from V_{cc} to 0 V but can never rise above the supply. Figure 7.31(b) illustrates this.

We can therefore say that class B bias provides 180° of output signal for 360° of input signal. Others say it distorts by 180°!

Class B bias is used for audio work but only in a circuit arrangement known as push-pull. This uses a system where the signal is divided into its individual positive and negative half cycles, these being fed to two separate transistors. Each transistor amplifies its half cycles and the respective outputs are then recombined (Figure 7.32).

Class B bias is used in radio systems to amplify signals at the final stages of transmission, and if a tuned load is used a push-pull configuration is not necessary.

Class C

Like class B bias the transistor is off in the absence of an input signal. However, in class B the base–emitter junction is at 0 V whereas in class C it is below 0 V – i.e. it has a negative voltage.

For the transistor to turn on when a signal is applied this negative voltage has to be overcome and only then will base current flow and amplification occur. The output signal is therefore a series of pulses that are less than 180° of the input signal. The principle of class C bias is illustrated in Figure 7.31(c).

Whilst class C bias is not useful for audio systems it does find wide use in oscillators, frequency modulation and frequency multiplier circuits. It is normally used with a tuned load.

Class AB

As the name suggests, class AB bias sits somewhere between A and B (Figure 7.31(d)). The transistor is therefore not fully on or off and the base–emitter junction voltage is somewhere between 0 and 0.6 V. Less of the input signal is required to turn the transistor on and the output consists of greater than 180° out but not the full 360°.

Characteristic summary

We can look at classes of bias (Table 7.1) in two ways: in words and practical circuits as we have just done, or by how the operating point (i.e. the

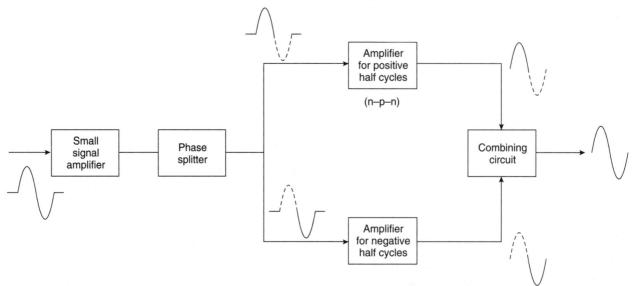

Figure 7.32   Simple push-pull ignoring phase change

Table 7.1

Bias type	Efficiency	Degrees out for 360° in	Typical uses of circuit
Class A	50%	360°	Small signal audio
Class B	78.5%	Slightly less than 180°	Audio (in push pull), radio transmitters
Class C		Less than 180°	Oscillators, frequency multipliers, some radio transmitters
Class AB		180°	As for Class B

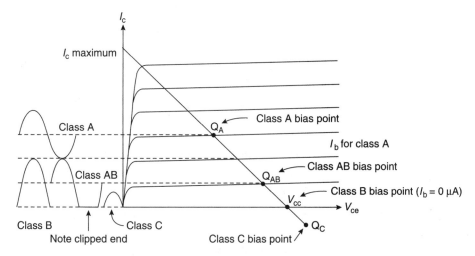

Figure 7.33

Q point) of the transistor shifts up and down the characteristic as we change the base–emitter bias voltage. This is shown in Figure 7.33.

The three amplifier configurations of a transistor

We have now seen that the transistor can act as an amplifier and we can change the class of bias according to the efficiency or shape of the output waveform that we require.

Additionally, we can alter the method of connecting the transistor so that instead of always applying the input signal to the base and obtaining the output from the collector we can use a different electrode to take the input and a different one to obtain the output signal.

In fact, the transistor can be connected in three different ways or configurations, depending on what sort of performance is required.

Figure 7.34(a) shows the common-emitter circuit – we have already performed calculations to find out the value of its components. It is referred to as

common emitter because the emitter electrode is common to both input and output signals.

The common collector or emitter follower

The emitter follower is shown in Figure 7.34(b). Note how the collector is connected directly to the supply and, whilst the input is applied to the base as before, the output is taken from the emitter.

The emitter follower provides a voltage gain of 1 (i.e. unity) and is used as a buffer amplifier as it has a high input impedance and a low output impedance.

The common-base amplifier

You can see from Figure 7.34(c) that the common-base amplifier differs from the previous two circuits because the input is applied to the emitter. This circuit arrangement is used at very high frequency as it minimises intercapacitance.

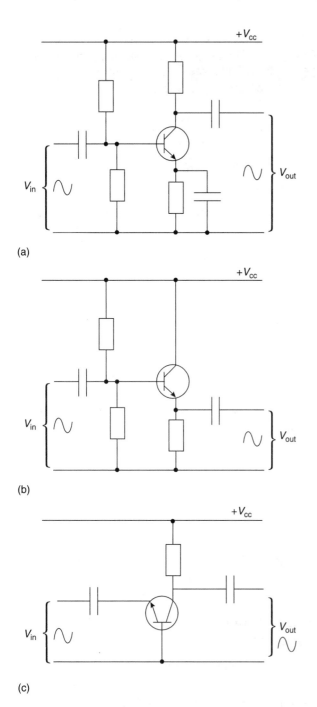

(a)

(b)

(c)

Figure 7.34 (a) The common-emitter amplifier; (b) the common-collector or emitter follower amplifier; (c) the common-base amplifier

Field effect transistors as amplifiers

Many of the rules that we have learnt with regard to the bipolar transistor as an amplifier are equally applicable to field effect transistors (FETs). As before, three configurations are possible but instead of common base, common emitter and common collector we now have

common drain
common source
common gate

Once again, the design of amplifier circuits is based around the use of the output characteristic, and the 'ground rules' of establishing Q points and allowing for maximum voltage swing still apply.

As before we deal with this topic in two sections. First we set up the junction field effect transistor (JFET) as a DC amplifier and see how to calculate the component values. When we have done this we examine how the amplifier will behave with a signal applied or, to put it professionally, under dynamic conditions.

The n-channel JFET as an amplifier

Notice how the supply rail is no longer called V_{cc} but is now known as V_{dd}. This is short for voltage from drain to drain.

The circuit in Figure 7.35 is the FET equivalent of the common-emitter transistor amplifier and is one of the most frequent that you will come across. As yet we have not applied an input signal to the circuit and are merely setting up the DC conditions.

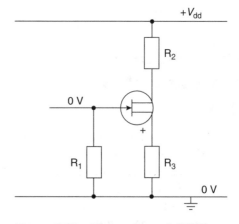

Figure 7.35 The n-channel JFET as an amplifier

To get the FET to conduct in the correct portion of its output characteristic it is essential that the gate–source voltage is at the appropriate level. For an n-channel device this means that the gate must be negative with respect to the source. You may think that this means that a negative potential must be incorporated into the circuit but another quick look at the figure shows you that this is not so. Instead, the required negative bias can be derived by placing a resistor in series with the source and the 0 V rail.

This source resistor R_3 (sometimes called R_s) carries the drain current and will therefore develop a voltage across it. The voltage is positive with respect to the 0 V rail and so the top of the source resistor assumes the polarity marked.

The gate–ground resistor R_1   The gate is connected to 0 V via R_1. As no appreciable current flows into the JFET because of its extremely high input impedance there will be a minimal voltage across R_1 and the potential across it will be virtually 0 V. Typical values of R_1 are 1 or 1.5 MΩ. R_1 is sometimes known as R_g for R_{gate}.

Calculating the source resistance R_3 (or R_s)   The value of the negative voltage between gate and source must be determined from the characteristic. Looking at the data given in Figure 7.36 let us assume that we want to bias the gate–source voltage at –1.0 V and the drain–source voltage is 8.5 V. The latter is chosen to ensure that we operate in the linear part of the characteristic and is half of the available supply remaining. That is,

$$V_{ds} = \frac{V_{dd} - V_s}{2}$$
$$= \frac{18 - 1}{2}$$
$$= \frac{17}{2} = 8.5 \text{ V}$$

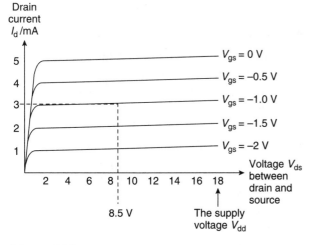

Figure 7.36

For these values we can see from Figure 7.36 that the quiescent drain current will be 3 mA.

The source resistance R_3 can be calculated from

$$R_3 = \frac{V_{ds}}{I_d}$$
$$= \frac{1 \text{ V}}{3 \text{ mA}} = 333 \, \Omega$$

Calculating the load resistance R_2   This resistor's value can be found by taking into account the information that we have already used and by referring to the characteristic.

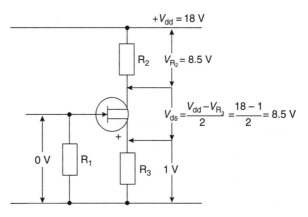

Figure 7.37

Figure 7.37 shows the voltages in the circuit bearing in mind that the source resistor has a potential across it of 1 V. We already know that the potential between the drain and the source is half the available supply, i.e. 8.5 V.

Guided example

An n-channel JFET is connected in the circuit arrangement shown in Figure 7.38. If the drain current is to be 5 mA, the voltage between the source and gate –2.5 V, and the supply rail is 20 V calculate the values of R_L and R_s. State a typical value for R_g.

V_{R_L} is 8.75 V. Note that $V_{R_L} + V_{ds} + V_{R_s} = V_{dd}$.

$$R_s = \frac{V_{gs}}{I_d} = \frac{2.5 \text{ V}}{5 \text{ mA}} = 500 \, \Omega$$

$$R_L = \frac{V_{R_L}}{I_d} = \frac{8.75 \text{ V}}{5 \text{ mA}} = 1.75 \text{ k}\Omega$$

$$R_g = 1 \text{ M}\Omega \text{ (typically)}$$

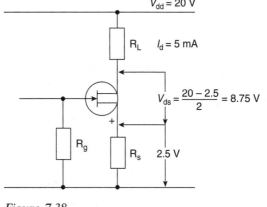

Figure 7.38

The voltage across the load resistor R_2 must also be 8.5 V as

$$V_{R_2} + V_{ds} + V_s = V_{dd}$$

$$8.5 + 8.5 + 1 = 18 \text{ V}$$

The current I_d through R_2 is 3 mA. Thus

$$R_2 = \frac{V_{R_2}}{I_d} = \frac{8.5}{3} = 2.83 \text{ k}\Omega$$

Putting field effect transistors under dynamic conditions

With any of the circuits that we have just examined we now have to apply an input signal just as we did with the bipolar transistor. For the same reasons as before it is necessary to include coupling (C_1 and C_3) and decoupling (C_2) capacitors and these are shown in the circuit diagram of Figure 7.39.

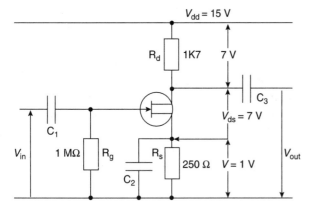

Figure 7.39

Drawing the load line

Once again we base our amplifier design work around the JFET's output characteristic so that we can form a mental picture of the largest input voltage that we can apply before the output will attempt to rise above the supply voltage and square off. It is therefore necessary to draw a load line on the characteristic (Figure 7.40).

Using the simple n-channel JFET in Figure 7.39 as an example we can find the two load line points.

Point one is the maximum voltage that can exist between drain and source, i.e. the supply V_{dd} (15 V).

Point two is the maximum drain current that can flow:

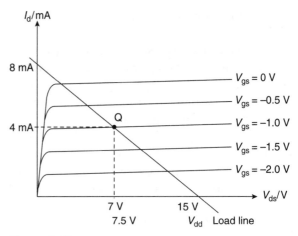

Figure 7.40

$$I_d = \frac{V_{dd}}{R_L + R_s}$$

$$= \frac{15}{(1.7 + 0.25) \text{ k}\Omega}$$

$$= \frac{15}{1.95 \text{ k}\Omega}$$

$$= 7.69 \text{ mA} \quad (\text{say } 8 \text{ mA})$$

As expected, the load line shows us that the Q point will be at a gate–source voltage of –1.0 V with V_{ds} being 7 V.

Working on the assumption that we do not want to run the risk of the circuit giving any distortion we can now look at the characteristic to determine the maximum peak to peak value of the signal to be amplified.

Application of an input signal

From Figure 7.39 we can see that the absolute maximum that the gate–source voltage can be driven through is 2 V peak to peak. That is, the peak value of 1 V would raise the gate–source voltage V_{gs} from –1 V to 0 V. In the opposite direction, as the input signal went negative, the maximum value it could reduce V_{gs} to is –2 V.

However, if we were to choose these values there is a great risk that clipping would result if the FET becomes overdriven. The purpose of the load line is to predict this.

It would therefore be much better to make sure that the peak to peak value of the input signal is not allowed to exceed 1 V, and this is shown in Figure 7.41. Under this condition the gate–source voltage V_{gs} will rise to –0.5 V and fall to –1.5 V. The portion of the characteristic operated on is always linear and there is therefore no risk of distortion.

The characteristic shows us the change of drain current that will result.

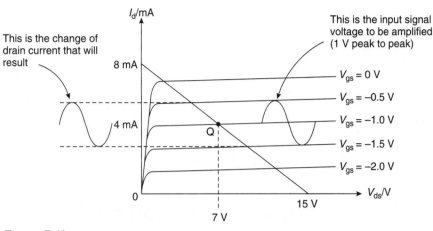

Figure 7.41

7.2 Operational amplifiers

Operational amplifiers – or opamps as they are usually referred to – were one of the first integrated circuits. They come under the category of linear integrated circuits.

Operational amplifiers are available in a variety of packages, some 8-pin dual-in-line (DIL), some 16 pin and even some in round 'can' arrangements that are often mistaken by the inexperienced for eight-legged transistors!

Inside an opamp

An opamp is treated by technicians as a 'black box'. That is, we do not have to know in detail what goes on inside the integrated circuit, just its block function. Additionally, we need to understand how to make it work for us by the connection of external components.

Figure 7.42 shows the block diagram of a typical opamp. The circuit can conveniently be divided into three blocks: a difference amplifier, a high gain amplifier and finally a buffer amplifier at the output.

The actual circuit diagram of what is inside a typical opamp is given in Figure 7.43 and all of the circuit can be contained inside an 8-pin DIL package!

The difference amplifier

The difference amplifier of the opamp contains the input terminals for the voltage to be processed. Note that the terminals are marked with plus and minus signs (Figure 7.42). Take care not to confuse

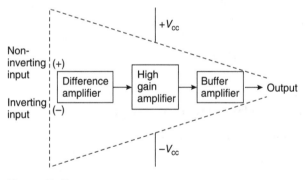

Figure 7.42

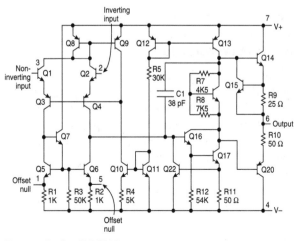

Figure 7.43   LM741 opamp

these with the supply rails (more later) which are a different thing entirely. The input impedance of the opamp is very high, normally in the mega-ohms region. This means that very little current will be drawn by the circuit. It is therefore a voltage-operated device.

The input with the minus sign is known as the inverting terminal. The input with the plus sign is known as the non-inverting terminal.

The difference amplifier examines the voltage levels at its two input terminals and makes available at the output the difference between them. So, for example, if a difference amplifier had 3 V on the plus (non-inverting) terminal and 1 V on the minus (inverting) terminal, the output of the difference amplifier would be 2 V; or, if the plus terminal had a potential of –5 V and the minus terminal a potential of –2 V the output would be –5 – (–2) = –3 V.

The high gain amplifier

The difference of the two inputs is then passed to the high gain voltage amplifier. The actual gain of this part of the circuit can be as high as a million (10^6).

This does not mean that if the input of the difference amplifier is 1 V a million volts will be available at the output! Of course, the maximum output will be limited by the supply voltage of the integrated circuit.

The buffer amplifier stage

Finally, after amplification the signal voltage is applied to the buffer amplifier stage. This section has a high input impedance but a low output impedance which is useful for drive current purposes. The circuit configuration of a typical output stage would be an emitter follower.

The supply voltage

Another point to note about the opamp is the supply voltage. This is usually a dual supply. A typical example is +9 V, 0 V and –9 V. Remember not to confuse the supply terminals with the inverting and non-inverting input terminals.

Dual rail supplies can be made using appropriate components (see page 135 for a typical circuit diagram) or by coupling two conventional supplies together as shown in Figure 7.44.

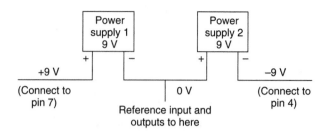

Figure 7.44   Running an opamp from two conventional supplies

Practical pinouts of the opamp

Many types of opamp are available but some standardisation of pinouts has been achieved by manufacturers. Figure 7.45 shows the arrangement for a (UA) 741 in 8-pin DIL mode.

The supply connections and the two input terminals account for four of the pins whilst pin 8 is not connected (NC). Pins 1 and 5 are used in conjunction with an external potentiometer to remove offset.

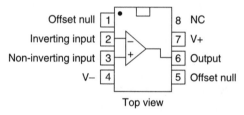

Figure 7.45   Practical pinouts of an opamp

Practical limitations of the opamp

From what we have already seen of these integrated circuits we can draw a few conclusions as to how we hope they will behave for us. In practice, they work slightly differently.

Offset

As the opamp only ever amplifies the difference in voltage between the two input terminals it follows that when both terminals are connected to 0 V the output of the integrated circuit should be 0 V (Figure 7.46).

In practice this is not always the case. Any small voltage that is present under these conditions is called 'offset'. Under some circumstances this doesn't matter but if the integrated circuit is being used to amplify microvolts or millivolts an offset of 1 V would be disastrous!

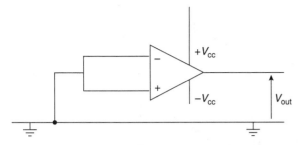

Figure 7.46 When connected as shown the output voltage should be 0 V. Any voltage measured is known as 'offset'

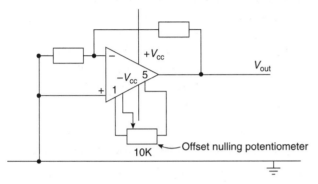

Figure 7.47

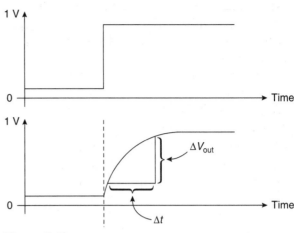

Figure 7.48

The gradient of the change in voltage can be calculated and this is known as the slew rate:

$$\text{slew rate} = \frac{\Delta V_{\text{out}}}{\Delta(\text{time})}$$

Slew rate can seriously affect the performance of an opamp at high frequencies.

Common-mode rejection ratio

As we have already seen, the output of an opamp is dependent on the difference in the potential of the two input terminals. If these terminals are at the same voltage or, to put it another way, the input signal is common to both terminals, no output should appear.

How well an opamp suppresses common-mode signals (i.e. the same signal at each input terminal) is known as the common-mode rejection ratio. This is usually quoted in decibels, and the higher the figure the better.

The opamp in open loop mode

The term open loop is used when the opamp has no other circuitry connected around it other than the power supply (Figure 7.49). Like this, maximum gain is available.

Manufacturers quote the gain of their opamps in open loop mode and usually provide a gain–

Fortunately, offset is easily removed by the connection of a variable resistor as shown in Figure 7.47. A 10 kΩ potentiometer is connected between the appropriate pins and the slider of the potentiometer is adjusted until 0 V output is obtained for 0 V input. This process is often referred to as offset nulling. The 10 kΩ potentiometer can be omitted if the opamp is to be used as an AC amplifier but it must be included for use as a DC amplifier.

Slew rate

You would expect any circuit to respond instantaneously when an input is applied. The output that it produces should faithfully represent the input with no distortion.

In an opamp this is not always so and the inability of the circuit to respond quickly to a sudden change of input voltage can seriously affect the shape of the output.

Slew rate is the maximum rate at which the output is capable of changing to follow a change in input voltage. Perhaps this is more easily understood by looking at Figure 7.48. The input to the opamp is a step as the voltage rises from 0 to 1 V.

At the output it takes time for the voltage to increase up to its final level and instead of the quick change that we are expecting the voltage rises over a period of time.

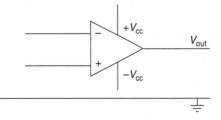

Figure 7.49 The opamp in open loop mode

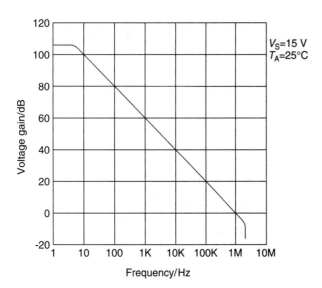

Figure 7.50   Open loop voltage as a function of frequency

frequency response graph. This shows that whilst the gain of the integrated circuit is extremely high at low frequencies it decreases, or rolls off, as frequency is increased. For example, in Figure 7.50, the gain at 1 Hz is over 100 dB. If the frequency of the input is increased to 10 kHz the maximum gain that can be achieved will drop to 40 dB.

If an opamp is operated in open loop mode the available gain is so high that the smallest of input signals will cause the output to rise to its maximum level. For example, if the difference voltage at the two input terminals is 1 mV and the open loop gain is 1×10^6 the output voltage will attempt to rise to

$$V_{out}(\text{theoretical}) = V_{in} \times \text{gain}$$
$$= 1 \text{ mV} \times 1 \times 10^6$$
$$= 1 \times 10^3$$
$$= 1000 \text{ V}$$

Quite obviously this figure is theoretical only! In practice, it can only increase to the supply voltage (i.e. $\pm V_{cc}$). It should also be remembered that if the input voltage is of the opposite polarity, e.g. 1 mV, then the same gain calculation will apply but the opamp will give out its maximum negative supply voltage:

$$V_{out} = V_{in} \times \text{gain}$$
$$= -1 \text{ mV} \times 10^6$$
$$= -1 \times 10^3 \text{ V}$$

The comparator

From the above you would think that the opamp in open loop mode is not used very often.

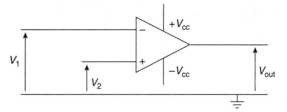

Figure 7.51   The comparator: if $V_1 > V_2$ then $V_{out} = +V_{cc}$; if $V_2 > V_1$ then $V_{out} = -V_{cc}$

In fact, it finds wide application as a comparator. The principle of this is shown in Figure 7.51.

If the voltage on the non-inverting terminal exceeds that of the inverting terminal the output rises to the positive supply rail. On the other hand, if the voltage at the inverting terminal exceeds the voltage of the non-inverting terminal then the opposite occurs and the output assumes the potential of the negative supply rail.

Practical use of the comparator

The comparator is one of the most important building blocks of control circuitry. The automatic porch light is an obvious example; a typical circuit diagram is given in Figure 7.52.

The LDR's resistance varies with the level of ambient light and this leads to a change in voltage at the non-inverting input of the comparator. The voltage at the inverting input is determined by the setting of the potentiometer. When the voltage at the non-inverting terminal exceeds that of the inverting terminal the output of the comparator trips (i.e. changes from low to high) and assumes the same value as the positive supply.

This voltage is now used to drive the transistor switch which, in turn, operates the relay. The contacts of this can be used to switch the mains.

The principle of this circuit can be applied to other sensors. For example, if the LDR is replaced by a thermistor a temperature-sensing circuit can be built.

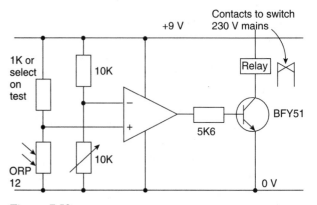

Figure 7.52

The opamp in closed loop mode

The term closed loop is used when some of the output signal is fed back to the input. Under most circumstances the fed-back signal is of opposite polarity to the input and so we have introduced negative feedback.

If the fed-back signal is in phase with the input then the circuit will oscillate.

The gain–bandwidth product

In any amplifying device the following statement holds true:

gain × bandwidth = constant

In an opamp the constant is generally taken to be the frequency at which the gain drops to 1. This is known as the **unity gain frequency** (UGF).

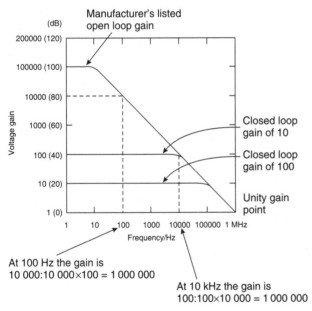

Figure 7.53

From the response curve in Figure 7.53 you can see that the frequency at which the gain falls to unity is almost 1 MHz. If we take this as the unity gain frequency we can say

gain × bandwidth = 1 MHz

From the response curve it is possible to predict the bandwidth at other gains. For example, from Figure 7.53 we can see that at a gain of 100 the maximum bandwidth is 10 kHz.

Instead of looking at the response curve we can calculate this using the formula

gain × bandwidth = 1 MHz (i.e. UGF)

If you designed a circuit that only required a bandwidth of 1 kHz the maximum available gain would be

$$\text{gain} = \frac{1 \text{ MHz}}{\text{bandwidth}}$$

$$= \frac{1 \text{ MHz}}{1 \text{ kHz}} = 1000$$

Feedback and gain of an opamp

In Figure 7.54 the non-inverting input of the opamp has been connected directly to ground. As this is at 0 V only the potential of the inverting input needs to be considered. A resistor (R_f) has been connected between the output and the input. As the inverting terminal is used at the input a negative feedback path has been set up.

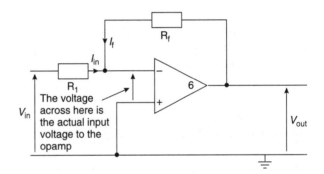

Figure 7.54

Let us make some assumptions.

(a) The input signal applied to the input terminal is 1 V.
(b) The output signal measured at the output is 10 V.

From this it follows that the closed loop gain of the device is

$$\text{gain} = \frac{V_{\text{out}}}{V_{\text{in}}} = \frac{10}{1} = 10$$

Now, we have already seen that the gain of the actual opamp itself is, say, 10^6. As our output signal is 10 V the actual signal applied to the input of the opamp can be found from

$$\text{gain} = \frac{\text{output}}{\text{input}}$$

$$10^6 = \frac{10 \text{ V}}{\text{actual input}}$$

$$\therefore \text{ actual input voltage} = \frac{10}{10^6} = 1 \times 10^{-5} \text{ V}$$

Thus the inverting terminal of the opamp is only 1×10^{-5} above ground potential of 0 V. We say that the input of the opamp is at **virtual earth**.

The next question that has to be answered is: what happened to the 1 V signal input we applied if only 1×10^{-5} V actually ended up at the input pin? The answer to this can be seen if you remember to treat the inverting input as being at almost 0 V. The input signal voltage is applied between earth and the inverting input. It therefore develops across R_1.

The output signal, of 10 V, is available between ground and pin 6. R_f is connected between the output and the inverting input which, as we have already said, is at virtually the same potential as earth. Therefore the output signal is developed across R_f.

We have previously mentioned the extremely high input impedance of the opamp. This effectively ensures that the current into its input is minimal which means that current flows via the resistors to the virtual earth point. From Kirchhoff's first law we know that the sum of currents at a junction is equal to zero and therefore

$$I_{in} = -I_f$$

The overall loop gain of any circuit is always the output signal divided by the input. Therefore

$$gain = \frac{V_{out}}{V_{in}}$$

Substituting for current gives

$$gain = \frac{-I_f R_f}{I_{in} R_1}$$

As $I_f = I_{in}$ we have

$$gain = -\frac{R_f}{R_1}$$

from which we can make the very important statement:

> voltage gain $= -\dfrac{R_f}{R_1}$
>
> The minus sign is used to indicate phase change.

In other words, with an opamp in closed loop mode the gain of the circuit is dependent on the ratio of the two resistors. Quite simple really! You have to remember that there are limitations to this, though. The supply voltage is one and the gain–bandwidth product of the opamp is another.

The inverting amplifier

The principle described gives us the simplest opamp circuit – the inverting amplifier (Figure 7.55).

$$gain = -\frac{R_f}{R_{in}} = -\frac{100 \text{ k}\Omega}{10 \text{ k}\Omega} = 10$$

(minus for phase inversion).

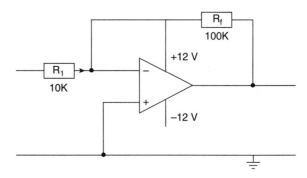

Figure 7.55

Guided example

From Figure 7.56

$$V_{out} = +1 \text{ mV} \times \left(-\frac{200}{1}\right)$$

Notice how the kΩ signs have been omitted as they cancel each other.

$$V_{out} = +1 \text{ mV} \times (-200)$$

$$= -200 \text{ mV}$$

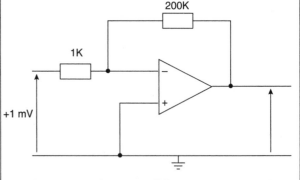

Figure 7.56   The gain of this circuit is (–)200

Amplification of AC or DC

The opamp can be used to amplify either DC or AC voltages. For AC voltages it is common practice to couple signals in and out via a capacitor, as shown in Figure 7.57. The actual value of the capacitor will be determined by the frequency range of the AC over which you are expecting the circuit normally to work.

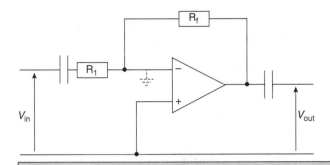

Figure 7.57

Practical 4

Note that we have used 741s for the practical experiments. However, virtually any opamp will do.

One of the advantages of opamps is that they lend themselves to practical work – there are so few components! Practical circuits are best constructed on prototype breadboard so that circuit changes can be made quickly.

Set up the circuit as shown in Figure 7.58. Be sure that you have connected the three-rail supply correctly.

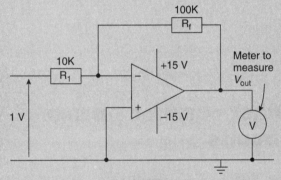

Figure 7.58

From the ratio of the two resistors you know that the circuit gain will be

$$-\frac{R_f}{R_1} = -\frac{100\,\text{k}\Omega}{10\,\text{k}\Omega} = -10$$

To test this apply an input voltage of 1 V and measure the output. It should be 10 V. Now try a different resistor for R_f – say, 120 kΩ. The output voltage should alter so that the gain becomes

$$\text{gain} = -\frac{120}{10} = -12$$

Now change the input so that a signal generator is connected as in Figure 7.59. Note the connection of the oscilloscope. Apply an input voltage of 1 V peak to peak at a frequency of 100 Hz and measure the output peak to peak voltage. This should be 10 V.

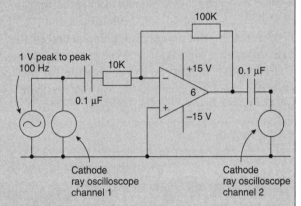

Figure 7.59

With the test equipment still connected it is possible to construct a table of readings that will allow a frequency response curve to be drawn. Set the frequency generator to each of the settings given in the table and at each new input frequency measure the peak to peak value of the output and record this.

Did you note the 180° phase change from input to output?

Your readings should decrease as the frequency of the input increases. This involves the gain–bandwidth product discussed on page 167.

The inverting amplifier is one of the most common circuit arrangements of the opamp. Although it is very useful at audio frequencies it has limited application at higher frequencies.

Frequency (kHz)	0.05	0.1	0.5	1	5	10	20	40
Pk–pk output								
Frequency (kHz)	60	80	100	200	400	600	800	1000
Pk–pk output								

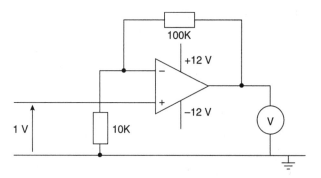

Figure 7.60   The non-inverting amplifier

The non-inverting amplifier

The non-inverting amplifier (Figure 7.60) does not change the phase of the signal from input to output. The amount of voltage fed back is determined by the potential dividing action of the two resistors R_f and R_1.

In a similar manner to the calculation for the inverting amplifier it can be shown that the gain of the circuit can be calculated from

$$gain = \frac{V_{out}}{V_{in}}$$

$$= \frac{R_f + R_1}{R_1}$$

$$= 1 + \frac{R_f}{R_1}$$

Guided example

From Figure 7.61

$$V_{out} = V_{in} \times \left(1 + \frac{R_f}{R_1}\right)$$

$$= 10\,mV \times \left(1 + \frac{20}{5}\right)$$

$$= 10\,mV \times 5$$

$$= 50\,mV$$

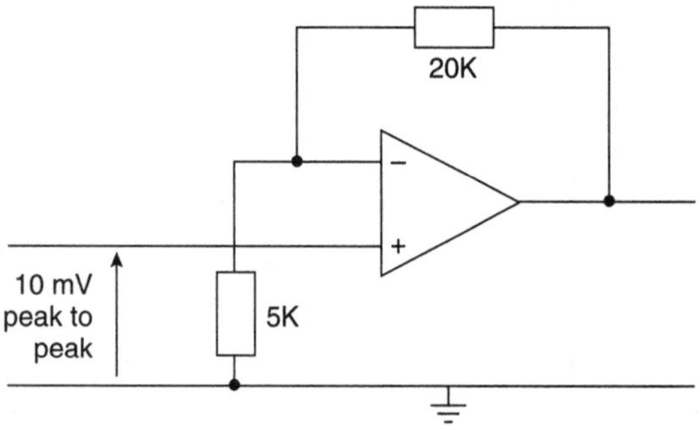

20K

10 mV
peak to
peak

5K

Figure 7.61

Practical 5

Using the components that you used for the inverting amplifier adapt the circuit so that it is wired as in Figure 7.60. Once again apply an input of 1 V and measure the output. It should be

$$V_{out} = V_{in} \times gain$$

$$= 1\,V \times (1 + R_f/R_1)$$

$$= 1\,V \times 11$$

$$= 11\,V$$

Again change the circuit by adding the coupling capacitors so that you can check that it amplifies AC.

Now set the signal generator to provide a square wave output. Apply this to the circuit at three different frequencies, e.g. 1 kHz, 10 kHz and 100 kHz. You should be able to see that the shape of the output alters from a good square wave towards a triangular shape. This, of course, is due to the slew rate of the opamp.

Other common opamp circuits

The difference amplifier

In the configuration of Figure 7.62 the opamp will take the difference in the two signal voltages applied to the input and amplify it.

If all the resistors are of the same value the output will simply be the difference. If, however, they are of different values amplification of the difference will occur.

If all the resistors are of equal value

$$V_{out} = V_1 - V_2$$

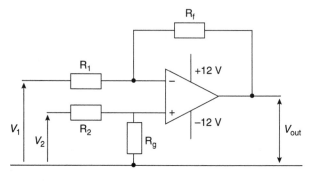

Figure 7.62

If the resistors are not all of equal value such that $R_f = R_g$ and $R_1 = R_2$, then

$$V_{out} = -\frac{R_f}{R_1}(V_1 - V_2)$$

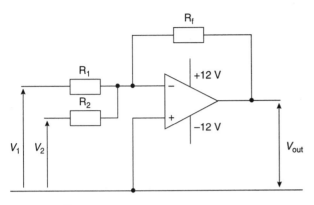

Figure 7.63

The summing amplifier

The circuit in Figure 7.63 adds input voltages together and, depending on the ratio of the resistors, can also amplify the sum of the voltages. Although only two inputs are shown, other resistors can be added to produce, say, a five-input summing amplifier.

Guided example

From Figure 7.64

$$-V_{out} = V_1\frac{R_f}{R_1} + V_2\frac{R_f}{R_2} + V_3\frac{R_f}{R_3}$$

$$= 0.1\frac{200}{10} + 0.3\frac{200}{20} + (-0.2)\frac{200}{40}$$

$$= 2 + 3 + (-1)$$

$$= 5 - 1 = 4$$

$$\therefore V_{out} = -4 \text{ V}$$

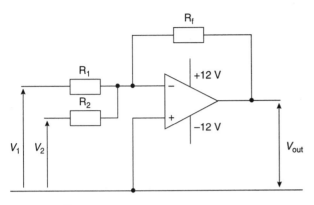

Figure 7.64

If all resistors are of equal value

$$V_{out} = -(V_1 + V_2)$$

(note the minus sign to signify a phase change).

The scaler adder

Scaler adder is the name given to a summing amplifier when the circuit uses resistors that are not all of the same value (Figure 7.65). Under these circumstances the output voltage becomes

$$-V_{out} = V_1\frac{R_f}{R_1} + V_2\frac{R_f}{R_2} + V_3\frac{R_f}{R_3}$$

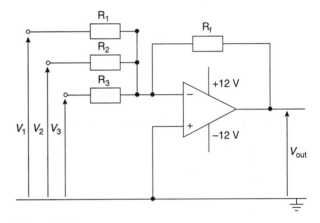

Figure 7.65

Audio mixers

The summing amplifier without gain or connected as a scaler adder finds wide application in the audio world where it is used to combine or mix input signals to obtain one output. A typical circuit is shown in Figure 7.66 (overleaf).

The output of the circuit in Figure 7.66 can feed the base and treble control arrangement in Figure 7.67 or this can be used as an independent circuit.

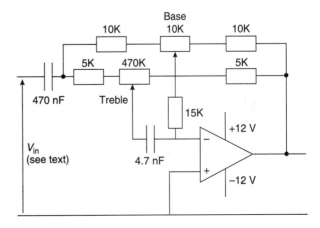

Figure 7.67

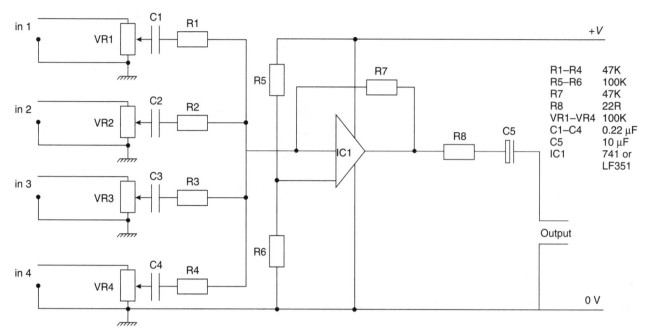

Figure 7.66

Practical 6

Summing amplifier

Set up the circuit in Figure 7.68. Note that the two power supplies are being used as independent input voltages. Set these to the values given in the table, each time making a note of the level of voltage at the output.

You can have further fun with this if you change the value of one of the input resistors (e.g. R_2) so that it is, say, 10 kΩ less than the others. This will configure the circuit as a scaler adder and the output voltages will alter accordingly.

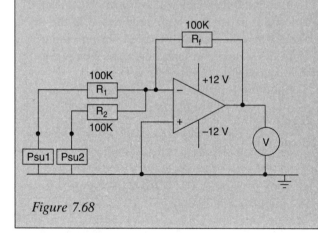

Figure 7.68

V_{in}	V_{out}	V_{in}	V_{out}
$V_1 = 1$ V		$V_1 = 2$ V	
$V_2 = 1$ V		$V_2 = 2$ V	
$V_1 = 2$ V		$V_1 = 4$ V	
$V_2 = 3$ V		$V_2 = 1$ V	
$V_1 = -3$ V		$V_1 = -3$ V	
$V_2 = 1$ V		$V_2 = -2$ V	
$V_1 = 2$ V		$V_1 = 1$ V	
$V_2 = -2$ V		$V_2 = 4$ V	

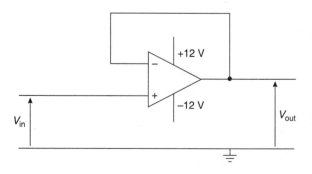

Figure 7.69

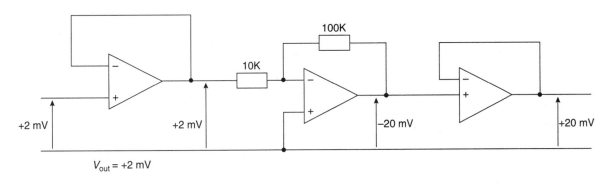

Figure 7.70

First voltage follower used as buffer amplifier

Inverting amplifier provides gain and changes phase of input by 180°

Second voltage follower to provide second phase change

The voltage follower

At first sight the method of connecting the opamp in Figure 7.69 appears a little peculiar. The feedback path from output to input has no resistor and therefore the whole of the output is used as feedback. Under these circumstances the circuit has no gain (i.e. the gain is unity) as $R_f = 0$ and $R_1 = \infty$.

The circuit is used, however, as a buffer amplifier (Figure 7.70) and has replaced the emitter follower in some circumstances. It has a very large input impedance and therefore does not load the circuit to which it is connected. The output impedance is low and suitable for matching to a loudspeaker or low impedance voltmeter.

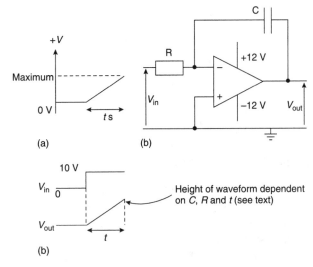

Figure 7.71

The integrator

In some applications such as a digital voltmeter or for sweeping a spot from one side of a cathode ray tube to the other in a television or oscilloscope a ramp-shaped waveform is required. An example of this is illustrated in Figure 7.71(a) which shows how the voltage rises from zero to its maximum value over a period of time (*t* seconds).

A ramp voltage is easily generated by charging a capacitor via a resistor. This is the principle that the integrator uses. The duration of the ramp is determined by the time constant formed by C and R when connected around the opamp as shown in Figures 7.71(b) and 7.71(c).

The value of output voltage at any time after a steady voltage has been applied to the input can be calculated from

A selection of opamps

$$V_{out} = -\frac{1}{CR} \times V_{in} \times t$$

Note the minus sign which is present to indicate the phase change that the output will have gone through. The formula tells us that the size of the output at any time will be dependent on the duration that the input voltage has been applied and, of course, the maximum value to which the output can rise, which is the supply voltage.

Guided example

In Figure 7.72 the value of R is 100 kΩ. If C has a value of 100 nF and the input voltage rises from 0 to 10 V the value of the output voltage after 1 ms will be

$$V_{out} = -\frac{1}{CR} \times V_{in} \times t$$

$$= -\frac{1}{100 \times 10^{-9} \times 100 \times 10^{3}}$$

$$\times 10\ V \times 1\ ms$$

$$= -1\ V$$

After 5 ms it will have risen to

$$V_{out} = -\frac{1}{10^{-2}} \times 10 \times 5 \times 10^{-3}$$

$$= -5\ V$$

After 1 s the output voltage will be equal to the negative supply (–9 V) but, theoretically, would have attempted to rise to

$$V_{out} = -\frac{1}{10^{-2}} \times 10 \times 1\ s$$

$$= -\frac{10}{10^{-2}}$$

$$= -100\ V$$

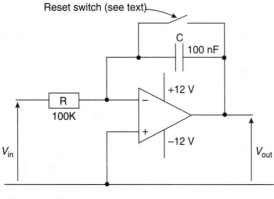

Figure 7.72

The integrator may be reset by placing a switch across C which, when closed, will short circuit it causing its discharge. This returns the integrator circuit back to its original state and causes the output to resume a state of 0 V. In a practical circuit the switch is more likely to be a transistor than a manually operated switch. By opening and closing the switch using a trigger pulse the output of the integrator will be a succession of ramps.

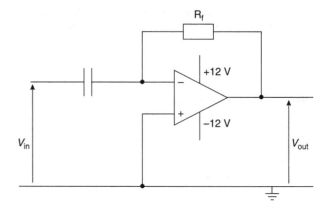

Figure 7.73

The differentiator

The differentiator circuit in Figure 7.73 is the opposite configuration to the integrator just discussed. The output voltage is proportional to the rate of change of the input signal multiplied by the time constant of C and R. Mathematically:

$$V_{out} = -CR\frac{dV}{dt}$$

In a practical application the differentiator is used to produce sharp triggering pulses which are applied to other circuits.

Public address amplifier

Guided example

In Figure 7.74 an integrator has a triangular input applied to it. The time constant formed by C and R is

$$10 \times 10^3 \times 0.22 \times 10^{-6} = 0.22 \times 10^{-2}$$

$$= 2.2 \text{ ms}$$

The time over which the waveform rises or falls (i.e. changes) is half the duration of one cycle, i.e.

$$\frac{\text{periodic time}}{2} = 0.5 \text{ ms}$$

The output of the integrator will assume a level of

$$- CR \times \frac{1 \text{ V}}{0.5 \text{ ms}}$$

$$= - 2.2 \times 10^{-3} \times \frac{1}{0.5 \times 10^{-3}}$$

$$= - 4.4 \text{ V}$$

As the frequency of the input is increased the rate of change of the input signal is increased. The size of the output voltage therefore increases without any change to the input apart from its frequency. If C and R are changed the shape of the output wave will be altered.

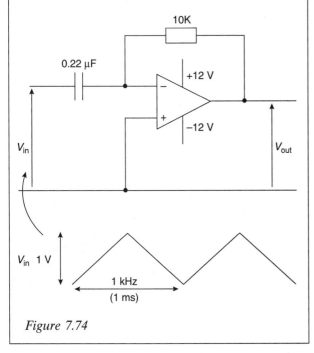

Figure 7.74

7.3 Transistor equivalent circuits

Norton AC equivalent circuit of a small signal amplifier

So far, all the amplifier analysis and the prediction of how amplifiers will behave has been done by referring to the characteristic and using this to predict performance.

The term AC equivalent circuit is used when an amplifier is examined solely from the way it will look to the signal voltage that is to be amplified. The DC conditions – such as the correct bias point and the resistor included to protect against thermal runaway – are not required as the equivalent circuit is used to analyse the dynamic behaviour of the circuit.

Before we can draw the circuit in this manner we have to establish a few facts.

Power supply impedance

Up to now we have always drawn the power supply to the circuit as two rails, the positive one being marked $+V_{cc}$ and the negative one 0 V. As we know, the voltages of these rails could very well be derived from the standard bridge rectifier and smoothing arrangement shown in Figure 7.75.

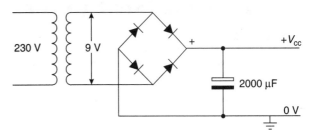

Figure 7.75

Looking at the circuit you can see that the value of the smoothing capacitor is 2000 μF and, as expected, it is connected between the positive and negative rails.

We have also always assumed that the 0 V rail is earth and we freely make statements such as 'the signal is shunted to earth'. Now, if we consider an audio frequency amplifier and a signal of 1 kHz the reactance of the smoothing capacitor is

$$X_C = \frac{1}{2\pi f C}$$

$$= \frac{1}{2\pi \times 10^3 \times 2000 \times 10^{-6}}$$

$$= 0.0796 \; \Omega$$

Therefore when we pass a signal via a decoupling capacitor to the earth rail the supply smoothing capacitor acts as a low impedance and the signal is also available on the positive supply rail.

That is, for all intents and purposes, the impedance of the supply presents a short circuit to the AC signal voltage between positive and negative rails.

We also know that the amplifier has an input impedance h_{ie} which we can obtain either from data issued by the transistor manufacturer or by plotting the input characteristic.

> The term h_{ie} is short for h parameter *input* impedance in the common-emitter mode. Thus h_{ib} would mean input impedance in common-base mode.

Finally, we have already established that the output current of the transistor is I_c and this is dependent on the transistor's current gain and the input current, i.e.

$$I_c = h_{fe} \times I_b$$

Deriving an AC equivalent circuit at the input to the amplifier

Figure 7.76(a) shows a conventional stabilised base bias common-emitter amplifier. If we now put ourselves in the position of the signal source to be connected across the input terminals AB it sees three components: the two base bias resistors and h_{ie}. This is illustrated in Figure 7.76(b).

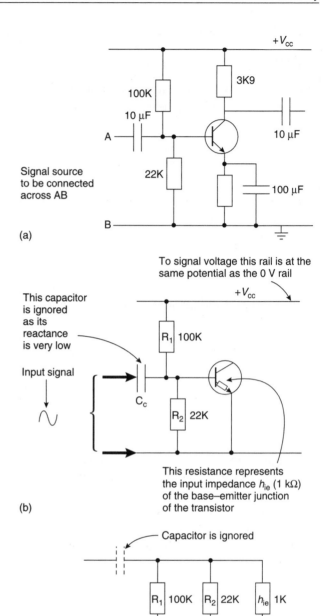

Figure 7.76 (a) The full circuit of the common-emitter amplifier; (b) how the circuit appears to the input signal; (c) simplified version of part (b)

As we have already shown, the low impedance of the supply smoothing capacitor causes both the 0 V rail and the $+V_{cc}$ rail to appear at the same potential to the signal. The components connected to either the 0 V rail or the $+V_{cc}$ rail thus appear in parallel with each other and so the circuit of Figure 7.76(b) can be redrawn as illustrated in Figure 7.76(c).

As this consists of resistances in parallel it is possible to work out their total equivalent resistance:

$$R_T = \frac{1}{1/R_1 + 1/R_2 + 1/h_{ie}}$$

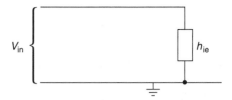

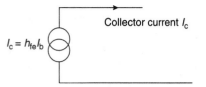

Figure 7.78

Figure 7.77   The simplified equivalent circuit of Figure 7.76(c) omitting coupling capacitor and base bias resistors

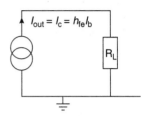

$$= \frac{1}{1/100\,\text{k}\Omega + 1/22\,\text{k}\Omega + 1/1\,\text{k}\Omega}$$

$$= 947\,\Omega$$

Notice how this equivalent resistance is approximately the same as h_{ie}. That is, the two bias resistors are very much greater than h_{ie} and therefore have a minimal effect on it. If we now disregard the larger resistors we can simplify the drawing of our equivalent circuit to Figure 7.77.

We have ignored the reactance of the coupling capacitors as this has been taken to be minimal at the frequency at which we are considering the amplifier to operate.

Thus it is possible, by considering the signal voltage, to redraw the circuit with only one component, the h_{ie} of the transistor. The signal applied at the base is developed across the impedance h_{ie} and this is the true input point of the transistor.

The AC equivalent circuit for the output of the amplifier

We now consider the output side of the transistor separately from the input side that we have just simplified. The collector current is $h_{ie} \times I_b$ and for convenience we regard this as a constant-current generator (Figure 7.78).

The transistor has two components that affect the flow of signal current at its output. One is the collector load resistance which we can readily identify. The other is the output conductance h_{oe}. We shall disregard the latter at this level of circuit analysis and consider the output current flowing via the collector load only.

In equivalent circuit terms we can therefore say that the constant-current generator that supplies the collector current works into a single resistor R_L. The output part of the equivalent circuit now appears as in Figure 7.79.

Putting the two sides together the whole equivalent circuit can be drawn as in Figure 7.80.

Figure 7.79   Output portion of the equivalent circuit

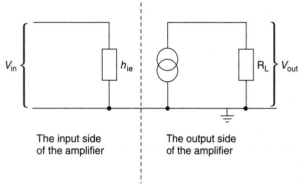

Figure 7.80

So far so good! We have now drawn the simplified equivalent circuit, but why and where does it get us?

Using the equivalent circuit

We can use the equivalent circuit to do all the calculations that we were previously having to extract from the characteristic. Using the circuit of Figure 7.80 and values taken from the amplifier that we started looking at in Figure 7.76(a) we can determine the performance of the circuit. Assuming an input signal of 20 mV peak to peak and a transistor with a current gain h_{fe} of 40 we can use the figures as follows.

The input current is the current that flows via the input impedance h_{ie} as a result of the input signal voltage – see Figure 7.81.

$$I_b = \frac{V_{signal}}{h_{ie}}$$

$$= \frac{20\,\text{mV}}{1\,\text{k}\Omega}$$

$$= 20\,\mu\text{A} \quad \text{(peak to peak)}$$

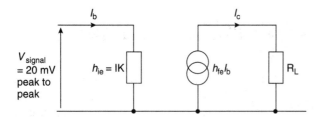

Figure 7.81

The **collector current** is the amplified base current:

$$I_c = h_{fe} I_b$$

$$= 40 \times 20 \text{ μA}$$

$$= 800 \text{ μA (peak to peak)}$$

The **signal output voltage** is the voltage across the collector load R_L and is determined by the size of R_L and the collector current:

$$V_{\text{signal out}} = I_c R_L$$

$$= 800 \text{ μA} \times 3.9 \text{ kΩ}$$

$$= 3.12 \text{ V peak to peak}$$

The **overall voltage gain of the amplifier** is the ratio of input signal (peak to peak) to output signal:

$$A_v = \frac{V_{\text{out}}}{V_{\text{in}}}$$

$$= \frac{3.12}{20 \text{ mV}} = 156$$

Alternatively, we can substitute from the equations already used:

$$\frac{V_{\text{out}}}{V_{\text{in}}} = \frac{I_c R_L}{I_b h_{ie}}$$

Now, $I_c = h_{fe} I_b$. Therefore

$$\frac{V_{\text{out}}}{V_{\text{in}}} = \frac{h_{fe} I_b R_L}{I_b h_{ie}}$$

Cancelling I_b we get

$$A_v = \frac{V_{\text{out}}}{V_{\text{in}}} = \frac{h_{fe} R_L}{h_{ie}}$$

(Substitute values from above to check: $A_v = h_{fe} R_L / h_{ie} = 40 \times 3.9 \text{ kΩ}/1 \text{ kΩ} = 156$.)

This formula is very useful as it allows us to predict the voltage gain of the amplifier by knowing the value of the transistor's parameters and selecting the appropriate value of load resistor. It saves a lot of headaches!

Guided example

Draw the equivalent circuit of the single-stage common-emitter amplifier shown in Figure 7.82. For an input voltage of 10 mV peak to peak, use the equivalent circuit to determine the voltage gain of the circuit and the size of the output signal.

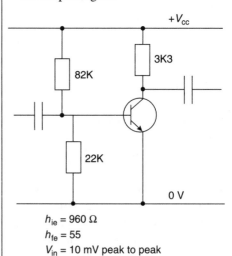

$h_{ie} = 960 \text{ Ω}$
$h_{fe} = 55$
$V_{in} = 10 \text{ mV peak to peak}$

Figure 7.82

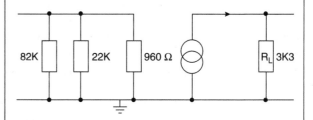

Figure 7.83

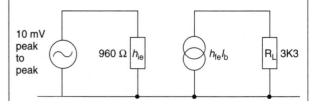

Figure 7.84

The circuit in Figure 7.83 simplifies to Figure 7.84. We have

$$\text{voltage gain} = \frac{V_{\text{out}}}{V_{\text{in}}} = \frac{I_c R_L}{10 \text{ mV}}$$

Now

$$I_c = h_{fe} I_b$$

and

$$I_b = \frac{V_{\text{in}}}{h_{ie}} = \frac{10 \text{ mV}}{960 \text{ Ω}} = 10.42 \text{ μA}$$

$$\therefore I_c = 55 \times 10.42 \,\mu\text{A} = 573.1 \,\mu\text{A}$$

$$\text{voltage gain} = \frac{V_{\text{out}}}{V_{\text{in}}}$$

$$= \frac{573.1 \times 10^{-6} \times 3.3 \times 10^3}{10\,\text{mV}}$$

$$= 189$$

$$V_{\text{out}} = I_c R_L$$

$$= 573.1 \times 10^{-6} \times 3.3 \times 10^3$$

$$= 189\,\text{V peak to peak}$$

Check using

$$A_v = \frac{h_{\text{fe}} R_L}{h_{\text{ie}}} = \frac{55 \times 3.3 \times 10^3}{960} = 189$$

$$V_{\text{out}} = V_{\text{in}} \times A_v$$

$$= 10\,\text{mV} \times 189$$

$$= 1.89\,\text{V peak to peak}$$

A two-stage amplifier

If an amplifier is cascaded (i.e. one stage follows another) the first amplifier's output feeds the second amplifier (Figure 7.85).

In equivalent circuit terms the input impedance of circuit 2 will appear in parallel with the collector load resistor of circuit 1 and this will affect the value of R_L. This is shown in Figure 7.86.

The gain of stage 1 when it feeds stage 2 can be calculated from

$$\frac{h_{\text{fe}} R_L}{h_{\text{ie}}}$$

where R_L is now the collector load in parallel with the input impedance of the following stage, i.e. R_L is in parallel with h_{ie_2}:

$$R_L = \frac{R_{L_1} h_{\text{ie}_2}}{R_{L_1} + h_{\text{ie}_2}}$$

Using the values in Figures 7.85 and 7.86 the gain of stage 1 when it feeds stage 2 will be

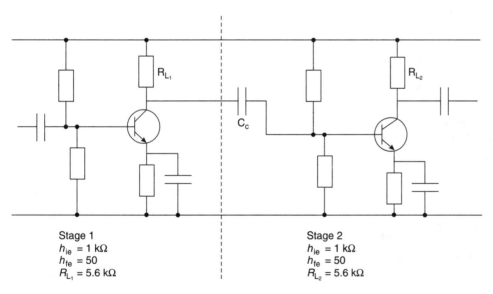

Stage 1
$h_{\text{ie}} = 1\,\text{k}\Omega$
$h_{\text{fe}} = 50$
$R_{L_1} = 5.6\,\text{k}\Omega$

Stage 2
$h_{\text{ie}} = 1\,\text{k}\Omega$
$h_{\text{fe}} = 50$
$R_{L_2} = 5.6\,\text{k}\Omega$

Figure 7.85

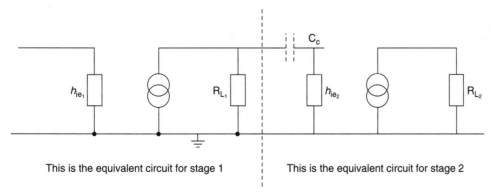

This is the equivalent circuit for stage 1   This is the equivalent circuit for stage 2

Figure 7.86

$$A_v \text{ (stage 1)} = \frac{h_{fe} R_L}{h_{ie}}$$

where

$$R_L = \frac{R_{L_1} h_{ie_2}}{R_{L_1} + h_{ie_2}}$$

$$= \frac{5.6 \times 10^3 \times 1 \times 10^3}{5.6 \times 10^3 + 1 \times 10^3}$$

$$= \frac{5.6 \times 10^6}{6.6 \times 10^3}$$

$$= 848 \, \Omega$$

Therefore

$$A_v \text{ (stage 1)} = \frac{50 \times 848}{1 \times 10^3}$$

$$= 42.4$$

However, if stage 1 was disconnected from stage 2 it would work only into its own collector load resistor and its gain would rise to

$$A_v = \frac{h_{fe} R_{L_1}}{h_{ie}}$$

$$= \frac{50 \times 5.6 \times 10^3}{1 \times 10^3}$$

$$= 280$$

Thus, the gain of the first stage of a cascaded amplifier will drop when it is connected to the second stage. Overall, however, the two-stage circuit will provide greater gain than each individual stage.

The Thévenin equivalent circuit of an amplifier

We have used the *h* parameter equivalent circuit to analyse how an amplifier operates under AC

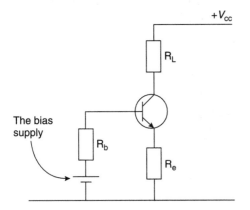

Figure 7.87

conditions and in doing this we ignored the bias supply.

The Thévenin equivalent circuit of an amplifier deals with voltages whereas the Norton model deals with currents. The equivalent circuit therefore has the bias supplies replaced by voltage generators.

Bias supply as a generator

If we once again look at a common-emitter amplifier with potential divider biasing the base

Guided example

A common-emitter transistor amplifier is shown in Figure 7.88(a). Draw the Thévenin equivalent circuit and calculate the values of the components it contains.

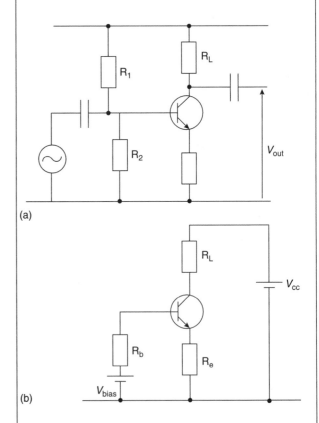

Figure 7.88   (a) Common-emitter transistor amplifier; (b) Thévenin equivalent circuit

The main part of this problem is to calculate the value of the bias supply resistance (see Figure 7.88(b)). This can be achieved by using the product over sum rule. That is,

$$R_b = \frac{R_1 \times R_2}{R_1 + R_2}$$

bias can be reduced to a DC generator in series with its resistance R_b and the collector supply connected via its load resistor R_L. The emitter resistor appears un-decoupled as the equivalent circuit is concerned with DC conditions only (Figure 7.87).

The value of R_b is the parallel equivalent of bias resistors R_1 and R_2 and can be calculated from

$$R_b = \frac{R_1 \times R_2}{R_1 + R_2}$$

The values of R_L and R_e are as in the circuit.

The equivalent circuit of the field effect transistor at the input (Norton model)

You have now seen that amplifier design principles do not change whether we consider conventional transistors or FETs. It is therefore possible to draw the equivalent circuit for an FET. In fact, in some ways it is simpler than the circuit we worked out for the bipolar transistor.

The signal voltage that we apply to the input of the FET is developed across the resistor connected between the gate and 0 V (Figure 7.89). This resistor is in parallel with the input impedance of the FET. We have shown the latter as dotted lines as it is not a physical component that you can find in the circuit.

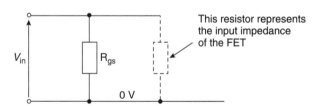

Figure 7.89

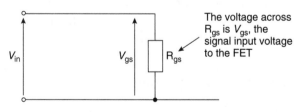

Figure 7.90

At this point it is handy to do a little bit of simplification. As the input impedance of the FET is so much higher than the value of the gate resistor we can ignore the former and assume that the input of the circuit appears as in Figure 7.90.

The equivalent circuit at the output

The amount that an FET amplifies a signal is set by the value of gm. This is the relationship between the change in signal voltage at the gate and the effect that it has on the level of drain current. Mathematically we said

$$gm = \frac{\Delta I_d}{\Delta V_{gs}}$$

> Sometimes component suppliers quote gm in its alternative form Y_{fs}.

This can, of course, be rewritten as

$$I_d = gm \; V_{gs}$$

The current that flows via the load resistor of the FET is I_d and so the output side of the transistor can be redrawn as in Figure 7.91. Putting the two sides of the equivalent circuit together it now appears as in Figure 7.92.

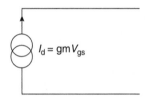

Figure 7.91

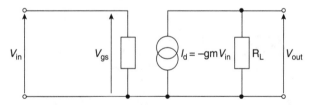

Figure 7.92

We can use this to perform calculations that we have previously made using the output characteristic and once again we produce a short formula that will enable us to find the voltage gain without too much trouble:

$$gain = \frac{V_{out}}{V_{in}} = \frac{I_d R_L}{V_{gs}}$$

Substituting for I_d gives

$$\frac{V_{out}}{V_{in}} = \frac{gm \; V_{gs} R_L}{V_{gs}}$$

> $\therefore$ voltage gain $= - \, gm \, R_L$

(The minus sign signifies phase inversion.) This formula is one of the most useful to use when considering FET amplifiers.

7.4 Types of feedback

Positive feedback

At one time or another you may well have been near an amplifier or in a situation where a public address system is being used and the microphone is allowed to come too close to a loudspeaker. The result is shown in Figure 7.93(a). The signal from the loudspeaker enters the microphone, is amplified and appears at the output of the loudspeaker where it immediately enters the microphone and so the

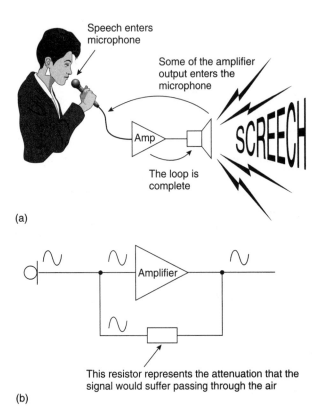

(a)

(b)

Figure 7.93   Positive feedback

process repeats. This is given the term feedback as the signal is applied (or fed back) from the output to the input.

From a technical point of view it is clear that the phase of the signal that is fed back is the same as that at the input, and this is shown in Figure 7.93(b). The total signal into the amplifier from the microphone is therefore the *sum* of the original signal plus the signal fed back. This type of loop is known as **positive feedback**.

The output of the amplifier as a result of a positive feedback loop rapidly grows in amplitude until it is limited to its maximum possible level, which is determined by the supply voltage. To us it is a howl and the noise is terrible!

However, positive feedback is useful to have in a circuit as all oscillators are based on the concept.

Negative feedback

At first sight the situation shown in Figure 7.94 appears to be exactly the same as the positive feedback arrangement that we have just discussed. Look closely, however, and you will see that the difference between the two diagrams is that the phase of the fed-back signal is opposite to that of the input signal.

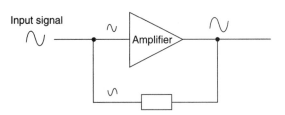

Figure 7.94   The concept of negative feedback

If we assume that only a proportion of the output signal is applied in anti-phase back to the input of the amplifier it will subtract from the input signal and the output of the amplifier will be less than it would have been if no signal was fed back. This loop is known as **negative feedback**.

A mathematical approach

What we have just described can be put into mathematical terms quite easily. With a bit of algebra we can use the final equation to predict how an amplifier will behave with negative feedback.

The situation is outlined in Figure 7.95. Note that the reducing block, or attenuator, introduces a phase change between the signal into it and the signal that is fed back. The amount by which the signal is reduced by the attenuator is given the

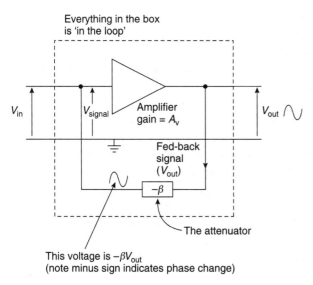

Figure 7.95

notation β. For example, if β reduced by half (or 50%) and if 1 V was applied to the attenuator the output would be

$$0.5 \times 1 \text{ V} = 0.5 \text{ V}$$

It is also possible to express the feedback decimal as a fraction and for this reason β is sometimes known as the feedback fraction. For example, for $\beta = 20\%$, as a decimal $\beta = 0.2$ and as a fraction $\beta = 1/5$.

Using Figure 7.95, the loop has an overall gain of A_v' were

$$A_v' = \frac{V_{out}}{V_{in}}$$

The signal applied to the amplifier input terminals is V_{signal}. But V_{signal} is the voltage applied to the loop (V_{in}) minus the voltage fed back in anti-phase:

$$V_{signal} = V_{in} - \beta V_{out}$$

The amplifier gain is the output voltage divided by the actual input voltage. Therefore

$$\text{amplifier gain} = A_v = \frac{V_{out}}{V_{in}}$$

Substituting for $V_{signal} = V_{in} - \beta V_{out}$ gives

$$A_v = \frac{V_{out}}{V_{in} - \beta V_{out}}$$

$$\therefore A_v(V_{in} - \beta V_{out}) = V_{out}$$

$$A_v V_{in} - \beta V_{out} A_v = V_{out}$$

$$A_v V_{in} = V_{out} + \beta V_{out} A_v$$

$$= V_{out}(1 + \beta A_v)$$

$$\therefore A_v = \frac{V_{out}}{V_{in}}(1 + \beta A_v)$$

$$\frac{V_{out}}{V_{in}} = \frac{A_v}{1 + \beta A_v}$$

As A_v' (loop gain) is equal to V_{out}/V_{in}, when (negative) feedback is applied to an amplifier of gain A_v the loop gain becomes

$$A_v' = \frac{A_v}{1 + \beta A_v}$$

This equation shows us quite clearly that the gain of the amplifier will be reduced when a proportion of the output signal is fed back in anti-phase to the input.

If the product βA_v is much greater than 1 the equation can be modified to

$$A_v' = \frac{A_v}{-\beta A_v}$$

(note that the A_v cancel) and from this it follows that the gain of the amplifier is determined by

$$A_v' = \frac{1}{-\beta}$$

> An amplifier in a loop situation can have its overall gain controlled by the feedback fraction.

Guided example

The amplifier in Figure 7.96 has a gain of 100 with the switch open (i.e. the open loop gain). When the feedback loop is brought into circuit by closing the switch, 20% of the output signal is fed back in anti-phase to the input. Calculate the gain of the amplifier under this condition.

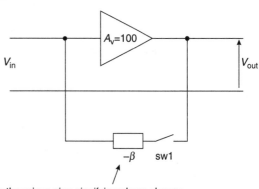

Note the minus sign signifying phase change

Figure 7.96

gain without feedback $= A_v = 100$

feedback fraction $= 20\% = \dfrac{20}{100} = 0.2$

The gain with feedback is

$$A_v' = \dfrac{A_v}{1 + \beta A_v}$$

$$= \dfrac{100}{1 + (0.2 \times 100)}$$

$$= \dfrac{100}{1 + 20} = \dfrac{100}{21} = 4.76$$

Summary

The general feedback formula for an amplifier is

$$A_v' = \dfrac{A_v}{1 \pm \beta A_v}$$

where A_v is the gain with no feedback, A_v' is the gain with feedback and β is the feedback fraction.

If the sign is negative it indicates positive feedback. If it is positive it indicates negative feedback.

Changing the phase of the fed-back signal (positive feedback)

Look again at Figure 7.95 and the subsequent derivation of the feedback formulae but now change the sign of the feedback fraction so that it is positive (i.e. no phase change occurs). We have

gain with feedback $= A_v' = \dfrac{V_{out}}{V_{in}}$

gain $= A_v = \dfrac{V_{out}}{V_{signal}}$

$$V_{signal} = V_{in} + \beta V_{out}$$

Note the positive sign as the phase has not been changed.

$$\therefore A_v = \dfrac{V_{out}}{V_{signal}}$$

$$= \dfrac{V_{out}}{V_{in} + \beta V_{out}}$$

$$A_v(V_{in} + \beta V_{out}) = V_{out}$$

$$A_v V_{in} = V_{out} - \beta V_{out} A_v$$

$$= V_{out}(1 - \beta A_v)$$

$$A_v = \dfrac{V_{out}}{V_{in}}(1 - \beta A_v)$$

$$A_v' = \dfrac{V_{out}}{V_{in}} = \dfrac{A_v}{1 - \beta A_v}$$

Assuming that the product βA_v lies between 0 and 1 (but is not 1) a situation now exists where the gain of the amplifier increases and we therefore have positive feedback.

Oscillators

An oscillator is a circuit which produces an AC waveform that is of constant frequency and amplitude. No input other than the power supply is applied to the circuit. Positive feedback is a requirement for oscillation to take place.

The effects of negative feedback

Gain and bandwidth

We have already seen that the gain decreases when negative feedback is applied. This has the effect of increasing the bandwidth of the amplifier, i.e. the gain–bandwidth product holds true.

Stabilisation

The circuit characteristics alter with negative feedback so that the closed loop gain is largely determined by the feedback fraction β. Instability of the amplifier due to ageing of components is therefore prevented and oscillation is unlikely to occur.

Distortion

Distortion is also reduced with negative feedback and the general feedback formula can be used to show this:

$$D' = \dfrac{D}{1 + \beta A_v}$$

where D is the distortion with no feedback and D' is the distortion with feedback.

Input and output impedances

When a circuit is modified to include negative feedback the output of the amplifier no longer develops solely in the load. This means that the output impedance must alter. Similarly, the input impedance is affected by the feedback network and this too changes.

Whether the input and output impedances rise or fall is determined by the method of applying negative feedback.

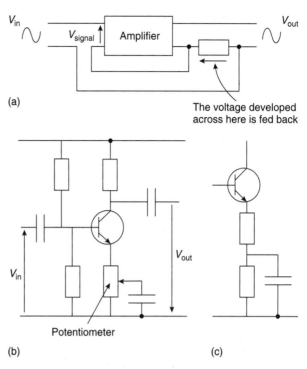

(a)

The voltage developed across here is fed back

Potentiometer

(b)   (c)

Figure 7.97   (a) Series current feedback; (b) the potentiometer partly decouples the emitter resistor, introducing negative feedback; (c) an alternative method is to split the emitter resistor into two halves and decouple one half

---

Guided example

An amplifier has a gain of 220 with no feedback and introduces distortion of 10%. If 12% of the output is applied in anti-phase to the input calculate (a) the new loop gain of the circuit and (b) the modified distortion figure.

(a)   Using the formula

$$A_v' = \frac{A_v}{1 + \beta A_v}$$

with $A_v = 220$ and $\beta = 0.12$ (12%), the new loop gain is

$$A_v' = \frac{220}{1 + 0.12 \times 220}$$

$$= 8.02$$

(b)   The modified distortion figure is given by

$$D' = \frac{D}{1 + \beta A_v}$$

With $D = 0.1$ (10%), $\beta = 0.12$ and $A_v = 220$, we have

$$D' = \frac{0.1}{1 + 0.12 \times 220}$$

$$= 0.0036$$

$$= 0.36\%$$

Methods of achieving negative feedback

There are four principal ways of applying negative feedback and, although each of them achieves the same effect on gain etc., the alteration of impedances is determined by the circuit configuration used.

Series current feedback

The circuit in Figure 7.97 derives its fed-back voltage from the output current and applies it in series with the input.

Parallel current feedback

The fed-back signal is derived in the same manner as for series current feedback but is applied in parallel to the input (Figure 7.98).

Series voltage feedback

The output signal of the amplifier is tapped across a potential divider and the proportion of voltage obtained is applied in series to the input of the amplifier (Figure 7.99).

Parallel voltage feedback

The proportion of the output signal required is tapped in the same way as for series voltage feedback but is applied in series with the input (Figure 7.100).

Finally, it is worth remembering that most designers would rather develop an amplifier with two stages than have a high gain single stage with no negative feedback. It must be useful!

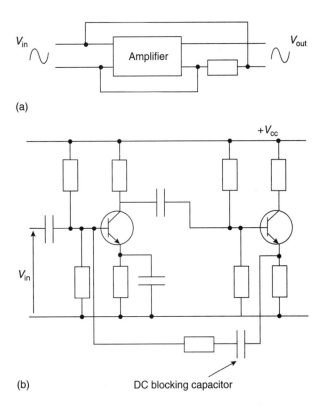

(a)

(b)   DC blocking capacitor

Figure 7.98   (a) Parallel current feedback; (b) practical circuit

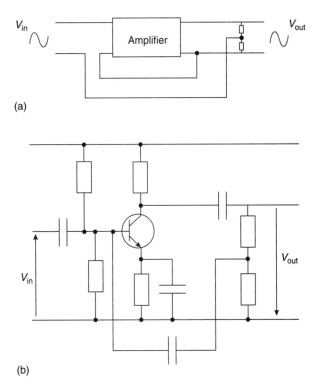

(a)

(b)

Figure 7.99   (a) Series voltage feedback; (b) practical circuit

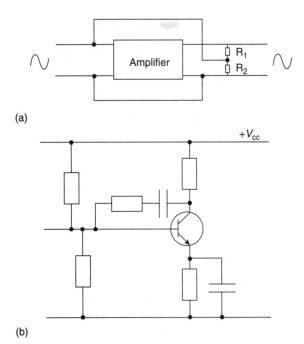

(a)

(b)

Figure 7.100   (a) Parallel voltage feedback; (b) practical circuit

Count Alessandro Giuseppe Antonio Anastaio Volta (1745–1827)

One of nine children, born in Lombardy to a noble family, Volta was appointed Professor of Physics in the High School at Como in 1774. He was fascinated by the new phenomenon of the age: **electricity**. It was Volta's early work on static electricity that led to the development of the capacitor. As he became more famous for his inventions he was made Professor at the University of Pavia in 1779. This is when he did his most important work. His friend Galvani had discovered experimentally that he could make muscles twitch by touching them two different metals. Volta took up this work and eventually produced the first electric battery. Without Volta's work there may not have been much of the electronics we know today. The great honour paid to Volta by his peers was to name the unit of electromotive force after him, and today we still use the **volt**.

Practical 7

The purpose of this practical is to prove that if the proportion of negative feedback is changed the gain of an amplifier will alter.

Construct the circuit in Figure 7.101. The amount of emitter resistance that is not decoupled can be altered by changing the setting of the variable resistor, i.e. we can adjust the proportion of series current feedback.

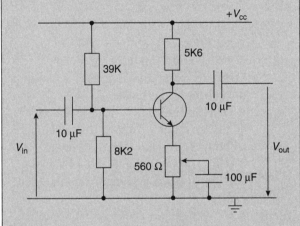

Figure 7.101

Condition for maximum gain

Apply an input signal of 1 kHz and adjust the slider of R_e so that maximum output signal is obtained. Vary the output of the signal generator until an undistorted output signal is seen on the oscilloscope and note the value of this.

Use this voltage and that of the input to calculate the gain of the amplifier:

$$\text{gain} = \frac{V_{out}}{V_{in}}$$

Now alter the setting of R_e until the output signal falls to approximately half of its maximum value. Once again use the value of this voltage to calculate the new gain of the circuit.

You now have two gain figures: one with no feedback and one with feedback. It is therefore possible to calculate the proportion of feedback applied by transposing the standard negative feedback formula. A_v is the figure with maximum output and A_v' is the figure when the output drops by 50%.

$$A_v' = \frac{A_v}{1 + \beta A_v}$$

$$\therefore A_v'(1 + \beta A_v) = A_v$$

$$\frac{A_v}{A_v'} = 1 + \beta A_v$$

$$\frac{A_v}{A_v'} - 1 = \beta A_v$$

$$\therefore \frac{A_v - A_v'}{A_v'} = \beta A_v$$

$$\beta = \frac{A_v - A_v'}{A_v A_v'}$$

Multiple choice questions

1 The opamp has
   (a)   low gain
   (b)   very low gain
   (c)   very high gain
   (d)   unity gain.

2 The opamp can be viewed as the following blocks assembled from input to output:
   (a)   high impedance differential amplifier → high gain amplifier → low impedance opamp
   (b)   low impedance differential amplifier → high gain differential amplifier → low gain opamp
   (c)   high impedance differential amplifier → low gain amplifier → high gain low impedance amplifier
   (d)   low impedance differential amplifier → low impedance amplifier → high gain output amplifier.

3 The gain of an opamp connected as a non-inverting amplifier can be expressed as
   (a) R_{out}/R_{in}
   (b) R_{in}/R_{out}
   (c) R_{in}/R_f
   (d) R_f/R_{in}.

4 The unity gain frequency of an opamp is
   (a)   10 kHz
   (b)   1000 kHz
   (c)   1000 MHz
   (d)   100 kHz.

5 Slew rate is
   (a)   change of time divided by change of voltage out
   (b)   a measure of how a rise of V_{in} causes amplification
   (c)   the maximum rate at which the output will change with varying V_{in}
   (d)   the maximum rate at which V_{out} will follow a change of V_{in}.

6 If 6 V is applied to the non-inverting terminal of an opamp and –6 V to the inverting terminal and the configuration is set for unity gain the output will be
   (a)   +6 V
   (b)   –6 V
   (c)   12 V
   (d)   0 V.

7 Offset voltage is easily controlled by
   (a)   adjusting supply voltage slightly using a 10 kΩ potentiometer
   (b)   using a 10 kΩ potentiometer between $-V_{cc}$ and the appropriate pins
   (c)   using a 10 kΩ potentiometer between $+V_{cc}$ and the appropriate pins
   (d)   none of these.

8 The common-mode rejection ratio of an opamp is important because
   (a)   it gives an indication of the opamp's ability to reject a voltage that is common to both input terminals
   (b)   it gives an indication of the opamp's ability to reject a voltage that is common to both input and output terminals
   (c)   it equals 10 log(voltage gain of signal applied to input terminals/common-mode gain)
   (d)   it is expressed in decibels and hence can easily be equated to the opamp gain.

9 Compensation components are added
   (a)   to prevent oscillation at low frequencies
   (b)   to allow for variations in supply voltages
   (c)   to reduce noise levels
   (d)   to aid impedance matching.

10 A typical opamp integrated circuit is
   (a)   147
   (b)   471
   (c)   741
   (d)   T03.

11 Which part of Figure 7.103 represents the response curve for the amplifier in Figure 7.102?

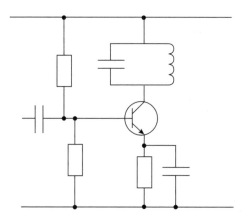

Figure 7.102

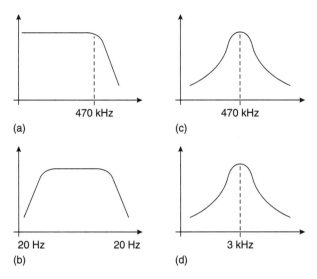

Figure 7.103

12 The load line points to be marked on the characteristic in Figure 7.104 for the circuit shown are

(a) 16 mA, 9 V
(b) 19 mA, 9 V
(c) 5 mA, 0 V
(d) 30 μA, 4.5 V.

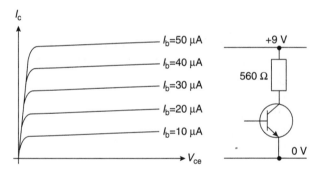

Figure 7.104

13 The value of C_1 in Figure 7.105 will be

(a) 176 μF
(b) 17.6 μF
(c) 1.76 μF
(d) 1.76 pF.

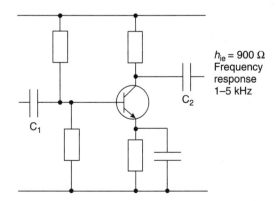

$h_{ie} = 900 \ \Omega$
Frequency response 1–5 kHz

Figure 7.105

14 If the voltages measured with respect to 0 V in Figure 7.106 are $x = 1.6$ V, $z = 1$ V, $y = 4.5$ V but there is no signal out of the amplifier a likely fault is

(a) C_3 short circuit
(b) C_2 short circuit
(c) C_1 open circuit
(d) C_3 open circuit.

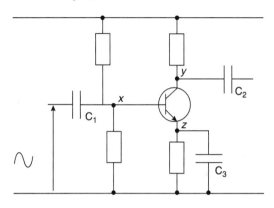

Figure 7.106

15 The load line point for the circuit in Figure 7.107 would be

(a) A
(b) B
(c) C
(d) D.

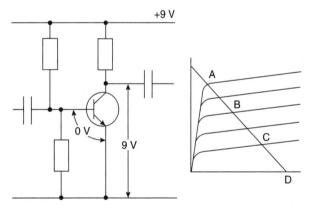

Voltages shown are quiescent

Figure 7.107

16 The circuit in Figure 7.108 can be used as

(a) a power amplifier
(b) a voltage amplifier
(c) a current attenuator
(d) a low impedance to high impedance matching circuit.

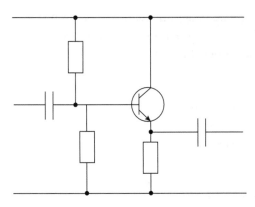

Figure 7.108

17 The circuit in Figure 7.109 is biased in
   (a)   class A
   (b)   class B
   (c)   class C
   (d)   class AB.

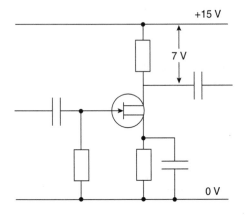

Figure 7.109

18 The circuit in Figure 7.110 will
   (a)   invert V_{out} by 90° with respect to V_{in}
   (b)   invert I_{out} by 0° with respect to I_{in}
   (c)   invert V_{out} by 360° with respect to V_{in}
   (d)   invert I_{out} by 180° with respect to V_{in}.

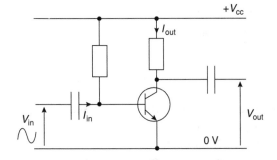

Figure 7.110

19 From Figure 7.111 the amplifier bandwidth is
   (a)   3.1 kHz
   (b)   3 kHz
   (c)   2.9 kHz
   (d)   1.5 kHz.

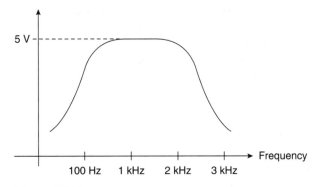

Figure 7.111

20 Upper frequency roll-off of a small signal
   amplifier is caused by
   (a)   low reactance of the coupling capacitors
   (b)   high impedance of the bias resistor's
         capacitance
   (c)   low value of the stray capacitance
   (d)   non-physical capacitance in the circuit.

21 The simplified equivalent circuit in Figure 7.112
   represents a single-stage bipolar transistor
   amplifier. The output of the constant-current
   generator is equal to
   (a) $h_{fe}I_b$
   (b) $h_{fe}I_e$
   (c) $h_{ie}I_b$
   (d) $h_{ie}I_c$.

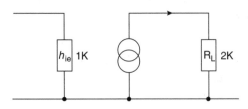

Figure 7.112

22 In Figure 7.113 the signal current that flows at
   the input of the amplifier is
   (a)   22.22 mA
   (b)   900 mA
   (c)   10 mA
   (d)   11.11 μA.

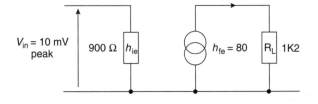

Figure 7.113

23 If the h_{fe} of the equivalent circuit in Figure 7.113 is 80 the collector current will be
   (a) 0.88 mA peak to peak
   (b) 0.88 mA peak
   (c) 1.2 mA peak
   (d) 80 μA peak.

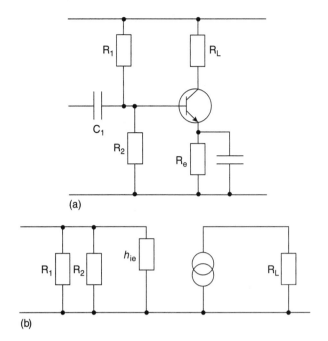

(a)

24 In the equivalent circuit in Figure 7.113 the signal voltage developed across the load will be
   (a) 1.2 V
   (b) 1.08 V
   (c) 0.8 V
   (d) 1.07 V.

(b)

Figure 7.114

25 Pick the following true statement. The transistor amplifier drawn in Figure 7.114(a) is represented by the simplified equivalent circuit of Figure 7.114(b). The bias resistors R_1 and R_2 may be ignored because
   (a) they are lower in value than h_{ie}
   (b) they are in parallel with C_1
   (c) they are very much larger than h_{ie}
   (d) their reactance is not frequency dependent.

26 One advantage of using an equivalent circuit is
   (a) the load impedance is constant
   (b) the amplifier frequency response is wide band
   (c) amplifier performance can be estimated without use of characteristics
   (d) the active device requires no supply.

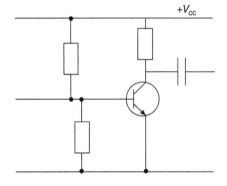

Figure 7.115

27 Which part of Figure 7.116 represents the Thévenin equivalent circuit for the amplifier circuit in Figure 7.115?

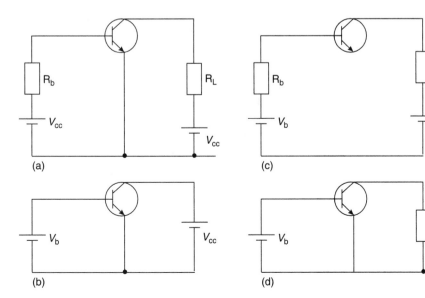

Figure 7.116

28 The equivalent circuit in Figure 7.117 is for
   (a) a bipolar transistor
   (b) a unipolar transistor
   (c) a stabilised transistor
   (d) a variable FET.

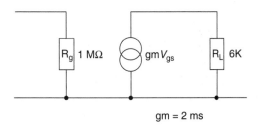

Figure 7.117

29 If the equivalent circuit in Figure 7.117 has an input voltage of 20 mV peak, the output voltage developed across the load will be
   (a) 120 mV peak
   (b) 480 mV peak
   (c) 240 mV peak to peak
   (d) 480 mV peak to peak.

30 The equivalent circuit in Figure 7.117 does not show the input impedance of the active device. This is because
   (a) it is very much smaller than V_{in}
   (b) it is very much larger than R_g
   (c) it is a constant-current generator
   (d) it has V_{dd} connected to it.

31 In Figure 7.118 the potential of R_2 will be approximately
   (a) 1.6 V
   (b) 0.6 V
   (c) 10 V
   (d) 1 V.

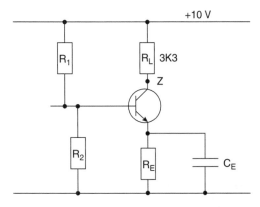

Figure 7.118

32 In Figure 7.118 the value of R_E will be approximately
   (a) 1.5K
   (b) 1K

(c) 3K3
(d) 0.73K.

33 In Figure 7.118 the quiescent base–emitter bias will be
   (a) 0 V
   (b) 0.6 V
   (c) 1.6 V
   (d) 3.2 V.

34 In Figure 7.118 the voltage between point Z and 0 V is found to be 0.3 V. A possible cause could be
   (a) R_E open circuit
   (b) R_L short circuit
   (c) R_L open circuit
   (d) C_E short circuit.

35 One feature of the bias configuration shown in Figure 7.119 is
   (a) it lacks stabilisation
   (b) it automatically compensates for changes of transistor
   (c) thermal runaway protection is not required
   (d) h_{FE} is reduced.

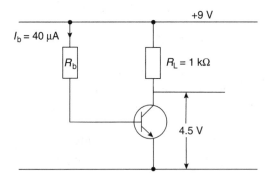

Figure 7.119

36 The current gain of the transistor in Figure 7.119 will be approximately
   (a) 112
   (b) 40
   (c) 100
   (d) 150.

37 The purpose of R_s in Figure 7.120 is
   (a) to protect against thermal runaway
   (b) to decrease negative gate–source bias
   (c) to bias the gate–source to the required voltage
   (d) to provide negative feedback.

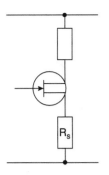

Figure 7.120

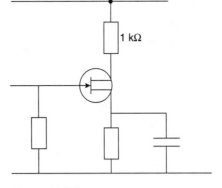

Figure 7.121

38 An FET has a gm of 20 ms. If the circuit
arrangement is as shown in Figure 7.121 the
voltage gain of the stage will be approximately
(a) 21
(b) 2100
(c) 20
(d) 1900.

40 Which of the circuits in Figure 7.122 are of a
small signal JFET amplifier?

39 An FET can be used as a variable resistor
where
(a) high power is dissipated
(b) electronic control is required
(c) thyristor control is included in series
(d) a low impedance is required.

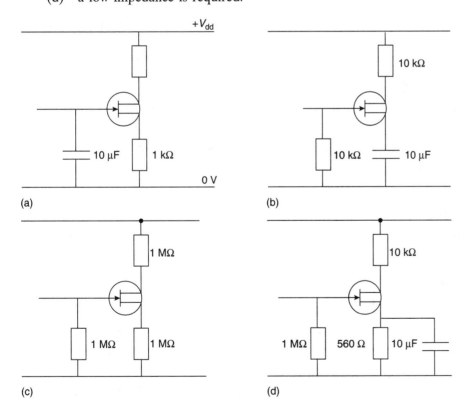

Figure 7.122

8

Digital electronics

8.1 Number systems

When we look at the number systems with which we count and calculate we notice two things about their structure:

(a) the number of digits we use;
(b) the weight, or significance, that each digit has by virtue of its position (i.e. the column it's in).

The number of digits in a system determines the system's **base** or **radix** and the value of each column is determined by that base. The best way to see this is to look at a system we already know.

The decimal system (or denary system)

The decimal system uses *ten* digits (0 to 9) and is therefore a base 10 system. What each of these digits represents depends on the column in which it appears. The significance of each column goes up in powers of 10.

A multi-digit number really means the sum of the powers of 10 with each power weighted by the digit in its column, e.g. 231 represents

$$1 \times 10^0 + 3 \times 10^1 + 2 \times 10^2$$

In this system $10^0 = 1$, $10^1 = 10$, $10^2 = 100$, $10^3 = 1000$ and so on, so we have $10 + 30 + 200 = 231$.

Note that the number in the right-hand column is the **least significant** number and the number in the left-hand column is the **most significant** number.

This will hold true for all the number systems we consider.

Binary numbers

The simplest operation for an electronic circuit is switching. A switch has two possible states – ON or OFF. In digital circuits, including computers, we use very large numbers of high speed switching circuits connected in particular ways to perform various operations.

In order to represent and analyse these circuits we need a system of arithmetic which can be entirely represented by *two states*. The binary system is such a system.

As a base 2 system it requires two digits and uses 0 or 1. Each column in the system is raised by a power of 2 as we move to the left (just like the decimal system is with tens).

For example, 1101_2 has a decimal value of

$$\begin{array}{cccc} 2^3 & 2^2 & 2^1 & 2^0 \\ 1 & 1 & 0 & 1 \end{array} = 8 + 4 + 0 + 1 = 13_{10}$$

Thus $1101_2 = 13_{10}$
Try another one, 1101101_2:

$$\begin{array}{ccccccc} 2^6 & 2^5 & 2^4 & 2^3 & 2^2 & 2^1 & 2^0 \\ 1 & 1 & 0 & 1 & 1 & 0 & 1 \end{array}$$

Thus

$$\begin{aligned} 1101101_2 &= 64 + 32 + 0 + 8 + 4 + 0 + 1 \\ &= 109_{10} \end{aligned}$$

In practice the binary digits 1 and 0 represent the switch states ON and OFF or voltage levels high and low and we refer to them as logic states or logic levels.

The 0 and 1 in this system are the two **binary digits**. These are called **bits**. Thus any binary number ranges from the most significant bit (MSB) to the least significant bit (LSB).

Binary count

To see how we count up in binary just consider the first few numbers and remember the system we use in decimal – see Table 8.1.

Table 8.1

Decimal	Binary
0	0
1	1
2	10
3	11
4	100
5	101
6	110
7	111
8	1000
9	1001
10	1010
11	1011
12	1100
13	1101
14	1110
15	1111
16	10000
17	10001
18	10010
19	10011
20	10100
21	10101 and so on . . .

It is worth noting, at this stage, that we can work out the maximum decimal number it is possible to represent with a given number of bits. Look at the list in Table 8.1 and you will see that

with 2 bits we can represent 4 states 0 to 3
with 3 bits we can represent 8 states 0 to 7
with 4 bits we can represent 16 states 0 to 15

The general case is that with N bits we can represent 2^N combinations of 0 and 1. Since 0 is the first state, the largest decimal number we can represent is $2^N - 1$. For example with an 8-bit binary number we could represent decimal numbers from 0 to 255 ($2^8 = 256$).

Conversions

Clearly we need to be able to convert between binary and decimal values. Most calculators provide these conversions for us nowadays but, in fact, they are easily performed on paper.

Decimal to binary

The conversion from decimal to binary can be done mathematically by dividing the decimal number by 2 and noting the remainder and repeating this on each successive quotient. For example, to convert the decimal 107:

Division	Quotient	Remainder
107/2	53	1
53/2	26	1
26/2	13	0
13/2	6	1
6/2	3	0
3/2	1	1
1/2	0	1

Thus $107_{10} = 1101011_2$.

There are two things to note at this point:

(a) Keep dividing by 2 until the quotient is zero.
(b) The most significant bit of the binary number is the *last* remainder.

Now let's try converting 1255_{10}:

1255/2	627	1	LSB
627/2	313	1	
313/2	156	1	
156/2	78	0	
78/2	39	0	
39/2	19	1	
19/2	9	1	
9/2	4	1	
4/2	2	0	
2/2	1	0	
1/2	0	1	MSB

Thus $1255_{10} = 10011100111_2$.

Binary to decimal

The binary to decimal conversion is a very simple process of adding the values of the columns in which a 1 occurs, giving each column its value according to its position. This is best seen by example.

Something which you may have noticed about our binary numbers is the value of 2^{10}. This is 1024, which is as close to 1000 as we can get in a binary column. This is often referred to as 1 binary k (kilo or thousand). Thus in memory systems, for example, when we say 4k of memory we really mean 4×1024. Normally 1k can be treated as a decimal thousand but when we deal in large numbers (several megabits) we should remember that we have 24 extra locations for every 1k and this can become a significant amount in large memory systems.

Guided examples

1   1101010

Allocate the powers of 2 for each column present. Then sum the columns in which a 1 is present.

```
1   2   4   8    16  32  64
0   1   0   1    0   1   1   = 64 + 32 + 8 + 2
                            = 106
```

2   11101101001

```
1  2  4  8  16  32  64  128  256  512  1024
1  0  0  1  0   1   1   0    1    1    1
```

$$= 1024 + 512 + 256 + 64 + 32 + 8 + 1$$

$$= 1897$$

3   101010101

```
1  2  4  8  16  32  64  128  256
1  0  1  0  1   0   1   0    1
```

$$= 256 + 64 + 16 + 4 + 1$$

$$= 341$$

See if you get the right answers to these:

4   1101

5   111001101

6   00010

7   1000

8   11111

[*Answers* **4** 13   **5** 461   **6** 2   **7** 8   **8** 31]

8.2 Boolean algebra, logic gates and truth tables

Basic laws of Boolean algebra

The mid-nineteenth-century mathematician G. Boole invented a system of algebra for the mathematical analysis of logic. Today we use his Boolean algebra to express the functions of our logic gates in digital electronic circuits, but students familiar with the theory of sets will recognise much of the arithmetic which today electronics engineers think of as their own.

We can break down the logic functions used in electronics into three fundamental types and then use combinations of these to generate other functions.

The AND function

AND is denoted in Boolean algebra by a dot between the two relevant variables. For example,

> a AND *b* AND *c* is written as *a.b.c*

If we examine the truth table for the AND function we see that an output of logic 1 is only obtained when all the inputs are present as logic 1 (in positive logic 1 is represented by the more positive of two possible voltage levels). Thus if the function is

$$F = a.b.c$$

F is only at logic 1 when *a* AND *b* AND *c* are at logic 1. The truth table (Table 8.2) holds true for any number of inputs.

The AND function may be thought of as acting like multiplication upon the variables.

The OR function

OR is denoted in Boolean algebra by a plus sign between the relevant variables. So

> a OR *b* OR *c* is written as *a + b + c*

The output of an OR gate would be at logic 1 if *a* OR *b* OR *c* were present or, indeed, any combination of the input variables.

Table 8.2

a	b	c	F
0	0	0	0
0	0	1	0
0	1	0	0
0	1	1	0
1	0	0	0
1	0	1	0
1	1	0	0
1	1	1	1

The function for a three-input OR gate would thus be

$$F = a + b + c$$

and Table 8.3 is the truth table.

Because we get a logic 1 output for any combination of inputs at logic 1 the gate is known as an inclusive OR gate.

OR may be considered as a summation of variables.

Table 8.3

a	b	c	F
0	0	0	0
0	0	1	1
0	1	0	1
0	1	1	1
1	0	0	1
1	0	1	1
1	1	0	1
1	1	1	1

The NOT function

The NOT function is signified in Boolean algebra by a line above the variable on which the function acts, e.g.

NOT a is written as $\bar{a}$

NOT is, in fact, an inversion of the variable. As an electronic operation NOT is simply a 180° phase shift of a variable. Thus NOT 1 is 0 and vice versa. This is demonstrated by the truth table:

$$F = \bar{a}$$

a	F
0	1
1	0

Note that NOT acts on a single variable.

By following an AND gate or an OR gate with a NOT gate we are able to produce the inverse of each function. NOT AND is called NAND and NOT OR is called NOR.

This is very useful in the implementation of circuits since we can produce any logic function using only NOR gates or, more commonly, only NAND gates, and for this reason they are known as universal logic gates.

The NOR function

As already explained the NOR function is the inverse of the OR function. In Boolean notation we see that

a NOR *b* NOR *c* is written as
$\overline{a + b + c}$

and as we would expect the function $F =$ has the truth table shown in Table 8.4.

Table 8.4

a	b	c	F
0	0	0	1
0	0	1	0
0	1	0	0
0	1	1	0
1	0	0	0
1	0	1	0
1	1	0	0
1	1	1	0

The NAND function

The NAND function gives us a truth table which is the inverse of the AND function. The operation may be thought of as NOT AND. In Boolean notation a NAND *b* NAND *c* is written $\overline{a.b.c}$

The function $F = \overline{a.b.c}$ has the truth table shown in Table 8.5.

Table 8.5

a	b	c	F
0	0	0	1
0	0	1	1
0	1	0	1
0	1	1	1
1	0	0	1
1	0	1	1
1	1	0	1
1	1	1	0

The exclusive OR function

The exclusive OR function gives us an output of logic 1 only when inputs *a* OR *b* are at logic 1. It gives a logic 0 output for any other condition, such as both inputs at logic 1. This is quite different from the case we considered earlier with the OR gate (inclusive OR).

This function can be generated in many different ways using the gates already considered but it is so useful that we have a special notation for it in Boolean algebra and it is available to us as a gate in its own right.

a EXOR *b* is written $a \oplus b$

$F = a \oplus b$

In order to evaluate logical statements and design circuits to implement these statements we need to know a few basic rules that apply to the manipulation of Boolean variables.

a	b	F
0	0	0
0	1	1
1	0	1
1	1	0

Some basic rules

Associative law

$$a.b.c = a.(c.b) = b.(a.c) \ldots$$

$$a + b + c = a + (b + c) = b + (a + c) \ldots$$

This is only true if the connections are the same, i.e.

$$a.b + \text{c} \neq a.(b + c)$$

Commutative law

$$a.b.c = a.c.b = b.a.c \ldots$$

$$a + b + c = b + c + a = c + a + b \ldots$$

Idempotent law

$$a.a.a.a = a$$

$$a + a + a + a + a = a$$

Complementation law

$$a.\bar{a} = 0 \qquad a + \bar{a} = 1$$

Constant with a variable

$$a.0 = 0 \qquad a + 0 = a$$

$$a.1 = a \qquad a + 1 = 1$$

Absorption law

$$a.(a + b) = a \qquad a + (a.b) = a$$

Distributive law

$$a.b + a.c = a.(b + c)$$

$$(a + b).(a + c) = a + (b.c)$$

Additional simplification rules

$$a.(\bar{a} + b) = a.b$$

$$a + \bar{a}.b = a + b$$

$$(a + b).(\bar{a} + c) = a.c + \bar{a}.b$$

$$(a + c).(\bar{a} + b) = a.b + \bar{a}.c$$

DeMorgan's law DeMorgan's law will prove to be very useful later in your studies and can be summarised as 'break the line and change the sign'.

$$\overline{a + b} = \bar{a}.\bar{b} \qquad \overline{a.b} = \bar{a} + \bar{b}$$

$$\bar{a}.b = \overline{a + \bar{b}} \qquad a + \bar{b} = \overline{\bar{a}b}$$

Sum of products We have already mentioned that AND is like a *product* of variables and OR is like a *sum* of variables. When a Boolean function is expressed as a collection of ANDed terms ORed together the expression is said to be in sum of product or **minterm** form. This is particularly useful since this is the form most easily derived from the truth table.

Function from a truth table   To obtain a minterm expression from a truth table we simply note each combination of input variables for which the output, or function, is at logic 1. The function is then described by one of these combinations OR another.

Table 8.6

a	b	c	F	Notes
0	0	0	0	
0	0	1	0	
0	1	0	1	$\bar{a}.b.\bar{c}$
0	1	1	0	
1	0	0	1	$a.\bar{b}.\bar{c}$
1	0	1	1	$a.\bar{b}.c$
1	1	0	0	
1	1	1	0	

For example, from Table 8.6

$$F = \bar{a}.b.\bar{c} + a.\bar{b}.\bar{c} + a.\bar{b}.c$$

As another example, from Table 8.7

$$F = \bar{a}.b.\bar{c} + \bar{a}.b.c + a.\bar{b}.\bar{c} + a.b.\bar{c}$$

Table 8.7

a	b	c	F
0	0	0	0
0	0	1	0
0	1	0	1
0	1	1	1
1	0	0	1
1	0	1	0
1	1	0	1
1	1	1	0

Positive logic

So far we have only considered the arithmetic and representation of our logic. Now we need to see how we may implement the logic electronically.

With the positive logic type of system the logic 0 is represented by the least positive of the two voltage levels (often 0 V) and the logic 1 is represented by the more positive voltage (Figure 8.1).

The precise voltage levels vary with the type of technology used to produce the gate.

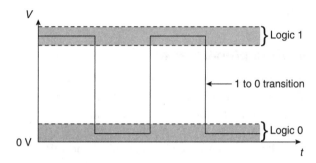

Figure 8.1

Negative logic

In the negative logic case the logic 1 is represented by the less positive of the two available logic levels (Figures 8.2 and 8.3).

Note that both voltages may be positive or negative in either type of logic. All that matters to the definition is whether the more positive represents 1 or 0. For now we shall only consider positive logic.

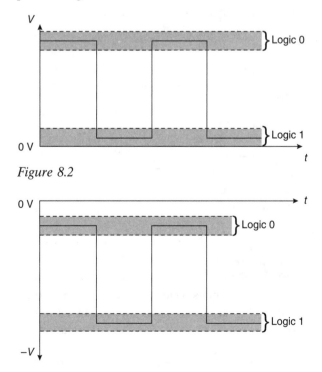

Figure 8.2

Figure 8.3

Universal logic

Both NAND and NOR are sometimes referred to as universal logic since any logic function at all can be implemented using only NAND or only NOR gates.

Manufacturers of integrated circuits provide chips with multiple gates, e.g. six NAND gates to a single package. Also, for reasons of manufacturing technology it is cheaper to fabricate some gates than others in integrated circuit form. It is thus common to see circuits produced in NAND only form.

NAND implementation

Converting from one form of logic to NAND is where we can really see the benefit of DeMorgan's law. For example, let's convert the following function to NAND only: $F = a.b + a.c + \bar{a}.b$.

We know that we need to get rid of the OR signs but we don't have any lines to break. We also know that double inversion doesn't alter the logic. So:

$$F = a.b + a.c + \bar{a}.b = \overline{\overline{a.b + a.c + \bar{a}.b}}$$

Now we can apply DeMorgan's law:

$$F = \overline{\overline{a.b} \cdot \overline{a.c} \cdot \overline{\bar{a}.b}}$$

This expression contains only NAND and so a circuit can be produced using only NAND (Figure 8.4).

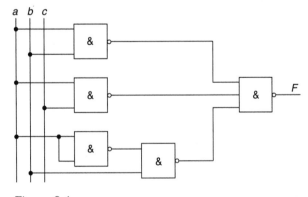

Figure 8.4

Logic gates

The switching circuits which we use to perform the logic functions are called gates. As we saw earlier these switches are two-state devices so operating in binary is logical.

Although there are standard symbols for the gates which perform our logical operations many manufacturers use a mixture of different symbols, the most common being the American style.

Each gate is designed such that it will only produce an output (logic 1) for given combinations of inputs (set at logic 1). Each gate is named after the function it performs and can be defined by its truth table.

For convenience each gate will be considered as a two-input device but in practice multiple inputs are available.

AND gate

The AND gate operates in a fashion similar to a series switch circuit where each switch represents one input variable (Figure 8.5).

As we can see from the switch circuit the gate output will only go high when *all* the inputs are high.

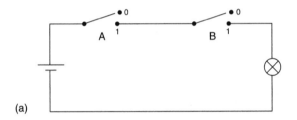

(a)

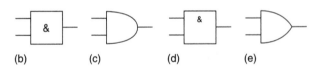

(b)   (c)   (d)   (e)

Figure 8.5   (a) Equivalent switch circuit of an AND gate. (b)–(e) Common symbols used for AND gates: (b) British Standards Institution; (c) old German standard; (d) new German Standard; (e) American Standards Association

Boolean expression $F = a.b$

Truth table

a	b	F
0	0	0
0	1	0
1	0	0
1	1	1

OR gate

Again the OR gate could be represented as a switch circuit but this time the switches are in parallel (Figure 8.6).

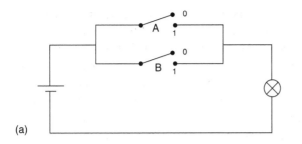

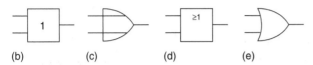

(a)

(b)   (c)   (d)   (e)

Figure 8.6   (a) Equivalent switch circuit of an OR gate. (b)–(e) Common symbols used for OR gates: (b) British Standards Insitution; (c) old German Standard; (d) new German Standard; (e) American Standards Association

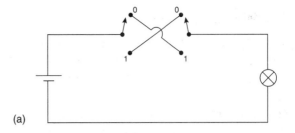

(a)

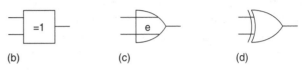

(b)   (c)   (d)

Figure 8.7   (a) Equivalent switch circuit of an EXOR gate. (b)–(d) Common symbols used for EXOR gates: (b) British Standards Institution; (c) German Standard; (d) American Standards Association

By considering the switch circuit we see that this gate will produce a logic 1 output when *any* of its inputs are at logic 1. Remember that this is an 'inclusive' OR function.

This gate is represented by the Boolean expression

$F = a + b$

The truth table for the two-input gate is

a	b	F
0	0	0
0	1	1
1	0	1
1	1	1

Exclusive OR gate (EXOR)

The exclusive OR gate is not so easily seen as a switching circuit but may be thought of as a type of two-way switch arrangement (Figure 8.7).

This gate removes the 'inclusive' output of the normal OR gate. It is an extremely useful gate for applications where one of two inputs is being selected in isolation, i.e. for determining conditions where inputs are *not* the same. It is often referred to as a 'non-equivalence' circuit.

The Boolean expression is

$F = a \oplus b$

and the truth table is

a	b	F
0	0	0
0	1	1
1	0	1
1	1	0

From the truth table we can see that the EXOR function is logically the same as $F = \bar{a}.b + a.\bar{b}$. This is often the way we see the EXOR function presented since this is how it appears from the truth table in 'sum of products' form. It is worth remembering so that we recognise it as EXOR.

The NOT gate

We can't show this function as a simple switch equivalent but by including a relay we can create the NOT effect (Figure 8.8). When the switch A is closed (logic 1) the coil is energised and the relay contact open circuits the lamp circuit. Thus the lamp is not lit (logic 0). When A is opened (logic 0) the contact is released and the lamp lights (logic 1).

The NOT gate inverts the input and for this reason the gate is often called an **inverter**. Note that since the function is a bit inversion the NOT gate is a single-input device.

The Boolean expression is

$F = \bar{a}$

and the truth table is

a	F
0	1
1	0

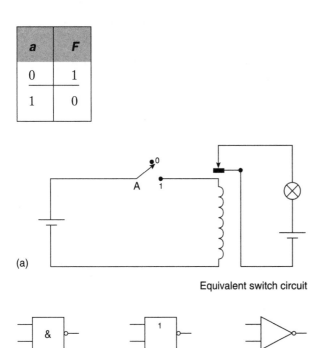

Equivalent switch circuit

(a)

(b)   (c)   (d)

Figure 8.8   (a) Equivalent switch circuit of a NOT gate. (b)–(d) Common symbols used for NOT gates: (b) British Standards Institution; (c) German Standard; (d) American Standards Association

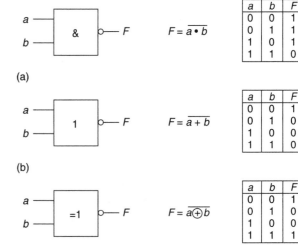

(a)

a	b	F
0	0	1
0	1	1
1	0	1
1	1	0

$F = \overline{a \cdot b}$

(b)

a	b	F
0	0	1
0	1	0
1	0	0
1	1	0

$F = \overline{a + b}$

(c)

a	b	F
0	0	1
0	1	0
1	0	0
1	1	1

$F = \overline{a \oplus b}$

Figure 8.9   (a) NAND gate; (b) NOR gate; (c) EXNOR gate

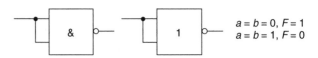

$a = b = 0, F = 1$
$a = b = 1, F = 0$

Figure 8.10

Double inversion

It should be noted that if we invert a variable twice we will not have to change the logic state of that variable. Remember that inversion means a phase shift on our pulse waveform of 180°. Thus if we double invert we shift a total of 360° (back to where we started). This is useful for introducing a line to break when we need to apply DeMorgan's law ($\overline{\overline{a}} = a$).

NAND, NOR, EXNOR gates

If we follow AND, OR or EXOR gates with an inverter they become NAND, NOR or EXNOR gates respectively. The inversion is denoted in all the various gate symbols by a small circle on the inverted terminal, in this case the output (Figure 8.9).

From the truth table we can see why the EXNOR gate is often called the **equivalence** circuit.

Since we often need to use the gates we have available to implement a given function it is worth noting that if we short circuit the inputs of a NAND or NOR gate the gate operates as a NOT gate (Figure 8.10).

Now we are in a position to consider a simple logic problem, draw a truth table, obtain the Boolean function and finally draw a circuit which will implement the function.

Practical 1

The purpose of this practical is to introduce the 7400, one of the most common transistor–transistor logic (TTL) integrated circuits. It may also be listed as 74LS00, 74HC00, 74HCT00. It is sometimes identified as a quad two-input NAND as it consists of four two-input gates (Figure 8.11).

When using any TTL integrated circuit it is important that the supply voltage is maintained at 5 V and connected with the correct polarity.

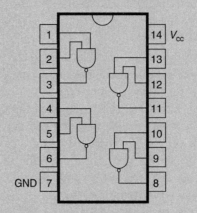

Figure 8.11   7400 transistor

Inverting using a NAND gate

The NOT gate gives an output that is the exact opposite of its input. In practice this can easily be achieved using a NAND gate (Figure 8.12).

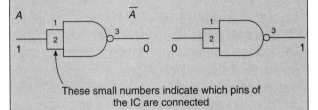

These small numbers indicate which pins of the IC are connected

Figure 8.12

Wire up the circuit as shown in Figure 8.13. When swA is *open* the input $A = 1$. The output indicated by the LED should show the opposite. The reverse applies. When swA is closed $A = 0$. The output now should equal 1.

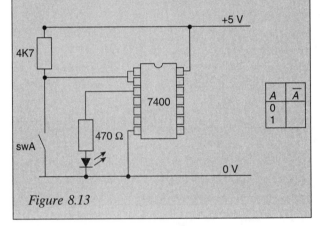

A	$\bar{A}$
0	
1	

Figure 8.13

Guided example

Consider a gas water heater. The gas valve supplying the burner needs to be opened when the hot tap on the bath is turned on or when the hot tap on the sink is turned on or both. Also, in the interest of safety, we don't want the gas to be supplied to the burners if the pilot light is out. We need to design the logic circuit which will provide the appropriate signal to enable the valve drive.

1   Allocate the variables: B, bath tap; S, sink tap; P, pilot light; G, gas valve. Logic 1 implies tap or valve open and pilot light on.

2   Draw the truth table (Table 8.8).

Table 8.8

B	S	P	G
0	0	0	0
0	0	1	0
0	1	0	0
0	1	1	1
1	0	0	0
1	0	1	1
1	1	0	0
1	1	1	1

3   Derive the function $F = \bar{B}.S.P + B.\bar{S}.P + B.S.P$.

4   Draw the circuit – Figure 8.14.

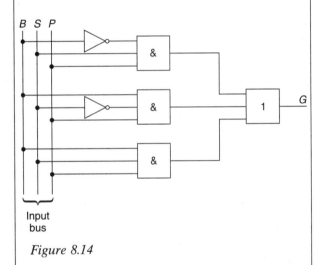

Input bus

Figure 8.14

Practical 2

OR function from NAND gates

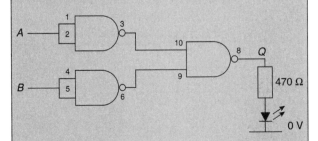

Figure 8.15   Circuit diagram for Practical 2; if the LED lights then $Q = 1$; if the LED does not light then $Q = 2$

The purpose of this practical is to demonstrate how an OR function can be obtained from interconnecting NAND gates. Once again we are using a 7400. Figure 8.15 gives the circuit diagram and Figure 8.16 the wiring diagram.

If swA is open, $A = 1$; if swA is closed, $A = 0$.

If swB is open, $B = 1$; if swB is closed, $B = 0$.

Alter the settings of A and B to simulate the input conditions to the gates. Then complete the truth table.

Now use the last gate of the 7400, between pins 13, 12 and 11, to invert the output of the combination, thereby giving a NOR function (Figure 8.17).

A	B	Q
0	0	
0	1	
1	0	
1	1	

A	B	Q
0	0	
0	1	
1	0	
1	1	

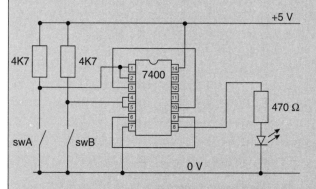

Figure 8.16   Wiring diagram for Practical 2

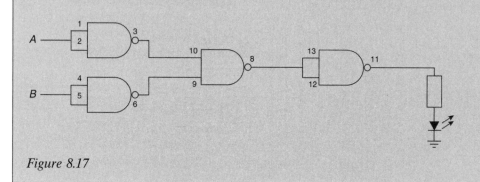

Figure 8.17

Practical 3

EXOR from NAND

This exercise is designed to show how the EXOR function can be produced using only NAND gates. Figure 8.18 gives the circuit diagram and Figure 8.19 the wiring diagram. Use swA and swB to simulate 0 or 1 at the input and thus complete the truth table.

A	B	Q
0	0	
0	1	
1	0	
1	1	

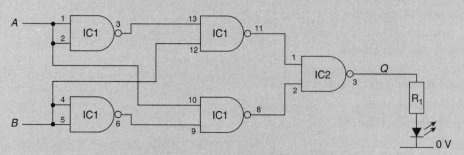

Figure 8.18   Circuit diagram for Practical 3: if the LED lights then $Q = 1$; if the LED does not light then $Q = 2$

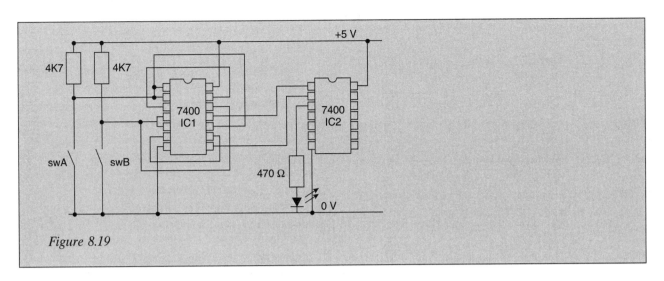

Figure 8.19

Minimisation

Very often the solution which we derive from a truth table is not the solution requiring the smallest number of gates. Also, the way in which a customer's specification is given means that it may even include variables which are irrelevant to the problem. Sometimes we can reduce the function simply by using the rules of Boolean algebra. However, in complicated functions it is not always apparent that a function may be minimised. There are many techniques for minimising a logic function. The one we consider here is a graphical method. It is easy to use and works well for problems involving up to four variables. The method can be used beyond this (up to six variables) but it becomes so cumbersome that it is easier to consider mathematical solutions.

Karnaugh mapping

In this method we draw a 'map' with a set of boxes, each of which represents one possible ANDed combination of input variables. The map is constructed such that adjacent boxes, vertically or horizontally, contain product terms which vary from their neighbour by only one variable.

Having drawn the map, we place a 1 in each box where the represented term is present in the function being mapped.

Next we 'loop' groups of adjacent 1s and finally eliminate any variables which change state within a loop, since if a variable can be 0 or 1 it is irrelevant (complementation law).

Remember that for n variables the number of input combinations is 2^n and this dictates the size of the map.

The best way to master Karnaugh mapping is by example. First let's concentrate on construction of the map. Figures 8.20, 8.21 and 8.22 show two-

Figure 8.20   A two-variable map

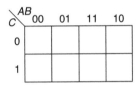

Figure 8.21   A three-variable map

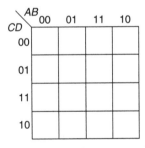

Figure 8.22   A four-variable map

variable, three-variable and four-variable maps respectively. Note that in the case of the three- and four-variable maps we use a Gray code marking. This ensures that *only one* variable changes as we move vertically or horizontally between boxes.

The Karnaugh map is drawn in a single plane but it should be thought of as a flattened out three-dimensional structure since boxes on opposite sides of the map and in the corners of the map are also treated as being adjacent.

Next we need to mark a function onto the map, e.g. a two-variable function $F = a.b + a.\bar{b}$. Put a 1 in the boxes which represent each of the terms present – see Figure 8.23.

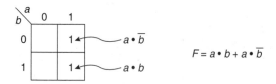

Figure 8.23

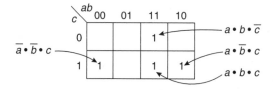

$$F = a \cdot b \cdot \overline{c} + a \cdot \overline{b} \cdot c + \overline{a} \cdot \overline{b} \cdot c + a \cdot b \cdot c$$

Figure 8.24

For a three-variable case, e.g. $F = a.b.\overline{c} + a.\overline{b}.c + \overline{a}.\overline{b}.c + a.b.c$, see Figure 8.24.

Supposing the function contains a term which does not contain all the variables, e.g. $F = a.b.c + a.\overline{b} + a.c$. We must supply the missing variable. This can be done by ANDing $(x + \overline{x})$ to the incomplete term where x is the missing term. Thus the function above becomes:

$$F = a.b.c + a.b.(c + \overline{c}) + a.c.(b + \overline{b})$$
$$= a.b.c + a.b.c + a.b.\overline{c} + a.c.b + a.\overline{b}.c$$
$$= a.b.c + a.b.\overline{c} + a.\overline{b}.c$$

In fact this is the same as placing a 1 in each box of the map where the incomplete term occurs, so we don't really need to expand the function formally. For example, for $F = a.b + a.c + a.\overline{b}$ see Figure 8.25.

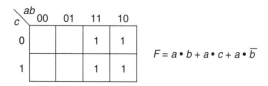

$$F = a \cdot b + a \cdot c + a \cdot \overline{b}$$

Figure 8.25

Next we need to look at looping. This is where some thought is required but there are a few simple rules we can observe.

(a) All 1s must be enclosed by a loop.
(b) Loops can only encircle 1, 2, 4 or 8 1s.
(c) A 1 may be included in several loops.
(d) Loops should be as big as possible.
(e) There should be as few loops as possible.

Don't forget that we can loop corners and opposite sides. Some examples are given in Figures 8.26–8.29.

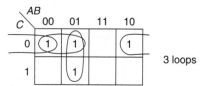

3 loops

Figure 8.26

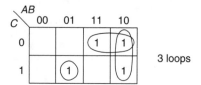

3 loops

Figure 8.27

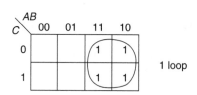

1 loop

Figure 8.28

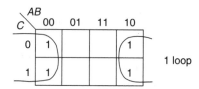

1 loop

Figure 8.29

There may be several ways in which a particular map can be looped but all will lead to a minimised sum of products if the rules are followed.

Lastly we need to see how terms are read from the loops. What we do is examine each loop to see

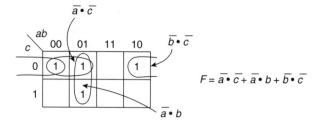

$$F = \overline{a} \cdot \overline{c} + \overline{a} \cdot b + \overline{b} \cdot \overline{c}$$

Figure 8.30

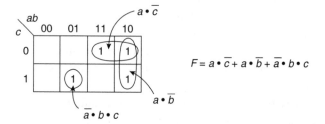

$$F = a \cdot \overline{c} + a \cdot \overline{b} + \overline{a} \cdot b \cdot c$$

Figure 8.31

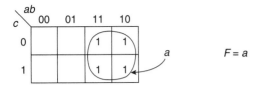

Figure 8.32

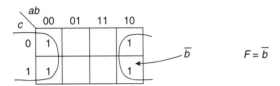

Figure 8.33

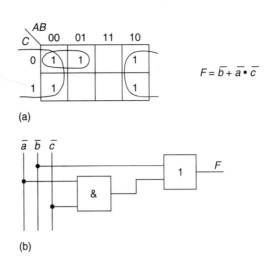

Figure 8.35

if any variable changes state within the loop. If it does we discard it from the term. If a loop encloses two boxes one variable can be eliminated; if four boxes are encircled two variables are eliminated and so on. Also each loop yields one term in our sum of products equation.

The functions for the four previous examples are given in Figures 8.30–8.33.

One of the reasons why engineers are interested in minimising a function is that when they build a logic circuit to implement the function they may be using a couple of gates more than they need to. This doesn't seem too important until we consider that the company they work for may be planning to produce a few million of these circuits.

Try designing a circuit to implement this function:

$$F = \bar{a}.\bar{b} + \bar{a}.b.\bar{c} + a.\bar{b}.\bar{c} + a.\bar{b}.c$$

From now on we'll assume that the inputs are available with their inversions on a bus (Figure 8.34).

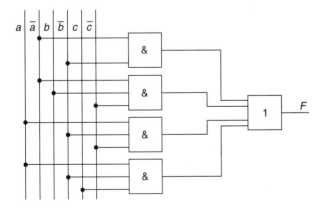

Figure 8.34

Now use Karnaugh to minimise the function and design a circuit to implement the minimised function (Figure 8.35).

Guided examples

What we need now is some practice. Try these without looking at the solutions.

Table 8.9

a	b	c	F
0	0	0	0
0	0	1	0
0	1	0	0
0	1	1	1
1	0	0	0
1	0	1	1
1	1	0	1
1	1	1	0

Table 8.10

a	b	c	F
0	0	0	1
0	0	1	1
0	1	0	0
0	1	1	1
1	0	0	0
1	0	1	1
1	1	0	0
1	1	1	1

Table 8.11

a	b	c	F
0	0	0	1
0	0	1	1
0	1	0	1
0	1	1	1
1	0	0	1
1	0	1	0
1	1	0	1
1	1	1	1

From the truth tables given in Tables 8.9–8.11:

(a) determine the sum of products form of the function;
(b) implement the circuit;
(c) minimise the function by Karnaugh;
(d) implement the minimised function;
(e) implement the minimised function using NAND gates only.

1   See Table 8.9.

2   See Table 8.10.

3   See Table 8.11.

1   (a) $F = \bar{a}.b.c + a.\bar{b}.c + a.\bar{b}.c + a.b.\bar{c}$

   (b)   See Figure 8.36.

   (c)   See Figure 8.37. This doesn't reduce any further.

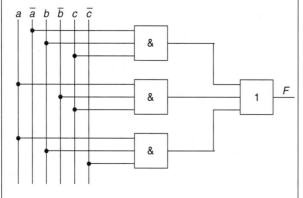

Figure 8.36

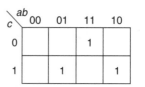

Figure 8.37

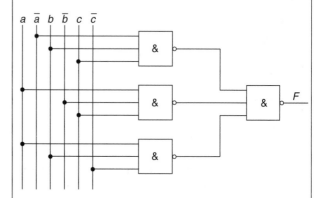

Figure 8.38

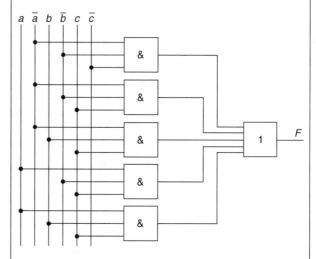

Figure 8.39

   (e) $F = \overline{\overline{\bar{a}.b.c + a.\bar{b}.c + a.b.\bar{c}}}$

      $= \overline{\overline{\bar{a}.b.c} \cdot \overline{a.\bar{b}.c} \cdot \overline{a.b.\bar{c}}}$

      See Figure 8.38.

2   (a) $F = \bar{a}.\bar{b}.\bar{c} + \bar{a}.\bar{b}.c + \bar{a}.b.c + a.\bar{b}.c + a.b.c$

   (b)   See Figure 8.39.

   (c)   See Figure 8.40. $F = \bar{a}.\bar{b} + c$.

   (d)   See Figure 8.41.

   (e) $F = \overline{\overline{\bar{a}.\bar{b} + c}} = \overline{\overline{\bar{a}.\bar{b}} \cdot \bar{c}}$

      See Figure 8.42.

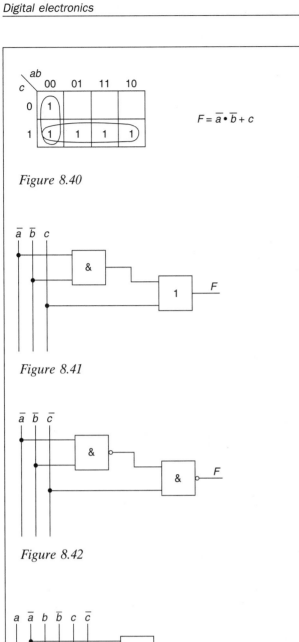

$F = \overline{a} \cdot \overline{b} + c$

Figure 8.40

Figure 8.41

Figure 8.42

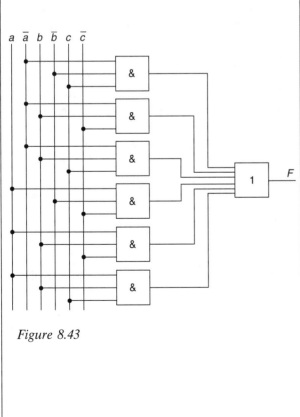

Figure 8.43

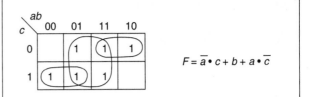

$F = \overline{a} \cdot c + b + a \cdot \overline{c}$

Figure 8.44

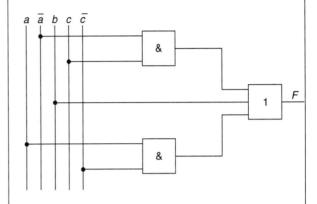

Figure 8.45

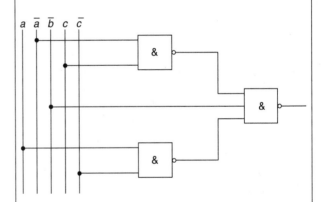

Figure 8.46

3 (a) $F = a.\overline{b}.\overline{c} + \overline{a}.b.\overline{c} + \overline{a}.b.c + a.b.\overline{c} + a.b.\overline{c} + a.b.c$

(b) See Figure 8.43.

(c) See Figure 8.44.

$F = \overline{a}.c + b + a.\overline{c}$

(d) See Figure 8.45.

(e) $F = \overline{a}.c + b + a.\overline{c}$

$= \overline{\overline{\overline{a}.c} \cdot \overline{b} \cdot \overline{a.\overline{c}}}$

See Figure 8.46.

OR–AND minimisation from Karnaugh

So far we have used Karnaugh maps to give us a minimal function as a sum of products (AND–OR) but by the same basic method we can derive a product of sum (OR–AND) form. All we need to do is loop the 0 states instead of the 1 states. When we read the loops a variable which does not change states is recorded if it is a 0 and inverted if it is a 1.

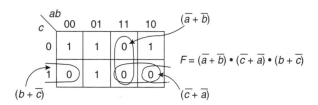

Figure 8.47

$$F = (\bar{a} + \bar{b}) \bullet (\bar{c} + \bar{a}) \bullet (b + \bar{c})$$

Consider the same map we looked at earlier in Figure 8.30, redrawn in Figure 8.47. When we considered this map earlier we got

$$F = \bar{a}.\bar{c} + \bar{a}.b + \bar{b}.\bar{c}$$

Let this be F_1 and let

$$F = (\bar{a} + \bar{b}).(\bar{c} + \bar{a}).(b + \bar{c})$$

be F_2. If we get the same truth table for both versions of the function then, by definition, the functions are equal – see Table 8.12.

The maps in Figures 8.31–8.33 are redrawn in Figures 8.48–8.50 respectively.

Try for yourself to generate the truth table for the example in Figure 8.48 and see if the product of sum form equals the sum of product form we got before. The examples in Figures 8.49 and 8.50 yield the same result directly.

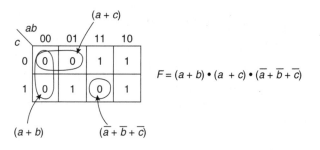

$$F = (a + b) \bullet (a + c) \bullet (\bar{a} + \bar{b} + \bar{c})$$

Figure 8.48

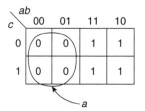

Figure 8.49

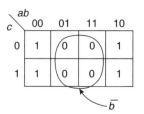

Figure 8.50

Redundancy

Because of the circuit design it is often the case that, in practice, some combinations of input variables can never occur in a particular application. These combinations are called 'can't happen' states. It may also be the case that some combinations of input are irrelevant since we are not interested in the resultant output states. These are called 'don't care' states. Both these types of input combination are **redundant**. These are normally marked on a Karnaugh map with an ×. When we come to minimise the function the ×s can be read as a logic 1 or a logic 0, whichever is more convenient.

Table 8.12

a	b	c	$\bar{a}$	$\bar{b}$	$\bar{c}$	$\bar{a}.\bar{c}$	$\bar{a}.b$	$\bar{b}.\bar{c}$	$\bar{a}+\bar{b}$	$\bar{c}+\bar{a}$	$b+\bar{c}$	F_1	F_2
0	0	0	1	1	1	1	0	1	1	1	1	1	1
0	0	1	1	1	0	0	0	0	1	1	0	0	0
0	1	0	1	0	1	1	1	0	1	1	1	1	1
0	1	1	1	0	0	0	1	0	1	1	1	1	1
1	0	0	0	1	1	0	0	1	1	1	1	1	1
1	0	1	0	1	0	0	0	0	1	0	0	0	0
1	1	0	0	0	1	0	0	0	0	1	1	0	0
1	1	1	0	0	0	0	0	0	0	0	1	0	0

Adding binary digits

One very useful circuit which is easily examined as a logic circuit is one which can add binary digits.

If we look first at simply adding 2 bits we can derive a truth table showing the expected outcome of each possible combination of input variables – Table 8.13. What we have here is two separate output lines: carry, which has the truth table of an AND gate, and sum, which has the truth table of an exclusive OR gate.

If we make this up into a circuit we have what is called the **half adder**.

Table 8.13

A	B	Sum (A⊕B)	Carry (A.B)
0	0	0	0
0	1	1	0
1	0	1	0
1	1	0	1

The half adder

The half adder circuit (Figure 8.51) is so commonly used that it has its own circuit symbol – see Figure 8.52.

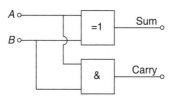

Figure 8.51

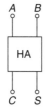

Figure 8.52

This is fine if all we ever want to add are two binary digits, but in reality we need to add larger numbers than this so we need a circuit that can take account of the carry bit generated from a lower order addition. This type of circuit is called a **full adder**.

Practical 4

The half adder

The circuit in Figure 8.53 uses an EXOR and an AND gate. An alternative way of producing it would be to use only NAND gates as shown in Figure 8.54 (overleaf).

The wiring diagram is given in Figure 8.55 (overleaf). Use swA and swB to provide the two input conditions for each of the inputs. Hence complete the truth table.

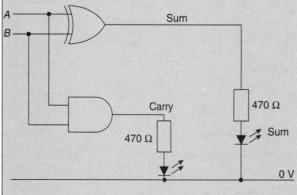

Figure 8.53

A	B	Sum	Carry
0	0		
0	1		
1	0		
1	1		

Full adder

To sort this out we need to look at the truth table for the addition of our two digits plus the possible third digit from a lower addition – see Table 8.14.

This full adder is a very important circuit, particularly in computing. We could make up a full adder using two half adders (Figure 8.56). To see if this circuit works we practise both our Boolean algebra and our truth table construction – see Figure 8.57 and Table 8.15 (page 214). Since we get the same answers as the full adder truth table we know the circuit works!

For reasons of cost effectiveness this is not practical and full adders are manufactured as integrated circuits; parallel binary adders can then be made up from cascaded full adders – see Figure 8.58.

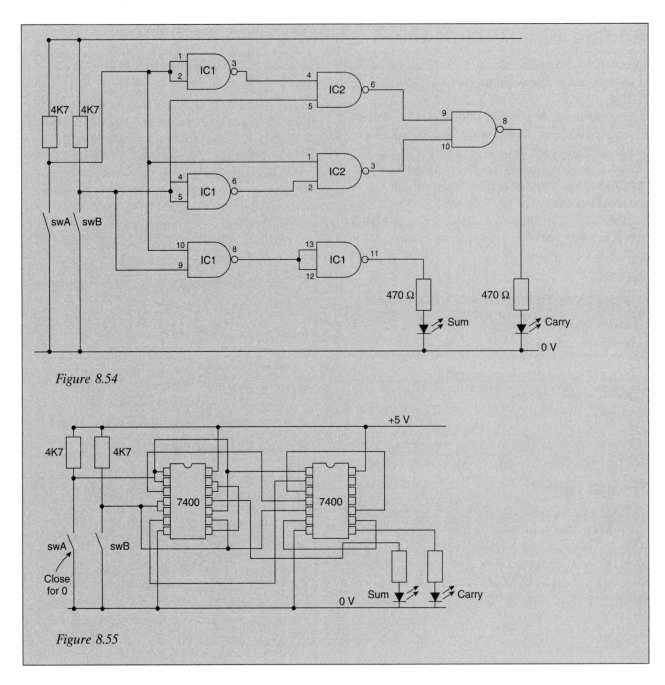

Figure 8.54

Figure 8.55

Table 8.14

A	B	C_{in}	Sum	C_{out}
0	0	0	0	0
0	0	1	1	0
0	1	0	1	0
0	1	1	0	1
1	0	0	1	0
1	0	1	0	1
1	1	0	0	1
1	1	1	1	1

As you would expect, there is no carry in to the least significant pair of digits so that input is earthed. Thereafter, each carry out is fed to the carry in of the next stage.

Sequential logic

Until now we have been considering **combinational logic**, i.e. combinations of gates such that the output of the circuit depends only on the state of the inputs. However, there is a whole range of logic circuits in which the output depends not only on the input state but also on the state of the output at the time of applying the input. Most of these circuits may be said to contain some form of memory and many of them operate in synchronism with a timing signal from a master clock.

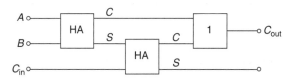

Figure 8.56

Figure 8.57

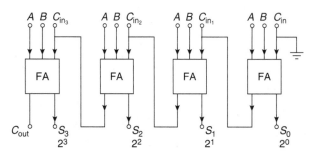

Figure 8.58

Practical 5

Full adder

The full adder circuit consists of two half adders, one feeding the other as shown in Figure 8.59. The assembly of NAND gates used to produce the carry output is, in fact, acting as an OR gate.

An easier method of using this circuit is to use a custom-produced integrated circuit such as the 7483. This package contains a 4-bit full

Figure 8.59

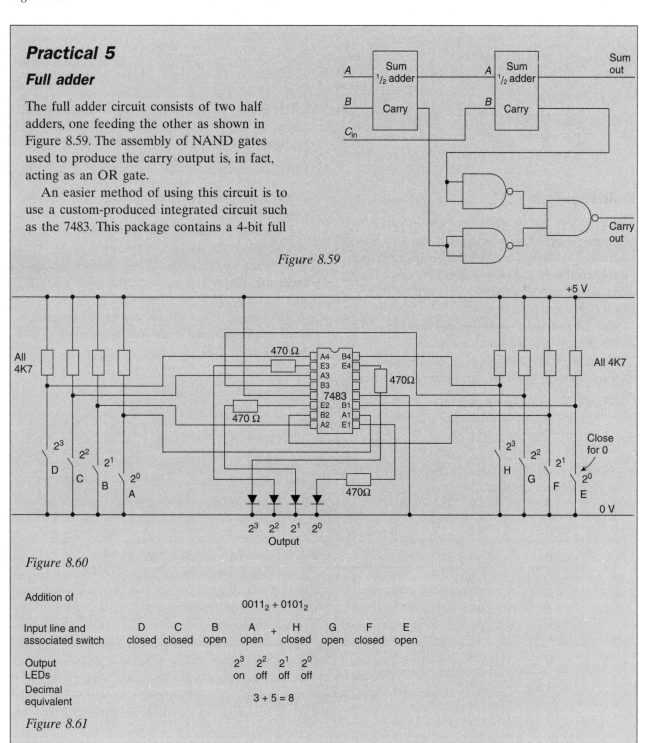

Figure 8.60

Addition of								
				$0011_2 + 0101_2$				
Input line and associated switch	D closed	C closed	B open	A open	+ H closed	G open	F closed	E open
Output LEDs				2^3 on	2^2 off	2^1 off	2^0 off	
Decimal equivalent				$3 + 5 = 8$				

Figure 8.61

adder. It adds together two 4-bit binary numbers and provides an output in binary form. Pin 14 goes high if the output exceeds 1111_2 (i.e. 15_{10}).

The wiring diagram is given in Figure 8.60. The input consists of two binary numbers, DCBA and HGFE. Note that A and E are the LSBs in each number. The integrated circuit sum outputs are arranged as follows:

Binary	2^3	2^2	2^1	2^0
Pin no.	15	2	6	9

The output is shown by the condition of the LEDs. Verify the circuit operation by setting switches as in Figure 8.61. Then note the state of the output LEDs. They should indicate as in the figure.

Practical 6

This exercise uses the 7490 and one other integrated circuit to produce the sequencing effect with LEDs. The second integrated circuit is a 'BCD to 1 out of 10' decoder. This means that for a binary level at the input the corresponding output pin will become active by going low.

For example, if in Figures 8.62 and 8.63 (page 215) the binary coded decimal (BCD) input is 0101_2 (i.e. 5_{10}), pin 5 will go low, all others being high.

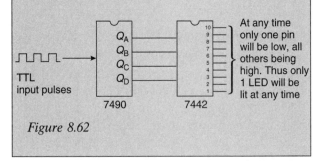

Figure 8.62

Multivibrators

Multivibrators can be made up from discrete components, opamps or logic gates, but they may all be treated as having two elements configured such that when the output of one element is high the other is low, and they may be switched to alter which element output is high.

Since the output may be high or low our multivibrators are two-state circuits.

There are three basic types of multivibrator and they are classified in terms of which of their two states is stable.

Astable multivibrator (free-running) As its name suggests, an astable has no stable state and switches continuously between its two possible states. The rate at which the circuit switches state is determined by the values of the interconnecting feedback components between the two elements that make up the multivibrator.

The output of this circuit is a fixed frequency, fixed amplitude pulse train. The astable is the basis of many types of pulse generator and clock circuit.

Table 8.15

A	B	C_{in}	$A \oplus B$	$A.B$	X $(A \oplus B).C_{in}$	Carry out $(A.B)+X$	Sum $(A \oplus B) \oplus C_{in}$
0	0	0	0	0	0	0	0
0	0	1	0	0	0	0	1
0	1	0	1	0	0	0	1
0	1	1	1	0	1	1	0
1	0	0	1	0	0	0	1
1	0	1	1	0	1	1	0
1	1	0	0	1	0	1	0
1	1	1	0	1	0	1	1

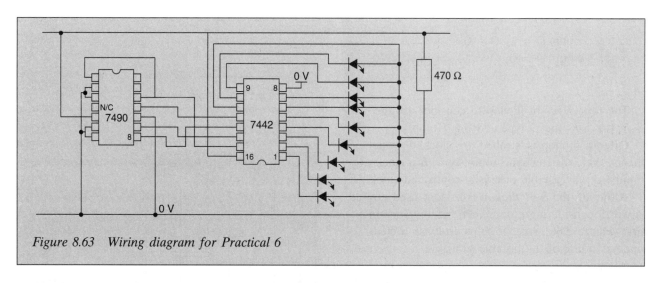

Figure 8.63   Wiring diagram for Practical 6

Practical 7

NAND gates connected as an astable multivibrator

The circuit in Figures 8.64 and 8.65 produces a series of pulses at an approximate pulse repetition frequency of 1 Hz and in consequence can be used to flash two LEDs. Note that the fourth gate is only acting as an inverter – if only one LED is required it need not be connected.

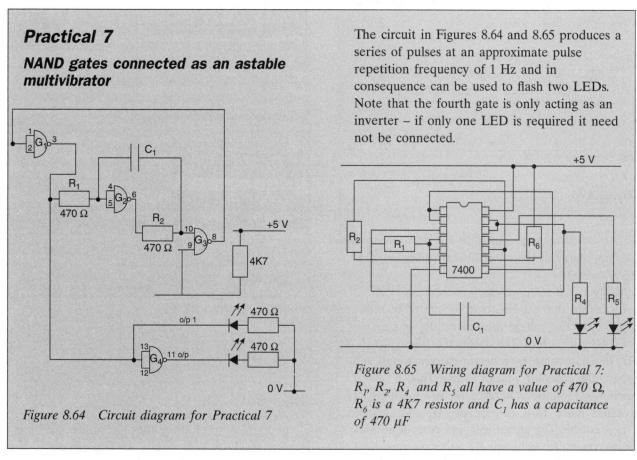

Figure 8.64   Circuit diagram for Practical 7

Figure 8.65   Wiring diagram for Practical 7: R_1, R_2, R_4 and R_5 all have a value of 470 Ω, R_6 is a 4K7 resistor and C_1 has a capacitance of 470 μF

Monostable multivibrator (one-shot)   This has only one stable state. If we apply an external pulse we can trigger the monostable into its other state but it will only remain there for a short period of time (determined by the interconnecting feedback components between the two elements). After this period has elapsed the circuit reverts to its original, stable, state where it will remain until triggered again.

Bistable multivibrator (flipflop)   This type of multivibrator is stable in either of its states. If triggered by an externally applied pulse it will

switch from its original state to the other state. It will now remain in this new state indefinitely or until triggered again, in which event it will switch back to its original state.

The flipflop forms the basis of static random access memory (RAM) and is used in a range of digital counters and registers. It is the flipflop which concerns us here in its application to sequential logic.

The flipflop has a set input, a reset input and two outputs which are normally labelled Q and $\overline{Q}$. By definition a flipflop is said to be

set   when $Q = 1$, $\overline{Q} = 0$
reset   when $Q = 0$, $\overline{Q} = 1$

The four types of flipflop to consider are the S–R, the J–K, the D-type and the T-type.

Often a flipflop is 'strobed' or 'clocked', which means that it is run synchronously with a clock input from an astable or crystal-controlled clock.

Although the **S–R flipflop** is seldom used now it is worth considering a discrete transistor version first (Figure 8.66), since it helps establish a clear understanding of the bistable principle.

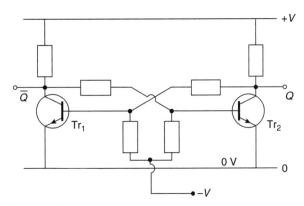

Figure 8.66

At switch on, one transistor will start to conduct slightly ahead of the other (owing to component tolerance etc.)

Consider that Tr_2 conducts more than Tr_1. This means that the collector voltage of Tr_2 will fall due to the voltage drop across R_4 as a result of collector current. This drives the base voltage of Tr_1 down, causing Tr_1 collector current to fall and hence the collector voltage to rise. This, in turn, increases the base voltage of Tr_2, causing it to conduct more. Thus, very rapidly, Tr_2 saturates and Tr_1 is cut off. The circuit will now remain in this state (reset). It could equally well have remained in the other state had Tr_1 conducted more initially.

If we now pulsed the ON transistor (Tr_2) OFF the circuit would change state rapidly by the regenerative process just described and, having settled, would remain with Tr_1 conducting and Tr_2 cut off, i.e. the flipflop would be set.

In some cases the 1, 1 state at the input of a flipflop may occur. Since we cannot allow an indeterminate state to occur we must look for another response from our flipflop. The answer is to use a **J–K stage** (Figure 8.67). This has a similar truth table (Table 8.16) to the S–R but with the difference that, on receipt of a 1, 1 input, the J–K output toggles, i.e. it always changes state.

Figure 8.67   Standard symbol

Table 8.16

J	K	Q	$\overline{Q}$
0	0	0	0
0	0	1	1
1	0	0	1
1	0	1	1
0	1	0	0
0	1	1	0
1	1	0	1
1	1	1	0

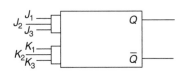

Figure 8.68   Gated J–K flipflop

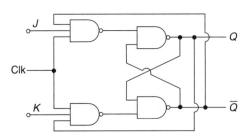

Figure 8.69

In addition to clocking the J–K we can also use 'gated' flipflops. With these, AND gates are incorporated in the input of the integrated circuit so that, in effect, the flipflop only sees its input (J or K) as being at logic 1 when *all* the AND inputs are at logic 1 (Figure 8.68).

A J–K can be obtained from an S–R by ANDing the S input and R input with the $\overline{Q}$ output and Q output respectively. A NAND gate version is shown in Figure 8.69. If you examine the circuit you will see that, basically, the input gates ensure that the flipflop inputs always see a 0 and a 1, even if the J–K inputs are 1, 1.

With a **D-type** flipflop we have a single trigger input (D) and it operates such that the Q output takes on the same logic state as the D input. Any change in state only occurs when a clock pulse is present.

The *D*-type can be obtained from an *S–R* or a *J–K* flipflop by connecting an inverter (NOT gate) between the inputs so that $S = \overline{R}$ (or $J = \overline{K}$) for any input state (Figure 8.70). If we look at the *S–R/J–K* truth table for this condition it shows that the *Q* output is always the same as the *D* input ($D = S = R$).

J	*K*	*Q*	$\overline{Q}$
0	1	0	0
1	0	0	1
0	1	1	0
1	0	1	1

The *D*-type is always clocked so the output state changes only occur when Clk = 1. When the clock is at 0 the output cannot follow the *D* input so the output is **latched.** The *D*-type has the following truth table.

Clk	*D*	*Q*	$\overline{Q}$
1	0	0	0
1	0	1	0
1	1	0	1
1	1	1	1

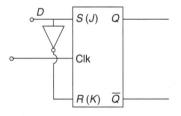

Figure 8.70

Both TTL and CMOS versions of the *D*-type are available and it is worth noting the manufacturers' distinction between 'flipflop' and 'latch', e.g. 7475 (TTL dual *D* flipflop) and 4042 (CMOS quad latch). The difference between a latch and a flipflop is that the flipflop is edge triggered. This means that its output can change state only on the clock pulse transition between 0 and 1. Usually, this is on the 1 to 0 transition. The latch can change state at any time whilst the clock input is at logic 1.

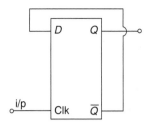

Figure 8.71

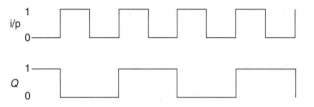

Figure 8.72

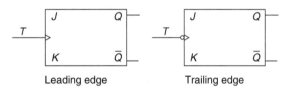

Leading edge   Trailing edge

Figure 8.73

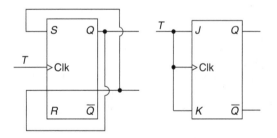

Figure 8.74

We can use the *D*-type as a divide by 2 circuit acting on the clock input. This is done by connecting the $\overline{Q}$ output to the *D* input (Figure 8.71).

Suppose, initially, $Q = 1$ and $\overline{Q} = D = 0$. The first clock pulse will cause the circuit to switch to $Q = 0$ and $\overline{Q} = D = 1$. The second clock pulse will cause the circuit to switch back to $Q = 1$ and $\overline{Q} = D = 0$ and so on. As we can see from the waveforms in Figure 8.72 the pulse repetition rate of the output is only half the repetition rate of the clock input.

***T*-type** flipflop (toggle) circuits change state on receipt of each clock puse. Versions are available to toggle on either the leading or the trailing edge of the clock pulse. Remember that a *J–K* will always toggle when both its inputs are at logic 1, so a *T*-type is easily obtained from a *J–K* or an *S–R*, as shown in Figures 8.73 and 8.74.

8.3 **Counters**

In modern electronic systems there are many applications where the ability to count is required. What is being counted is normally the number of pulses occurring in a given time but, in a digital system, the pulses may be representing many forms of data.

There are many forms of digital counting circuit but generally they all employ the flipflop as their basic circuit element. In their turn counters form the building blocks of other systems. They are employed in straight counting in any one of a number of code patterns such as BCD or binary or modulo-N. They are used in time and frequency measurement, in waveform generation, in frequency division and in many more applications.

We can treat counters, at this stage, as a series of flipflops (usually J–K) connected in cascade so that the output of one flipflop feeds the input of the next and so on down the line.

Our counters can be run **synchronously** or **asynchronously**.

Synchronous counters are connected so that all the flipflops act at the same time at an instant determined by a pulse from a master clock. These types give the faster count but the circuits tend to be more complex, and hence more expensive.

Asynchronous (or non-synchronous) counters are called **ripple-through counters** because each flipflop operates in turn along the line so data appear to ripple through the circuit. Since each stage changes state in turn we get a relatively slow count, but often speed is not the prime concern in choosing a circuit for a particular application.

Asynchronous counters

If we examine the behaviour of a single J–K when both its inputs are held at logic 1 we see that it acts as a divide by 2 circuit. That is, its output has a pulse repetition rate which is half that of the incoming clock pulse train.

The waveforms shown in Figure 8.75 assume a trailing-edge triggered J–K (triggered on a 1 to 0 transition) which is usually the case in our counters.

If we start with the J–K reset the Q output goes from 0 to 1 in response to the first clock pulse and

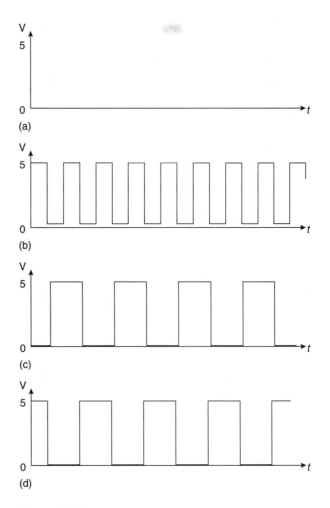

Figure 8.75

from 1 back to 0 on the second clock pulse. If we want to record the count of more than two pulses we need to add more flipflops. The maximum count size for our circuit is $2^n - 1$ where n is the number of flipflops in the circuit.

The circuit shown in Figure 8.76 has four flipflops so it could give a maximum count of $2^4 = 16$, but remember that this is 0 to 15 giving 16 output conditions. The LEDs connected to each output will light up to indicate a logic 1 on their respective Q outputs but, in practice, the output could be fed to another circuit or a display decoder etc.

Since all the J–K inputs are held constant at logic 1 the stages will toggle on the trailing edge of the pulse applied to their clock inputs.

Assume that initially all states are reset ($Q_A = Q_B = Q_C = Q_D = 0$). The trailing edge of the first clock pulse will cause flipflop A to toggle, so Q_A goes to logic 1. On the trailing edge of the second clock pulse A toggles and Q_A goes to logic 0. This change in Q_A presents a trailing edge to the clock input of flipflop B so Q_B goes to logic 1. The third clock pulse toggles A so now Q_A and Q_B are at logic 1.

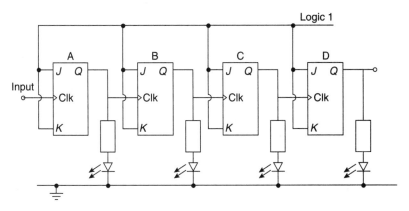

Figure 8.76

When the fourth clock pulse occurs its trailing edge toggles A so Q_A goes to logic 0 and this trailing edge toggles B so Q_B goes to a logic 0. This change in Q_B presents a trailing edge to the clock input of flipflop C so it toggles and Q_C goes to a logic 1 with all other Q outputs at logic 0.

This process continues until the trailing edge of the fifteenth clock pulse occurs. This sets A for the last time and now all the stages are set.

Table 8.17 shows that, as you would expect, the next (sixteenth) clock pulse resets all the flipflops and the count starts again from zero.

If we look at the pulse waveforms for each flipflop and remember that the LED will be lit when Q is at logic 1 we can see that we have a straightforward count of pulses in binary form. Note that A operates twice as often as B and four times as often as C and so on.

The speed of the count is determined by the clock rate. This has a maximum limit because each flipflop introduces an additional propagation delay and the minimum clock period must be greater than the total propagation delay of the circuit. The dotted line in Figure 8.77 illustrates the cumulative effect of these delays.

This type of counter is sometimes referred to as an **up counter** since it counts up from zero. However, if we connected the $\overline{Q}$ output of each flipflop to the clock input of the next we would have a **down-counter** counting down from 15 to 0.

The four-stage ripple-through counter considered

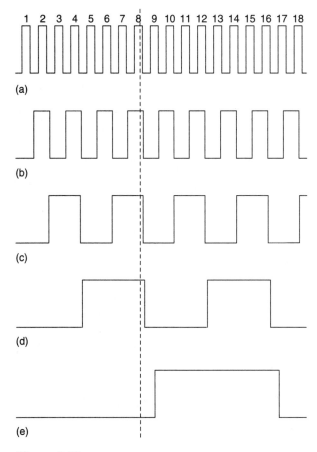

Figure 8.77

Table 8.17

							Clock pulses										
	0	*1*	*2*	*3*	*4*	*5*	*6*	*7*	*8*	*9*	*10*	*11*	*12*	*13*	*14*	*15*	*16*
Q_A	0	1	0	1	0	1	0	1	0	1	0	1	0	1	0	1	0
Q_B	0	0	1	1	0	0	1	1	0	0	1	1	0	0	1	1	0
Q_C	0	0	0	0	1	1	1	1	0	0	0	0	1	1	1	1	0
Q_D	0	0	0	0	0	0	0	0	1	1	1	1	1	1	1	1	0

Practical 8

Asynchronous counter

This practical uses 74107s to build an asynchronous counter (Figures 8.78 and 8.79, opposite). The circuit function is similar to that shown in Practical 5 on page 213. Once again a truth table can be drawn (Table 8.18) to indicate the number of input pulses. Don't forget to debounce the input if via a single switch.

Table 8.18

Number of pulses at input	State of output LEDs			
	2^3	2^2	2^1	2^0
0				
1				
2				
3				
4				
5				
6				
7				
8				
9				
10				
11				
12				
13				
14				
15				

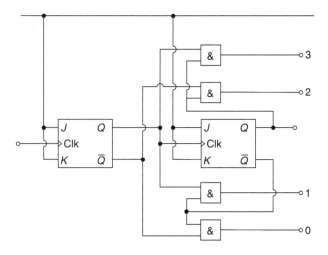

Figure 8.80

gives a straight binary count output. Often we need an output in some other form such as decimal or BCD. This is achieved by adding a decoder circuit to each flipflop output so that a unique output is obtained for each input clock pulse. A simple example is a two-stage counter giving a count from 0 to 3 and decoded with AND gates to give a decimal count (Figure 8.80).

Rather than have counters which count in groups of two, four, eight, sixteen etc. it is more common for us to require counts of ten or even twelve. We know that we cannot count to a number greater than 2^n with n flipflops but it is possible to stop the count short of its maximum.

Counts of less than 2^n

For counts of less than 2^n the technique is to select the number of flipflops which gives a maximum count size as close to and greater than the required count. Then we modify the circuit so that all the count stages above the required maximum are left out. The standard ways to do this use logic gates to feedback or feedforward at a particular count or to trigger the reset or preset on the counter at the chosen count size.

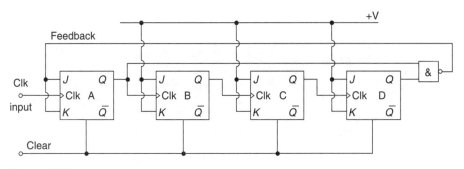

Figure 8.81

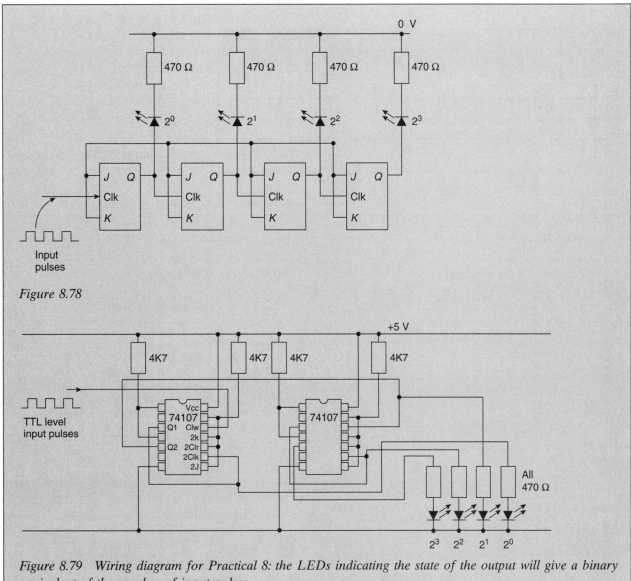

Figure 8.78

Figure 8.79   Wiring diagram for Practical 8: the LEDs indicating the state of the output will give a binary equivalent of the number of input pulses

Feedback decade counter

Decade counters, as their name suggests, count in tens (0 to 9). The nearest value above this that is a power of 2 is 16. So we need four flipflops (Figure 8.81).

If we look at the circuit operation we see that it counts in the normal way from 0 to 9 (1001). At this point the NAND gate has both its inputs set to logic 1 for the first time. The NAND output changes to logic 0 and since this feeds the J–K input to the first flipflop the count stops. Now a clear pulse would be required to restart the count. The count sequence is as shown in Table 8.19.

Many of the commercially available integrated circuit counters incorporate features such as preset, reset (clear) and enable lines etc. and these can also be used to adjust our count to less than 2^n.

Practical 9

Using a decade counter

Rather than using individual J–K flipflops to construct a counter it is common practice to use a dedicated integrated circuit. One of the most common is the 7490. This integrated

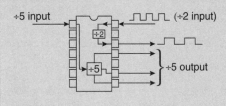

Figure 8.82

Table 8.19

	Clock pulses										
	0	**1**	**2**	**3**	**4**	**5**	**6**	**7**	**8**	**9**	**10**
Q_A	0	1	0	1	0	1	0	1	0	1	0
Q_B	0	0	1	1	0	0	1	1	0	0	1
Q_C	0	0	0	0	1	1	1	1	0	0	0
Q_D	0	0	0	0	0	0	0	0	1	1	0

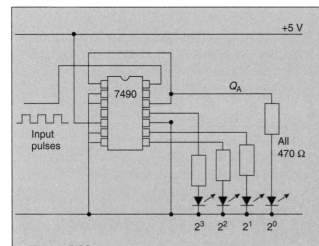

Figure 8.83

circuit contains two separate counters, one containing a divide by 5 circuit, the other a divide by 2 (see Figure 8.82).

Normal practice is to connect the output of the divide by 2 circuit into the divide by 5 input (i.e. pin 12 to pin 1) thus producing a divide by 10 circuit. The output is available in BCD form on pins 12, 9, 8 and 11, these pin numbers corresponding to 2^0, 2^1, 2^2 and 2^3 respectively. The circuit in Figure 8.83 uses the 7490 to count up to 10 and then reset.

Wire up the circuit as shown in Figure 8.83. The input can consist of a series of pulses or the action of a single switch incorporating debounce as shown in Figure 8.84. (Hint: The AND gate could be replaced with two NAND gates.)

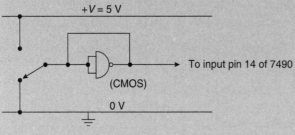

Figure 8.84 Switch debounce circuit using one AND gate

With each input pulse the LEDs should indicate one increment in binary as the truth table (Table 8.20) shows.

Table 8.20

Number of pulses at input	State of output LEDs			
	2^3	2^2	2^1	2^0
0	0	0	0	0
1	0	0	0	1
2	0	0	1	0
3	0	0	1	1
4	0	1	0	0
5	0	1	0	1
6	0	1	1	0
7	0	1	1	1
8	1	0	0	0
9	1	0	0	1
10	1	0	1	0
11	1	0	1	1
12	1	1	0	0
13	1	1	0	1
14	1	1	1	0
15	1	1	1	1

Reset and preset

When we considered the *J–K* flipflop we did not allow for the fact that we may want to have a known state of *Q* output before we apply logic level 1 to *J* and *K*. This can be done by including preset and reset inputs so that the state of *Q* can be determined by an input independent of the clock. The basic *J–K* circuit is modified as shown in Figure 8.85.

For example, suppose we wish to set the initial condition of the flipflop to *Q* = 0, i.e. clear the flipflop so that *Q* = 0, Clk = 0.

This is done by setting the clear input to logic 0 and the preset input to logic 1. Now Clk = 0, Cr = 0, Pr = 1.

Since Cr = 0 the output of NAND gate D must be logic 1 ($\overline{Q}$). Since the clock is at logic 0 the output of NAND gate A must be logic 1. So, all the inputs to NAND gate C are at logic 1 and hence its output must be at logic 0 ($\overline{Q}$), i.e. reset.

In the same way we can argue the condition for preset: Clk = 0, Cr = 1, Pr = 0. Since Pr = 0 the output of NAND gate C is logic 1 (*Q*). Since Clk = 0 the output of NAND gate B is logic 1. Cr = 1 and so all inputs to NAND gate D are

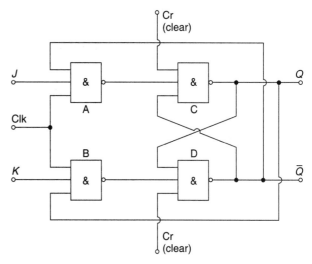

Figure 8.85

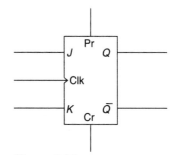

Figure 8.86

Practical 10

Resetting a counter

If you examine the counter you will see that pins 13 and 10 are returned high via a 4K7 pull-up resistor. These two pins are the clear pins for the two individual flipflops within the 74107. If the pins are taken low, even for an instant, the flipflops clear or reset, causing the *Q* outputs to go to 0 regardless of the condition of the clock input. This can be used to cause the counter to reset at any pre-decided number if an external gate is incorporated as shown in Figures 8.87 and 8.88.

The output of the NAND gate is always high except when its two inputs are both logic 1. This only occurs when the counter changes to 1001_2 (i.e. 10_{10}). At this instant the circuit resets to 0000. The LEDs indicating the counter output never show a state of 10_{10} but indicate up to the previous count, i.e. 9_{10}.

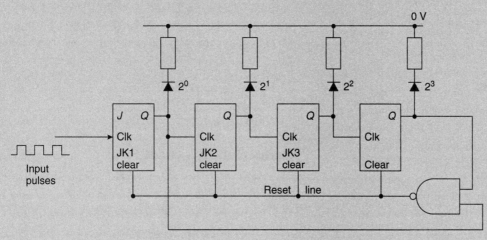

Figure 8.87 Circuit diagram for Practical 10. The reset line is normally high; it momentarily becomes low when the output of the NAND gate pulls it down

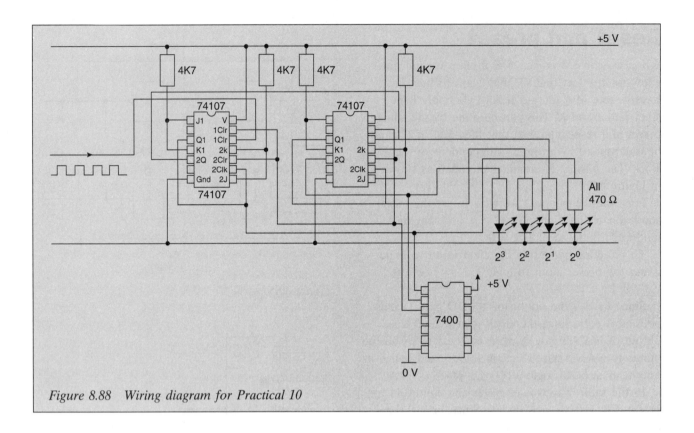

Figure 8.88   Wiring diagram for Practical 10

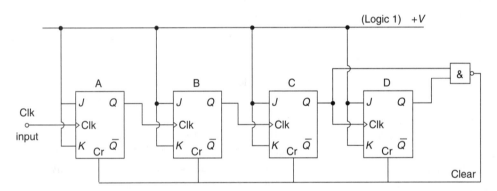

Figure 8.89

at logic 1 and its output is at logic 0 ($\overline{Q}$), i.e.
preset.

The flipflop symbol is modified as in Figure 8.86
to take account of the extra inputs.

Reduction by reset

Again, if we want a count size of N then we need n
counters where $2^n > N$. The way we set the count
size to N is to trigger the reset pins on all the
flipflops when the count goes to $N + 1$. This is
achieved by connecting all the Q outputs which are
at logic 1 when the count is $N + 1$ to a NAND gate
and feeding the NAND output to the reset line. For
once, this is easier done than said!

For example, consider a four-stage counter
(maximum count $2^4 = 16$) which we wish to modify
to a count size of 12 (0 to 11).

When the counter gets to 12 ($N + 1$) the Q
outputs of flipflops C and D will be at logic 1 so
we connect them to the NAND as shown in Figure
8.89. Now on the twelfth clock pulse the NAND
gate has both its inputs at logic 1 so its output
drops to logic 0 and triggers the reset. Thus the
count is now

0, 1, 2, 3, 4, 5, 6, 7, 8, 9, 10, 11, 0, 1, 2, 3, 4 etc.

Reduction by preset

The principle is the same again but this time we
force the flipflops with a Q output at logic 0 to set
at a particular count size. The trailing edge of the
next clock pulse then resets the counter and the
count starts again. The idea is demonstrated in a
three-stage counter set to count to 5 (divide by 6)
(Figure 8.90).

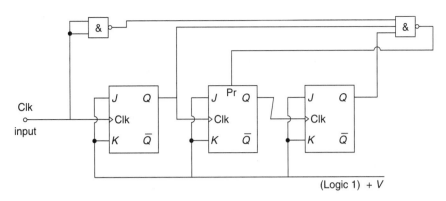

Figure 8.90

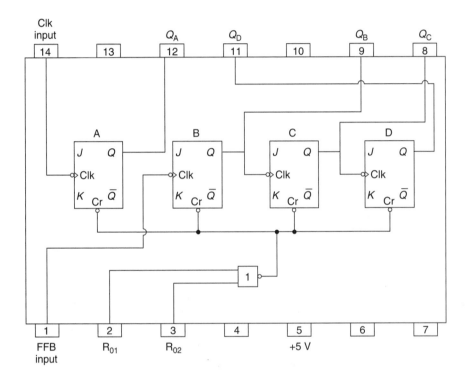

Figure 8.91

Counters are readily available as integrated circuit packages in both TTL and CMOS and manufacturers offer a range of 'in-built' facilities. In most cases the package is versatile in that, by choosing to make certain combinations of external connection, we can obtain the size or type of count we require.

An example of a chip which clearly conforms to the principles we have outlined is the TTL package 7493 (Figure 8.91).

The 7493 is described by the manufacturer as a binary divide by 16 ripple counter (not presettable). In fact, the chip contains two separate counters, a divide by 2 and a divide by 8. Flipflops B, C and D are internally connected to form a three-stage (divide by 8) ripple-through counter. Flipflop A is a divide by 2.

By connecting the Q output of flipflop A (pin 12) to the clock input of flipflop B (pin 1) and using pin 14 as the clock input we have a 0 to 15 (divide by 16) counter. For a full count pins 2 and 3 must be held at logic 0. These are the reset or clear inputs. If either or both pins are driven logic high then the counter resets. These inputs, via the internal NAND gate, allow us to modify the count size as already explained.

The counter is trailing-edge triggered and the package draws a current of 31 mA with a maximum toggle frequency of around 18 MHz.

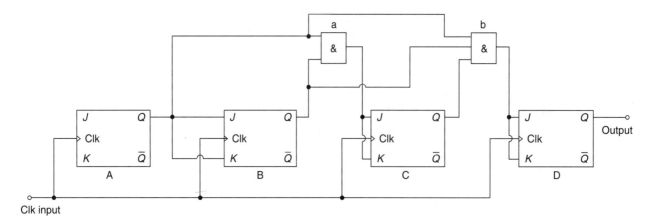

Figure 8.92

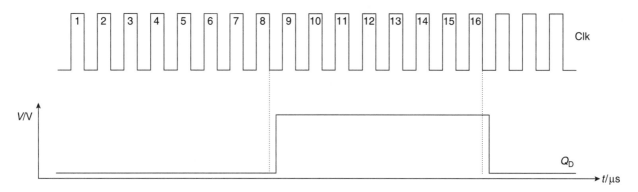

Figure 8.93

Synchronous counters

We can see that the counting rate of ripple counters is comparatively slow. If we arranged the circuit so that all the flipflops were acted on by the clock simultaneously, the speed could be dramatically increased. This will make the circuits more complicated and costly but if speed is a requirement then synchronous counters are the answer.

Figure 8.92 shows a divide by 16 counter. All the clock inputs are fed together and the short-circuited J–K inputs of each flipflop have their logic state determined by the Q output of all the previous stages.

Since the stages are all clocked at once the limiting factor on clock rate is now the propagation delay of one flipflop.

Let us start with all the flipflops reset so that the count is 0. When the trailing edge of the first clock pulse occurs flipflop A will toggle ($Q_A = 1$, Q_B etc. = 0).

On the trailing edge of the second clock pulse flipflop A will toggle and Q_A falls to 0, and since J and K of flipflop B were held at logic 1, flipflop B will toggle ($Q_A = 0$, $Q_B = 1$ $Q_C = Q_D = 0$).

We can see that now AND gate a has one input high and one low. This means that flipflop C will not toggle on the next clock pulse. On the trailing edge of the third clock pulse flipflop A toggles but B does not since its J and K inputs were at logic 0. Now we have $Q_A = 1$, $Q_B = 1$, $Q_C = Q_D = 0$. This means that the J and K inputs of flipflop C are held at logic 1 via the first AND gate.

As the trailing edge of the fourth clock pulse occurs flipflop A toggles to reset, flipflop B also toggles to reset and flipflop C toggles to set. Now only Q_C is at logic 1.

This process continues until, at the trailing edge of the sixteenth clock pulse, the whole counter is reset and the count begins again (Figure 8.93).

Synchronous decade counter (reset)

We can reduce the count of a synchronous counter just as we did with asynchronous counters – see Figure 8.94.

Down counters

So far, every counter we have considered has counted up from zero. These are called **up counters**.

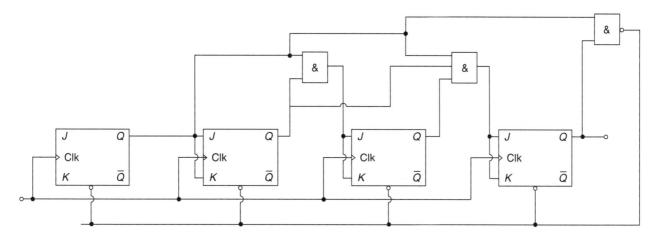

Figure 8.94

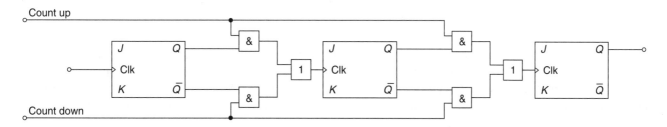

Figure 8.95

There are some applications where we may wish to count down from some number to zero.

If we look at the problem we see that the solution is obvious. As our Q outputs change from all 0 to, eventually, all logic 1, so our $\overline{Q}$ outputs must have changed from all logic 1 down to, eventually, all 0. So, if we connected the $\overline{Q}$ outputs instead of the Q outputs we would have a **down counter**.

Up–down counters

By adding a few logic gates we could arrange for our circuit to act as either an up counter or a down counter according to our requirements (Figure 8.95). Applying a logic 1 to the count up or count down line will enable the appropriate pair of AND gates and thereafter the counter operates as normal.

Consider that we want to count down. The counter is initially set so that all Q outputs are at logic 1, with a logic 1 on the count down line (and logic 0 on the count up line).

The count is initially 111 (7). The first clock pulse resets flipflop A so $\overline{Q}_A$ rises to logic 1. The count is now 110 (6). On the second clock pulse flipflop A sets so $\overline{Q}_A$ goes to logic 0. This trailing edge is applied to the clock input of flipflop B and

it toggles to reset so $\overline{Q}_B$ goes to logic 1. The count from the Q outputs is now 101 (5).

This count continues until all the flipflops are reset, at which point all $\overline{Q}$ outputs are at logic 1 and the count (from the Q outputs) is 000. The next clock pulse will set A which sends $\overline{Q}_A$ to logic 0 and the resulting trailing edge causes B to toggle and so on back to a count of 111.

Shift registers

If we remember that the output of a flipflop is either a logic 0 or logic 1 we can see that it could be used to act as a 1-bit memory. When the flipflop is set we have 'stored' a logic 1 and when the flipflop is reset we have stored a logic 0. In fact the flipflop is the basic storage element used in static RAM. If a single flipflop can store 1 bit, then n flipflops could be used to store an n-bit data word. When we arrange flipflops in this way we have a **register**.

In order to read data into the register serially (one bit after another) we need to shift the data from the input through the register in a similar way to our ripple-through counters. This is where we get the name 'shift register'.

Initially, consider a simple register to shift a 4-bit word right (Figure 8.96).

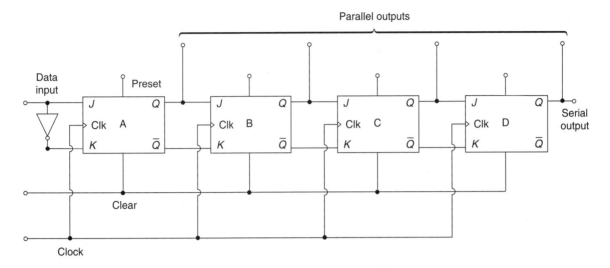

Figure 8.96

We can see that flipflop A is set up to operate as a *D*-type and both preset and clear terminals are provided so that the logic state can be set independently of the clock. Usually, the clear are connected together to give a register clear input. Assume that the register is initially clear (Q_A, Q_B, Q_C, Q_D = 0). Now, as an example, assume the 4-bit word to be stored is 1011_2.

After the first clock pulse, A is set ($Q_A = J_B$ = 1). After two clock pulses B is also set ($Q_A = Q_B = J_C = 1$). Remember the data are being applied to the input serially so, when the third clock pulse occurs, the input to flipflop A is $J = 0$, $K = 1$; also $J_B = 1$ and $J_C = 1$ while $K_B = 0$ and $K_C = 0$.

On the trailing edge of this third clock pulse flipflop A resets and flipflop C sets. This gives an output state $Q_A = Q_D = 0$, $Q_B = Q_C = 1$. The state of the inputs is that $J_B = 0$ while $J_C = J_D = 1$.

The last bit to be stored is a logic 1 and this is now applied to the *J* input of flipflop A. On the trailing edge of the fourth clock pulse A sets, B resets and C and D remain unchanged.

Examination of the register shows that the word is now stored as the *Q* outputs of the four flipflops. If we allow clock pulses to continue to be applied but the data are zero the register will empty in four more clock pulses.

What is happening is that flipflop A records the data at the input and each clock pulse shifts the data one place to the right.

For different applications shift registers are available that operate on the principle of moving the data to the left.

The ways in which data can be written into or read from a shift register give us four basic arrangements.

Serial in/parallel out In this case the data are applied to the input as a pulse train and shifted in 1 bit at a time. When the complete word is stored in the register all the *Q* outputs are read at once.

Parallel in/serial out Here we clear the register and then the word is stored by simultaneously using the preset inputs to set each flipflop where a logic 1 is required. Data are then read out 1 bit at a time, under control of the clock.

Serial in/serial out This is sometimes used as a delay or a simple temporary store. It is worth noting that the data in this case can only be read in the order of the input.

Parallel in/parallel out This is used as a store and is the sort of arrangement used in some microprocessor registers.

As well as shifting data we also use registers as a straightforward store (Figure 8.97).

Shift registers could be made up from commercially available flipflop integrated circuits but in fact a range of both complementary metal–oxide–semiconductor (CMOS) and TTL registers is available. The 4035 is a CMOS example which allows shift right only. Most shift registers shift in one direction only although some, such as the TTL 7495, provide the facility for switching the shift direction.

The 4035 (Figure 8.98) is a parallel in/parallel out four-stage shift register but can be configured to any other mode of operation (e.g. serial in/serial out). This chip requires a clock rise time of less than 5 µs. The maximum clock frequency (at 10 V) is 3 MHz with a current of around

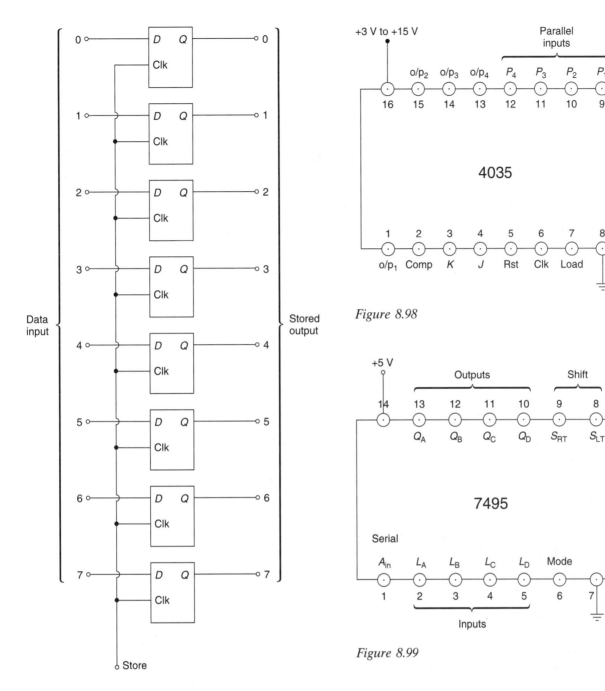

Figure 8.97

Figure 8.98

Figure 8.99

4 mA. Compare this with the speed and current consumption of the TTL 7495 (Figure 8.99). This is also a 4-bit parallel in/parallel out register but has a maximum clock rate of 36 MHz at a current per package of 39 mA. The principle of switching the shift direction is again a matter of using logic gate control.

There are two data input lines: one for serial data to be shifted right and one for serial data to be shifted left. The direction is controlled by the logic levels on the AND gates applied via the two lines shown in Figure 8.100.

The circuit is arranged so that the logic levels on these lines are always the complement of each other. When the top AND gates are enabled (logic 1 on both inputs) the data right input is connected to the D input of flipflop A and its Q output is connected to the input to flipflop B and so on.

When the bottom gates are enabled the data left input is connected to the input of flipflop D and its Q output is fed back via the lower AND gate to the input to flipflop C and so on.

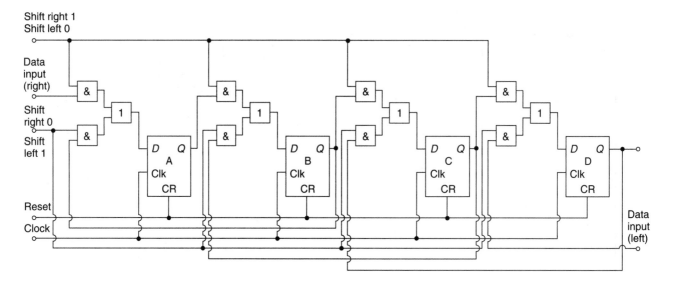

Figure 8.100

Multiple choice questions

1 The result of the sum 8_{10} + 110 is
(a) 1110_2
(b) 11_{10}
(c) 110_{10}
(d) 111_2.

2 The Boolean expression that represents the combination in Figure 8.101 is
(a) $Q = A.B + \overline{C}$
(b) $Q = A + C + B$
(c) $Q = A + B.\overline{C}$
(d) $Q = A.B.\overline{C}$.

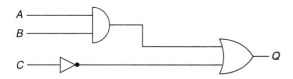

Figure 8.101

3 The truth table for the gate in Figure 8.102 is

(a)

A	B	Q
0	0	1
0	1	0
1	0	1
1	1	1

(b)

A	B	Q
0	0	0
0	1	1
1	0	1
1	1	0

Figure 8.102

(c)

A	B	Q
0	0	1
0	1	1
1	0	1
1	1	1

(d)

A	B	Q
0	0	0
0	1	1
1	0	1
1	1	1

4 The waveform that will be obtained from the output of the circuit in Figure 8.103 is which of the parts in Figure 8.104?

5 The circuit in Figure 8.105 has eight clock pulses applied to the input. The resulting states of the LEDs are

	LED1	LED2	LED3	LED4
(a)	ON	OFF	ON	OFF
(b)	OFF	ON	OFF	ON
(c)	OFF	OFF	OFF	ON
(d)	ON	OFF	OFF	ON

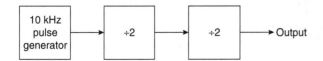

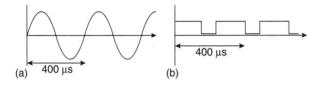

Figure 8.103

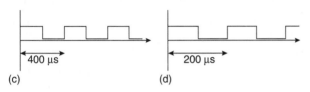

(a)   400 μs   (b)

(c)   400 μs   (d)   200 μs

Figure 8.104

6 One disadvantage of an asynchronous counter is
   (a) it is not a very fast circuit
   (b) the propagation delay is minimal
   (c) the circuit is not available in integrated circuit form
   (d) only LEDs can be used as a readout.

7 The counter circuit in Figure 8.106 will count from
   (a) $0 \to 10$
   (b) $0 \to 8$
   (c) $1 \to 9$
   (d) $0 \to 9$.

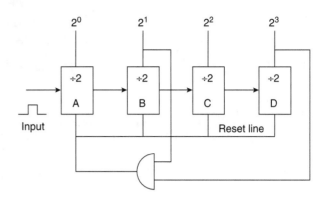

Figure 8.106

8 DeMorgan's law states that
   (a) $\overline{A.B} = A.B$
   (b) $\overline{A + B} = \overline{A}.\overline{B}$
   (c) $A.B = A + B$
   (d) $\overline{A + B} = A + B$.

9 An up–down counter is one which
   (a) resets on an up or a down count
   (b) counts in decimal
   (c) will increment or decrement
   (d) clocks every alternate pulse.

10 One purpose of a shift register is
   (a) to toggle outputs
   (b) to delay data by one clock pulse
   (c) to accept only logic 1
   (d) to reset after 2^{n+1} pulses.

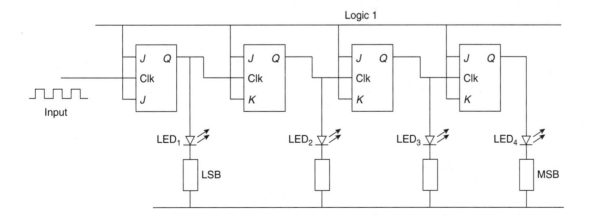

Figure 8.105

CHAPTER

9

Information transmission

9.1 Communication engineering and information transmission systems

The passing of information or data from one point to another is an integral part of everyday life. Indeed, it is quite remarkable to think that the first domestic broadcast of a radio signal is generally accepted to have been in 1919 and of a domestic television signal 1936, and over the relatively short time span of 60 years we have moved into the age of computer communications, electronic mail and satellite transmissions.

The transmission of information may be achieved in two ways using either DC or AC voltages to effect communication.

Information transmission using DC signals

The simplest transmission system that we can consider is probably the lighthouse which uses the process of switching a lamp on and off to convey information to ships at sea about the exact part of the land that they are passing.

Such a system is very much the same if used in conjunction with transmission lines. In the example in Figure 9.1, the buzzer at the far end of the cable (i.e. the load) will sound when the switch is in the closed position. The voltage (i.e. the source) to operate the circuit is supplied by the battery which only provides current when the buzzer is activated.

Examined electronically, the system is essentially interrupting and passing a current, the flow of which is used to operate the sounder. Observed graphically, the process can be resolved to Figure 9.1(b).

This principle formed the basis of the wired telegraph which used manual operators to send and receive DC pulses arranged in a system that followed the Morse code.

Other systems that use DC to signal include some telex machines and certain methods of telephone switching where the call connection information consists of short bursts or pulses of DC voltage.

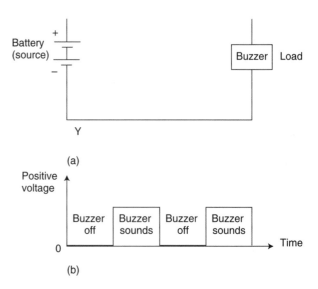

Figure 9.1

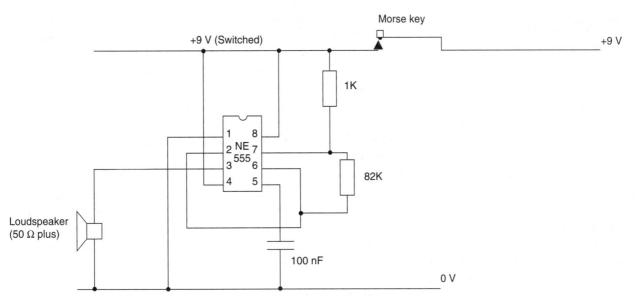

Figure 9.2   This circuit using the 555 can operate as an oscillator and can be used to signal information such as Morse code

The polarity of DC signalling

When DC is used to convey information, the polarity of the DC can also be used. The word 'polarity' refers to the direction in which the voltage used for signalling is connected to the line. It is not normally used when a DC signalling system consists of just a light.

In Figure 9.1(a) the connection of the source (i.e. battery) to the line is conventional and the applied voltage at point X is positive with respect to point Y. As seen graphically in Figure 9.1(b) this method of DC signalling uses a positive voltage. Note that the polarity of the source can be reversed which will give the opposite effect. In this case point X is now negative with respect to point Y and, graphically, the difference can easily be recognised (Figure 9.3).

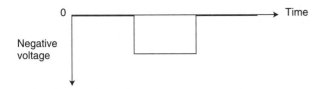

Figure 9.3   The concept of a negative voltage for signalling

Notice how the voltage that causes the signalling to occur is always positive or negative and is consistently either above or below the zero line and never crosses through it. It is therefore DC.

The limitations of DC signalling

The use of DC voltages to signal information is not extensive for a number of reasons.

(a) A DC system requires transmission lines to connect the near and far ends unless it signals via light.
(b) Although easy to produce, DC cannot readily be amplified, which causes problems where the system in use suffers from attenuation.
(c) Most transmission lines contain transformers which are used for a number of purposes including impedance matching and altering the level of voltages. DC cannot pass through a transformer and requires the use of expensive repeaters.
(d) The majority of the noise that transmission systems suffer from is of a pulse nature. With a DC system of transmission the presence of sufficiently large noise voltages will cause the system to assume that there is information present when, in fact, there is none (Figure 9.4).

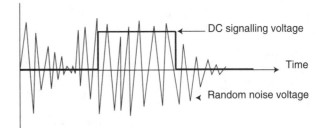

The noise voltage is read as a signal
even when the signalling voltage is 0 V

Figure 9.4

AC signals

Voice information is naturally in AC (analogue) form.

Most of us know that in a speech transmission circuit the very first component is the microphone. Its job is to convert into a voltage the changing air pressure that occurs as a result of our speaking. The output of a microphone therefore consists of a voltage pattern (sometimes called a speech pattern) which directly represents the way in which we speak.

As we change the loudness of our speech the height or peak to peak value of the voltage alters, whereas if we change the pitch of our voice the periodic time of the pattern and hence its frequency changes – see pages 70–71 for definitions of peak to peak and periodic time/frequency.

Notice from Figures 9.5 and 9.6 that, as we change the pitch of our voice, the number of cycles in a given time alters. For a very low tone of voice the oscilloscope may display one cycle per 10 ms waveforms whereas, if the voice is altered to a higher pitch, the number of waveforms would increase.

The calculations relating frequency and periodic time that were introduced in Chapter 4 (page 71) still hold true. Thus from the microphone pattern the frequency range or **bandwidth** of a person's speech may be obtained.

Although we all have different voices (and some people's are instantly recognisable) the majority of us speak in the frequency range 100–2000 Hz – a bandwidth of 1.9 kHz. This is sometimes referred to as the **baseband**.

Our hearing operates over a much wider span of frequencies and, at birth, is generally taken to be between 20 Hz and 20 kHz. As we grow older the bandwidth deteriorates and the majority of adults operate with a hearing range of 30 Hz to 16 kHz.

An important point to be noted from this is that it is not necessary for a person to hear the whole bandwidth of speech to understand conversations or music. This fact has been capitalised on by telecommunication systems which process speech between the frequencies of 300 Hz and 3.4 kHz. Known as 'commercial speech', this is the frequency range transmitted by telephone and radiocommunication systems. Note that for domestic radio and television broadcasting the frequency range used is much larger but is still not the full 20 Hz to 20 kHz range.

> Remember that it is not only audio AC signals that are transmitted from one point to another. AC tones may be used to represent digital levels of 1 and 0 and then transmitted (see later).

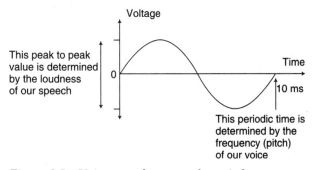

Figure 9.5   Voice waveform at a low pitch – someone speaking at 100 Hz

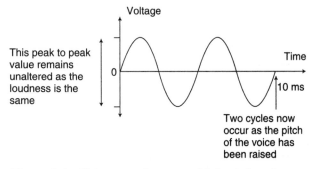

Figure 9.6   Voice waveform at a high pitch – the frequency is now 200 Hz

Baseband signals

Telecommunication engineers often talk of the baseband signal in a system. Essentially, this is the electrical representation of the signal that is to be transmitted. In a radio studio it is the output of the CD player or microphone that is fed to the transmitter. In a video signal it is the voltage out of the camera that represents the scene being filmed. In a telephone system it is the signal from the microphone.

Obviously, different baseband signals have different frequency ranges or bandwidths and here are a few examples:

Audio signal range	10 Hz to 20 kHz
Typical hi-fi amplifier	20 Hz to 20 kHz
Typical CD player	15 Hz to 22 kHz
Average adult hearing range	30 Hz to 16 kHz
Telephone (commercial speech)	300 Hz to 3.4 kHz
Video signal, 625 line UK system	0–5.5 MHz

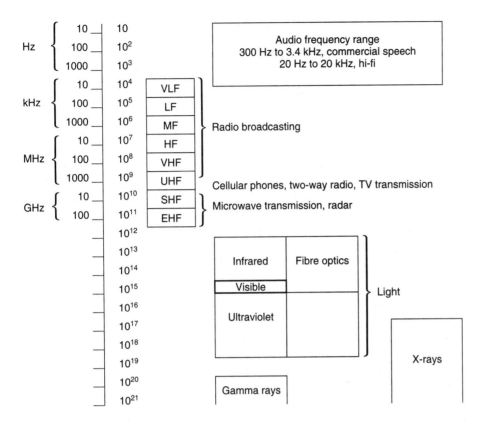

Figure 9.7   The frequency spectrum

The frequency spectrum

The frequency spectrum is the name given to a chart or graph which shows the relationship between signals at different frequencies. It starts at zero hertz and finishes at infinity!

In practice it is useful because at a glance it puts into perspective where signals lie in relationship to one another. A simple version is shown in Figure 9.7. The audio frequency range that we have just been talking about sits within one section. This can be lifted out and expanded to show graphically the difference between our hearing range and the frequencies between which most of us speak (Figure 9.8).

Video signals

A hi-fi signal contains information that is only audio, i.e. the music that we want to hear. A video signal, however, has to convey two types of information – the sound and the vision. To achieve this the complete or composite video signal actually contains two signals, one for the audio and one for the picture.

When looked at on an oscilloscope the vision part of the video signal is completely different from a simple audio signal. Over and above the voltage levels that will represent the brightness of the picture it contains synchronising information to ensure that in the receiver each line of the picture begins and ends at the same time as in the camera that is doing the filming. For this reason the time of one cycle of video (i.e. its frequency) is of importance (Figure 9.9).

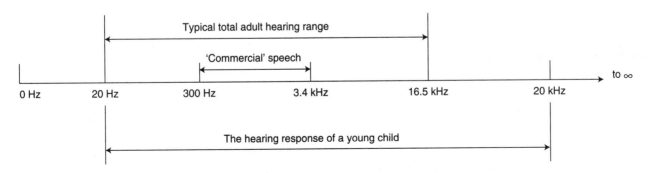

Figure 9.8   The audio frequency spectrum

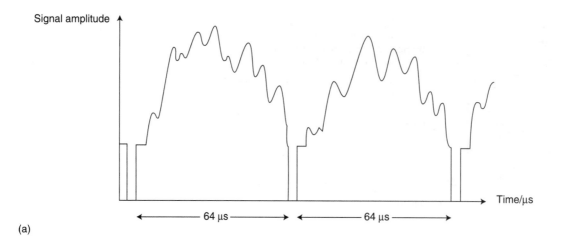

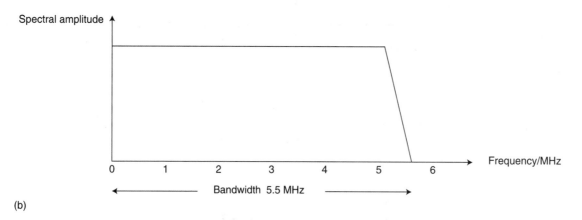

Figure 9.9   (a)   Video baseband signal and (b) video base bandwidth for the UK 625-line colour TV system

Notice that parts of the waveform are flat (i.e. they have the same voltage level over a period of time). This is obviously DC and so the lowest frequency of the waveform is 0 Hz. The upper frequency can be calculated and proved to be 5.5 MHz. The spectrum representation is shown in Figure 9.9(b).

The frequency of one line of video is easily found as

$$\text{frequency} = \frac{1}{\text{duration of one line}}$$

$$= \frac{1}{64 \ \mu\text{s}} = 15\ 625 \text{ Hz}$$

Digital signals

The difference between an analogue and a digital system

The analogue system   If you look at the signals that we have considered up to now the height or amplitude of the voltage directly represents the

loudness or intensity of the signal. Theoretically, then, the amplitude of the signal can be increased and increased until an infinite voltage level is reached. Such a system is said to be analogue. One example of an analogue system is where a vinyl record is played back on a hi-fi system. The principle of this is illustrated in Figure 9.10. The figure shows that the output of the stylus is a voltage that is directly proportional to the amplitude and frequency of the groove in the record. This voltage is passed through a series of amplifiers until it is of sufficient peak to peak value to drive a loudspeaker.

The digital system   Let us now look at another audio system but one which is completely digital – the CD player – and compare the types of voltages and signals that we should expect with the analogue system just described.

In Figure 9.11 the laser and associated sensor provides an output voltage that is in digital form. The difference here compared with the analogue voltage from the stylus is that the output is a series of pulses that represent the voltage originally recorded.

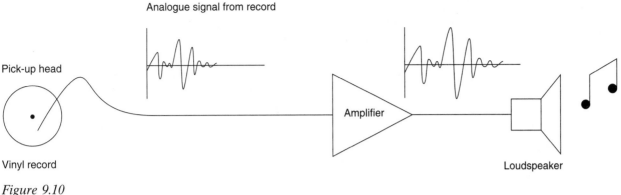

Figure 9.10

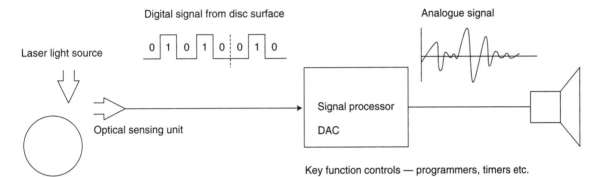

Figure 9.11

This pulse train consisting of only two levels, high or low, is applied to the digital to analogue converter which reverses the process and provides an analogue output voltage suitable for final amplification.

A comparison of the systems

At first sight it is easily appreciated that the digital system is more complicated than the analogue system. The advantages that it has, however, far outweigh the extra circuitry and expense.

One of the problems with an analogue system is noise or interference. Any quick burst of interference will appear as a noise 'spike' and immediately add to the signal voltage that is being processed (see Figure 9.12). You can imagine the effect that this would have on the signal voltage. It appears on top of the voltage that is to be processed and appears at the output of the system as a pop or a more continuous form of interference.

Problems such as noise are overcome by the digital system. When the compact disc is recorded the analogue music waveform undergoes the process of analogue to digital conversion at source so no risk of interference at this stage is possible. In playback, digital pulses are sensed by the laser and its associated reader and the signal is only returned to analogue form just prior to final amplification.

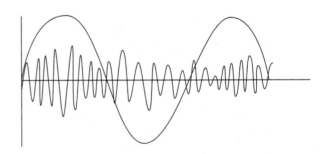

Figure 9.12 *Effects of noise on signals from analogue systems*

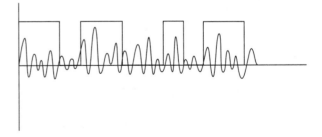

Figure 9.13 *Effects of noise on signals from digital systems*

Freedom from noise

Digital systems also have a property grandly referred to as 'noise immunity'. Consider again the noise spike that was first shown in Figure 9.12. This time we have placed it on a digital signal in Figure 9.13.

Several points are clear. The spike is of very short duration compared with the length of one of the highs or one of the lows. When the spike occurs at a point where the signal is high it has no effect as the system only registers voltages as being present or absent, i.e. ones and zeros. Where the spike occurs when the signal is a zero its length is so short compared with the length of the pulse that it has little or no effect.

If the duration of the spike is equal in length to the time that a pulse is low it will still have no audible affect as the frequency of the pulses (i.e. the sampling rate) is so high that the chance of the same low being corrupted twice in succession is virtually zero.

The principles just described allow the transmission of high quality signals that can be processed with no risk of distortion through interference. The advantages therefore apply to other forms of transmission media such as cable or radio.

9.2 Transmitting AC signals

One of the simplest circuits that transmits an AC signal is the one-way intercom (Figures 9.14 and 9.15). In professional circles the term simplex is used to denote a communication link that is in a single direction. If the link is two way – such as the normal telephone – it is said to be duplex.

The microphone provides a voltage out that directly represents the voice of the operator. This voltage pattern is connected via a pair of wires to an amplifier where it is increased to sufficient level for it to drive the loudspeaker. The amplifier is usually as near to the microphone as possible, as the natural resistance of the connecting cable would attenuate the microphone signal to a level where it was either 'lost' or became swamped by noise.

Although the concept is very simple it does pose certain problems. With a telephone system, for example, it would mean that each telephone would require a dedicated pair of wires for every other telephone connected to it. Obviously, such a system is impractical, and although all conversation and music occur within the same frequency limits cables carry more than one signal simultaneously. The same concept applies to radio transmission. We can listen to various radio stations at different frequencies on the dial but the speech or music that they are transmitting all originates in the audio frequency range.

What is modulation?

The process in which speech is changed from its original frequency to another at which it is transmitted is known as modulation. Modulation occurs at the transmitting or sending end of a circuit and is the superimposing of information onto a carrier wave. The opposite of modulation, which occurs at the distant end of a link, reverses the process and the original information superimposed onto the carrier is converted back into speech, music or data. This is known as demodulation.

Types of modulation

You will have undoubtedly heard of some of the methods of modulation as there are two types that are commonly used for domestic broadcasting – amplitude modulation (AM) and frequency modulation (FM). In addition to these there are other examples including pulse and phase modulation.

Figure 9.16 illustrates the concept of modulation. The information to be transmitted, known as the modulating signal, forms one input to the modulator. The other input is the carrier and is normally at a higher frequency than the modulating frequency. The output of the modulator will depend on the types of input applied.

Amplitude modulation

In AM the amplitude of the carrier is changed by the modulating signal. The result of the process of modulation can be examined in two ways – either by looking graphically at the output of a modulator on an oscilloscope or by examining the output by using a frequency spectrum analyser. The latter is a device which displays waveforms in their relative positions in the frequency spectrum.

It is simplest to examine the process of AM by considering a single audio tone applied to the modulator. Such a tone could come from a test oscillator (a typical frequency in broadcasting for a

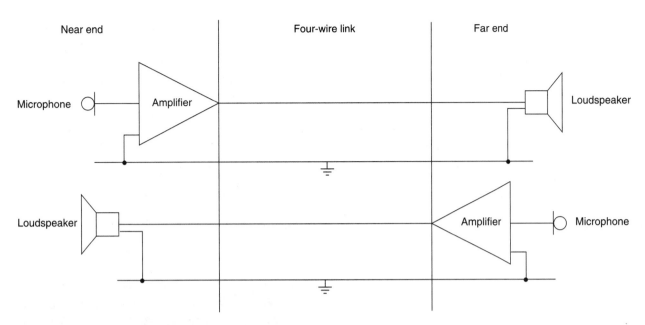

Figure 9.14

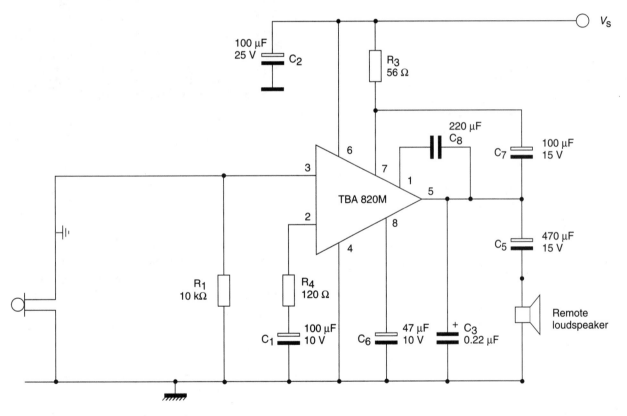

Figure 9.15   A suitable circuit for an intercom

test tone is 1 kHz) or even from someone whistling at an even pitch and loudness (i.e. amplitude) down a microphone.

The two inputs to the modulator are shown in Figure 9.17. One is the audio note that is to be transmitted, known as the modulating audio (f_m), a steady tone of, say, 600 Hz. This frequency is sometimes called the **baseband frequency**. The other input originates from an oscillator which provides the carrier frequency (f_c). In the case of our example let's say that the carrier frequency is 100 kHz.

The modulator operates such that the height or amplitude of the carrier frequency is controlled by the peak value of the modulating audio. The resultant waveform out of the modulator is a

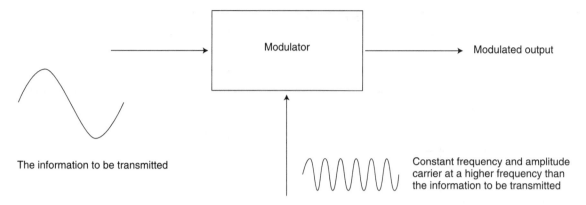

Figure 9.16

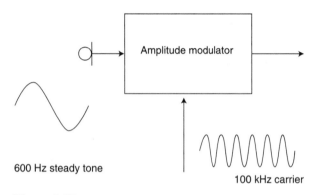

Figure 9.17

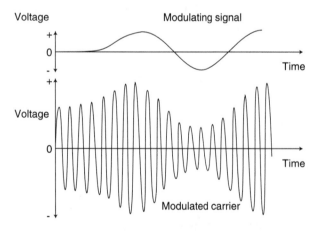

Figure 9.18

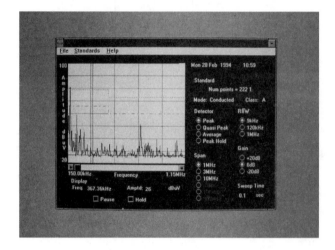

Spectrum analyser

Practical 1

The circuit shown in Figure 9.19 (opposite) is a simple amplitude modulator. Although typical frequencies and peak to peak values of inputs are suggested, build the circuit and experiment with other values to show the effects of distortion produced by over-modulation.

carrier wave the amplitude of which varies at the rate of the change in height of the modulating audio. Its actual shape is illustrated in Figure 9.18.

Notice in Figure 9.18 that, when the peak value of the modulating audio decreases, the same happens to the carrier wave's amplitude.

It is the outer shape of the modulated carrier that directly resembles the tone that was used to achieve modulation and it is this envelope that is detected in the receiver and used to obtain the original modulating audio from the transmitted carrier.

The products of amplitude modulation

Examined mathematically, the output of the modulator is found to consist of four frequencies:

(a) the carrier f_c;
(b) the carrier plus the modulating audio $(f_c + f_m)$, known as the upper side frequency;
(c) the carrier minus the modulating audio $(f_c - f_m)$, known as the lower side frequency;
(d) the modulating audio signal f_m.

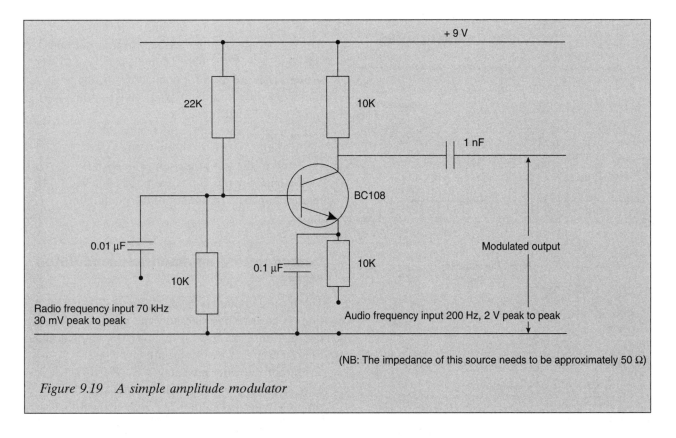

Figure 9.19   A simple amplitude modulator

Displayed as a frequency spectrum these would appear as in Figure 9.20.

Note that it is quite common to ignore the modulating audio as its frequency lies so far away from those of the other outputs.

The bandwidth of the modulated signal is from the lower side frequency to the upper side frequency which equates to twice the modulating audio frequency.

100% modulation

A little thought applied to Figure 9.19 should tell you that there must be a limit that the amplitude of the modulating audio should not be allowed to

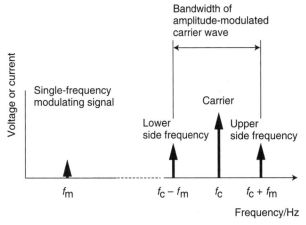

Figure 9.20   Frequency spectrum of an amplitude-modulated wave for a single-frequency modulating signal

---

Guided example

A carrier of 1000 kHz is amplitude modulated by a single tone of 1 kHz. The products of modulation are

$$f_m = 1 \text{ kHz}$$

$$f_c = 1000 \text{ kHz}$$

$$f_c + f_m = 1000 + 1 = 1001 \text{ kHz}$$

$$f_c - f_m = 1000 - 1 = 999 \text{ kHz}$$

$f_c - f_m$ ⟋ f_c ⟍ $f_c + f_m$
999 kHz   1000 kHz   1001 kHz

The bandwidth is 1001 − 999 = 2 kHz = $2 f_m$.

---

exceed because distortion to the envelope of the modulated waveform will occur. The maximum amplitude of modulating audio allowable before this happens is said to produce a depth of modulation of 100% (Figure 9.21(a)). A depth of greater than 100% is known as over-modulation, a typical example of which is shown in Figure 9.21(b). Over-modulation leads to the transmission of harmonics, causing interference to other signals.

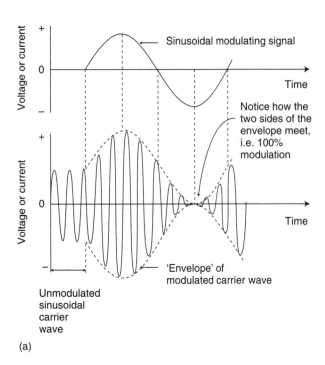

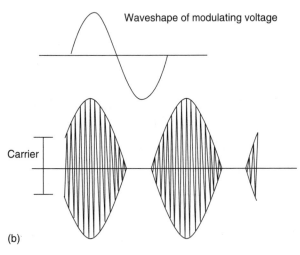

Figure 9.21   (a)   Graphical representation of an amplitude-modulated carrier wave; (b) an over-modulated signal – the modulation envelope is not an accurate reproduction of the waveform of the modulating voltage (this, or any type of distortion occurring during the modulation process, generates spurious sidebands or 'splatter')

Modulating with a range of frequencies

As already discussed, music or voice consists not of one steady frequency but of a range of frequencies. Modulating with a frequency range alters the products of modulation from two side frequencies equally placed on either side of the carrier to **sidebands** which appear as in Figure 9.22.

The contents of each sideband are the modulating audio frequencies superimposed onto the carrier.

Each sideband contains identical information and hence it is only strictly necessary to transmit one sideband. This is the basis of single sideband (SSB) systems that are used for commercial traffic (e.g. frequency division multiplexed cable transmission) but not for broadcast services.

Figure 9.22 shows that the bandwidth of the modulated carrier is from the bottom of the lower sideband to the top of the upper sideband. Mathematically this still corresponds to a width of twice the highest frequency of the modulating audio.

Demodulating an amplitude-modulated signal

The term demodulation (also often called detection) is used to describe how the process of modulation is reversed to recover the original audio information that was transmitted.

One of the chief advantages of AM is that it is easy and cheap to demodulate. A look at the simple circuit in Figure 9.23 shows that all that is

---

Guided example

A carrier of 7000 kHz is amplitude modulated by an audio signal of bandwidth 100 Hz to 2.5 Hz. The products of modulation are

f_c = 7000 kHz (7 MHz)

Upper sideband

$f_c + f_{m_1}$ = 7000 + 0.1 = 7000.1 kHz

$f_c + f_{m_2}$ = 7000 + 2.5 = 7002.5 kHz

Lower sideband

$f_c - f_{m_1}$ = 7000 – 0.1 = 6999.9 kHz

$f_c - f_{m_2}$ = 7000 – 2.5 = 6997.5 kHz

Spectral representation

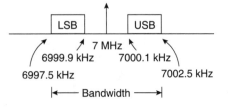

The bandwidth is 7002.5 – 6997.5 = 5 kHz = 2 × highest f_m.

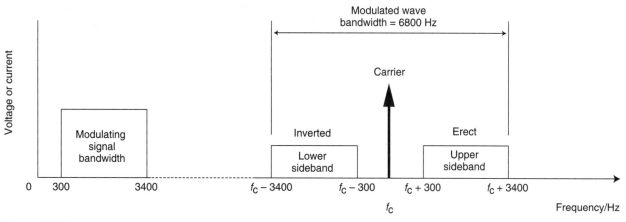

Figure 9.22

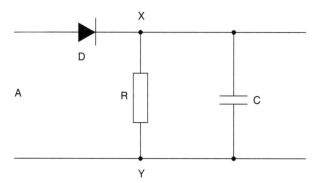

Figure 9.23 The diode detector

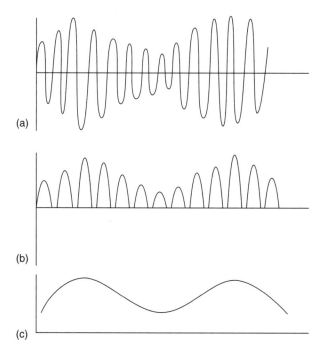

Figure 9.24 (a) Amplified AM wave at desired frequency; (b) output at XY in Figure 9.23 with C not in the circuit; (c) output at XY in Figure 9.23 with C in the circuit; the CR time constant is chosen so that C discharges to follow the modulation envelope

needed is a diode and a few other components – hardly complicated circuitry!

If we consider an amplitude-modulated waveform applied to the input to the circuit the action of the diode will be to perform half-wave rectification. The waveform now present is shown in Figure 9.24(a).

The charge and discharge of C now follows the envelope of the half-wave rectified waveform. As can be seen from Figure 9.24(b) the voltage across it thus resembles that of the original modulating audio and hence the original audio information that was shifted to a higher frequency carrier can be retrieved.

In an AM radio the demodulator is followed by an audio amplifier so that the demodulated audio can be brought up to a suitable peak to peak value to drive a loudspeaker. On its own the simple diode demodulator has several uses – as a 'crystal' set, a simple field strength meter to indicate the power of a transmission and so on.

The crystal set

Figure 9.25 shows a circuit for the simplest radio receiver that can be built. It consists of three sections:

(a) the aerial and tuning;
(b) the demodulator;
(c) the headphones.

Although it is simple to build the circuit can give surprisingly good results if the broadcasts it is tuned to are strong enough. Note that it will not drive a loudspeaker directly and the headphones should be high impedance (not 8 Ω standard).

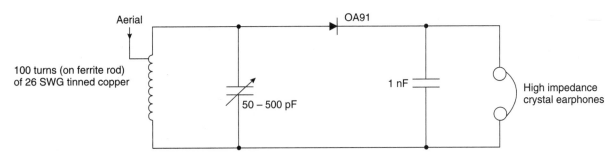

Figure 9.25

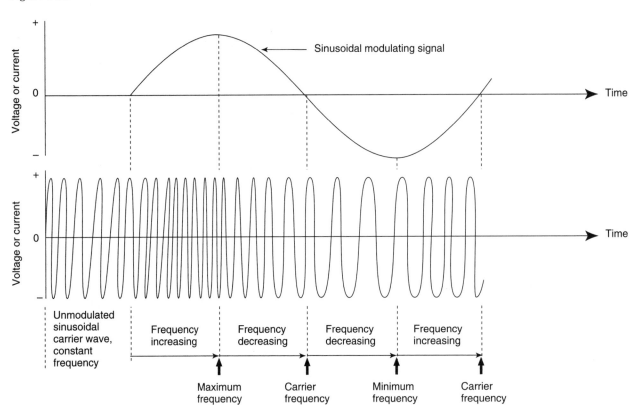

Figure 9.26   Graphical representation of a frequency-modulated carrier wave

Frequency modulation

In the same manner that the amplitude of a carrier wave can be altered so that it represents the height of the modulating audio an approach can be adopted where the peak to peak value of the carrier wave always remains constant but its frequency is changed in sympathy with the changes in amplitude of the modulating audio. This is the basis of FM.

Figure 9.26 illustrates the principle of FM. When the amplitude of the modulating audio changes, the frequency of the carrier constantly alters. As the amplitude increases towards a positive maximum the frequency of the modulated carrier increases and, conversely, as the amplitude of the modulating audio declines from a positive maximum towards its negative peak the frequency of the modulated carrier decreases. Notice that, in contrast with AM, the amplitude of the carrier never alters.

The products of frequency modulation

Thus in FM the modulated carrier constantly changes frequency. The limits between which it varies are determined by the peak and maximum negative values of the modulating audio. For one cycle of modulating audio, therefore, the carrier alters to a minimum below and a maximum above its unmodulated value. The range of alteration, or **deviation** as it is normally known, is equal above and below the nominal value of the carrier if the modulating audio is symmetrical.

The products of modulation of an FM wave differ from those of an AM wave in that they consist of multiples of the modulating frequency placed either side of the carrier. There are thus two side frequencies for each modulating frequency, one above and one below the carrier. The bandwidth of an FM wave is therefore much larger than that

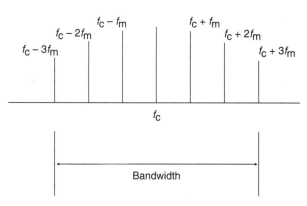

Figure 9.27

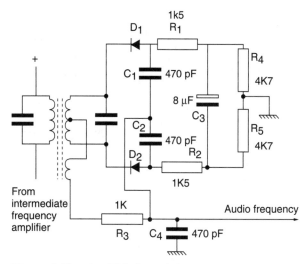

Figure 9.28   An FM demodulator

Guided example

A signal of 20 Hz to 15 kHz is used to frequency modulate a carrier of 100 MHz. If the rated system deviation is ±50 kHz the bandwidth is

$$2(f_{d_{max}} + f_{max}) = 2(50 + 15) = 130 \text{ kHz}$$

---

occupied by an AM wave. The concept is illustrated in Figure 9.27.

In theory the bandwidth is infinite but in practice it tends to be limited to

$$2(f_{d_{max}} + f_{max})$$

where $f_{d_{max}}$ is the rated system deviation and f_{max} is the highest modulating frequency. For example, the BBC has a deviation of ±75 kHz and the highest modulating frequency is 15 kHz. The bandwidth is therefore 2(75 + 15) = 180 kHz.

The demodulation of a frequency-modulated signal

We have already seen that the demodulation of an AM wave is very simple. Furthermore, it is easy to build a crystal set from just a few components. The detection of FM is much more complicated and the description of the circuit operation is somewhat lengthy!

The circuit of a typical discrete component FM detector is shown in Figure 9.28. Remembering that with FM the frequency of the modulated carrier is dependent on the instantaneous amplitude of the audio, the output of the FM detector is either positive or negative according to the input frequency. The response curve is S-shaped as shown in Figure 9.29.

Note that it is much more difficult to set up an FM detector than an AM detector.

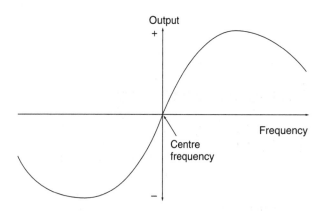

Figure 9.29

Amplitude modulation versus frequency modulation

Both AM and FM are used for commercial broadcasting. Each has advantages and disadvantages when comparisons are made.

One of the most common forms of interference in a communication system is pulses of voltage which add to the changes in amplitude of the carrier and appear as noise and interference on the demodulated waveform. With an FM wave it is relatively easy to suppress this type of noise as only changes in frequency of the received carrier are detected, not variations in amplitude.

The bandwidth occupied by an FM wave is very much greater than that of an AM wave but stereo broadcasting is easily achieved with FM. This has implications for the use of frequency spectrum space.

The modulation and detection of AM is simple and cheap compared with FM.

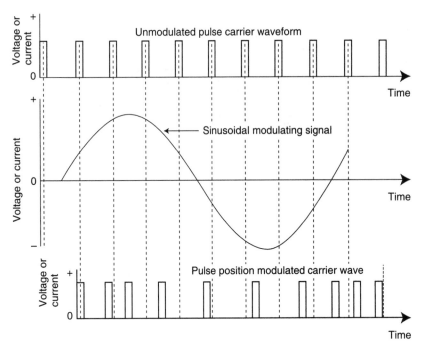

Figure 9.30   Pulse position modulation

Pulse modulation

Pulse modulation differs from AM and FM as there are several different ways of achieving it. Three systems of pulse modulation will now be considered; pulse position modulation (PPM), pulse width modulation (PWM) and pulse amplitude modulation (PAM).

Of these three, PPM and PWM are digital whereas PAM is analogue. PAM is widely used in communications after digitisation.

Pulse position modulation

PPM alters the position of the carrier wave pulse rather than its width or height. The principle is illustrated in Figure 9.30. PPM is little used compared with PAM and PWM.

Pulse width modulation

Unlike the systems previously considered the carrier in Figure 9.32 consists not of a continuous

Practical 2

The circuit in Figure 9.31 will produce a pulse position modulated waveform. You can build it in two forms. Circuit (a) requires an external input for modulation. Circuit (b) allows a self-contained demonstration circuit to be constructed.

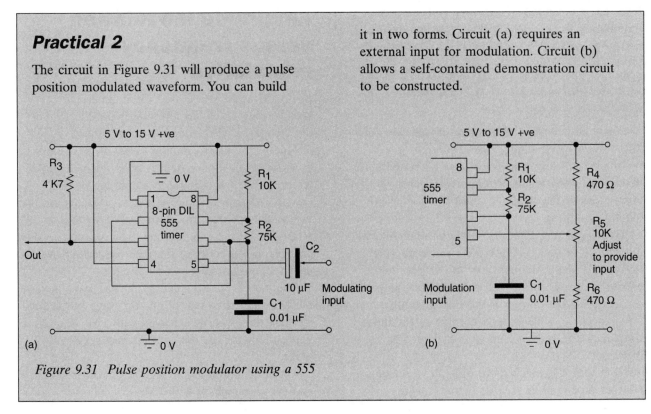

Figure 9.31   Pulse position modulator using a 555

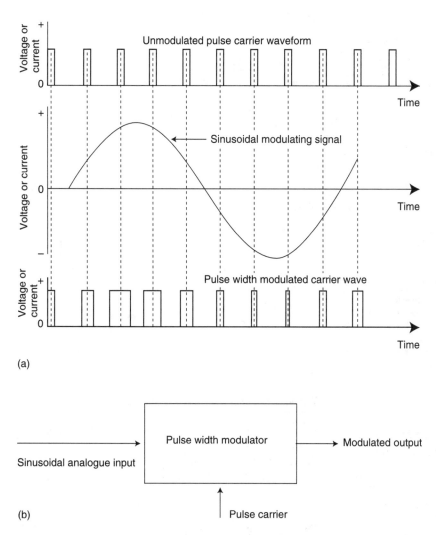

(a)

(b)

Figure 9.32 Pulse width modulation

sinewave but of a series of pulses that are at a constant frequency and amplitude.

When this carrier is applied to the modulator together with the audio to be transmitted, the resultant output resembles the original carrier only inasmuch as it still consists of pulses that all have the same height. The width, or duration, of the pulse is altered so that this reflects the amplitude of the modulating waveform. For example, as the modulating waveform alters from 0 V amplitude towards a positive peak the pulse width of the modulated carrier increases. Conversely, when the modulating waveform goes negative the reverse occurs and the width of the pulse diminishes.

The output train of modulated pulses is therefore digital as the information is either present or not present.

As a system for conveying audio information PWM is not one of the best. If it was used the detector would have to be capable of accurately measuring the duration of the received pulse and converting this back into its audio equivalent.

However, PWM is used in speed and temperature control systems where the average value of the pulse is of consequence and not the actual width at any one instant. As no detector stage is used the system can remain simple.

Pulse amplitude modulation

PAM is illustrated in Figure 9.34. The audio signal to be modulated is applied to the modulator along

---

Practical 3

Pulse width modulation

The circuit in Figure 9.33 will provide an output pulse train that is variable in width according to the modulation input waveform.

IC_1 is configured as a 1 kHz astable multivibrator providing the carrier and triggers IC_2 which is connected as a monostable.

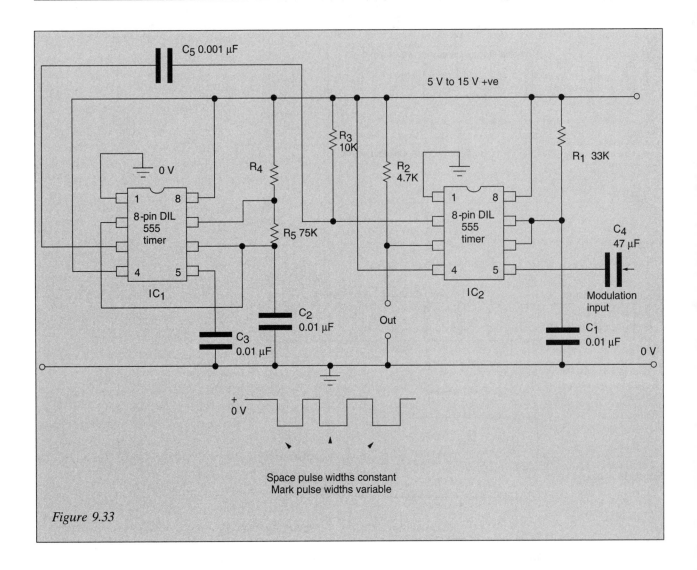

Figure 9.33

Space pulse widths constant
Mark pulse widths variable

---

with the carrier which consists, as in PWM, of a train of regular pulses.

Examination of the modulated carrier output shows that it consists of a regular pulse width but at any time its height, or amplitude, is proportional to the modulating audio. Each pulse of the modulated carrier is known as a sample.

The modulated pulse waveform is still an analogue signal and, as such, will be susceptible to all the problems of noise and distortion to which this type of waveform is prone.

For this reason PAM is invariably used in conjunction with a second stage of circuitry which is known as quantisation.

Quantisation

Quantisation is the word that is used to describe how the analogue format of a pulse amplitude modulated carrier is converted or **encoded** into a digital signal that consists of a string of binary numbers.

We have already seen that a signal which has undergone PAM is still in analogue format.

The next stage of the process is to apply this PAM waveform to a circuit which will give an output voltage at each sample time. This voltage should be proportional to the height of the sample.

First, a voltage is nominated to the total height of the samples – in Figure 9.35 the overall voltage present is 8 V and 1 V sub-divisions are shown. Note that the level of the voltage must exceed any noise voltages that may be present.

The binary representation of each voltage level is given next to it. For example, at the seventh sample the voltage is at a height of 5 V or, in its binary equivalent, 0101_2. The signal has thus been encoded into digital form.

At each sample time, the binary equivalent of the height of the sample is available as the output of the quantisation circuit. Eventually this will be transmitted down the line or over free space.

The resulting pulse train is shown in Figure 9.36, time related to the sample points of the original analogue waveform and the quantisation level taken at the sample point.

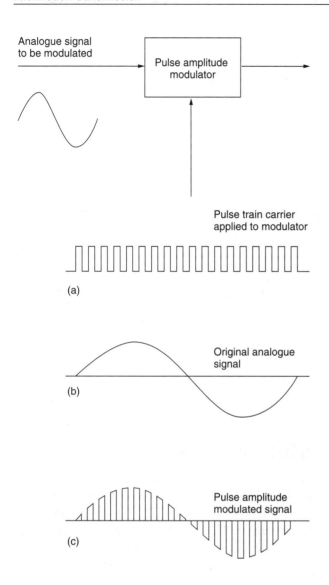

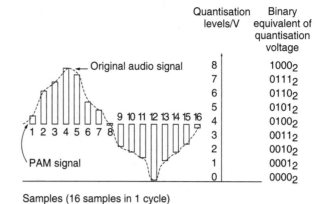

Figure 9.35

(a)

(b)

(c)

Figure 9.34 Pulse amplitude modulation

You should now be able to see that the original analogue waveform has been translated into a digital format which can be transmitted without the corruption and distortion problems to which analogue signals are susceptible.

The method outlined so far (Figure 9.37) has to be refined somewhat for a practical system. A number of factors have to be taken into account such as the sampling rate and duration compared with the frequency of the wave that is undergoing quantisation. The accepted rule is that the minimum sampling rate must be at least twice the highest frequency of the audio baseband signal to be transmitted. You have also probably noticed that at the sampling instant the quantisation level is taken as the nearest to the height of the pulse amplitude signal. This is another reason why the number of samples taken must exceed the baseband frequency by at least a factor of 2.

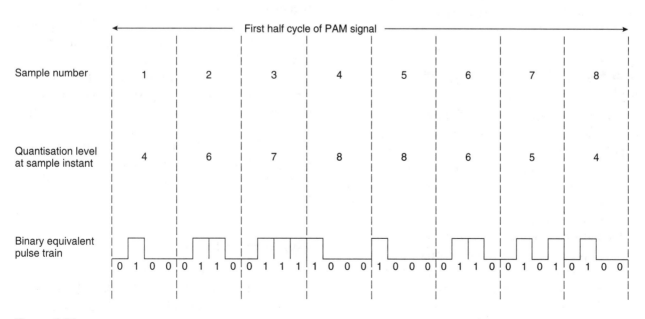

Figure 9.36

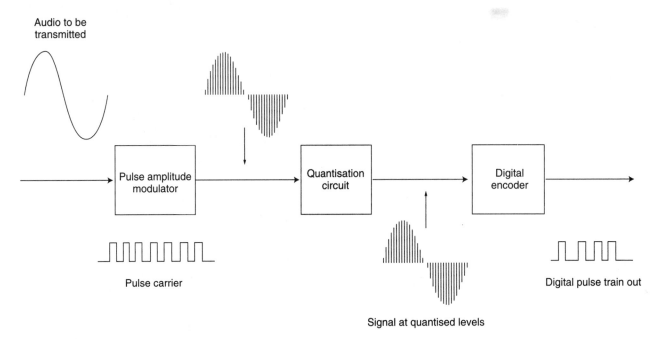

Figure 9.37   Digitising an audio signal for transmission

Sampling rate calculation

From the above statement,

> a signal of bandwidth *B* hertz requires a **minimum** sampling rate of 2*B* hertz.

For example, for a commercial speech signal of 300–3.4 kHz, the bandwidth is (3400–300) Hz = 3100 Hz. The minimum sampling rate is therefore 3100 × 2 = 6200 samples per second.

British Telecom have standardised their sample rate at 8000 per second. A total of 128 quantisation levels is used (i.e. 2^7), requiring an 8-bit system.

Transmitting the binary pulse train

Life would be simple if the digital signal that has been produced as a result of quantisation could be applied directly to a line transmission system.

However, a digital signal is DC as it is all above 0 V. As we have already discussed, the transmission of a DC signal is difficult via a line because of the presence of transformers, capacitors etc.

We have now reached the situation where the encoded pulse train that represents the original audio information must be modulated to allow transmission, either over line or over free space. To achieve this, shift keying is used.

Shift keying

There are several methods of shift keying, namely amplitude, frequency and phase. All achieve the same result of converting a digital signal into a format that will allow it to be transmitted either via the public switched telephone network (PSTN) or via free space (i.e. a radio transmission).

Amplitude shift keying

Amplitude shift keying is illustrated in Figure 9.38(a). The digital signal is applied to a circuit together with a carrier at a constant audio frequency and amplitude. When the digital signal is at level 1 the carrier appears at the output of the circuit but when the digital signal drops to level 0 no carrier is transmitted. Bursts of carrier are transmitted (or squirted!) down the line. At the far end the process has to be reversed to recover the digital signal.

A potential disadvantage of this method of shift keying is that any noise during a period of no carrier transmission could cause the wrong code to be detected.

Phase shift keying

In phase shift keying a constant carrier is transmitted down the line but its phase is altered to represent the difference between the digital levels of the signal.

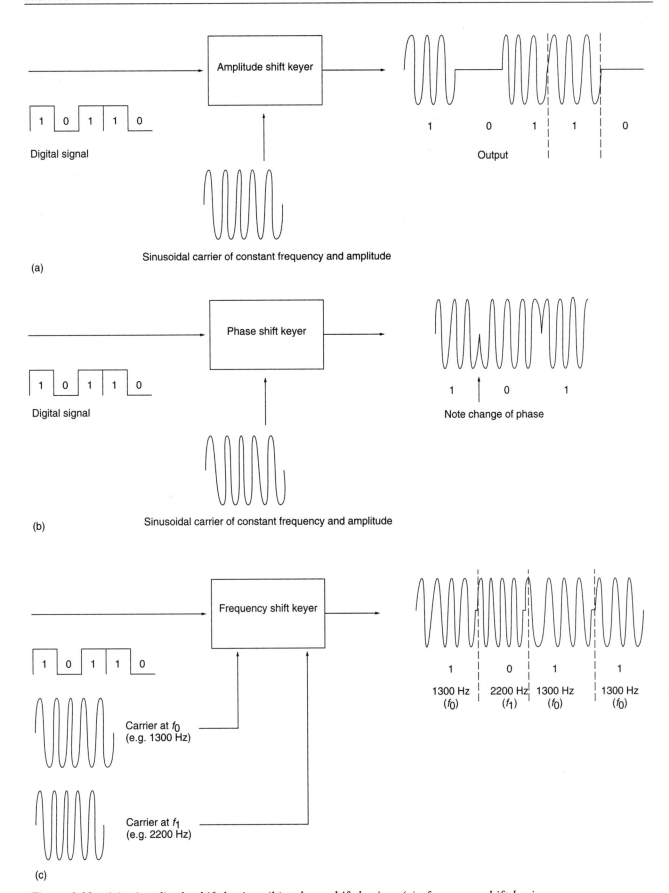

Figure 9.38   (a) Amplitude shift keying; (b) phase shift keying; (c) frequency shift keying

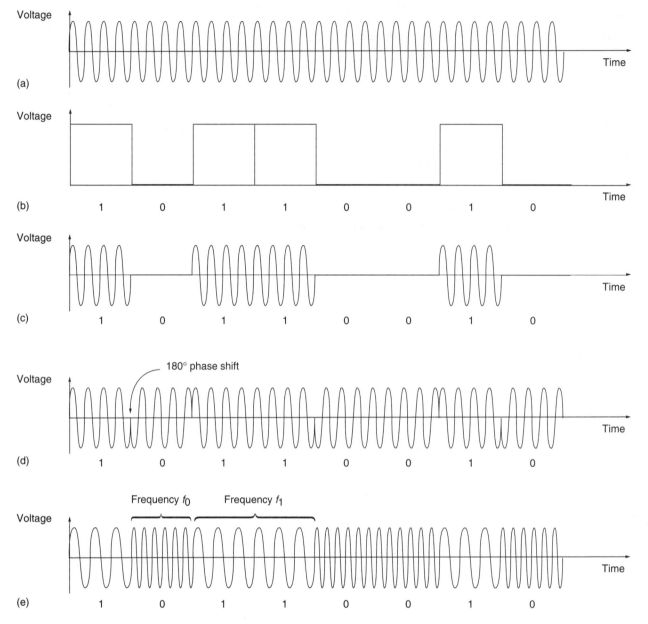

Figure 9.39   (a) Normal carrier wave; (b) digital signal, binary message 10110010; (c) amplitude shift keying; (d) phase shift keying; (e) frequency shift keying

Figure 9.38(b) shows how the phase of the carrier changes by 180° when the digital signal moves from 1 to 0 or vice versa.

Frequency shift keying

Frequency shift keying is one of the most common methods and finds wide application in computer modems and in the transmission of digital signals over radio.

As illustrated in Figure 9.38(c) two carriers are used, one of frequency f_0 and one of frequency f_1. For example, f_0 could be 1300 Hz and f_1 could be 2200 Hz.

When the digital signal is at level 0 one carrier, say 2200 Hz, is transmitted. At the instant that it

changes to level 1 the other carrier, 1300 Hz, is transmitted. The signal applied to the line therefore consists of two constantly changing audio tones. The principle is illustrated in Figure 9.38(c).

Figure 9.39 gives a ready comparison of the three types of shift keying together with the carrier input and the digital waveform to be modulated.

Multiplexing

The term multiplexing is used to describe a transmission medium that is carrying more than one signal simultaneously. Multiplexing is divided into two types: frequency division (FDM) and time division (TDM).

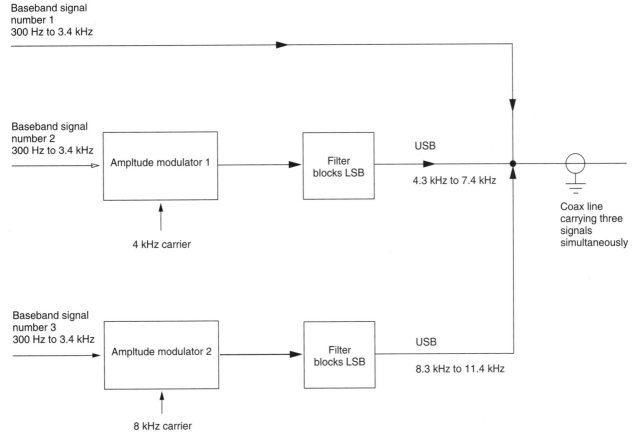

Figure 9.40

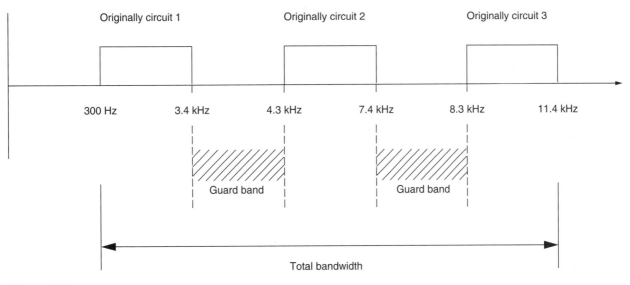

Figure 9.41

Frequency division multiplexing

Although you may not know it, you are already familiar with this form of multiplexing. Radio and television transmission over free space carries many signals simultaneously. These signals all originate in the same baseband of audio or video in the frequency spectrum. Separation of each signal is ensured by modulating them onto different carrier frequencies.

This principle can also be applied to line transmission. Figure 9.40 outlines the system. Three audio signals each of commercial speech are to be transmitted via the same transmission line. Signal number 1 is applied to the line with no modulation, i.e. it is transmitted at its baseband frequency of 300 Hz to 3.4 kHz. The remaining two signals are modulated each onto a different carrier frequency. Baseband signal number 2 is applied to an

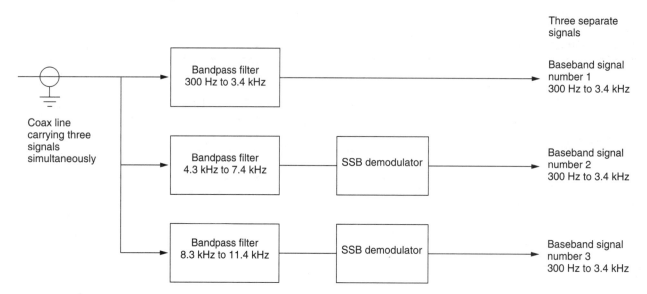

Figure 9.42

amplitude modulator which has a carrier frequency of 4 kHz. Baseband signal number 3 is applied to a second amplitude modulator, the carrier input of which is at a frequency of 8 kHz.

Assuming that the output of the amplitude modulators are filtered so that only one of the two sidebands produced is processed, the overall signal applied to the line will consist of three separate signals each at different frequencies. The frequency spectrum clearly shows this and is illustrated in Figure 9.41. Note the guard band that divides each of the signals. Its presence helps to ensure that crosstalk between signals is minimised. It can also be used to contain certain signalling information.

Retrieving the baseband signals after transmission
At the far end of the line the process has to be reversed so that the three original baseband signals can be processed to different destinations. This involves separating the two carriers and the signal at its baseband frequency and then demodulating the first two. A simple system is illustrated in Figure 9.42.

Although only a simple FDM system has been described the concept of different carrier frequencies can be extended so that a line carries hundreds of signals arranged in groups and supergroups. In theory the number of carriers could be extended over a vast frequency range but in practice the bandwidth of the line (determined by, amongst other things, its capacitance and inductance – primary line coefficients) limits the number of channels that can be simultaneously accommodated. Note that signals may be voice or data but the system is analogue and as such has its inherent disadvantages.

Summary An FDM system always transmits each baseband signal simultaneously. One can be at its original frequency; the others are placed on carriers. The frequency spectrum slot for each signal is totally dedicated and remains open even when breaks in baseband signal (such as pauses in conversation) occur. The system is analogue.

Time division multiplexing

TDM is different from FDM in that at any time only one signal is applied to the line. It is a digital system and has a greater capacity than FDM. It is not used in broadcasting but is widely applied for the commercial distribution of signals by telecommunication companies.

We have already seen how an analogue baseband signal can be put through a process of PAM and associated quantisation to produce the digital equivalent which is a continuous pulse train of ones and zeros.

A TDM system will take the pulse trains, divide them into sections each of so many bits and apply them consecutively to the line so that it only carries one signal at any time.

A simple TDM system that has to handle three 'conversations' is illustrated in Figure 9.43.

Each conversation has been digitised and as a result there are three different pulse trains. Each train is applied to a gate which controls when the pulses can be placed on the line. The clock pulses that open each gate are time sequenced so that it is impossible for more than one gate to allow information through at any time.

Looking at a time slot of the information that the line carries therefore shows sections of the digital pulses (i.e. bits) representing the three

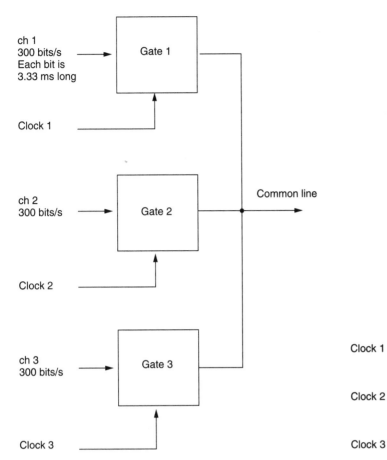

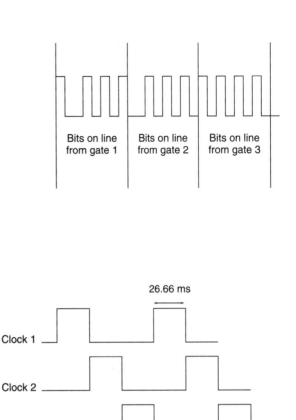

Figure 9.43   A practical TDM system

original conversations. One bit stream follows another and after the third conversation has had its section of bits transmitted the clock sequence repeats and bits from conversation number one are again placed on the line.

Obviously, the system has to be extremely fast so that the gaps in the transmission of bits from a baseband signal are not noticed by the human ear after demultiplexing at the far end of the line.

Summary   TDM is a digital system and as such has the advantage over analogue FDM of high noise immunity. As all signals are at the same frequency the total bandwidth of the line can be used, thus enabling a fast data rate. By a system known as bit interleaving, when a pause in conversation occurs the time slot that the signal would have occupied on the line is dedicated to an alternative signal. This greatly improves line-carrying capacity. TDM is more complex and expensive than FDM but for data transmission has become standard when used in conjunction with error correction systems.

Practical 4

ZN414 radio

This practical is of interest as it covers a number of theoretical topics. The ZN414 is a self-contained AM radio in three-pin integrated circuit form that provides an audio frequency output. The circuit is divided into two sections (Figure 9.44): radio frequency and audio frequency. Details of the audio part can be found on page 239 (simple intercom).

The radio section is of special interest as it is tuned by adjusting the bias on a pair of varicap diodes via the setting of RV_1's slider. R_1 acts as ballast resistor for D_1 which provides the stabilised supply for the ZN414.

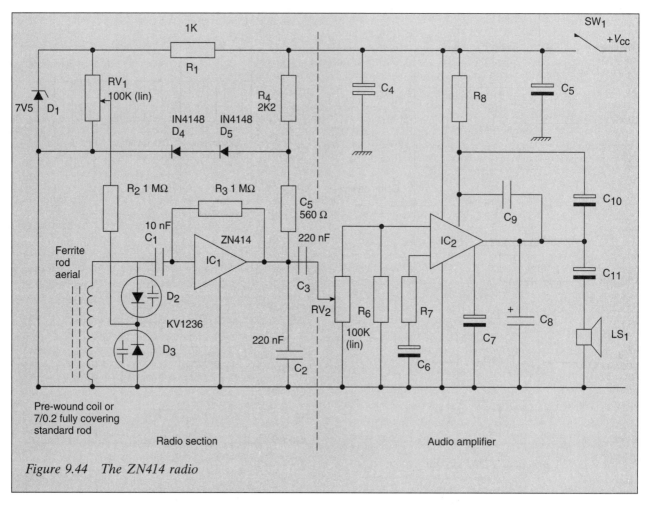

1K

R₁

RV₁
100K (lin)

R₄
2K2

C₄

R₈

C₅

SW₁
+V_cc

7V5 D₁

IN4148
D₄

IN4148
D₅

R₂ 1 MΩ

R₃ 1 MΩ

C₅
560 Ω

C₁₀

10 nF
C₁

ZN414

IC₁

220 nF

C₉

IC₂

Ferrite
rod
aerial

D₂

C₃

C₁₁

KV1236

RV₂

R₆

R₇

C₈

LS₁

D₃

100K
(lin)

C₇

220 nF

C₆

C₂

Pre-wound coil or
7/0.2 fully covering
standard rod

Radio section

Audio amplifier

Figure 9.44   The ZN414 radio

9.3 **The medium of transmission**

The term 'transmission medium' refers to the medium via which information is sent from one point to another.

We have already talked of the simplest signalling system of all, the lighthouse. This uses air or **free space** to convey information. A radio signal also travels over free space but for much further distances than light.

A telephone system may well use cable to link two points. However, the type of cable may differ along the route of the call according to local conditions. Alternatively, it could use a combination of fibre optics, satellite radio and cable.

Each medium has its own merits and inherent weaknesses. It is a case of choosing the most

appropriate medium to set up a communications link. It is no good using cable to communicate with vehicles!

Transmission by line

The simplest form of establishing a communications link using wire is to take two separate wires and run them independently from source to destination (Figure 9.45).

In practice it is only too obvious that adopting this strategy would give a very limited system. Assuming that the wires are just bare copper they cannot be allowed to touch each other or, indeed, any other conductor.

To overcome these problems most cable systems follow the pattern outlined in Figure 9.46 where the two conductors are insulated and enclosed in a sheath made of a malleable material such as PVC. As most systems use two conductors, cables are made by twisting the wires together. This allows easy routing of more than one set of conductors within a single outer sheath and is often referred to as 'twisted pair'. The number of twisted pairs within one cable may run into hundreds and the diameter of the outer sheath may be 10–15 cm (see Figure 9.47).

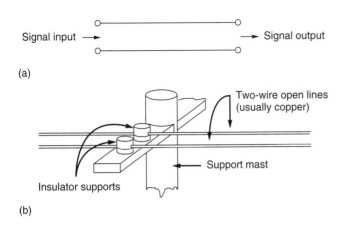

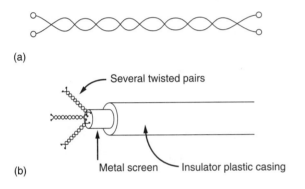

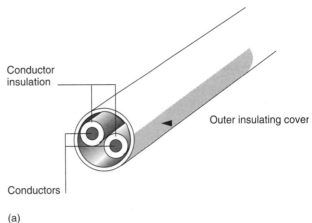

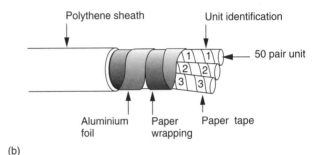

(a)

Figure 9.45   (a)   Symbol used to represent a transmission line in a circuit; (b)   example of a single-pair open-wire transmission line

Figure 9.46   (a)   Basic twisted pair configuration; (b)   example of common cable construction

Figure 9.47   (a) Audio-frequency unit-twin cable; (b) 50-pair units are made up into a complete cable; (c)   a 50-pair unit

One of the disadvantages of using two conductors as in twisted pair is that each conductor is susceptible to interference from external magnetic fields which induces a noise voltage on the line. One method of overcoming this is to use cable manufactured as outlined in Figure 9.48. Known as coaxial cable (coax) the outer of the two conductors (which is usually in braid form) is held at earth potential whilst the inner conductor carries the signal voltage. Another form of coaxial cable is often called screened lead. This is used for audio work.

The insulation that separates the inner conductor from the outer can be made of a number of materials and is known as the dielectric. The choice of dielectric is important as at high frequencies it has significant capacitance which can lead to loss of AC signals.

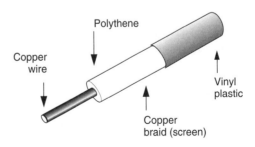

Figure 9.48   Construction of flexible coaxial cable (solid dielectric)

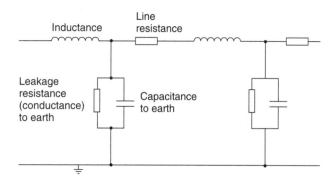

Figure 9.49   The primary line coefficients represent the electrical equivalent of a transmission line

Primary line coefficients

Every cable also has the natural resistance of the conductors and, between the two conductors, inductive coupling. The ever present factors of capacitance, resistance and inductance are known as the primary line coefficients. It is quite common to draw these when representing a piece of cable, as shown in Figure 9.49.

The value of the line coefficients can significantly affect the way a piece of cable will behave once a signal is applied to it. They can limit the bandwidth, attenuate the signal or alter the phase of the signals applied. Obviously this has to be kept in mind when choosing a cable for a particular purpose.

The effects of capacitance are significant at high (radio) frequencies and so the bandwidth of a cable can be limited by its physical construction. This has serious implications when signals are multiplexed as the number of signals that can simultaneously travel on one cable is limited by its characteristics.

The resistance of the conductors, however, will lead to attenuation of signals at all frequencies, and if the signal being conveyed is of particularly small value it is important to choose a cable of low resistance so that the attenuation the signal will suffer is limited.

If the cable link is over a significant distance repeater stations (i.e. amplifiers) are incorporated so that attenuation loss is compensated for.

Fibre optics

An alternative approach to conventional cable manufactured from copper is to use fibre optics.

If you look carefully at the frequency spectrum diagram given on page 235 you will see that as frequency increases the regions of infrared, visible light and, eventually, ultraviolet are reached. From this it follows that light is just another form of electromagnetic radiation and thus it is possible to modulate it to carry information. Prior to the invention of fibre optics early efforts at transmitting signals via light were made using tubes with reflecting mirrors to accommodate curves and angles. This method of using light transmission was not very satisfactory and it was not until about the mid-1960s that the discovery of very pliable optical cable manufactured from glass fibre made the use of the technology feasible.

Since then fibre optics have escalated in importance and are now taken for granted as another medium of communication. A simple digital fibre optic system is shown in Figure 9.50.

The audio information is encoded into digital form and then amplified. The signal now present is used to modulate the light source and the result is a continuous pulse train which is applied to the minute strands of glass fibre cable that propagates the light to the distant end. The light source may be either an LED or a laser. The former is cheaper but has a limited modulation rate whereas the latter is easily modulated, has a wide bandwidth and is highly efficient.

At the far end of the system the pulse train is received by a photodiode detector, the output signal of which is passed to the demodulator. The original transmitted signal is therefore recovered.

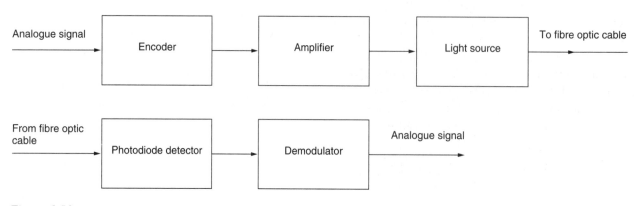

Figure 9.50

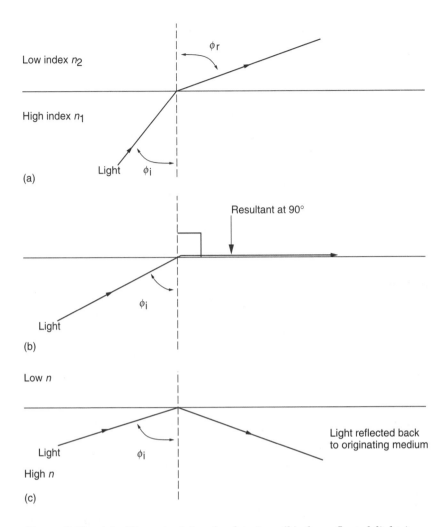

Figure 9.51 (a) *The principle of refraction; (b) the reflected light is propagated at 90° to the vertical when* ϕ_i *equals the critical angle; (c) total internal reflection (* ϕ_i *is greater than the critical angle)*

Although fibre optic systems have very much lower losses than conventional cables, 'in line' amplification is required. Repeater (sometimes known as regenerator) stations are incorporated

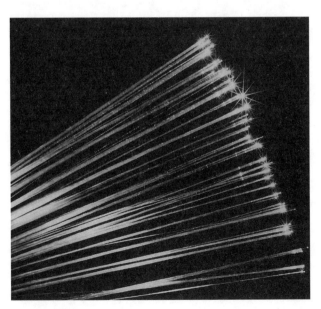

Optical fibres

where the signal is demodulated, amplified and remodulated and then once again applied to the fibre optic cable for onward transmission.

Fibre optic light propagation

The transmission of light via a fibre optic cable uses the principle of refraction, i.e. when light passes from one medium to another with a different refractive index its direction of travel alters. Figure 9.51(a) shows this principle.

The critical angle is the angle that the incident light makes with the medium when the reflected light is propagated at 90° to the vertical (see Figure 9.51(b)).

Assuming that the critical angle is exceeded the refracted light will be propagated back into the medium from which it originated. When the angle that light enters the fibre exceeds the critical angle, total internal reflection occurs and the light is reflected back into the originating medium (Figure 9.51(c)). At the opposite side of the cable another total internal reflection will occur and so the light passes down the cable. This is the principle by which a fibre optic cable conveys a modulated ray of light.

Fibre optic cable

The principle of propagation along a fibre dictates that the cable must be constructed using two media with different refractive indices. In practice, cables are classified into two types: step index and graded index.

Step index cable   This type of fibre optic cable is circular and consists of two materials each with a different refractive index. The change from one material to the other is abrupt and hence a graph shows a step function, from which the cable takes its name. The principle is illustrated in Figure 9.52.

Figure 9.51(b) shows that, assuming that the take-off angle of the ray does not exceed ϕ_i, the light will be reflected down the cable. Only a single – or mono – ray (as opposed to a diverse beam) needs to be propagated and this is achieved by ensuring that the wavelength of the light is the same as the diameter of the core of the cable.

If a number of rays from a single light source are propagated along the fibre, dispersion problems can arise. This is known as multimode propagation; the principle is shown in Figure 9.53. It follows that the propagation time for various rays to reach the far end of the optical cable will be different and this reduces the bandwidth.

Graded index cable   Unlike step index fibre optic cable where the refractive index changes abruptly from the inner to the outer cable, in graded index cable the process of change is gradual. This is illustrated in Figure 9.54.

Graded index fibre optic cable has the advantage that the bandwidth is large and this makes it the most commonly installed.

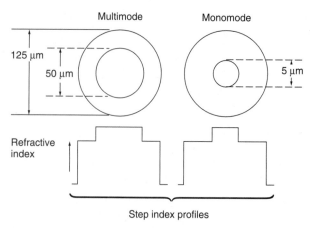

Figure 9.52

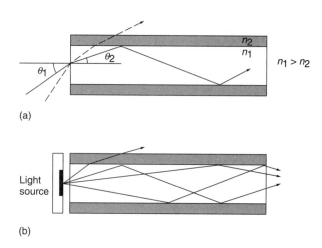

Figure 9.53   (a)   Ray diagram of a step index fibre; (b)   launch conditions into a step index fibre showing generation of multiple modes

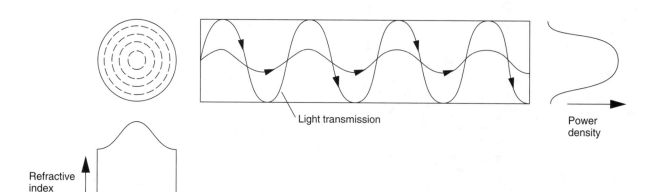

Figure 9.54

BT engineers laying optical fibre cable near Ambleside in the Lake District

The pros and cons of fibre optics

The three biggest enemies of transmission using conventional copper cables are *attenuation*, *interference* (including *crosstalk*) and *noise*.

Attenuation

As we have already discussed, attenuation in coax or twisted pair copper cable is due to the resistance of the copper cable used in its construction.

Whilst it is inaccurate to say that fibre optics do not suffer from attenuation, the loss measured over several kilometres is very small compared with that in coax or twisted pair copper cables. The losses that do occur are due to absorption of the transmitted light by the cable, scattering of the transmitted light (not all of the 'ray' is reflected onwards down the cable) and radiation – at a sharp bend in the cable the light does not propagate onwards but radiates from the point of the bend.

The significantly smaller attenuation of fibre optics means that fewer repeater stations are required, a further saving in cost.

Crosstalk

Crosstalk is the term given when a signal from one cable is induced in another. This can easily occur where several copper cables run adjacent to each other, possibly in the same sheath, and the changing magnetic field resulting from a signal on one cable cuts the next cable and induces interference in it. This can be a real problem when conventional cables such as multi-twisted pair in one sheath are used.

By using fibre optics each light transmission is contained within the cable and none escapes through the cladding. This source of interference is therefore removed.

Noise

The majority of noise induced in a conventional cable originates from changing magnetic fields and is man-made. Typical sources include electromagnetic pulses from power transmission lines, machinery, motors etc.

Practical 5

The circuit in Figure 9.55 will enable you to build and test a simple fibre optic link to carry audio frequencies. Once built, try increasing the frequency of the input beyond audio to determine the upper frequency limit.

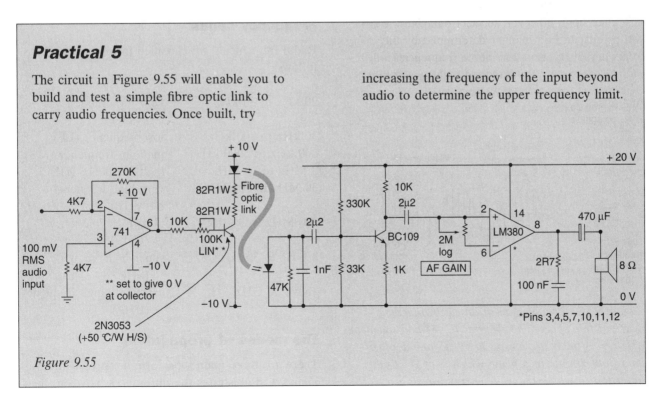

Figure 9.55

With fibre optics and light as a transmission medium the information carried is unaffected by external magnetic fields. It therefore suffers from very low noise interference. In a hostile environment such as a factory or ship etc. this can be of significant importance.

Bandwidth

Perhaps the biggest benefit of all is that the bandwidth of a fibre optic system is not constrained by line constants such as capacitance. It is therefore possible to multiplex the system to transmit thousands of signals simultaneously over one strand of fibre optic thinner than a human hair – an inconceivable idea in the early days of telecommunications!

Radio transmission via free space

An electromagnetic wave will propagate from an aerial via free space (i.e. the atmosphere) provided that its frequency is high enough (Figures 9.56 and 9.57). In general radio signals are taken to be signals that propagate from frequencies of approximately 16 kHz upwards.

Once radiated an electromagnetic wave can be treated in a similar manner to light. That is, it travels at the same speed of 3×10^8 m/s, is refracted when passing into a medium of different refractive index and is attenuated over a distance. At certain frequencies it can be reflected by objects or screened from others.

Unlike light, however, an electromagnetic wave will propagate in a manner determined by the frequency of transmission. Some frequencies will radiate over many thousands of miles whilst others

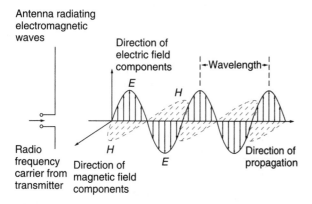

Figure 9.56 Propagation of an electromagnetic wave in free space. The electric (E, →) and magnetic (H, – – –) fields are always at 90° to one another and both vibrate in a plane which is at 90° to the direction in which the wave energy travels

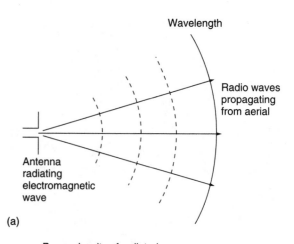

(a)

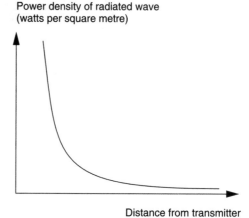

(b)   Distance from transmitter

Figure 9.57 (a) Radio waves spreading out from an antenna; (b) variation of power density of waves with distance from the radiation source

provide only a relatively local service. Additionally, the distance over which a signal can travel can be affected by the time of day or night.

Frequency bands

Radio frequencies are classified into sections as follows:

20 kHz to 30 kHz	very low frequency (VLF)
30 kHz to 300 kHz	low frequency (LF)
300 kHz to 3000 kHz	medium frequency (MF)
3 MHz to 30 MHz	high frequency (HF)
30 MHz to 300 MHz	very high frequency (VHF)
300 MHz to 3 GHz	ultra high frequency (UHF)
3 GHz to 30 GHz	super high frequency (SHF)
above 30 GHz	extremely high frequency (EHF)

The modes of propagation

There are three main types of radio propagation. Figure 9.58 illustrates the differences between them.

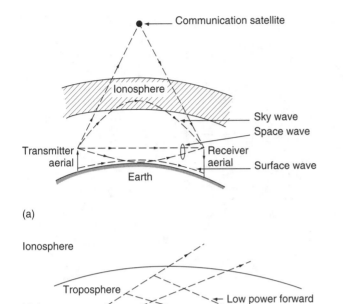

(a)

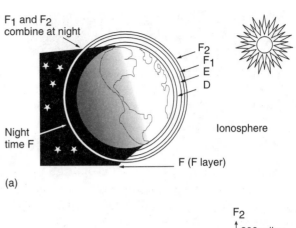

(a)

(b)

Figure 9.58 (a) Methods of radio propagation; (b) scatter propagation

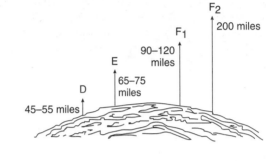

(b)

Figure 9.59   The ionosphere comprises several layers of ionised particles at different heights from the earth's surface. At night the F_1 and F_2 layers combine to form a single layer and the D and E layers disappear

Surface wave propagation   This is used in the LF and VLF bands. The radio wave travels close to the surface of the earth and follows its curvature. In the LF and VLF bands the distance that the surface wave will travel is considerable and a coverage of thousands of miles is not unusual. Surface waves also have the advantage that they can penetrate water.

At MF surface wave propagation is still effective and can be used for broadcasting but, beyond this band, as frequency is increased its effectiveness quickly declines until it does not propagate many metres beyond the transmitter.

Sky wave propagation   Sky wave propagation relies on layers of gases above the atmosphere of the earth known as the ionosphere. This region is subject to ultraviolet radiation from the sun and therefore its electron density constantly changes.

From about 3 MHz to 30 MHz, when an electromagnetic wave is radiated towards the ionosphere it encounters layers of ionised gases each with a different refractive index. These layers are shown in Figure 9.59. The electromagnetic wave is therefore refracted and eventually returned to earth. The distance that a radio signal can travel via sky waves is considerable and, if multiple hops occur, worldwide coverage can easily be achieved (Figure 9.60).

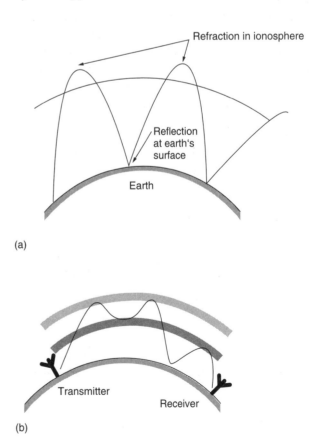

(a)

(b)

Figure 9.60   (a) A radio wave being propagated via multiple hops; (b) the signal may also bounce between ionospheric layers

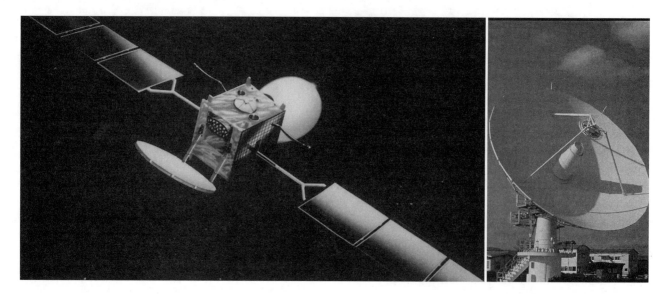

Inmarsat-3 satellite and ground station

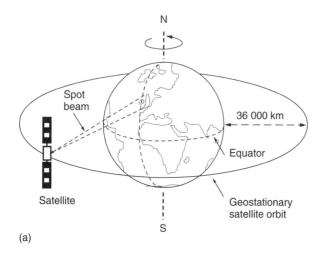

(a)

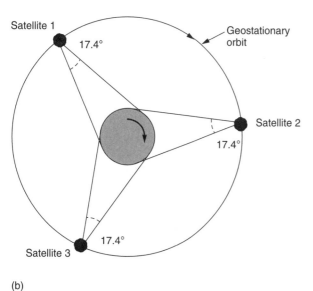

(b)

The disadvantage of sky wave communication is that the state of the ionosphere is constantly changing. This, in turn, alters the distance over which a radio signal at a certain frequency will travel. Because of this it is usually necessary to change the frequency of transmission depending on the time of day and year. This is not critical with other modes of propagation.

Space wave propagation   Space wave propagation is sometimes known as line of sight (LOS) and occurs when the frequency of transmission is raised above about 30 MHz. As the wave travels in a straight line from the transmitting aerial it is essential that the receiving aerial can 'see' that of the transmitter.

Space wave propagation is used at VHF and UHF. On the earth the distance over which communication can be established is limited by the curvature of the earth and the height at which the transmitting and receiving aerials can be mounted. A distance of 20 km is considered normal. For coverage beyond this, networks of relay stations are used.

Space waves are also the mode of propagation used for satellite communications. Above 30 MHz signals pass straight through the ionosphere with no refraction and thus it is possible to link up with communication satellites. Note that ground to air systems can also use space wave propagation.

Scatter propagation   Highly directional aerials are used to direct a radio signal of (effective) high

Figure 9.61   (a) Communication via satellite using the geostationary orbit. The satellites appear stationary with respect to the earth and thereby eliminate any tracking by transmitter and receiver earth stations. (b) World-wide communication can be achieved using three satellites spaced 120° apart in geostationary orbit

power at an area of the horizon just under the ionosphere which is known as the troposphere. A small amount of the signal is reflected in the forward direction and picked up by high gain dish aerials working into low noise amplifiers. The principle is shown in Figure 9.58(b).

Tropospheric scatter finds wide applications linking together two fixed installations such as oil platforms where communication needs to be continuous without the alteration of frequency that sky wave propagation involves.

All modes of propagation can be made directional by the design of the aerial from which the signal is radiated. However, electromagnetic waves are susceptible to interference from other magnetic fields, especially when AM is used. The problem is not so acute with frequency modulated signals but when data are sent via radio it is normal to include some form of error correction to ensure that signals are subject to minimal corruption.

Communication via satellites

Continuous radiocommunication can also be achieved by the use of space wave propagation and satellites in space. Assuming that the satellites are placed in geostationary orbit some 22 282 miles or 35 860 km above the earth they will rotate at the same speed as the earth. Viewed from the surface of the earth they thus appear stationary.

A space wave transmission can then be directed at the satellite where it will be received, amplified and re-transmitted back to earth. Typical frequencies are 6 GHz for the uplink to the satellite and 4 GHz for the downlink back to earth.

For almost 100% coverage of the earth's surface three satellites are required spaced as shown in Figure 9.61(b). They are located directly above the equator of the earth.

Satellite transmission is also widely used for domestic television broadcasting using geostationary satellites.

Orbiting satellites that rotate at a speed different from that of the earth are also in use for such purposes as weather observation, position fixing systems and photography of the earth's surface.

The frequency spectrum over which radio signals can radiate is crowded and space for transmission is allocated by international agreement. As different types of transmission require different bandwidths, segregation of signal types, their bandwidth and modulation system is attempted. For this reason, at MF and HF FM is not used. At VHF where the bandwidth available is large high quality FM can be employed.

9.4 Units of loss and gain within communication systems

Figure 9.62 shows a communication system with a number of repeater stations. What is the overall gain of the system?

Figure 9.62

If you answered 60 you are correct. However, if you thought that the overall gain was 15 you made the common mistake of adding each of the individual amplification factors together, which is wrong!

If we consider an input signal of 1 mV peak to peak applied to the system the picture becomes a little clearer. After the first amplifier the output signal is 10 mV, after the second it is 30 mV and at the final stage the signal is amplified by a factor of 2 to give its final value of 60 mV.

The overall gain of the system is the ratio of the output signal divided by the size of the input. Expressed mathematically we have

$$\text{voltage gain} = \frac{\text{peak to peak output signal (mV)}}{\text{peak to peak input signal (mV)}}$$

In our example the ratio is 60. That is, an input signal is amplified 60 times and appears at the output 60 times bigger than the input.

An alternative way of expressing the same ratio is to use units based on logarithms. First employed in the 1920s these have the advantage that, unlike in our example, individual amplifier gains may be added. Also, our own ears behave in a logarithmic manner.

Two formulae are used for decibels:

$$\text{dB} = 10 \log_{10}\left(\frac{P_{\text{out}}}{P_{\text{in}}}\right)$$

or

$$\text{dB} = 20 \log\left(\frac{V_{\text{out}}}{V_{\text{in}}}\right)$$

In our original example, the gain of each amplifier can be calculated in decibels as follows.

Amplifier 1

$$\text{gain} = 20 \log \left(\frac{V_{\text{out}}}{V_{\text{in}}} \right)$$

$$= 20 \log \left(\frac{10 \text{ mV}}{1 \text{ mV}} \right)$$

$$= 20 \text{ dB}$$

Amplifier 2

$$\text{gain} = 20 \log \left(\frac{V_{\text{out}}}{V_{\text{in}}} \right)$$

$$= 20 \log \left(\frac{30 \text{ mV}}{1 \text{ mV}} \right)$$

$$= 9.54 \text{ dB}$$

Amplifier 3

$$\text{gain} = 20 \log \left(\frac{V_{\text{out}}}{V_{\text{in}}} \right)$$

$$= 20 \log \left(\frac{60 \text{ mV}}{30 \text{ mV}} \right)$$

$$= 6.02 \text{ dB}$$

The overall gain can now be found in one of two ways. The ratio of the output signal to the input can be used:

$$\text{overall gain} = 20 \log \left(\frac{V_{\text{out}}}{V_{\text{in}}} \right)$$

$$= 20 \log \left(\frac{60 \text{ mV}}{1 \text{ mV}} \right)$$

$$= 35.56 \text{ dB}$$

Or the individual decibel gains of the amplifiers can be added (remember that this was not possible when each amplifier had its gain expressed as a ratio):

$$\text{gain}_{\text{amp 1}} + \text{gain}_{\text{amp 2}} + \text{gain}_{\text{amp 3}}$$

$$= 20 \text{ dB} + 9.54 \text{ dB} + 6.02 \text{ dB}$$

$$= 35.56 \text{ dB}$$

The use of decibels is only valid if *the input and output impedances are equal* (*matched*).

Decibels are not a measure of power or voltage but of increase in the level of a signal compared with an input signal. It is irrelevant to say that a signal is 3 dB but it is quite proper to say that a signal of 2 W has been increased by 3 dB to 4 W.

Here are some Guided Examples on the use of decibels.

Guided examples

1 An amplifier has an input power level of 4 W. The output power level is measured at 8 W. Assuming the input and output impedances are matched the gain of the amplifier in decibels is

$$\text{gain} = 10 \log \left(\frac{P_{\text{out}}}{P_{\text{in}}} \right)$$

$$= 10 \log \left(\frac{4}{2} \right)$$

$$= 3 \text{ dB}$$

(**NB:** A doubling of power equals +3 dB.)

2 An amplifier system has an input power level of 1 W. When the output power level is measured in a matched impedance it is found to be 17 W. The gain of the amplifier in decibels is

$$\text{gain} = 10 \log \left(\frac{P_{\text{out}}}{P_{\text{in}}} \right)$$

$$= 10 \log \left(\frac{17}{1} \right)$$

$$= 12.3 \text{ dB}$$

3 An amplifier has an input applied to it of 1 V peak to peak. The output signal is measured across a matched impedance at 2 V peak to peak. The gain of the amplifier in decibels is

$$\text{gain} = 20 \log \left(\frac{V_{\text{out}}}{V_{\text{in}}} \right)$$

$$= 20 \log \left(\frac{2}{1} \right)$$

$$= 6.02 \text{ dB}$$

(**NB**: A doubling of voltage equals 6 dB.)

Table 9.1 provides a ready comparison of power or voltage ratios with their decibel equivalents and is a useful reference source.

It is also quite possible to express a drop in power or voltage using decibels. You may remember that the bandwidth of an amplifier is measured where the output falls to –3 dB of the input which corresponds to 0.707 of the input.

If decibels are used to show a loss they are preceded by a minus sign as the following examples show.

Guided examples

1 A signal of 30 V is applied to a line transmission system. When measured in a matched impedance the output voltage is found to be 20 V. The decibel loss of the system is

$$\text{loss} = 20 \log\left(\frac{V_{\text{out}}}{V_{\text{in}}}\right)$$

$$= 20 \log\left(\frac{20 \text{ V}}{30 \text{ V}}\right)$$

$$= -3.52 \text{ dB}$$

2 A system causes a power level to drop from 25 W at the input to 1 mW at the output. The decibel loss is

$$\text{loss} = 10 \log\left(\frac{P_{\text{out}}}{P_{\text{in}}}\right)$$

$$= 10 \log\left(\frac{1 \text{ mW}}{2.5 \text{ W}}\right)$$

$$= 10 \log (4 \times 10^{-5})$$

$$= -44 \text{ dB}$$

Marchese Guglielmo Marconi (1874–1937)

Marconi was an Italian electrical engineer who was inspired by a paper on electromagnetic waves by Hertz. He worked on the method of wave production started by Hertz and gradually perfected a method of transmission and reception of these waves (radio waves). His work culminated in a Morse code transmissin of radio waves from the southwest tip of England to Newfoundland on 12 December 1901. This may reasonably be called the birth of radio, although it was Reginald Aubry Fessenden, an American, who actually used a carrier wave to convey sound information.

Table 9.1 Ratios of power and voltage in terms of decibels

Decibels	Power ratio	Voltage ratio	Decibels	Power ratio	Voltage ratio
1	1.26	1.12	15	31.6	5.62
2	1.58	1.26	20	100	10
3	2.00	1.41	30	1000	31.6
4	2.51	1.58	40	10^4	10^2
5	3.16	1.78	50	10^5	316
6	3.98	2.00	60	10^6	10^3
7	5.01	2.24	70	10^7	3160
8	6.31	2.51	80	10^8	10^4
9	7.94	2.82	90	10^9	31600
10	10.00	3.16	100	10^{10}	10^5

Multiple choice questions

1 The purpose of modulating a baseband signal is
(a) to broaden the bandwidth to improve quality
(b) to place it into the audio transmission band
(c) to enable multiplexing to occur
(d) to impress it onto a carrier for transmission.

2 The outputs of the modulator shown in Figure 9.63 will be
(a) 1 kHz, 500 kHz, 502 kHz, 498 kHz
(b) 1 kHz, 499 kHz, 0.5 MHz, 0.51 MHz
(c) 0.001 MHz, 0. 499 MHz, 500 kHz, 505 kHz
(d) 500 kHz, 1 kHz

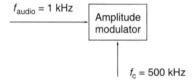

Figure 9.63

3 The waveform given in Figure 9.64 shows
(a) pulse width modulation
(b) amplitude modulation
(c) frequency modulation
(d) quad modulation.

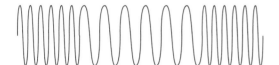

Figure 9.64

4 Which of the following types of modulation is most commonly used in digital transmission of audio signals?
(a) pulse amplitude modulation
(b) pulse width modulation
(c) pulse position modulation
(d) pulse frequency modulation.

5 The process of quantisation is
(a) digitising an analogue signal for transmission
(b) measuring an analogue to digital conversion
(c) quantifying the bit rate
(d) a method of time division multiplexing.

6 The minimum sampling rate when quantising a signal is
(a) equal to the bandwidth
(b) twice the bandwidth
(c) the reciprocal of the bandwidth
(d) twice the lowest frequency component.

7 Frequency division multiplexing is
(a) limited by the sampling rate
(b) a digital system for optical fibre networks
(c) used in multichannel computer networks
(d) an analogue system.

8 Time division multiplexing is
(a) used with frequency modulation
(b) a digital system
(c) a method of narrow band modulation
(d) used on short-wave radio bands.

9 In a TDM system each baseband signal is allocated
(a) a different time slot
(b) a different frequency band
(c) a different modulation system
(d) an alternative channel.

10 Stereo transmission uses
(a) pulse amplitude modulation
(b) pulse width modulation
(c) amplitude modulation
(d) frequency modulation.

11 Short wave radio communication occurs on the
(a) HF band
(b) LF band
(c) VHF band
(d) MF band.

12 The primary coefficients of a transmission line are
(a) an indication of line efficiency
(b) the first lumped resistance constant
(c) a multiple of the line bandwidth
(d) determined by physical construction.

13 One advantage of fibre optic over coaxial cable is that
(a) physical joining of cable is easier
(b) bandwidth capacity is greater
(c) attenuation is easily corrected
(d) baseband signals can be applied direct to the cable.

14 Satellite communication uses
   (a) ionospheric propagation
   (b) space wave propagation
   (c) surface wave propagation
   (d) reflected ionospheric ray propagation.

15 The transmission of a signal via a fibre optic system is likely to use
   (a) digital modulation
   (b) analogue modulation
   (c) cross modulation
   (d) hybrid modulation.

16 One disadvantage of step index fibre optic cable is that
   (a) it only accommodates analogue signals
   (b) it suffers a high degree of crosstalk
   (c) its bandwidth is large compared with graded index cable
   (d) its bandwidth is limited compared with graded index cable.

17 Most telecommunications which use satellite are via a geostationary satellite which
   (a) is stationary in space
   (b) is located above the polar caps
   (c) rotates anticlockwise when compared with the earth's movement
   (d) rotates about the earth at the same speed as the earth.

18 The ionosphere is
   (a) a means of propagation
   (b) a layer of gases above the earth
   (c) normally able to return space waves to earth
   (d) a method of satellite propagation.

19 Radio signals are likely to propagate from an aerial if the transmission frequency is greater than
   (a) 20 Hz
   (b) 20 MHz
   (c) 20 kHz
   (d) 200 kHz.

20 VHF broadcasts are to be found between
   (a) 30 MHz and 300 MHz
   (b) 3 kHz and 30 MHz
   (c) 300 MHz and 600 MHz
   (d) 600 MHz and 1 GHz.

21 The decibel is meaningless if no reference level is quoted because
   (a) the individual gains are added together
   (b) it is the ratio of two power levels

   (c) it provides an indication of loudness
   (d) the impedances will not be matched.

22 A system that produces attenuation would have a 'gain' of
   (a) 0 dB
   (b) negative decibels
   (c) positive decibels
   (d) equal decibels.

23 The gain of the system X in Figure 9.65 is
   (a) 0 dB
   (b) 3 dB
   (c) 30 dB
   (d) 1 dB.

Figure 9.65

24 The input voltage to the system in Figure 9.66 expressed as a peak value is
   (a) 5 V
   (b) 2.5 V
   (c) 2 V
   (d) 1.25 V.

Figure 9.66

25 The input power to system X in Figure 9.67 is
   (a) 80.72 W
   (b) 2.54 W
   (c) 1.27 W
   (d) 1.6 W.

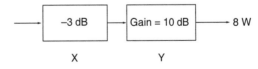

Figure 9.67

26 A telephone line system is fed with an input signal of 20 mV peak to peak. The output signal at the far end is measured as 1 mV peak to peak. The decibel loss of the system is
   (a) –26 dB
   (b) –21 dB
   (c) –19 dB
   (d) –20 dB.

27 An amplifier is fed with an input signal of 35 mV peak. The output is developed across a matched resistance of 1 kΩ and causes 1 mA RMS of load current to flow. The decibel gain of the amplifier is
  (a) 35 dB
  (b) 21 dB
  (c) 10 dB
  (d) 32 dB.

28 The unit of decibels is
  (a) linear
  (b) reciprocal
  (c) logarithmic
  (d) exponential.

29 Decibels are useful in audio work because
  (a) the human ear responds in a linear manner at all frequencies
  (b) an increase in a sound level does not cause an identical increase in hearing
  (c) all hi-fi equipment responds in decibels
  (d) attenuation in amplification is unusual.

30 The overall gain of the amplifier Z in Figure 9.68 is
  (a) 1.07 dB
  (b) 1.13 dB
  (c) 0.08 dB
  (d) 2.21 dB.

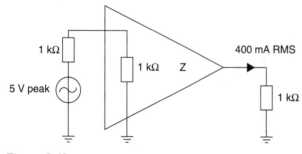

Figure 9.68

CHAPTER

10
Microelectronics

10.1 Micro-processors

Over the last few years electronic systems have become more and more dependent on micro-processors to provide control. Since they have become cheaper and more reliable the ubiquitous microprocessor has become a component that all electronics engineers must understand.

To this end, we first need to come to terms with the fact that the long dominance of the technology by the Americans has left us with a minefield of jargon, acronyms and terminology. At first this jargon seems a bit exclusive and daunting, but once we cut through it we find it's just electronics.

The difference between electronics and microelectronics is really just 'chip' technology. Resistors, capacitors, transistors etc. all operate in the same basic way but, instead of being separate (discrete) components they are integrated onto a single slice of silicon. Tens of thousands of them, together with all the circuit interconnections, are made on a tiny, wafer thin, slice of silicon. That's what makes it 'micro'.

The circuit is encapsulated in plastic and legs are included to allow easy connection to the outside world. This is the 'integrated circuit' (IC) which has become known to the public as the 'silicon chip'.

As a very rough guide we can break microelectronics into four basic areas: wired logic, custom chips, semi-custom chips, microprocessors.

Wired logic

Wired logic generally refers to a circuit built on a printed circuit board (PCB) from standard chips. These circuits tend to be used to perform fairly simple functions. Simple to design and implement, no software requirement and cheap are all benefits of wired logic. However, they are not open to modification or expansion without redesign and they use more components and manufacturing time than the other microelectronic options.

Custom chips

Generally, we can take the whole function of a wired logic circuit and integrate it onto a single chip. This gives a great improvement in reliability and efficiency. The problem is that, because it is a special chip designed for one purpose, the design and development costs are very high. In some cases custom chips find such a large market for their application that they become standard chips and high volume production covers the initial design cost.

Semi-custom chips

Semi-custom chips came into their own with computer-aided chip design systems which use a library of standard logic functions and combinations.

The principle is to produce an uncommitted logic array (ULA) which is a chip with an array of complete logic elements such as gates, half adders, input/output etc. which are not interconnected.

The manufacturer can take a standard ULA from his range and provide the connections that make the chip suitable for a particular customer's requirements.

Microprocessors

We are most interested in the microprocessor at this stage.

All three of the circuit types we have mentioned so far are produced to perform a particular function. If the function changes or the customer's needs change we have to dump the chip and redesign our system around a new chip.

With a microprocessor we can change the function of the system to any one of many applications without a single hardware (electronic component) change. All we need to do is change the software (program). This is a cheaper option for any user with, perhaps, many hundreds of these systems in use.

The microprocessor is a microelectronic chip designed to be the 'thinking' part of a microcomputer. This is called the central processing unit (CPU) of the computer. Of course, it doesn't think, it just performs the usual digital logic functions, but so rapidly that it is able to compute large problems faster than the human brain.

Before we discuss the microcomputer further it is worth looking at the scale of integration used in microelectronics. The term 'scale of integration' means how many components are packed into the chip. This is measured in several different ways such as the number of active devices or the number of binary digits or the number of complete logic cells on a chip.

The most common definition of category is shown in Table 10.1.

Table 10.1 Categories of integration

Small scale integration (SSI)

Chips containing a few logic gates (generally 1–20). There are not many SSI chips around now

---

Medium scale integration (MSI)

Chips containing standard logic function blocks such as flipflops and decoders. They contain between 20 and 100 logic gates. Most standard logic chips are MSI

Large scale integration (LSI)

A chip with between 100 and 1000 gates is usually described as LSI. A wider definition allows most microprocessors to be described as LSI, but with the development of VLSI most microprocessors now live under that definition

---

Very large scale integration (VLSI)

A chip with more than 1000 gates, often up to tens of thousands. Large digital blocks are integrated as VLSI chips such as a complete CPU, larege memory chips and even single-chip microcomputers

---

Fabrication technology

The early microprocessors used pMOS technology which means that the active device was a p-channel metal–oxide–semiconductor (FET). The problem with them is that they usually need a negative supply voltage and often several different supply rails. The good thing about them is that the technology is well established and they are fairly cheap to produce.

A lot of the more modern processors use nMOS (n-channel FET) technology. They generally operate from a single +5 V supply but it has to be well stabilised (about ±5% tolerance).

Examples of nMOS processors include the Mostec 6502, used in the BBC computers and many entertainment systems, and the INTEL 8085, 8086 and 8088 chips which found use in industrial control and the IBM PC.

The cost to the customer of nMOS technology is usually as low as pMOS technology because very large volume production is involved.

Another major type in use is CMOS (complementary MOS). This offers a combination of both p-channel and n-channel FETs in a single device. CMOS offers very low power consumption but the price we pay for that is loss of speed of operation. CMOS tends to be the choice for processors that are to operate in portable equipment from a battery supply. With all the MOS types of device we need to exercise a little care in handling because, although they usually have diode protection built in, they are easily damaged by static charge.

The last group of processors use bipolar technology for their logic, e.g. transistor–transistor logic (TTL), integrated injection logic (I^2L) and emitter-coupled logic (ECL). Bipolar devices take up more room on a chip than FET devices so there is a lower packing density with usually less complex devices. Also bipolar chips tend to require more power. Their big advantage is their high speed of operation.

Lastly, before we discuss details we need to understand the term **word length**.

Word length

A word, or data word, is a group of binary digits (bits). These words can be of any length but microprocessors tend to operate on particular sizes of word. Generally there are 4-bit processors, 8-bit such as the 8085, the 6502 and many of the processors used for control applications, 16-bit processors which form the basis of the earlier IBM PCs like the 286 machines and 32-bit processors around which the later 486 machines are built.

Processors with other word lengths are available but tend to be non-standard.

In this book we concentrate on the 8-bit processor.

Computer codes

In order for a computer to process data, we must encode the data in some way. At the level of electronic circuits all computers operate in binary. For humans this is a complicated and tedious business. To help make the connection between the computer's binary and our decimal, several systems of encoding have been developed. We consider the three most common since they demonstrate the principle of data encoding fairly simply.

Octal

Octal is a number system using a radix, or base, of 8 and was developed in the early days of computers. The system uses the numerals 0 to 7 inclusive, and since $8 = 2^3$ each octal digit can be represented within the computer by a 3-bit binary code. The column values increase in powers of 8 (Table 10.2).

Table 10.2

Decimal	Octal	Binary
0	0	000
1	1	001
2	2	010
3	3	011
4	4	100
5	5	101
6	6	110
7	7	111
8	10	001 000
9	11	001 001
10	12	001 010
11	13	001 011
.	.	.
.	.	.
.	.	.
126	176	001 111 110
128	200	020 000 000
.	.	.
.	.	.
.	.	.

The conversions between number systems can be done formally using standard algorithms but a simpler approach can usually be found. The conversions between decimal and octal use the same principle as binary conversions but 8 is now the significant number. The algorithm for converting integers of any base to decimal is as follows.

> Multiply the most significant digit by the base and add the next most significant digit. Now multiply this by the base, add the next digit on the right and so on until the last digit is added. The final sum is the decimal equivalent.

Let's apply this to octal numbers. Octal number 3201, for example, becomes

    3 × 8
    24 + 2
    26 × 8
    208 + 0
    208 × 8
    1664 + 1
    1665 Decimal equivalent

This is really equivalent to allocating powers of 8 to each column and adding them up as we did for binary to decimal conversion. For example,

    512 64 8 1
      3   2 0 1

giving

    1536 + 128 + 0 + 1 = 1665

For conversion from decimal to octal we use the same method as we used for decimal to binary, only this time we keep dividing by 8 and noting the remainders. The remainders, in reverse order, are then the required octal number.

1665_{10}		Remainder
	$1665 \div 8$	
	208	1
	$208 \div 8$	
	26	0
	$26 \div 8$	
	3	2
	$3 \div 8$	
	0	3

Now, in reverse order, we have 3201_8.

In the case of octal to binary and vice versa it is worth noting the direct representation of each octal digit in binary by breaking the binary number into 3-bit codes. For example,

    octal 325

goes to

    binary 011 010 101

Similarly, binary 1011010111 becomes

001 011 010 111

which can be converted direct to octal as

  1   3   2   7

This technique of grouping bits into distinct groups is an extremely useful idea, since most of the codes we have to deal with are based on discrete bit-sized groups.

Hexadecimal numbers

Hexadecimal (hex for short) is one of the most important number systems for electronics engineers and technicians because it is the basis of machine code programming on microcomputers and microprocessor-based systems.

Hex is a base 16 number system. This means we need 16 characters to represent numbers in the system. Since our normal numbers extend only from 0 to 9 we use alphanumeric representation, i.e. a combination of numbers and letters.

In hex we use the numbers 0 to 9 as usual and then we use the letters A to F. Since we can count in a single column from 0 to 15 we need a 4-bit binary code to represent each hex digit (Table 10.3).

Table 10.3

Decimal	Hexadecimal	Binary
0	0	0000
1	1	0001
2	2	0010
3	3	0011
4	4	0100
5	5	0101
6	6	0110
7	7	0111
8	8	1000
9	9	1001
10	A	1010
11	B	1011
12	C	1100
13	D	1101
14	E	1110
15	F	1111

As before each column increases by a power of 16 so, for example,

Decimal	Hexadecimal	Binary
16	10	0001 0000
27	1B	0001 1011
129	81	1000 0001
255	FF	1111 1111
256	100	0001 0000 0000

and so on.

We can use the methods already discussed for conversion between binary, hex and decimal but this time remember the radix is 16 and the binary groups are 4 bits long.

Exercise

Try completing the table below using the rules and short cuts you have learnt. Just in case you are stuck the answers are given below.

Decimal	Binary	Hexadecimal	Octal
21			
	110101		
		2C	
			230
1502			

Answers
Left to right and line by line: 10101, 15, 25, 53, 35, 65, 44, 101100, 54, 152, 1001100, 98, 010111011111, 5DE, 2736

Binary coded decimal (BCD)

As we have seen, there are several different ways of representing data in binary form. One important way to encode our data for use in computing is to code our decimal numbers digit by digit as a straight binary equivalent. This means representing numbers 0 to 9 so we need 4 bits to represent each digit. This is called binary coded decimal (BCD). Two of the more common 4-bit codes are as follows.

In the **weighted (8–4–2–1) BCD** each binary digit is given its normal weighting and any number up to 9 is coded in straight binary. For example,

$$134_{10} = 000100110100$$

For clarity we can break the binary number into 4-bit groups and see the direct relationship between the decimal digits and the binary groups. For example

$$247_{10} = 0010\ 0100\ 0111$$
$$1543_{10} = 0001\ 0101\ 0100\ 0011 \dots$$

Note that the gaps are not usually there.

The **non-weighted XS–3** code (or 'excess three') is derived from the 8–4–2–1 weighted code but a 3 is added to each digit value. So, for example,

$$247_{10} = 0010\ 0100\ 0111$$
$$+\quad 11\quad 11\quad 11$$
$$\quad 0101\ 0111\ 1010$$

This code offers certain advantages over 8–4–2–1 when arithmetic is being performed with the data.

As with everything in engineering there are both advantages and disadvantages when comparing BCD with straight binary. The conversion between decimal and BCD is much simpler than between decimal and straight binary but straight binary usually requires fewer bits to represent a number and arithmetic is usually easier in straight binary.

It is worth noting that a 4-bit code would allow 2^4 or 16 combinations and BCD only needs ten. The remaining six could be used to represent other things such as positive or negative data.

Table 10.4 Six-bit BCD set

Character	Zone	Numeric	Octal	Character	Zone	Numeric	Octal
A	11	0001	61	1	00	0001	01
B	11	0010	62	2	00	0010	02
C	11	0011	63	3	00	0011	03
D	11	0100	64	4	00	0100	04
E	11	0101	65	5	00	0101	05
F	11	0110	66	6	00	0110	06
G	11	0111	67	7	00	0111	07
H	11	1000	70	8	00	1000	10
I	11	1001	71	9	00	1001	11
				0	00	1010	12
J	10	0001	41				
K	10	0010	42	*	11	0000	60
L	10	0011	43	–	10	0000	40
M	10	0100	44	×	10	1100	54
N	10	0101	45	/	01	0001	21
O	10	0110	46	=	00	1011	13
P	10	0111	47	(	01	1100	34
Q	10	1000	50	)	11	1100	74
R	10	1001	51	.	11	1011	73
				:	10	1110	56
S	01	0010	22	$	10	1011	53
T	01	0011	23	Blank	00	0000	00
U	01	0100	24				
V	01	0101	25				
W	01	0110	26				
X	01	0111	27				
Y	01	1000	30				
Z	01	1001	31				

Generally when BCD is referred to it is 8–4–2–1 code unless otherwise stated.

Six-bit BCD   As well as numbers, computers also have to handle letters and symbols. Everything must be in the form of binary code so we need more than a 4-bit code.

With a 6-bit code we have $2^6 = 64$ discrete codes available. This would allow us to code 10 digits, 26 characters and 28 special symbols, such as punctuation.

The code works by adding 2 bits, called zone bits, to the 8–4–2–1 numeric bits. Digits are then coded with zone bits 00 and the usual 8–4–2–1 bits except 0 which is coded 1010 (10_{10}). Next a code is generated for each letter of the alphabet and the additional symbols. Although the code is effectively split into 2 bits/4 bits all 6 bits can be represented by two octal digits and, for convenience, this is often how the code is entered.

The bare code is as shown in Table 10.4 but in practice the code appears as a 7-bit code because a 'check' or **parity** bit is added:

Parity	Zone	Numeric
P	AB	8–4–2–1

The parity bit is added so that the computer has some check on whether or not data are valid. For each character the parity bit is set at 0 or 1 to make the sum of the 1s odd or even according to whether the system operates on odd or even parity.

For example, if we are using an odd parity system, the characters 8, 9, D, F and W would be stored as

	Parity	Zone	Numeric
8	0	00	1000
9	1	00	1001
D	0	11	0100
F	1	11	0110
W	0	01	0110

Many types of error checking codes are used in computing but one of the simplest and most common is the parity check. The idea is that prior to sending a data word a parity encoder adds a 0 or 1 to make the total number of 1s in the word odd. When the word is recieved a parity checker adds up the 1s and if the sum is even then an error has occurred. Both odd and even parity systems are used in practice. Parity checking is limited in its ability to detect errors since any even number of bits lost will not show up as a parity error.

Eight-bit BCD codes   With modern data processing and word processing a 64-character set is not sufficient, with 10 digits, upper and lower case letters etc., so it is common to find 8-bit codes in

Table 10.5

Character	Zone	Numeric	Hex
0	0101	0000	50
1	0101	0001	51
2	0101	0010	52
3	0101	0011	53
4	0101	0100	54
5	0101	0101	55
6	0101	0110	56
7	0101	0111	57
8	0101	1000	58
9	0101	1001	59
A	1010	0001	A1
B	1010	0010	A2
.	.	.	.
.	.	.	.
.	.	.	.
Y	1011	1001	B9
Z	1011	1010	BA
.	.	.	.
.	.	.	.
.	.	.	.

use. Each 8-bit word (**byte**) consists of four zone bits and four 8–4–2–1 numeric bits.

If we look back at hex we see that each hex digit consists of 4 bits. Now a byte can be conveniently represented by two hex digits, the first giving the zone bits and the second the numeric bits. Again, the computer adds a parity bit to this code. By far the most commonly used 8-bit code is **ASCII–8**.

ASCII stands for American Standard Code for Information Interchange. There are various versions in use but this is as close to a standard for alphanumeric codes as we have. Table 10.5 gives an example of some ASCII codes.

Basic microcomputer

The minimum requirements for a microcomputer are shown in Figure 10.1.

A microcomputer has to contain:

● a **CPU** (which is the microprocessor, controlling operations and decoding and executing instructions);

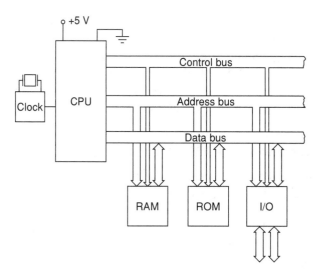

Figure 10.1 Minimum requirements for a microcomputer

- a **memory** section containing ROM and RAM (where program is stored permanently and temporarily, respectively);
- an **input/output** (I/O) (which allows the system to receive information from, and pass data to, the outside world);
- a **bus system** (which provides the connection between the various sections of the system for data communications – some texts refer to the bus as the **data highway**).

The system needs a **data bus** which carries data from one section to another, an **address bus** which allows the CPU to talk to the appropriate memory location and a **control bus** which carries the signals determining data transfer direction, timing and all the other complex controlling functions.

These buses are really just a set of conductors between various sections. The bus is said to have a 'width'. The bus width simply tells us how many conductors there are in the bus. If we use the 8085 8-bit processor as an example we see it operates with an 8-bit data bus (that is what we expect for a processor with an 8-bit data word length). It operates into a 6- to 8-bit control bus and a 16-bit address bus.

The word placed on the address bus or the data bus is written or read as a whole but the control bus is more like a collection of wires and each may go high or low at any time, independently of the others, as control functions dictate.

The memory

We already mentioned the need for RAM and ROM so we should clarify what they are.

RAM stands for **random access memory**. This means memory where we can get at (access) any

particular memory location in the range at random. In other words, we do not need to go through each location sequentially. Even ROM allows random access so the strict definition of RAM is pretty useless!

By common usage the term RAM has come to mean read/write memory. This means that the user and the CPU can write data into the memory and read data from it.

RAM is where the program's transient data reside whilst the CPU is running them. When we write a program into the microcomputer we are storing it in RAM. It is important to remember that RAM is only for temporary storage of data. This is because RAM is **volatile**, i.e. when the power supply is removed the stored data are lost.

There, you are getting to grips with the jargon already!

ROM stands for **read only memory**. This means that the CPU or the user can get at data from ROM to read and use but they can't write to it so they can't alter what's there.

ROMs are programmed at manufacture and they are non-volatile. All the programs which your system needs permanently to operate will be stored in the ROM section of the memory.

An example of ROM is the stored constants on your pocket calculator. You can switch off and take out the battery for a week. When you put the battery back and switch on, your calculator still knows the value of π. That is because it is stored in ROM.

A system can address a certain amount of memory, determined by the address bus width. For example, a 16-bit address bus would allow $2^{16} = 64k$ discrete addresses. However, we may not want to use all of the range in a system and also we need to allocate certain addresses to certain jobs. In order to show the system users what addresses are at their disposal the designer or manufacturer uses a memory map.

Memory mapping

In order to operate the system we need to know where the user RAM is located and where room exists for expansion, if any.

Remember that all our addresses are in hexadecimal numbers, so our 16-bit bus allows us to address memory from 0000 to FFFF which is $2^{16} = 65\ 536$ or 64k (remember that 1024 is 1 binary k).

In Figure 10.2 we have 4k bytes of ROM and 1k byte of RAM, i.e. 1k of locations each 1 byte (8 bits) long. Thus each location can store a 1-byte data word. In this map the rest of the addressable space is unused.

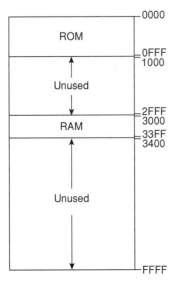

Figure 10.2

Address decoding

Each discrete combination of bits on the address bus has to access a particular location. These codes are directed to the appropriate address by a decoder. A decoder is simply a logic network which has a separate output for each possible data word at its input.

If we consider a 2-bit address, we could have 2^2 = 4 addresses.

$$
\left.
\begin{array}{cc}
A_1 & A_0 \\
0 & 0 \\
0 & 1 \\
1 & 0 \\
1 & 1
\end{array}
\right\}
\begin{array}{l}
\text{address lines} \\
\\
\text{codes or addresses}
\end{array}
$$

The 2-bit to 4-line decoder circuit shown in Figure 10.3 is using a simple logic arrangement in order to illustrate the principle. In a practical decoder other factors are taken into account.

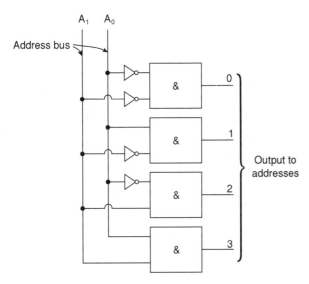

Figure 10.3   Simple address decoder

Similarly, with a 3-bit decoder we would have eight addresses and so on.

As the number of addresses increases, so the complexity and cost of the decoding increases. To help with this we need to select, carefully, where we place our memory within the map.

Location of RAM

If the RAM is in chips of 1k, then we need ten address lines to address all the locations in the chip. Those same ten address lines (A_0 to A_9) could be decoded to address each 1k chip in the system. If we choose the right start address for each chip we can use the other lines in the address bus just to select which chip is being addressed.

The 1k needs a start address that is a power of 2×1024; then only one more line is needed to address it. That is, if it starts at 1024 we need A_{10} as well as A_0–A_9; if we locate it at 8192 we need A_{13} together with A_0–A_9.

As an example, consider a 5-bit bus addressing 8-byte chips (Figure 10.4 and Table 10.6). The pattern for the three least significant bits just keeps repeating and can address all 8 bytes within a chip. Separately, we can decode the most significant 2 bits to enable each chip in turn.

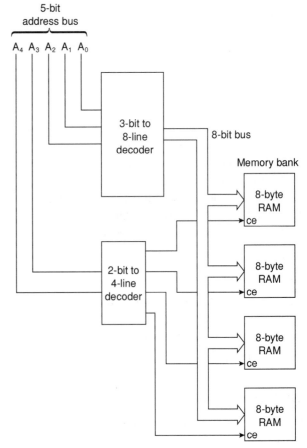

Figure 10.4   Five-bit bus addressing 8-byte chips; ce, chip enable

Table 10.6

A_4	A_3	A_2	A_1	A_0	
0	0	0	0	0	Least significant 3-bit pattern
0	0	0	0	1	
0	0	0	1	0	
0	0	0	1	1	Once
0	0	1	0	0	
0	0	1	0	1	
0	0	1	1	0	
0	0	1	1	1	
0	1	0	0	0	
0	1	0	0	1	
0	1	0	1	0	
0	1	0	1	1	
0	1	1	0	0	Twice
0	1	1	0	1	
0	1	1	1	0	
0	1	1	1	1	
1	0	0	0	0	
1	0	0	0	1	
1	0	0	1	0	
1	0	0	1	1	Three times
1	0	1	0	0	
1	0	1	0	1	
1	0	1	1	0	
1	0	1	1	1	
1	1	0	0	0	
1	1	0	0	1	
1	1	0	1	0	
1	1	0	1	1	Four times
1	1	1	0	0	
1	1	1	0	1	
1	1	1	1	0	
1	1	1	1	1	

A similar argument applies to the location of ROM. This type of planning in the map helps reduce hardware cost and keep decoder complexity down.

Input/output (I/O)

The I/O lets the CPU interface with the outside world but in order to use it the CPU must know where it is. There are basically two ways of organising the I/O. We can use it as **isolated** or **memory mapped**.

As the name suggests, memory mapped I/O is allocated a spare place in the system memory map and can then be addressed in the same way as memory. This has the advantage that all the instructions available to the microprocessor are available to use with outside devices (**peripherals**)

via the I/O. The disadvantage is that, where memory space is precious, we are giving some of the available address range to the I/O.

With isolated I/O no memory space is taken but we have a very limited list of instructions. With the 8085, for example, only two instructions are available, IN and OUT. These take data from the input port into a register called the **accumulator** or take data from the accumulator to the port. Often this is all we want and no memory space has been lost. Intel provides us with up to 255 possible peripheral addresses on the 8085.

Practical systems often operate with a combination of both isolated and memory mapped I/O.

Many processors offer MEMREQ and IOREQ lines, or their equivalent (memory request or I/O request). These are the control lines which determine whether a data transfer is to memory or I/O. The 8085 has a single pinout IO/$\overline{\text{M}}$ which is logic high for input/output and logic low for memory. This technique helps keep the pin count low.

Once again the choice of location for the mapped I/O is important since it will help to reduce decoding circuit complexity. Remember that when the $\overline{\text{M}}$ input to the processor is active we may be addressing memory or memory mapped I/O.

By placing the I/O from E000 to FFFF (Figure 10.5) we know that whenever the three most significant bits of the address bus are all at logic 1 we must be talking to the peripherals.

This means that we can easily sort out data transfers to the peripherals by using a simple four-input AND gate (Figure 10.6).

All that is now left in the system for us to look at is the microprocessor itself. From now on we

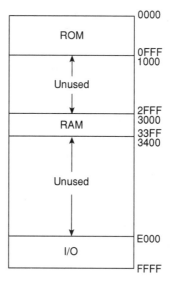

Figure 10.5

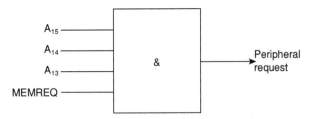

Figure 10.6

shall consider only the 8085 as being representative of all 8-bit processors. The principles covered here can be applied to other types.

Microprocessor architecture

The pinout of the 8085 is shown in Figure 10.7. Some of the pins we have mentioned already and some are obvious; some we will leave altogether at this stage.

Internally, most processors offer similar features but the layout and nomenclature vary. Figure 10.8 looks pretty daunting but if we pick off the units one at a time we soon see that, although complicated, it is understandable.

First we see that a lot of sections in the microprocessor are, in fact, **registers** of one kind or another. So what is a register?

In its simplest form a register is a set of flipflops which can be set or reset to record or temporarily store data. For example, if we have four flipflops in a register and we set the first and third and reset the second and fourth we have stored the 4-bit data word 1010. Set means that the output of the flipflop is at logic 1 and reset means that the flipflop output is at logic 0.

In our example microprocessor most of the internal registers are 8 bit. This means they consist of eight flipflops and can store an 8-bit word.

Now we know what a register is we can start to look at the block diagram in more detail.

The arithmetic and logic unit (ALU)   This is the circuit which, as its name suggests, carries out the arithmetic and logical operations required on data supplied to it.

In use the ALU appears to be very clever indeed but in reality it does simple things like addition, inversion and logic operations. However, it does them so fast that we get the impression that the micro is better at maths than we are.

The data which the ALU operates on come from two sources: the accumulator and the temporary register.

The accumulator (register A)   This is an 8-bit register which can be loaded with data directly by

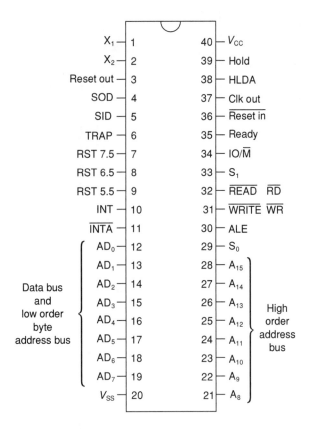

Figure 10.7   The pinout of the 8085

the programmer. Data stored in the accumulator have direct access to the ALU. We could use this register for temporary storage of data – but with care. As well as providing the ALU with data to operate on, the accumulator is also the register the ALU writes to. Thus the result of any ALU operation is written directly to the accumulator and would overwrite any data already stored there.

The temporary (TMP) register   This is the sort of register sometimes referred to as **invisible** or **transparent**. What this means is that the programmer cannot directly access it so it is not 'visible'.

The purpose of the TMP register is to hold the other data word when, for example, 2 bytes are to be added together.

If the programmer instructed the microprocessor to add a data byte from one location to the data byte held in the accumulator the data byte from the other location would have to be moved into TMP first so that the ALU had access to both it and the byte in register A.

The flag register (register F)   The flag register looks like any other 8-bit register but the data word it holds needs to be read bit by bit instead of as a whole.

The job of this register is to record the status of the program at any given point in its operation, the state of play as it were.

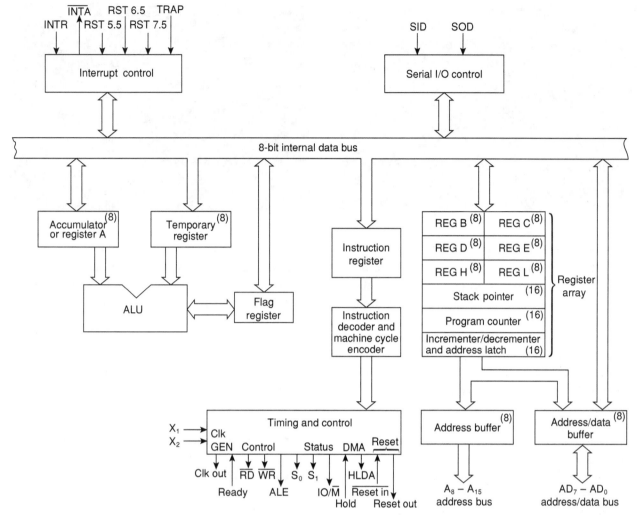

Figure 10.8

When the ALU performs an operation we need to know the magnitude of the result which is stored in the accumulator but also whether it is positive or negative. If we compare 2 data bytes and by subtraction we determine that they are equal we need to record the 0. If we add 2 bytes together and the result generates a carry bit we need to know this, and so on.

The flag register is the one which tells us these things (Figure 10.9).

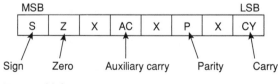

Figure 10.9

Notice that not all the bits are used in the 8085. The layout, order and number of flags used varies from processor to processor.

If the word stored in the flag register at a particular point in the program was 3C we would need to convert this from hexadecimal to binary to read the state of each individual flag:

$$3C_{16} = 00111100_2$$

This tells us that the sign and zero flags are reset, the auxiliary carry and parity flags are set and the carry flag is reset.

Sign flag   This tells us when a negative result is obtained from an ALU operation. This is set to a logic 1 if the most significant bit of the byte we are considering is 1.

Zero flag   This is set to logic 1 if the result of the operation performed by the ALU yields all zeros.

Auxiliary carry   This flag records a carry from a lower order addition, i.e. when a carry out of bit 3 (the most significant bit of the low order nibble) occurs as a result of an addition.

This flag becomes important when we use binary coded decimal (BCD) arithmetic.

Microcomputer chips

Parity flag This flag tells us whether we have odd or even parity. This means an odd or even number of ones as a result of an operation. Parity is used as a bit error detection method in data communications where the transmitted and received word must have the same parity.

In the 8085 the parity flag is set for even parity and reset for odd.

The carry flag This flag is set if, when an addition is performed, we generate a carry. We might also note that when a subtraction is used the carry flag can act as a 'borrow' and in this way we can take a large number from a smaller one and in excess of 8 bits.

The flag register is used by 'conditional' instructions. For example, if we use the instruction JNZ *address* (jump to the specified address if not zero) the CPU knows whether or not to jump by checking the state of the zero flag.

The instruction register This holds the instruction when it is fetched from memory prior to execution.

The instruction decoder An instruction is applied to the microprocessor in the form of a two-digit hexadecimal code. Data are applied in exactly the same form. The processor knows that the first byte it sees is an instruction and from then on it can identify each byte as an instruction, data or address byte based on order.

The instruction byte is called the op-code and the instruction decoder has to control the operation of the registers and the ALU in response to the particular op-code involved.

The register set The 8085 offers six general-purpose 8-bit registers and instructions are available which allow the programmer to use these registers in pairs to hold 16-bit data.

The accumulator and flags form one pair A–F but as we have already seen they are somewhat special. The next pair are B–C, then D–E and finally H–L.

The reason for H and L not following the alphabetic progression is that, although they can be used as two general-purpose 8-bit registers or a single 16-bit pair, they also have a special purpose. They can be used to store a memory address (16-bit) and that address can then be referred to in the program simply as M (memory). This is a technique used in programming called indirect register addressing which we shall look at in more detail later.

The point now is that the two registers are used in this way to hold the high and low order bytes of the address and hence their names.

The stack pointer This is a 16-bit register dedicated to a particular job. The job is to hold the address of the top of the stack.

A stack is an area of RAM which the programmer designates as a stack area. The stack operates as a last-in first-out (LIFO) store and data are **pushed** onto the stack and **popped** off it. The stack is created by placing the start of stack address in the stack pointer at the start of program.

Each time we add a data byte to the stack with a push the stack moves down by one address and the stack pointer is automatically decremented (one is taken away).

Each time we reduce the stack by a data byte with a pop instruction the stack pointer is incremented (one is added).

In this way the location of the last byte of data added to the stack is always held in the stack pointer.

The program counter This is also a dedicated 16-bit register and its job is to hold the address of the next instruction in the program so that after executing an instruction the CPU knows where to go to get the next one.

The increment/decrement address latch   This is used by the processor as part of its internal house-keeping operations in connection with the handling of memory addresses. The programmer has no access to this directly.

Interrupt control   There are several conditions under which we want to halt program operation either permanently or temporarily. The subject of interrupts will be looked at in detail later. Suffice it to say, at this stage, that the control of interrupt signals is carried out by this section.

Timing and control section   This is the part that keeps all the various actions and moves synchronised and ordered.

The crystal-controlled clock provides a constant frequency pulse train from which the control unit takes its timing.

The control unit also takes care of the read/write pulses for registers and memory and I/O devices. These pulses are output to the control bus.

Many other jobs are covered by the control unit such as automatic incrementing and decrementing of the program counter.

Multiplexing   In addition to the units shown there is also multiplexing between the low order byte of the address bus and the data bus. This means that the pin count of the 8085 is kept down by using a multiplexer to switch eight of the pins between address and data bus.

We have been looking at an 8-bit microprocessor as a simple example of basic structure. It is important to remember that for computing applications 16-bit and 32-bit processors are in use and their increased word size brings with it an increase in bus width, register size and address range.

All these factors combine to allow larger word lengths and therefore more data to be processed in a given time. Add to this the steady increase in processor clock rates that has occurred in the last few years and we begin to appreciate the massive gain in operating speed of readily available mass-produced processors.

Computer language

In order for us to communicate with the processor or with the computer we need a form of 'language'. These languages can be divided into two groups.

High level language

When we refer to high level languages, we mean those which are not machine dependent. This means that a program written in one of these languages can be run on any computer, using any processor, provided that the system includes the necessary translation for that language. These are easy programming languages for us because they allow a type of English to be used.

Well-known high level languages include BASIC, PASCAL, C, ADA, COBOL, FORTRAN etc.

Some of these languages need a system with a **compiler** and some a **line interpreter** and so on. All of these are really programs which convert the high level language into a form the processor can understand.

One disadvantage of high level language programming was often that it produced longer run-time programs than could be achieved in machine code. With the advent of **optimising compilers** this is now arguable.

Low level language

We already know that, at the real working level of our electronic processors, everything operates in binary. This means that we need to talk to the processor in binary. Unfortunately, this would prove too daunting a task for most humans, so we distance ourselves slightly by using **machine code**.

Machine code

Machine code is totally specific to a particular type of processor and is therefore low level. For each processor a list is made of all the codes to which the processor responds, i.e. all the instructions it understands. This list is called the instruction set for the processor.

In order to make life a little easier for humans the codes are hexadecimal (base 16 numbers). This means that each hexadecimal digit represents 4 bits. So a byte can be represented by a two-digit hexadecimal number. The manufacturer of the microprocessor issues an instruction set which lists the hexadecimal code for all the instructions that the processor understands.

Assembly language

Assembly language is also a low level language because it is processor dependent but it is a compromise between machine code and high level since it allows the programmer to use mnemonics for instructions. The system must incorporate a program which can convert these mnemonics to machine code for us. This is called an **assembler** and each processor type has to have its own assembler written specifically for it.

As engineers we are usually more interested in low level programming, for fault detection etc., although all electronics engineers should be able to program in a high level language as well.

If we look at a few example instructions from the 8085 instruction set all this may become clearer.

If we wanted to put the number 5 into register A (the accumulator) and put the number 6 into register B and then add them together we could give the instructions in assembly language and then assemble them or we could use the instruction set to look up the machine code for each instruction and write the program in hexadecimal. This process is called **hand assembly**. Finally, if the system allowed it, we could write the program in binary (see Table 10.7).

Just a simple program like this should convince you that programming in binary would be a nightmare. Just imagine a hundred line program in binary! Worse still imagine that when you run it there is a fault (or bug) and you have to check through it to find, maybe, a 1-bit error. You would be a wreck!

Note that the instruction to move a number into register B has the code 06 and this happened also to be the data we wanted to move. As we stated earlier, the CPU knows which is an instruction and which is data simply by the order in which it receives them.

Assembly instructions are made up of distinct parts:

(a) the **op-code** which is the operation code, e.g. MVI A;
(b) the **data** – this accompanies some op-code, e.g. 05;

(c) the address bytes. This is needed where an op-code refers to a memory address.

The 8085 offers single-byte, 2-byte and 3-byte instructions. For example,

- ADD B is a single-byte instruction with an op-code only (80);
- MVI A,05 has 2 bytes, the op-code (3E) and the data (05);
- LDA 3020 has 3 bytes, the op-code (3A) which tells the processor to load register A with the contents of the memory at the 2-byte address given (30) (20).

A peculiarity of this processor is that the address is written in machine code with the low order byte first, e.g.

$$\left.\begin{array}{c} 3A \\ 20 \\ 30 \end{array}\right\} \quad \text{LDA 3020H (H signifies hexadecimal)}$$

All processors offer multibyte instructions in their instruction sets and we must refer to the manufacturer's data to be sure we are using the available instructions efficiently.

Instruction sets are usually divided into groups to make use of the set a little easier. Typically, these groups are as follows:

- Data transfer, which deals with the movement of data between registers, keyboard, memory etc.
- Arithmetic and logic, which provides for addition, subtraction, logical OR, incrementing etc.
- Branch control, which allows conditional instructions such as jumps, calls, returns etc.
- Machine control, which allows for the use of stacks, input/output etc.

Table 10.7

Command	Assembly	Machine code	Binary
Move the number 5 into register A immediately	MVI A,05	3E	00111110
		05	00000101
Move the number 6 into register B immediately	MVI B,06	06	00001010
		06	00001010
Add them together	ADD B	80	10000000

Mnemonic	Op-code	Time	Mnemonic	Op-code	Time	Mnemonic	Op-code	Time	Mnemonic	Op-code	Time
AC1 D8	CE	7	DCX H	2B	6	MOV D,D	52	4	PUSH H	E5	12
ADC A	8F	4	DCX SP	3B	6	MOV D,E	53	4	PUSH PSW	F5	12
ADC B	88	4	DI	F3	4	MOV D,H	54	4	RAL	17	4
ADC C	89	4	E1	FB	4	MOV D,L	55	4	RAR	1F	4
ADC D	8A	4	HLT	76	5	MOV D,M	56	7	RC	D8	6/12
ADC E	8B	4	IN A8	DB	10	MOV E,A	5F	4	RET	C9	10
ADC H	8C	4	INR A	3C	4	MOV E,B	58	4	RIM	20	4
ADC L	8D	4	INR B	04	4	MOV E,C	59	4	RLC	07	4
ADC M	8E	7	INR C	0C	4	MOV E,D	5A	4	RM	F8	6/12
ADD A	87	4	INR D	14	4	MOV E,E	5B	4	RNC	D0	6/12
ADD B	80	4	INR E	1C	4	MOV E,H	5C	4	RNZ	C0	6/12
ADD C	81	4	INR H	24	4	MOV E,L	5D	4	RP	F0	6/12
ADD D	82	4	INR L	2C	4	MOV E,M	5E	7	RPE	E8	6/12
ADD E	83	4	INR M	34	10	MOV H,A	67	4	RPO	E0	6/12
ADD H	84	4	INX B	03	6	MOV H,B	60	4	RRC	0F	4
ADD L	85	4	INX D	13	6	MOV H,C	61	4	RST 0	C7	12
ADD M	86	7	INX H	23	6	MOV H,D	62	4	RST 1	CF	12
ADI D8	C6	7	INX SP	33	6	MOV H,E	63	4	RST 2	D7	12
ANA A	A7	4	JC A16	DA	7/10	MOV H,H	64	4	RST 3	DF	12
ANA B	A0	4	JM A16	FA	7/10	MOV H,L	65	4	RST 4	E7	12
ANA C	A1	4	JMP A16	C3	10	MOV H,M	66	7	RST 5	EF	12
ANA D	A2	4	JNC A16	D2	7/10	MOV L,A	6F	4	RST 6	F7	12
ANA E	A3	4	JNZ A16	C2	7/10	MOV L,B	68	4	RST 7	FF	12
ANA H	A4	4	JP A16	F2	7/10	MOV L,C	69	4	RZ	C8	6/12
ANA L	A5	4	JPE A16	EA	7/10	MOV L,D	6A	4	SBB A	9F	4
ANA M	A6	7	JPO A16	E2	7/10	MOV L,E	6B	4	SBB B	98	4
ANI D8	E6	7	JZ A16	CA	7/10	MOV L,H	6C	4	SBB C	99	4
CALL A16	CD	18	LDA A16	3A	13	MOV L,L	6D	4	SBB D	9A	4
CC A16	DC	9/18	LDAX B	0A	7	MOV L,M	6E	7	SBB E	9B	4
CM A16	FC	9/18	LDAX D	1A	7	MOV M,A	77	7	SBB H	9C	4
CMA	2F	4	LHLD A16	2A	16	MOV M,B	70	7	SBB L	9D	4
CMC	3F	4	LXI B,D16	01	10	MOV M,C	71	7	SBB M	9E	7
CMP A	BF	4	LXI D,D16	11	10	MOV M,D	72	7	SBI D8	DE	7
CMP B	B8	4	LXI H,D16	21	10	MOV M,E	73	7	SHLD A16	22	16
CMP C	B9	4	LXI SP,D16	31	10	MOV M,H	74	7	SIM	30	4
CMP D	BA	4	MOV A,A	7F	4	MOV M,L	75	7	SPHL	F9	6
CMP E	BB	4	MOV A,B	78	4	MVI A,D8	3E	7	STA A16	32	13
CMP H	BC	4	MOV A,C	79	4	MVI B,D8	06	7	STAX B	02	7
CMP L	BD	4	MOV A,D	7A	4	MVI C,D8	0E	7	STAX D	12	7
CMP M	BE	7	MOV A,E	7B	4	MVI D,D8	16	7	STC	37	4
CNC A16	D4	9/18	MOV A,H	7C	4	MVI E,D8	1E	7	SUB A	97	4
CNZ A16	C4	9/18	MOV A,L	7D	4	MVI H,D8	26	7	SUB B	90	4
CP A16	F4	9/18	MOV A,M	7E	7	MVI L,D8	2E	7	SUB C	91	4
CPE A16	EC	9/18	MOV B,A	47	4	MVI M,D8	36	10	SUB D	92	4
CPI D8	FE	7	MOV B,B	40	4	NOP	00	4	SUB E	93	4
CPO A16	E4	9/18	MOV B,C	41	4	ORA A	B7	4	SUB H	94	4
CZ A16	CC	9/18	MOV B,D	42	4	ORA B	B0	4	SUB L	95	4
DAA	27	4	MOV B,E	43	4	ORA C	B1	4	SUB M	96	7
DAD B	09	10	MOV B,H	44	4	ORA D	B2	4	SUI D8	D6	7
DAD D	19	10	MOV B,L	45	4	ORA E	B3	4	XCHG	EB	4
DAD H	29	10	MOV B,M	46	7	ORA H	B4	4	XRA A	AF	4
DAD SP	39	10	MOV C,A	4F	4	ORA L	B5	4	XRA B	A8	4
DCR A	3D	4	MOV C,B	48	4	ORA M	B6	7	XRA C	A9	4
DCR B	05	4	MOV C,C,	49	4	ORI D8	F6	7	XRA D	AA	4
DCR C	0D	4	MOV C,D	4A	4	OUT A8	D3	10	XRA E	AB	4
DCR D	15	4	MOV C,E	4B	4	PCHL	E9	6	XRA H	AC	4
DCR E	1D	4	MOV C,H	4C	4	POP B	C1	10	XRA L	AD	4
DCR H	25	4	MOV C,L	4D	4	POP D	D1	10	XRA M	AE	7
DCR L	2D	4	MOV C,M	4E	7	POP H	E1	10	XRI D8	EE	7
DCR M	35	10	MOV D,A	57	4	POP PSW	F1	10	XTHL	E3	16
DCX B	0B	6	MOV D,B	50	4	PUSH B	C5	12			
DCX D	1B	6	MOV D,C	51	4	PUSH D	D5	12			

D8, 8-bit data; A8, 8-bit I/O address; D16, 16-bit data; A16, 16-bit memory address. Time is the execution time in machine cycles; where two times are given, the longer time is if action is performed.

Figure 10.10   Op-codes in alphabetical order

In addition to the basic form of instruction set (Figure 10.10) RISC chips have now appeared on the market. RISC stands for reduced instruction set command whilst CISC is complex instruction set command. RISC chips came about as a result of the computer analysis of machine code programs which showed that a few instructions were used many times in various programs whilst some were not used at all. Each type has its place in the market for different applications and the argument over relative merit still continues in many quarters.

Program operation

Now that we have seen what an instruction looks like in machine code, we need to examine the way in which the microprocessor deals with that instruction during a program run.

The program, having been entered, is stored in the system RAM. This memory is connected to the CPU via the data bus and the address bus. The data bus allows the op-code and data to be brought from memory to the CPU a byte at a time (in our 8-bit processor). The address bus allows the correct memory location to be accessed for this op-code/data.

Obviously, the instruction must be 'fetched' from memory before it can be 'executed'. Then the next instruction is fetched and so on. This repeated cycle of operation is called the fetch–execute cycle.

Fetch–execute cycle

Under control of the clock and control unit the processor will fetch an op-code which must then be decoded. Depending on what the op-code was, there may be one or two more fetches to bring in data or an address. This is determined by the op-code being the first byte of a 1-, 2- or 3-byte instruction.

After fetching and decoding is complete the next operation is execution of the instruction. The time taken for this part of the fetch–execute cycle also depends on the instruction. Most manufacturers publish a list of the number of clock cycles required for each instruction in the set. If we know the clock frequency we can multiply the number of cycles by the period of the clock to obtain the time taken for each instruction. This is useful when we need to write delay routines.

When we are designing programs it is often necessary to program efficiently. Program efficiency can be measured against many different criteria but usually we are concerned with efficient memory use and execution speed.

Memory usage can be reduced by thinking carefully about the structure of the program and the type of instructions used.

The time taken for a program to run can be calculated from the number of machine cycles involved and often we can reduce this by rearranging the way in which we tackle each part of the program in turn. For example, where two 2-byte instructions have been used we might have achieved the same end using three 1-byte instructions which would reduce the execution time. This type of subtle program change will only come with experience.

As an example we could look at the fetch–execute cycle for an instruction to add from memory.

Fetch

1. Contents of the PC are put on the address bus.
   This means that the address held in the program counter is placed on the bus so that the next instruction can be accessed.

2. Contents of the memory are placed onto the data bus.
   Remember that the instruction is in the form of a two-digit hexadecimal code and is applied via the data bus to the CPU.

3. Data bus contents are transferred to the instruction decoder.
   This is required so that the op-code can be decoded.

4. The PC is incremented.
   This is done by the control unit so that the program counter is holding the address of the next program byte.

Decode

1. Decode the instruction and set up the registers.
   In this case the instruction is a 3-byte instruction so that after decoding the CPU knows that additional fetch cycles are required.

Fetch (data)

1. Contents of the PC are put onto the address bus.

2. Contents of the memory are put onto the data bus.

3. Data bus contents are transferred to the MAR (low).
   The MAR is a memory address register (16-bit) which holds the 2 bytes of an address prior to its use in the program.

4. The program counter is incremented.

5. Steps 1 and 2 are repeated to obtain the other byte of the address.

6. Data bus contents are transferred to the MAR (high byte).

Execute

1. The contents of the MAR, both bytes, are placed onto the address bus.

2. The contents of the memory, at this address, are placed onto the data bus.

3. The contents of the data bus are transferred to the ALU.

4. The A register contents are sent to the ALU. This is via the temporary register.

5. The addition is carried out and the result is stored in the accumulator.

6. The program counter is incremented.

Types of memory

We have already considered the fact that our on-board memory is split into RAM and ROM but many types of chip are available to provide this memory. There is also a need for mass storage of data and we have a range of back-up memory in the form of hard and floppy disc systems and magnetic tape etc.

ROM

The purpose of the ROM is to hold permanently required data. This enables the system to perform its task without the need to enter data each time. In a dedicated system the program would be stored in ROM but even in personal computers some program routines are stored in ROM to allow, for example, the keyboard to be scanned and the screen display routines to operate.

The simplest type of ROM structure to understand is a semiconductor type called a **diode matrix** ROM. The idea is to use a mesh of wires arranged in rows and columns. We make the rows the inputs and the columns the outputs. Where we want logic 1 to be stored we provide diode connections between input and output.

As an example we could look at a 4-bit by 8 array. This means the device holds eight 4-bit words.

For each address within the ROM, one input line would be driven to logic 1 by the address decoder.

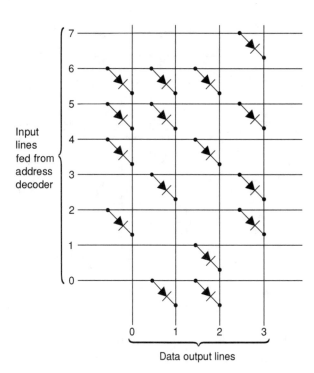

Figure 10.11

Wherever a diode made a connection between that input line and an output line the output line or lines would be at logic 1. All the other lines would be held at logic 0.

From Figure 10.11 we can see that if input line 2 is selected the output will be 1001, if input line 4 is selected the word output is 1010, line 5 gives 1101 and so on.

This type of ROM is simple and inexpensive but because it is relatively slow and relatively large currents are required from the input drivers to supply the output it is rarely seen nowadays.

In order to reduce the number of word lines required the address decoding is often broken down into row and column addressing.

Typically, the number of words available in a memory is a power of 2. If we have n address lines we will have 2^n addressable locations. By splitting the address decoding we can reduce the number of word lines required from 2^n to $2 \times 2^{n/2}$. It is worth repeating, at this point, that most manufacturers sell their memory chips in Ks or Megs. 1k is not 1000 but 1024 (2^{10}). When we start to look at several megabytes of memory those extra 24 per thousand become a significant amount of extra memory.

Masked ROM

When a high volume production of ROM chips is required the technique used involves a photographic mask.

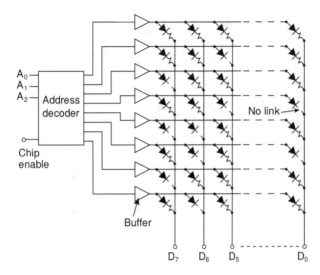

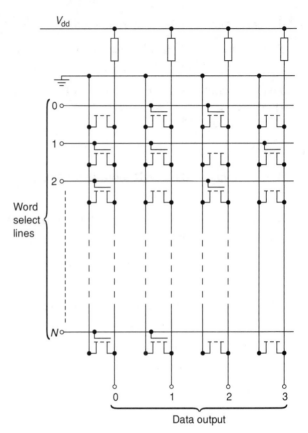

Figure 10.12

The data that are required to be stored are determined and checked by the customer. They are then sent to the manufacturer who produces a mask such that when the ROM is produced the storage elements will be at logic 1 only where the mask permits. The expensive part of this process is the mask production and checking for data accuracy, so it would not be an economic proposition for the production of less than about a thousand chips. For bulk production the development costs are soon recovered and the cost per chip becomes competitive.

The type of technology used to produce these ROM chips varies from type to type.

One system uses a very similar idea to the diode matrix ROM where conducting links make the connection between the input lines and the output lines and these links exist only where the photographic mask permits; it 'masks out' the positions where a link is *not* required and the associated data output line will then be at logic 0 (Figure 10.12).

Another production method involves FET technology (MOS), where the manufacturer's mask dictates where FET gates are connected or left floating (Figure 10.13).

The resistors at the top would normally be MOSFETs since they take up far less space when fabricated as an integrated circuit. They act as non-linear resistors, permanently on, but the non-linearity does not matter since the circuit operates digitally, either on or off.

When an input line is energised (logic 1) then, assuming *n*-channel devices, the FETs with gates connected will turn on and they will conduct, taking the output line down to earth (logic 0). Those FETs where the gate is floating will stay off and the associated output lines will stay at logic 1.

Figure 10.13

Programmable read only memory (PROM)

If we do not want to produce a large number of ROM chips with the same data we could use a PROM. These are chips which can be programmed by the user. Once programmed the stored data cannot be altered, so they act as permanent storage devices just like masked ROM. Like all ROM they are non-volatile (loss of supply does not mean loss of stored data).

The PROM chip is programmed by blowing fusible links incorporated in the integrated circuit; once blown the change is permanent. The links are blown, where required, by passing a large current through them.

The chip is manufactured with a link in each cell, sometimes in the collector and sometimes in the emitter (Figure 10.14). The link is made by depositing nichrome or polysilicon on the chip circuit. This link has a very narrow spot where the programming current (typically 50 mA) will blow it. Usually a proprietary PROM programmer is used to blow the links, but it could be done using bit-by-bit blowing by switching the necessary current to each memory cell in turn manually. When the chip is in use as a memory the operating current is far too small to affect the fusible links.

Where the link is in series with the collector the data line stays at logic 1 once the link is blown,

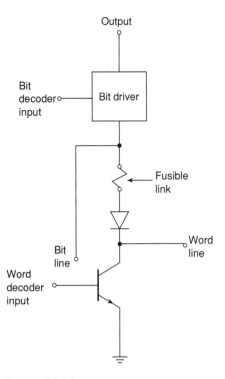

Figure 10.14

since the transistor base–emitter can be forward biased but the collector is permanently open circuit (Figure 10.15). Where the link is in the emitter, the cell in which the fuse is blown will have an output at logic 0. These types of memory chip are particularly useful for one-off projects where the requirement is for permanent non-volatile storage but only for a single chip.

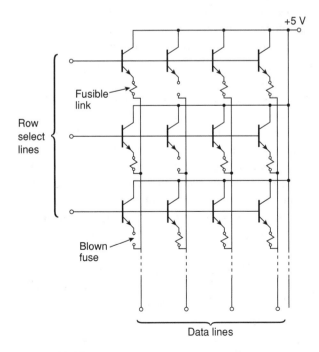

Figure 10.15

Erasable programmable read only memory (EPROM)

The EPROM can be used in a similar way to ROM but has the advantage of being field programmable, like PROM. The difference is that, after being programmed, the EPROM can be wiped clean (erased) and then programmed again if required. EPROM uses a technology called FAMOS (floating gate avalanche metal–oxide–semiconductor). The principal element of this memory is like a pMOS FET but with a floating gate, isolated from the substrate by a layer of silicon dioxide.

After manufacture the FET output, having an uncharged gate, is at logic 1. This can be programmed to logic 0 by pulsing the gate with a long duration pulse (about 50 ms) of about 25 V. This sets off an avalanche effect and the electrons injected into the gate leave it negatively charged. The resistance between the gate and the channel is very high because of the silicon dioxide layer so the stored charge cannot leak away. In fact it does leak away but so slowly that it would take tens of years before the charge was lost. This means that, in effect, the stored data are permanent.

These EPROM chips are made with a clear window in the top so that the device can be exposed to ultraviolet light in order to erase the stored data. This is done by taking the chip out of the circuit and placing it in an ultraviolet light box. The very short wavelength energy from the light source effectively knocks the stored electrons out of the gate region and allows the charge to leak away. To stop this happening accidentally in sunlight a piece of black tape is normally stuck over the window once the chip is programmed.

The disadvantage of this type of EPROM is the need to remove it from the circuit for erasure and the fact that it allows only bulk erasure, i.e. all the data must be lost even if only 1 bit required alteration. The solution to this is to use a PROM that can be bit reprogrammed *in situ*.

Electrically alterable PROM

Electrically alterable PROM devices go by several names: electrically erasable programmable read only memories (EEPROM or even E^2PROM) or, from the title, EAROM or, because of the way they are used, read mostly memory.

The idea is that, by using the control lines provided, each individual cell can be programmed or reprogrammed by applying a voltage pulse to it. Like the EPROM this is about 25 V but the process makes use of the tunnel effect rather than avalanche.

Table 10.8   Typical access/cycle times for a range of memory types

Memory type/technology	Access time	Cycle time	Power	
			Active	**Standby**
N-channel static RAM	120-250 ns	120-250 ns	1 W	850 mW
NMOS dynamic RAM	120-200 ns	375 ns	462 mW	20 mW
N-channel MOS ROM	250-300 ns	375-450 ns	220 mW	35 mW
UV EPROM	350-450 ns	–	525 mW	132 mW
EEPROM (EAROM)	around 250 ns	–	700 mW	350 mW

These chips offer many advantages and can be erased and rewritten several thousand times in their useful lifetime. The only disadvantage is, perhaps, their relatively high cost.

In terms of memory operating speed two basic definitions are required: access time and cycle time.

Access time   The exact definition of memory access time tends to vary between manufacturers but it is most useful to consider it as the time taken between addressing the device and display of the information. Another way to put this is that it is the time between an access request to a particular location and the time when that information or data is read.

Cycle time   For some types of memory the cycle time is defined as the minimum time required between memory accesses.

The access time for memory varies considerably depending upon the type of memory technology used and, to some extent, the manufacturer. It is difficult to specify 'typical' values for access times but the list in Table 10.8 gives an indication.

RAM

Random access (or, as we now know, read/write) memory is available using a range of technologies which offer different speeds, power consumption and other characteristics associated with electronics. However, at a fundamental level we can classify RAM as being one of two types of technology: static or dynamic.

Static RAM (SRAM)   The basis of the static RAM type of memory is the flipflop or bistable multivibrator. It can be set to logic 1 or reset to logic 0. A static RAM chip effectively contains thousands of these single-bit storage elements (e.g. a 4k RAM). SRAM is asynchronous and so does not require a clock, and the stored contents will remain stable forever as long as the power is maintained.

Dynamic RAM (DRAM)   In the dynamic RAM type of device data are stored as a charge. The capacitance between the gate and substrate of a MOS transistor (MOSFET) is used as the storage element for a single data bit.

The big advantage of DRAM is that the storage element is much smaller than the flipflop in SRAM. Thus there is a much higher packing density, i.e. more bits stored per unit area of chip. As an example of the difference, a 64k-bit DRAM uses the same chip area as a 16k-bit SRAM. In addition to packing density DRAM also operates at higher speed than SRAM.

Well, we know enough about engineering now to know that with those advantages there must be disadvantages.

The disadvantage of DRAM is the circuit complexity required. This is because the charge stored in the capacitive element leaks away in a few milliseconds and therefore the stored data are lost. To avoid this we need to repeatedly rewrite the stored data. This process is called **refreshing** the memory and is carried out every one or two milliseconds by reading the memory, a row or column at a time, and then rewriting it. This need to refresh has two disadvantages: one is the need for refresh circuitry although this is often included in the chip nowadays, and the second is the fact that the process slows down the speed at which the processor executes because of the delay in accessing the memory during the refreshing period.

Despite these disadvantages the packing density means that DRAM offers a cost-effective way of providing large memory. With the demand for RAM space increasing, DRAM accounts for a large part of the market now. SRAM is still used but tends to be for small memory applications.

10.2 Introduction to machine code programming

Now that we have seen the way in which various components are combined to make the microprocessor-based system and the microcomputer we need to know how to talk to it. At the lowest level of communication we need to program in machine code.

The only way to learn how to program is to do it, but at least we can look at some of the ground rules.

The development of a machine code program takes place in three stages: the algorithm, the flowchart and the code.

Algorithm

An algorithm is a step-by-step list of procedures for solving a problem. In a way, it outlines the method of solution, not the detail.

For example, if we had to add 2 data bytes from memory the algorithm might be as follows.

1. Get first byte from memory and store in a register.
2. Get second byte from memory and store in another register.
3. Add the contents of one register to the contents of the other.

How we actually do this would depend on the type of facilities offered by the particular processor concerned.

Flowchart

A flowchart is a diagram showing the 'flow' of program operation, a type of block diagram of the order in which we intend to carry out the required steps of the algorithm. The flowchart can be considered as a graphical way of presenting an algorithm.

Once we have developed a flowchart that makes sense the final stage of coding the program is very straightforward.

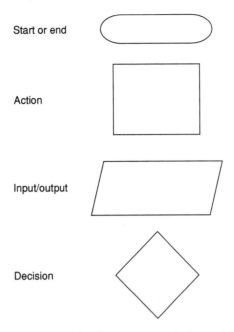

Figure 10.16   Common symbols used to construct a flowchart

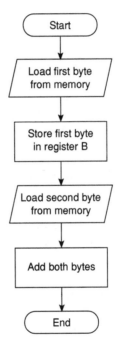

Figure 10.17

In order to construct a flowchart we need to know the symbols used; some of the common ones are shown in Figure 10.16.

If we look again at the example used for the algorithm we can produce a simple flowchart as in Figure 10.17.

Coding

Coding is the last stage of program development. By using the instruction set supplied by the manufacturer for a particular type of micro-

Table 10.9

Memory address	Assembly mnemonic	Machine code	Comment
3000H	SUB A	97	Subtract A from itself to clear the accumulator. This is not necessary in this case, but is 'good practice' as a general rule
3001H	LDA 3500	3A	Load the accumulator with the contents of the memory location 3500H
3002H		00	
3003H		35	
3004H	MOV B,A	47	Move the data in A to register B
3005H	LDA 350F	3A	Load the second byte into the accumulator
3506H		0F	
3507H		35	
3508H	ADD B	80	Add the byte in register B to the byte in register A
3509H	HLT	76	Reset. End of program

processor we encode the program in hexadecimal. This is the executable code which we run.

Working from the Intel 8085 instruction set we can code the example program. We need to store each instruction of our program in user RAM, and often it is helpful to include comments to clarify what we have done.

Assume that user RAM starts at address 3000H and that the 2 data bytes are stored at address 3500H and address 350FH. (Note that the H on the end of the address is just to tell us that it is in hexadecimal.)

We can bring data into the accumulator directly from memory and all arithmetical operations act on the accumulator. So, one method of solution would be as in Table 10.9.

It is important to note two points about the way we need to talk to the 8085:

(a) MOV B,A means copy data *to* B *from* A;
(b) When we code an address the Intel chip wants this as *low byte* followed by *high byte*.

So a three-byte instruction LDA 3500 is coded, 1 byte per address, as

```
3A   op-code
00   low byte of address
35   high byte of address
```

As another example of program construction consider the following problem.

Five data bytes are stored in consecutive RAM locations starting at address 350A. We wish to add them all together and store the result at address 3510.

In order to code this efficiently we need to know something about the ways in which we are allowed to address data within the system. Without knowing it, we have already used a few of the available modes of address but this problem calls for a mode we mentioned briefly but never examined.

Address modes

Whenever we use an instruction that refers to an 'operand' (the data the op-code acts on) there must be some information to tell the CPU where the operand is. Usually this location will be a memory address or a register.

To allow flexibility in programming, processors provide a range of address modes. Some processors offer a massive range of sophisticated modes but the 8085 provides only four modes which cover the basic requirements of any system.

Register We have already used this mode. Here the operand is held in a register and the address part of the instruction gives the name of the register, e.g. add B.

Immediate In this mode the operand itself is given in the instruction. These are the **move immediate** instructions MVI. For example, to move the operand (data byte) 25H immediately into register C we would use the immediate address mode instruction MVI A,25H.

Direct address mode In this case the memory address where the operand is stored is given directly in the instruction. This means a 3-byte instruction, e.g. LDA 3050H which tells the processor to copy data from address 3050H to the accumulator. We have already used this mode.

Indirect register addressing This is the one we need for the example. If we store a memory address in the H–L register pair, that location can then be referred to in the program simply as M.

So, for example, if we wrote the address 3050 into the H–L pair by using the instruction LXI H,3050 (load immediately the H–L pair with the address 3050H – note that X in the op-code signifies a 16-bit pair of registers), then we could move the data from this address into register A by using the command MOV A,M.

This seems unnecessarily complicated but, in fact, this address mode is very useful, especially for a programming technique known as **looping**.

So let's look at that problem again: 5 data bytes are stored in consecutive RAM locations starting at address 350A. We wish to add them all together and store the result at address 3510.

We need to tell the CPU where the first byte is stored by putting the address (350A) into the H–L pair. Then each time we want data we just go to the next consecutive address and we can do this by incrementing the H–L pair.

How many times do we increment it? Well, we have to pick up 5 bytes so we could set up register C as a counter by putting 5 into it (using immediate addressing) and decrementing C every time we take data out of the memory.

Incrementing and decrementing just means adding one and subtracting one respectively.

Now we are really getting into this. Let's prepare our program. The algorithm is as follows.

1. Store first byte address.
2. Set C as the counter.
3. Move data from memory to register B.
4. Add B.
5. Increment H–L.
6. Decrement C.
7. Test to see if the counter is at zero.
8. If not do steps 3 to 7 again.
9. When the counter is at zero copy the contents of A to memory.

The flowchart is given in Figure 10.18 and the code is shown in Table 10.10.

Now we have seen how to develop a program all we need is practice. This can only be mastered by using a machine to run programs and debug them when they don't work.

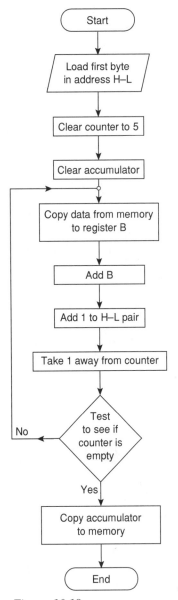

Figure 10.18

Table 10.10

Memory address	Assembly language	Machine code	Comment
3000H 3001H 3002H	LXI H,350A	21 0A 35	Load first byte address into the H–L pair
3003H 3004H	MVI C,05H	0E 05	Put 5 into the counter
3005H	SUB A	97	Clear accumulator
3006H 3007H	MOV B,M ADD B	46 80	Copy first byte to B
3008H	INX H	23	Move pointer to next byte
3009H	DCR C	0D	Reduce counter
3009H 300AH 300BH	JNZ 3006H	C2 06 30	Check counter for zero and go to 3006 if not
300CH	MOV M,A	7E	Store result in memory
300DH	HLT	76	Stop

So far we have looked at the requirements of a system, the internal features of some of the system components and, briefly, how to program the system. Now we need to consider the joining of the system to the outside world, **interfacing**.

The ways in which we transfer data between our microprocessor system and the outside world depend on exactly what form the outside world takes.

One thing we need to remember is that in most cases the outside world operates as an analogue environment. This means that often we need to convert between analogue and digital signals or values as we move between system and output or input. To do this we need converters.

10.3 Converters

Digital to analogue converters (DACs)

In the real world most things are analogue, i.e. they are continuously variable. They are not digital in their action. For example, temperature changes tend not to be discrete with discontinuities; when we increase or decrease the speed of some mechanical component in a system we do it gradually.

However, most of our electronic control and all of our processing tends to be done digitally. There are many types of circuit available to convert between the two so we shall examine only a few of the common methods.

Binary-weighted resistor DAC

The principle here is simple. Each bit of a digital word has a significance based on its position within the word, ranging from the least significant bit (LSB), which represents 2^0, to the most significant bit (MSB), which represents 2^n (where n is the number of bits in the word). So if we apply the bits to an amplifier, in such a way that the LSB is applied to the input with maximum attenuation and each successive bit is applied with successively less attenuation until we get to the MSB which receives minimum attenuation, the output of the amplifier

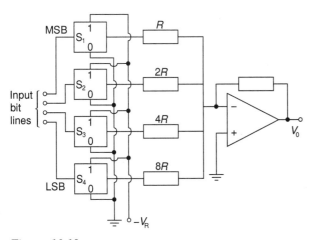

Figure 10.19

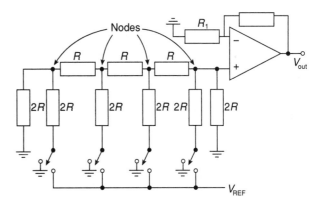

Figure 10.20

will have a value corresponding to the digital value of the applied word.

This is harder to say than to do!

The network of resistors at the input provides the required attenuation but we need their values to be related by some binary relationship. The obvious way to do this is to make each value twice the previous value (Figure 10.19).

If we have a fixed reference voltage which is connected to the series resistor by a digitally controlled switch, whenever a logic 1 is present we can see that the output voltage of the opamp will be proportional to the value of the applied digital word. The amplifier is acting as a sort of current-to-voltage converter.

Whenever a logic 1 is applied to a bit line the digitally controlled switch connects the associated series resistor to logic 0 (earth).

The problem with this type of converter is the resistors. We cannot buy standard values since they are not available in a range of binary values. Also, for the converter to be accurate we need resistors that track accurately with temperature. This means that the change in value of resistance with temperature must be uniform. This is very difficult to achieve.

One clever solution to these problems is to redesign the circuit to become what we call a ladder converter.

R–2R ladder-type DAC

In the R–$2R$ ladder-type circuit the resistor network is arranged so that we need twice as many resistors but only two values are required, R and $2R$ (Figure 10.20). The ladder is a current-splitting network so the ratio of the resistors is more important than the actual values.

The clever aspect of this circuit is that from any mode the resistance looking in any direction is $2R$.

Any switch connected to the reference voltage is at logic 1 and the series resistance between each node means that as we move further away from the amplifier input the significance of a logic 1 decreases. The output will be of the form $V_{out} = 2^{n-1}V$ which is the form we want.

Analogue to digital converters (ADCs)

In many practical systems the input is derived from a transducer and this input is analogue. To convert it to digital form for processing we again have many methods. The common converters use the principles involved in one of the following.

Counting ADC

The counting type of converter incorporates a DAC, a binary counter, an AND gate and an opamp used as a comparator (Figure 10.21). Quite a lot of the electronics you have learned applied in one go!

Initially the counter is set to zero by applying a clear pulse. The applied analogue voltage is greater than zero so the comparator produces an output which is applied as a logic 1 to the AND gate.

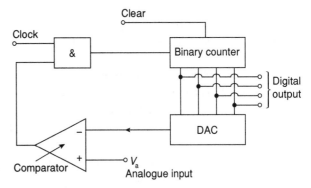

Figure 10.21

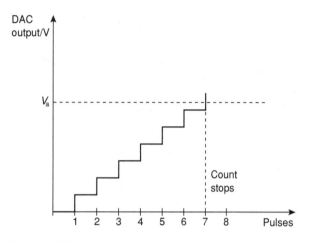

Figure 10.22

The clock generates a constant frequency pulse train so that every time a pulse occurs the AND gate output goes to logic 1 and the counter counts it.

As the count increases from zero the output of the DAC starts to increase from zero with a sort of staircase form (Figure 10.22).

As long as the analogue input voltage (V_a) is larger than the digital voltage from the DAC, the comparator will give an output of logic 1. This means that the AND gate output will be at logic 1 every time a clock pulse occurs and every clock pulse will be counted.

When the count reaches a certain value the DAC output will be equal to the analogue input voltage. At this point the comparator output falls to logic 0 and the AND gate is disabled. Now no more clock pulses are passed to the counter and the count stops.

The output of the counter is a digital word representing the value of the analogue input voltage. The counter can now be reset and the count started again.

The digital output will only be approximately the same as the analogue input because the accuracy depends on the size of the step between two digits. Basically the more bits there are in the digital output word, the more accurate the conversion (Figure 10.23). The problem is that as the word length increases so does the circuit complexity and cost. We know the level of acceptable accuracy for a given job and we choose our converter accordingly.

This circuit is fine if we have a fixed analogue input voltage but if the input is varying with time we cannot use it to convert the data continuously so we need to sample the data at fixed intervals. How often we sample depends on the conversion time of the circuit. This is easily found for this type of converter. If the maximum analogue voltage is represented by n pulses and the clock period is

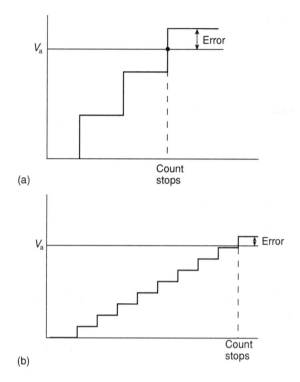

Figure 10.23

T seconds then the conversion time (and minimum time between samples) is nT seconds.

A better version of the counting ADC uses an up–down counter instead of an up counter. This type of converter is called a tracking or servo-counting ADC.

Tracking or servo-counting ADC

You will see that the circuit for a tracking ADC does not have a start command (clear pulse) and there is no need for an AND gate (Figure 10.24).

When the output of the ADC is less than the analogue input voltage the comparator output will set the counter to count up. This means that with each clock pulse the ADC output will increase. At some point the ADC output will become greater than the analogue input voltage and the

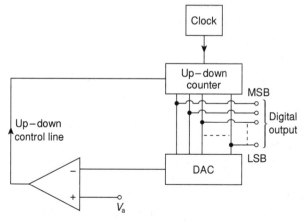

Figure 10.24

comparator output changes to set the counter counting down. However, it will only count down one count (1 LSB). This causes the comparator to set the count to up again. The digital output will vary ±1 LSB around the correct value.

For small changes of analogue input the conversion time is short so we can use this as a tracking ADC.

Parallel comparator ADC (flash converter)

The parallel comparator ADC gives a very fast conversion often referred to as **bin conversion**. This is because the analogue input is sorted into a given range or bin.

The best way to see how it operates is to look at a simple 3-bit converter (Figure 10.25). A practical (8-bit or more) converter is just a scaled up version but the principle is the same.

The analogue input voltage is applied simultaneously to a bank of comparators. The non-inverting inputs to the comparators are connected to a fixed voltage via a series resistor circuit so that each of them has an equally spaced threshold voltage ($V/8$, $2V/8$ etc.). Thus as V_a exceeds some of these the comparators will have an output of logic 1. Those which have a threshold greater than V_a will have an output of logic 0.

The output of the circuit for each available combination of comparator output is shown in the form of a truth table (Table 10.11).

If we take a case where the applied input V_a is greater than $2V/8$ but less than $3V/8$ then D_2 and D_1 will be at logic 1 and all others will be at logic 0. This gives an output of 2 for our 3-bit word and we know V_a lies somewhere between $2V/8$ and $3V/8$ volts.

Single-slope ADC

The single-slope ADC is a type of counting ADC but we make use of the fact that if we integrate a constant we get a linear ramp output from the integrator.

Both the integrator and the counter are initially reset by the logic control circuit (Figure 10.26).

With a fixed reference voltage applied to its input the integrator output is a linear ramp increasing from zero. This is applied to one input of a comparator. The other input of the comparator has the analogue voltage V_a applied to it. Initially V_a is larger than the integrator output and so the comparator output is at logic 1. This enables the AND gate and every time a clock pulse occurs it is applied to the counter and counted.

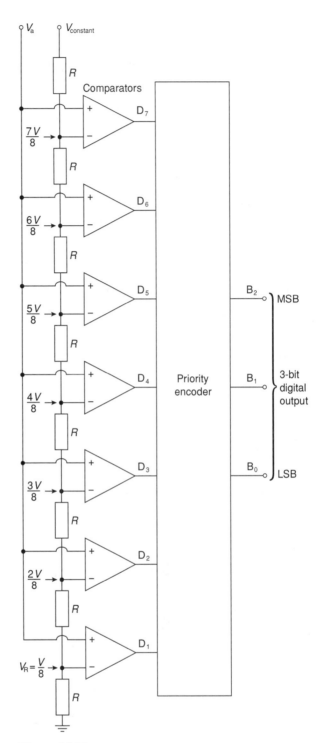

Figure 10.25

When the ramp voltage reaches a value equal to V_a the comparator output falls to logic 0, the AND gate is disabled, the clock pulses are no longer passed to the counter and the count stops.

This circuit gives a fairly slow conversion and suffers from non-linearity of the ramp and changes in clock regularity with temperature. There are ways round most of these problems using a dual-slope converter, which is a variation on this theme but we shall not cover it here.

Table 10.11

D_7	D_6	D_5	D_4	D_3	D_2	D_1	B_2	B_1	B_0
0	0	0	0	0	0	0	0	0	0
0	0	0	0	0	0	1	0	0	1
0	0	0	0	0	1	1	0	1	0
0	0	0	0	1	1	1	0	1	1
0	0	0	1	1	1	1	1	0	0
0	0	1	1	1	1	1	1	0	1
0	1	1	1	1	1	1	1	1	0
1	1	1	1	1	1	1	1	1	1

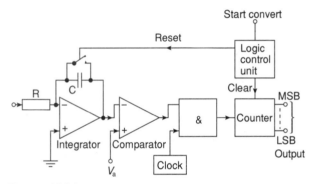

Figure 10.26

Some associated terminology

One of the concerns around choice of ADC or DAC is the question of accuracy and error. All types have a finite accuracy and a number of factors which introduce error.

In ADC systems three types of error occur by virtue of the system.

Quantisation error   The process of breaking an analogue signal into separate or discrete voltage levels to form digital code is called **quantisation**. The quantisation error is the smallest analogue input to which an output signal can be approximated.

This error has a maximum value of ±1 LSB. The size of the error depends on how many bits there are. The more bits there are in the converter, the smaller is the quantisation error. This is what was illustrated in Figure 10.23.

Sampling error   This happens because, if the conversion time is fairly long, the input will have changed in value. This means that the maximum frequency of input that we can convert is limited by the sampling rate, which in turn is limited by the conversion time.

Electronic error   This is really a term used for all the collective errors that occur when we pass a signal through circuits. It includes such things as non-linearity, propagation delay, attenuation, phase shift and so on.

Some of the terms used in connection with DAC are a little trickier to follow.

Resolution   A converter with a resolution of 12 bits uses a 12-bit word to represent an analogue signal. The more bits, the better the resolution.

Offset   When all the digital inputs to a DAC are at zero the analogue output should be zero. Sometimes a small voltage or current is present at the output for zero input – this is called the offset. Usually this can be trimmed out at the buffer amplifier of the converter.

Settling time   This is the time it takes for the analogue output to settle to a steady state after a change in the digital input has occurred. The worst case is when every bit of the input changes from 1 to 0 or vice versa. Settling times vary from about 0.1 μs to about 2 μs.

Sometimes a manufacturer will quote the settling time for an LSB change. This, of course, gives the best figure for this parameter.

Analogue output resistance   This is the resistance seen at the output of the DAC looking back. Typically this is around 5 kΩ so we need to have some buffering at the output.

Reading input and displaying output

If we wanted to look at the logic state of the output of our computer the simplest way is to connect an LED to each bus line, eight in the case of our 8085 example processor. An LED that is emitting light shows a logic 1 and logic 0 is signified by a diode which is off.

This is fine if all we want to see is the logic state. A more complex and more useful display is a seven-segment display (Figure 10.27). These allow decimal numbers to be displayed but of course we need suitable drivers connected between the bus and the display to convert the binary output to an equivalent decimal display.

When we want to input to the computer we need to have some form of code. We could just convert numbers to their binary equivalent but we also need to represent letters and punctuation etc. The most common way of doing this is to use ASCII – the American Standard Code for Information Interchange – which we looked at earlier.

By using a suitable program subroutine in the microcomputer monitor we can detect when a particular key is pressed on the keyboard. For that particular key the appropriate ASCII code is generated and transmitted along the data bus.

One way that we can detect which key has been pressed is to software poll for the interrupt that the key generates. We shall look at polling later.

The monitor program can also arrange to move the cursor to the start of the next line when a line

is complete. The cursor is also generated as an ASCII character like any other.

The characters are made up from a matrix of dots. The commonly used ones are seven rows by five columns and nine rows by seven columns.

Each dot has to be stored in ROM as a logic 1 for a bright spot on the cathode ray tube screen or as a logic 0 for a blank. This means that character generators require a lot of memory. Modern MOSFET memories allow us to have single-chip character generators that offer 128 character 9×7 fonts very cheaply. These characters as logic bits are fed into a shift register and applied serially to the cathode ray tube or printer.

We know that to talk to the peripherals we need I/O devices and we have looked at shift registers and the facility they offer for changing our data from serial to parallel or vice versa. However, we need to catch up on a bit more jargon about the way they are organised.

When we need to connect a serial peripheral device to our microprocessor system we use an interface adapter which basically consists of shift registers, some buffering and maybe some voltage level shifters so that different logic families can talk to each other, e.g. TTL to MOS. Most of the interface adapters can be programmed themselves.

Generally the transfer of data between the computer and the peripheral is asynchronous. This involves a technique known as handshaking.

If we sent the ASCII characters as continuous strings of bits the CPU would have to be synchronised to the sending peripheral so that it knew when a character started and ended. To get round this problem asynchronous transfers use start and stop control bits at the beginning and end of each character. Thus the CPU is stopped at the end of each character and so keeps in step with the sending device.

The devices that take care of this are quite sophisticated.

Asynchronous communications interface adapter (ACIA)   The ACIA can convert received serial data, together with the start and stop bits, into parallel data output. It will confirm that the transmission is error free and generate the interrupt signal. The ACIA will also take the parallel data from the bus, convert it to serial data and add the stop and start bits and error checking bits (such as parity).

Universal asynchronous receiver and transmitter (UART)   This is a MOS/LSI chip which can also receive and transmit asynchronous serial data in all the standard formats and perform the serial to parallel change and vice versa.

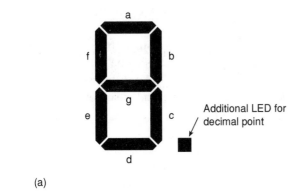

(a)

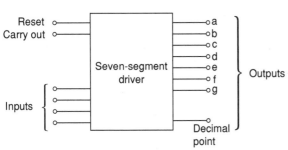

(b)

Figure 10.27

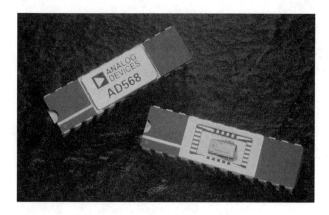

A digital to analogue converter

Parallel input, parallel output interface (PIO) This contains several parallel registers acting as output ports, together with the logic circuits for the interrupts.

Sometimes we use synchronous data transfer, e.g. between the CPU and the floppy disc controller. With synchronous transmission of data there is no requirement for sending the start and stop bits but the peripheral has to be synchronised to the CPU.

Universal synchronous/asynchronous receiver and transmitter (USART) This device can convert parallel data into any serial format required, synchronous or asynchronous.

Synchronising the transfer

Generally, most peripheral devices do not operate at the same speed as the microcomputer nor from the same clock. We may have a situation where data are read twice because the sending device is so slow or we may find that data are lost because the sending device is too fast and sends a second data byte before the first has been read.

There are several ways of synchronising the transfer to try and avoid these problems.

Polling This is a technique by which a software routine enables the CPU to go repeatedly to each peripheral device in turn and check to see if it is ready to transfer data. A control line called the **status line** is checked to see if a data transfer is required at each peripheral.

Handshaking This is a sort of mutual agreement between the computer and the peripheral as to the timing of transfer. Each data transfer channel has two handshake lines.

A logic 1 on one line indicates 'ready to send' while a logic 1 on the other line shows 'data received'. In this way the CPU and the peripheral remain synchronised by telling each other their current condition.

Interrupts In this system each peripheral is connected to an interrupt request pin on the CPU (INT or IREQ) and signals that it is ready for data transfer by changing the logic level on this pin. When this occurs the main program is interrupted and an interrupt service routine (ISR) runs to carry out the transfer. At the end of the ISR the CPU returns to the main program at the point where it was interrupted.

Buffer memory This is a method used when the device receiving the data is too slow for the CPU to be hung up by one of the other methods. A printer is a typical example of a buffered peripheral device. The idea is that the CPU downloads the data to the buffer memory at its own rate and then the printer takes the data from the buffer at its own, much slower, rate.

Direct memory access (DMA) This is the reverse of the last situation. When a peripheral device can transfer data at a much higher rate than the CPU can cope with it we use DMA. A hard disc drive is an example of such a device. When it wishes to transfer data the CPU is effectively put on hold and disconnected from the data and address buses; a DMA controller puts the data direct to memory via the system bus.

This provides very rapid data transfer and uses one of two common techniques. **Cycle stealing** is a method where the DMA controller identifies the cycles when the bus is unused by the CPU. This is used for the transfer of single bytes of data. When a large amount of data is to be transferred the DMA hangs up the CPU and transfers the whole block of data. This method is sometimes called **burst transfer**.

CHAPTER

11

Test meters

11.1 The moving coil meter

The moving coil meter is commonly found in electronic test equipment in a wide variety of forms displaying indications of voltage, current, ohms, decibels, power and more.

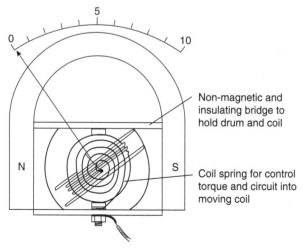

Figure 11.1 The moving coil meter

The construction and operation of the meter

The fundamental construction of a moving coil meter is outlined in Figure 11.1. Between the two poles of the permanent magnet a coil is pivoted around a drum. This coil is able to rotate in a clockwise direction only and is held in position by light springs so that if it is moved it always returns to its position of rest. These springs are also used to make an electrical connection to the coil itself.

The presence of the permanent magnet sets up lines of magnetic flux which flow across the opening where the coil is mounted. The meter relies on the principle that when a direct current is passed through a conductor a magnetic field is set up around the conductor. In this case, the conductor is the moving coil. The magnetic field that is now present around the coil interacts with that of the permanent magnet and causes the coil to turn on its pivot. When the current is interrupted the magnetic field of the coil disappears and the springs ensure that the coil is returned to its position of rest.

The movement of the coil is linear and proportional to the amount of current that flows through the coil. If a pointer is attached to the coil it will move as the coil rotates and can therefore be used to indicate the movement of the coil which, in turn, is proportional to the current flowing.

Selecting a meter

If we think about the meter just described, the amount of current that has to flow through the meter coil to cause it to deflect is quite small. Figure 11.2 details the specifications of typical readily available meters. It shows that the current needed to cause a deflection is of the order of 100 μA or 1 mA depending on the type of meter considered. It also gives the resistance of the coil: e.g. 1800 Ω and 75 Ω.

The labels on the figure read:
- Non-magnetic and insulating bridge to hold drum and coil
- Coil spring for control torque and circuit into moving coil

We are working
using these figures

technical specification					
size	sensitivity	coil resistance	accu-racy	application	scale length
E	100 µA	1800 Ω ±15%	2%	Voltmeter	40 mm
E	1 mA	75 Ω ±1%	2%	Ammeter	40 mm
F	100 µA	1300 Ω ±15%	2%	Voltmeter	55 mm
F	1 mA	75 Ω ±1%	2%	Ammeter	55 mm
G	100 µA	1300 Ω ±15%	2%	Voltmeter	73 mm
G	1 mA	75 Ω ±1%	2%	Ammeter	73 mm
G	50-0-50 µA	1300 Ω ±15%	2%	Centre-Zero	73 mm
H	50 µA	2700 Ω ±15%	1·5%	Voltmeter	100 mm
H	100 µA	1300 Ω ±15%	1·5%	Voltmeter	100 mm
H	1 mA	75 Ω ±1%	1·5%	Ammeter	100 mm

Figure 11.2

Full scale deflection voltage

The term 'full scale deflection' is used to describe the meter when the pointer is at its furthest point of travel – normally the right-hand side of the scale. This occurs when the meter coil is passing the maximum current that it can safely and continuously handle.

The voltage across the coil when the pointer is at maximum is known as the full scale deflection voltage (FSD voltage). Using the values outlined in Figure 11.2 this voltage is easily calculated using Ohm's law: for $I_{FSD} = 1$ mA and resistance R of the coil 75 Ω,

$$V = I \times R$$

$$\therefore \ V_{FSD} = 1 \text{ mA} \times 75 \text{ Ω}$$

$$= 75 \text{ mV}$$

A little thought should show you that, regardless of what is written on the scale of a meter and the units used, the meter is only handling minimal current to achieve FSD – in our case with a voltage across the coil of 75 mV as a current of 1 mA flows.

The question that now has to be tackled is what to do with the rest of the current or voltage that cannot be passed via the meter coil. It has to go somewhere!

11.2 Extending the range of a moving coil meter

Extending the current range   302
Extending the voltage range   303

A very common problem encountered by electronics enthusiasts and professional technicians alike is how to use a meter to indicate a current or voltage other than the natural FSD parameters of the meter.

The answer is to incorporate a resistor either in parallel or in series with the meter.

Extending the current range

The current range can be extended by placing a resistor in parallel with the meter but external to it. Such a resistor is known as a shunt and its positioning is shown in Figure 11.3.

Taking the meter specifications outlined in Figure 11.2 we shall assume that we want the meter to be able to indicate up to 1 A at FSD.

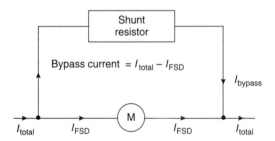

Figure 11.3   Extending the current range of a meter

From the table, the FSD current of the meter is 1 mA and the resistance of the coil is 75 Ω. The total current to be indicated is 1 A = 1000 mA. This needs to be split so that only 1 mA passes through the meter's coil and the remainder flows via the shunt (see Figure 11.4).

To extend a meter to indicate higher currents a resistor known as a **shunt** is included in parallel with the meter.

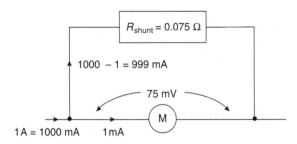

Figure 11.4

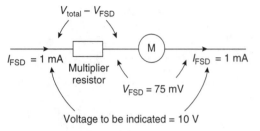

Figure 11.5 Extending the voltage range of a meter

The voltage across the coil at FSD can be calculated using the coil's resistance and I_{FSD}. In turn, this voltage can be used to calculate the value of the shunt resistor:

$$V_{FSD} = I_{FSD} \times R_{meter}$$
$$= 1 \text{ mA} \times 75 \text{ }\Omega$$
$$= 75 \text{ mV}$$

$$R_{shunt} = \frac{V}{I} = \frac{75 \text{ mV}}{999 \text{ mA}} = 0.075 \text{ }\Omega$$

Extending the voltage range

The meter can also be extended to indicate voltages higher than V_{FSD} by including a resistor in series with the meter. This is known as a multiplier resistor and the excess voltage is dropped across it. Its position is shown in Figure 11.5.

Taking the meter specifications outlined in Figure 11.2 we shall assume that we want to extend the meter to indicate voltages up to 10 V at FSD. From the specifications in the table we know the coil resistance and I_{FSD} and, as already seen, it is a simple matter to work out the FSD voltage from this.

The purpose of the multiplier resistor is to draw a voltage equal to the difference between the voltage to be measured and V_{FSD}. The procedure is illustrated in Figure 11.5. From the figure,

$$V_{total} - V_{FSD} = 10 \text{ V} - 75 \text{ mV} = 9.925 \text{ V}$$

So

$$R_{multiplier} = \frac{V}{I} = \frac{9.925 \text{ V}}{1 \text{ mA}} = 9.925 \text{ k}\Omega$$

> To extend the meter to read voltage a resistor has to be incorporated in series with the meter. This is known as a **multiplier resistor.**

11.3 The ohm-meter

The ohm-meter uses either a moving coil meter or a digital meter to indicate resistance in a circuit. It operates by including in series with the meter a battery which provides a fixed voltage. A simple arrangement is shown in Figure 11.6.

When a resistor is connected across the terminals of the meter the current that flows causes the meter to indicate. By connecting accurately known values of resistance across the terminals the reading of the meter may be calibrated in ohms and an indication of resistance value given.

A point to notice about an analogue resistance meter is that the scale reads backwards and is non-linear compared with the voltage or current reading. (Look carefully at the scale reproduced in the photo.) The reason for this is simple. If there is $0 \text{ }\Omega$ resistance between the terminals they must be short circuited. Under this condition maximum current must flow via the meter and hence FSD will be indicated by the pointer.

When using an analogue meter it is important that the pointer is aligned on the zero at the right-hand side of the scale before any resistance measurements are taken. This is easily done by shorting the probes together (i.e. connecting the positive lead to the negative) and adjusting the variable resistor until the pointer lines up. If this is not done, resistance readings will be inaccurate.

The principle of operation of the ohm-meter using an internal battery to supply a voltage applies

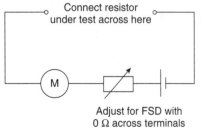

Figure 11.6

AVO 8 analogue multimeter

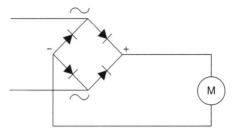

Figure 11.7

Figure 11.7 illustrates how this can be achieved. The bridge rectifier provides full wave rectification and, whilst the DC is raw (i.e. it is not smoothed), it is good enough for the meter to give a reading.

There is an interesting question to be tackled here. As the AC has been rectified and turned into DC but the meter scale is calibrated in AC, is it indicating RMS, peak, peak to peak or average?

The answer is that the meter is calibrated in RMS but is actually reading an average value of the raw DC. The readings that you obtain are therefore an indication of RMS but are only accurate if the input is sinusoidal.

even if the indicating device is digital. In this case the scale of the meter will give an indication of the resistance not (normally) in ohms but usually in kilo-ohms, mega-ohms or in fractions of a kilo-ohm if the reading is below 1000 Ω.

When the meter has a resistance connected across its terminals that is too large for it to indicate, the scale will usually read '1' which is taken to mean 'turn up to the next scale'. If the '1' is still present then the scale has to be increased by one range and so on until a reading is given.

Digital meters are extremely easy to use for resistance measurement in comparison with analogue meters.

11.4 Adapting a meter to read alternating current

Turn back to the description of how a meter works and you will see that it can only indicate if a DC voltage is applied to it. If an AC voltage is to be measured it has to be converted to DC before it is applied to the meter, which will then show its value.

11.5 The multimeter

The multimeter is the most essential piece of fault finding equipment that a technician can have. It is a single meter with a switch to adapt the meter to read current, voltage (AC or DC), resistance and perhaps even frequency and capacitance.

A very simple circuit of a multimeter is given in Figure 11.8 which shows how one indicating device can be used for a multitude of purposes.

Which multimeter to buy?

Look in any electronics supplier's catalogue and you will find many multimeters to choose from. The problem you are faced with is which one is best value for money or, if money is no object, which should you buy.

The answer to this question lies in considering the effect that the meter will have on the circuit that it is being used to test. This is determined by the **impedance** of the meter.

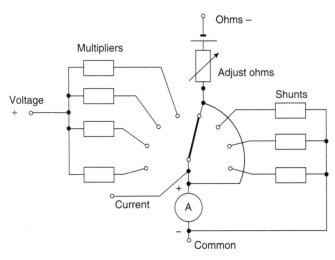

Figure 11.8

Impedance when measuring voltage

When a meter is put in a circuit to measure voltage it is important that the meter has as high a resistance as possible. This can easily be explained by looking at the following example.

In Figure 11.9 two resistors are in series across the 9 V supply. Using Ohm's law it is possible to calculate the theoretical voltage that is present across each resistor:

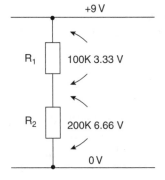

Figure 11.9

$$V_{R_1} = 10 \times \frac{R_1}{R_1 + R_2}$$

$$= 10 \times 0.33$$

$$= 3.33 \text{ V}$$

$$V_{R_2} = 10 \times \frac{R_1}{R_1 + R_2}$$

$$= 10 \times 0.66$$

$$= 6.66 \text{ V}$$

If a meter is added to the circuit to show the voltage across the 200 kΩ resistor the arrangement will alter so that it now appears as in Figure 11.10(a).

This shows that to all intents and purposes the circuit now comprises three resistances, the two original ones and that of the meter. As the meter is in parallel with the resistor the effective resistance of the combination can be calculated. Assuming that the meter has a resistance of 200 kΩ

$$\frac{1}{R_{comb}} = \frac{1}{R_2} + \frac{1}{R_{meter}}$$

$$= \frac{1}{200 \text{ k}\Omega} + \frac{1}{200 \text{ k}\Omega}$$

$$= \frac{1}{100 \text{ k}\Omega}$$

$$\therefore R_{comb} = 100 \text{ k}\Omega$$

The equivalent circuit is given in Figure 11.10(b). The overall circuit resistance has thus been altered and so the total voltage present will redistribute itself as shown in Figure 11.11.

If the meter had a resistance greater than 200 kΩ it would affect the circuit conditions less. So it follows that when selecting a meter the highest impedance possible should be chosen.

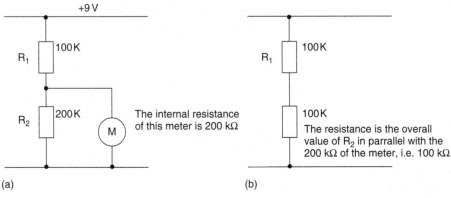

(a)   (b)

Figure 11.10

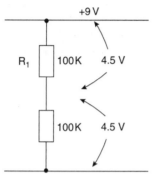

Figure 11.11

11.6 Meter loading

Ohms per volt   306

Meter loading is the term given to the effect that a meter has on a circuit once it is connected. If a meter loads the circuit by a large amount the readings that it gives will be inaccurate.

Ohms per volt

Analogue multimeters are specified not in simple terms of one value of impedance but in ohms per volt. This effectively says that the impedance of the meter is dependent on the range that the meter is switched to. A typical figure is 20 kΩ per volt (20 kΩ/V). This translates to 20 000 Ω for each volt that the scale can indicate. So, if the meter is switched to the 100 V range it will have an impedance of

$$20 \text{ k}\Omega \times 100 \text{ V} = 2000 \text{ k}\Omega = 2 \text{ M}\Omega$$

If switched to a range that could display a maximum of 300 V the impedance of the meter would be that much higher. From this, it is fair to say that the higher the range selected the less the meter will affect the circuit.

> When using a meter always start on the highest range and switch down until a reading is obtained.

Digital meters

The ohms per volt of a digital meter is very much higher than the ohms per volt of an analogue meter as the internal circuitry is electronic rather than passive. A value of 10 MΩ input impedance is not unusual and hence the effect on the circuit is usually so minimal that it can be disregarded.

Practical 1

The purpose of this practical is to demonstrate the effect of meter loading on a circuit and how it can upset circuit conditions. You will need two meters, one digital and one analogue.

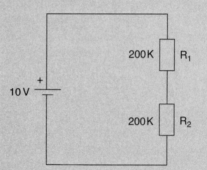

Figure 11.12

Examine the circuit shown in Figure 11.12. Calculate the theoretical voltage across each resistor using Ohm's law. Enter your answer in the appropriate part of the results.

Now connect up the circuit as in Figure 11.12. First, use the analogue meter to measure the voltage across R_1 and record this in the appropriate part of the results table. Now repeat this and measure the voltage across R_2.

When you have done this change over to using the digital meter and once again measure the voltage across each of the two resistors.

If you have understood the section on the difference in meters you will know that the results obtained will be dependent on the impedance of the meter that is being used. When writing this book we used an AVO 8 analogue meter (20 kΩ/V) and a Maplin M-6000 (10 MΩ).

Our own calculated results were easy! No maths was used as two equal value resistors across a supply always split the supply so that half of it appears across each resistor, i.e. 5 V.

Our practical results were as shown in the following table.

The reasons for the results obtained are as follows.

When using the analogue meter it was on the 10 V range and the meter's ohms per volt is 20 kΩ. The actual meter resistance introduced into the circuit was therefore 200 kΩ. When this is in parallel with the

200 kΩ resistance of R_1 or R_2 the conditions
of the circuit alter to those in Figure 11.13.
The voltage displayed is therefore never the
expected reading of 5 V.

The resistance of the digital meter is so
much higher (MΩ/V) that there is little effect
on the conditions of the circuit and the
voltage reading is almost equal to the
calculated value.

	Using digital meter	Using analogue meter	Cal-culated value
Voltage across R_1			
Voltage across R_2			

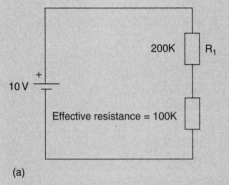

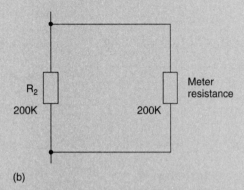

(a) (b)

Figure 11.13 (a) The effect of using an analogue meter in a circuit; (b) the effective resistance is calculated from the two parallel resistors

	Using digital meter	Using analogue meter	Calculated value
Voltage across R_1	5 V	3.33 V	5 V
Voltage across R_2	5 V	6.66 V	5 V

Some digital meters are 'auto-ranging'. This
means that they will always display the reading
without manual selection of range – a very useful
facility.

11.7 The cathode ray oscilloscope

When a multimeter is switched to the voltage
ranges it can indicate the value of the voltage
under test, and whether it is DC or AC, but that is
the limit of its ability. Indeed, for most cases this
is sufficient and the meter is one of the most
essential pieces of kit for an electronics service
technician.

There are occasions, however, in servicing and
investigating equipment and circuits when more
needs to be known about a voltage than a meter can
tell us. If the voltage is AC is it sinewave shaped or
square? How long does each cycle take to complete?
What is the peak to peak value and, sometimes, what
is the phase of one voltage compared with another at
a different point in the circuit?

The oscilloscope is a very versatile instrument as
it can display all the above information by giving us
a graphical real-time electronic picture of a voltage.

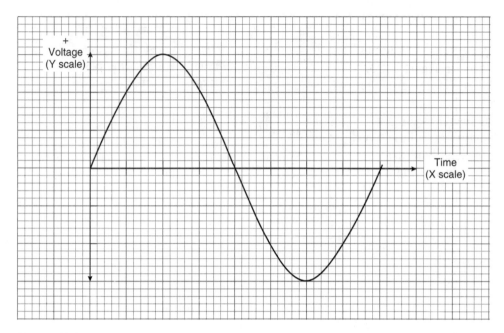

Figure 11.14

As with any graph, its interpretation is determined by the scales that are attached to the *x* and *y* axes. When using the oscilloscope you have the ability to alter these scales.

Figure 11.14 shows a sinewave displayed on a graticule with two scales as found on an oscilloscope. The horizontal scale measures time and is marked – or calibrated – in milliseconds per division. In fact, each division represents 2 ms. The vertical scale is calibrated in volts and here each division represents 2 V.

From Figure 11.14 it is quite easy to find the details of the voltage. For example, reading the horizontal (sometimes called X) scale, the time of one cycle can be determined:

> one complete cycle occupies 8 divisions
> each division represents 2 ms

Therefore,

> periodic time = 8 divisions × 2 ms
>
> = 16 ms

Turning our attention to the vertical, or Y, scale, the voltage of the waveform can be found:

> the peak to peak value of the waveform
>   occupies 6 divisions
> each division represents 2 V

Therefore,

> peak to peak voltage = 6 divisions × 2 V
>
> = 12 V

Now we have used the oscilloscope graticule to discover the details of the voltage the data can be used for other purposes. For example, once we know the duration of one cycle it is only a matter of using the formula to find the frequency. In our example,

$$\text{frequency} = \frac{1}{\text{periodic time}}$$

$$= \frac{1}{16\,\text{ms}} = 62.5\,\text{Hz}$$

The peak to peak voltage can be used to calculate the RMS, peak or average of the waveform as explained in Chapter 4, Section 4.1.

> peak to peak = 12 V
>
> ∴ peak = (12 V)/2 = 6 V
>
> RMS = 0.707 × peak
>
> ∴ RMS = 0.707 × 6 = 4.242 V
>
> average = 0.637 × peak
>
> ∴ average = 0.637 × 6 V = 3.822 V

If you had no trouble in understanding how the time and voltages of the waveform in Figure 11.14 were determined you should have no trouble in using an oscilloscope.

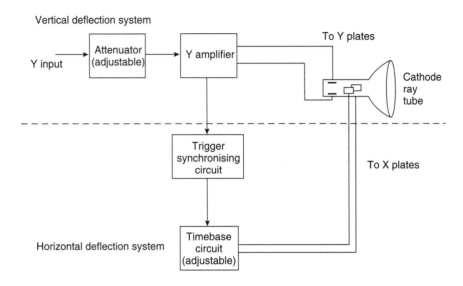

Figure 11.15

The circuitry of the oscilloscope

A simplified block diagram of an oscilloscope is shown in Figure 11.15. There are essentially two component parts: the vertical and the horizontal deflection systems.

Horizontal deflection of the trace (or spot) is achieved by applying an internally generated ramp voltage to the X plates of the cathode ray tube. This voltage has the effect of drawing the spot from one side of the screen to the other. As it moves across the screen it leaves a visible line which is known as the trace. When the spot reaches the right-hand edge of the screen it is returned to the left-hand side in order that it can repeat its sweep. During this period, known as the flyback, the screen is blanked so that no trace is visible.

The rate at which the spot moves across the screen is adjustable by altering the timebase circuit. This allows the oscilloscope to display waveforms (or traces) of different frequencies.

As the spot moves in a horizontal way it is also deflected vertically by the voltage that is applied to the Y plates or horizontal deflection system. To allow the oscilloscope to accommodate various levels of input voltage an attenuator/amplifier is provided so that, regardless of the applied voltage, the actual signal applied to the plates is always within allowable limits.

The controls of an oscilloscope

Although all oscilloscopes display and measure voltages there appear to be a bewildering number of controls on some which are quite off-putting. However, the fundamentals of all oscilloscopes are the same and so we give a summary of the controls and their function, grouped into sections.

Controls affecting the viewing of the trace

Intensity   The intensity control adjusts the brightness of the trace to a suitable level.

Focus   This concentrates the electron beam so that it produces a 'clean' line on the screen as it sweeps.

Illumination   The illumination control adjusts the brightness of the graticule placed in front of the screen to aid the taking of readings.

Trigger   This control should be adjusted until the trace appears stationary on the screen. If it is not correctly set the trace will appear to move continually from left to right, making it impossible to take accurate readings. Note that the trigger control usually works in conjunction with one that is marked input. The input control should be set to the channel via which the input is applied. It is no good attempting to trigger an oscilloscope that has an input on channel 1 if the trigger is working from channel 2.

Controls which affect the reading of the trace

Vertical or Y scale adjustment   This control is normally marked or calibrated in either volts per

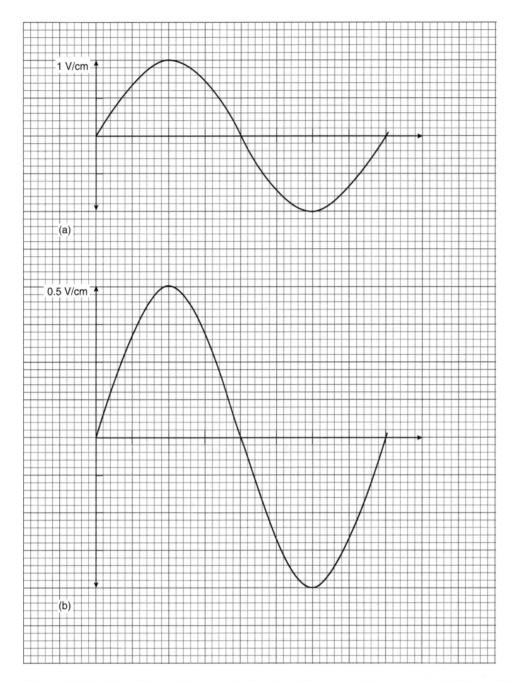

Figure 11.16   The effect of altering the Y scale adjustment: (a) scale set at 1 V/cm; (b) scale set at 0.5 V/cm

division or volts per centimetre. Before an oscilloscope can be used to take a reading it has to be read. The setting to which it is adjusted will tell the operator how to interpret the voltage waveform displayed on the screen.

Alteration of the control will make the size of the waveform change. It is important to understand that if you do this you are not changing the size of the input waveform to the oscilloscope, only the scale of the graph that you are viewing.

This is shown in Figure 11.16 where a sinewave with a peak to peak value of 4 V is shown displayed twice, once with the Y scale set at 1 V per centimetre and once with it set at 0.5 V per centimetre. Naturally, the sinewave in Figure

11.16(b) is twice the height of that in Figure 11.16(a) but note that the time or X scale of the waveform has not altered as only the Y or voltage scale has been adjusted.

It is quite possible that an oscilloscope will have two Y channels, thereby allowing it to operate in 'dual beam' mode.

Horizontal or X scale adjustment   This control is calibrated in time per division or time per centimetre. In the same way that the vertical scale has to be read before interpreting the display, so must the horizontal. The control is also known as the timebase as its adjustment alters the time that the spot takes to move across the screen.

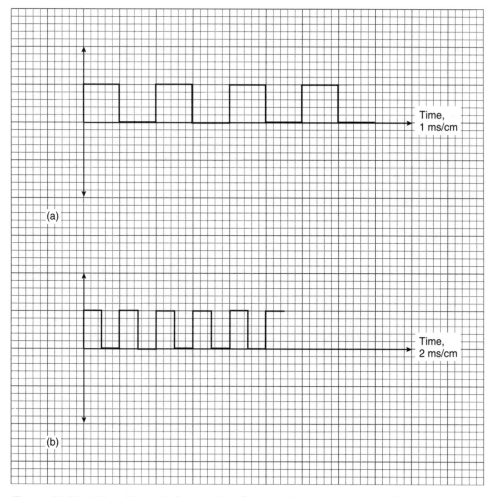

Figure 11.17   The effect of altering the X scale adjustment: (a) timebase set to 1 ms/cm; (b) timebase set to 2 ms/cm

Whilst the calibration of the vertical scale is always in volts or millivolts the timebase is marked in both milliseconds (ms) and microseconds (µs). Be careful when reading its setting to make sure that you have looked at it accurately.

Alteration of the control will adjust the number of cycles of waveform displayed on the screen. The effect is shown in Figures 11.17(a) and 11.17(b) where the same waveform is displayed twice, once with the timebase set to 1 ms/cm and once with it set to 2 ms/cm.

You can readily see the effect that this has had on the display. Remember that adjustment of the timebase has not altered the input waveform in any way, merely the manner in which it is displayed.

Dual timebase oscilloscopes

When servicing a piece of electronic equipment or examining how it operates it is quite often useful if you are able to look at two waveforms simultaneously. For example, if you suspect that an audio amplifier is causing distortion this is only possible to prove with certainty if the output signal of the amplifier is viewed with the input signal available for instantaneous comparison.

To accommodate this most oscilloscopes have what is known as a dual beam or dual timebase mode. When selected, two traces appear on the screen at the same time. One trace will display the waveform that is input on Y channel 1 and the other the input on Y channel 2 (Figure 11.18). Comparisons of the two waveforms can thus be easily made. In addition to their amplitudes and shapes it is also possible to compare the time or phase difference between them.

AC or DC levels

An oscilloscope is normally used to display and interpret information on AC waveforms. It can be used to gain information about DC levels as well. As the graphical pattern of a DC voltage is a straight line, the oscilloscope displays it as such. To the inexperienced user it often appears that the oscilloscope has nothing on its screen other than the free running timebase.

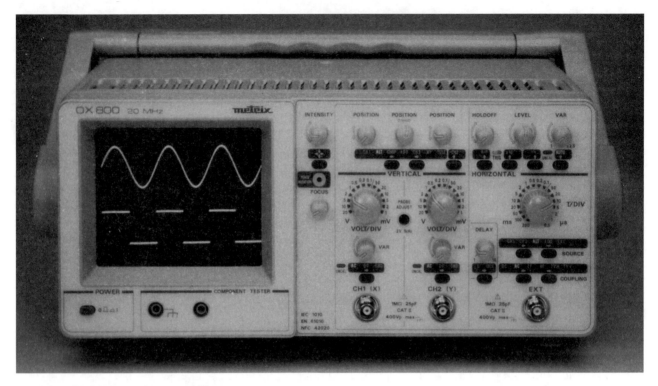

A Metrix 20 MHz analogue oscilloscope

To determine what DC is present the oscilloscope should have its input select switch set to DC coupling rather than AC. This will allow any DC voltage present to move the vertical position of the trace up the screen (for a positive voltage) or down the screen (for a negative voltage) . The actual DC voltage present is therefore the difference in the vertical position of the trace when the input select control is shifted between DC and AC.

Figure 11.19 shows the effect of a DC level present at the input to one channel of an oscilloscope. In Figure 11.19(a) the oscilloscope is AC coupled and the waveform is displayed with no DC level taken into account. In Figure 11.19(b) the coupling has been altered to DC and now the waveform appears higher up the screen.

Note that if you do not appreciate the effect that the DC/AC input select switch has, the trace of the oscilloscope may disappear when the oscilloscope is connected into the circuit. The DC level pushes the trace beyond the limits of the screen.

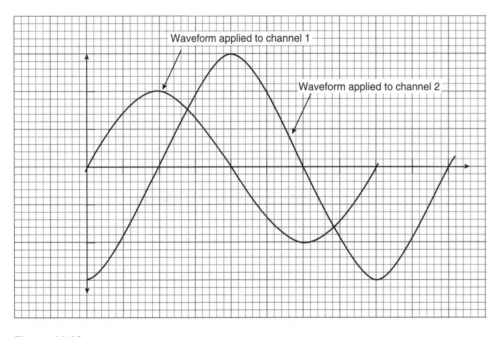

Figure 11.18

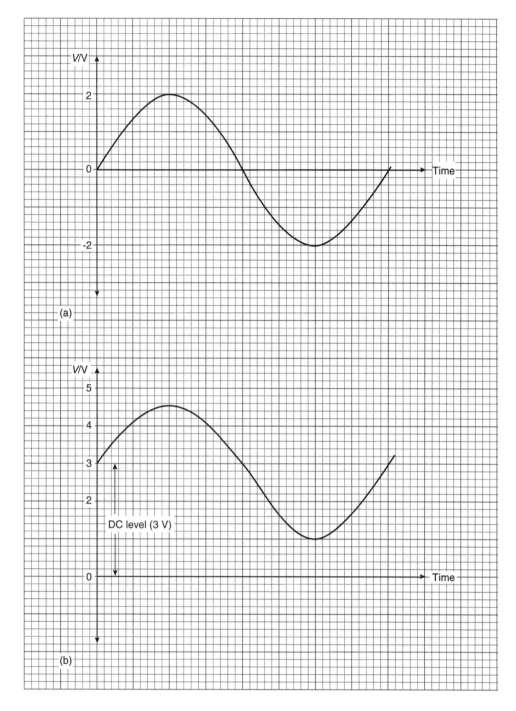

Figure 11.19   *The effect of applying a DC level to the input of one channel of an oscilloscope: (a) waveform is symmetrical about 0 V, i.e. there is no DC level; (b) waveform is symmetrical about 3 V DC, i.e. a 3 V DC level has been applied; note that its peak to peak value has not altered*

Practical 2

Displaying waveforms of different peak to peak values

This practical will allow you to see different peak to peak values of voltage on your oscilloscope.

Connect the circuit up as in Figure 11.20. The series resistors act as an attenuator or network to reduce the applied voltage. As they are all of the same value the voltage across them with respect to earth will successively decrease.

Measure the voltage at points A, B and C

in turn. You should see that the peak to peak value of the trace reduces each time.

When you have established this, connect channel 1 of your oscilloscope across points A and D and channel 2 across points D and C. Use the settings of the Y channel to work out the value of the peak to peak voltage of each trace and hence the overall reduction or attenuation in voltage that has occurred. (We obtained a reduction of 3.33 V.)

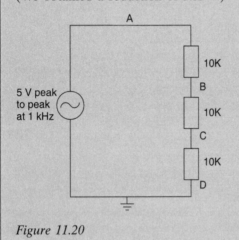

Figure 11.20

Practical 3

Displaying DC on the oscilloscope

The purpose of this practical is to use your oscilloscope to display different DC levels so that you will know what to expect when you come across this fault.

Connect up the three resistors as shown in Figure 11.21. Now adjust the controls of the oscilloscope so that a steady continuous trace is displayed.

With the input select switch set to ground use the Y shift to adjust the position of the

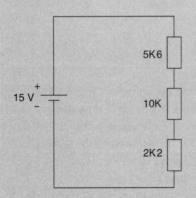

Figure 11.21

trace to coincide with the lowest horizontal line on the graticule. When you have done this, reset the input switch to DC.

Now connect the oscilloscope probes across each of the resistors in turn, each time noting the number of centimetres that the trace jumps up the graticule.

You can try this again with a different value of input voltage – say 20 V. This will alter the number of squares that the trace jumps.

Practical 4

Investigating phase shift

This practical will allow you to examine phase shifts on your oscilloscope.

Connect up the circuit as in Figure 11.22. Notice that channel 1 will show the input to the circuit (which is the output of the signal generator) whilst channel 2 is connected to show what is happening at the output.

The value of the capacitors and resistors are not critical but each resistor must be of equal value, as must each capacitor.

The result of this is that the oscilloscope should show two traces – the input and the output. The latter should have a phase difference compared with the input. The difference should be measurable in time using the X scale.

As a matter of interest the frequency at which the phase difference should be zero can be calculated using the formula $1/2\pi CR$ ($C = C_1 = C_2$; $R = R_1 = R_2$). With the values given in Figure 11.22 use of the formula indicates that the phase difference should be zero at a frequency of 1.06 kHz.

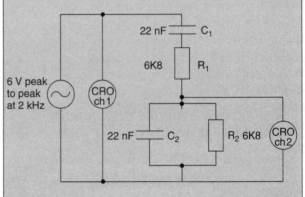

Figure 11.22

11.8 The signal generator

The controls of the signal generator 315

Whilst an oscilloscope is used to display a waveform or voltage that is present in a circuit, the signal generator is used to provide AC voltages that, normally, are adjustable in both peak to peak value and frequency.

A signal generator finds wide use in the testing of devices where an input is required to make the circuit operate. At audio frequency this could be, for example, amplifiers and cassette recorders. At higher frequencies it could be to test a radio receiver or frequency counter. The higher the output frequency that a generator has to provide, the more expensive it will be.

The number of controls on a signal generator is minimal compared with those on an oscilloscope. The frequency is usually set between limits by the adjustment of a range switch. The exact frequency of the output is then selected by a dial which is calibrated or, in more expensive devices, works in conjunction with a digital readout.

The controls of the signal generator

Different manufacturers mark the controls of their products in different ways although they have much in common. In the descriptions that follow the terms given to the controls may not exactly match the signal generator that you have access to.

Frequency selection

The range of frequencies over which the signal generator can provide an output is usually selected with the aid of **frequency range** switches which may be rotary or interlocking push button.

Each position of the switch gives the maximum and minimum frequencies that the output can provide when that setting is chosen (see 6 in Figure 11.23). The exact output frequency is set by using a second control which normally takes the form of a rotary dial (8). In the example shown in Figure 11.23 the generator is set to provide an output of 28 kHz.

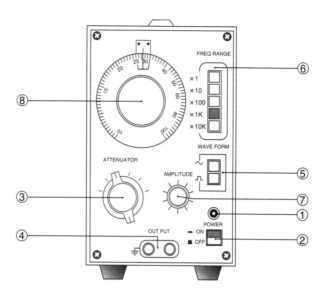

Figure 11.23   Front panel of a signal generator: 1, 'on' indicator; 2, power on/off; 3, attenuator or output coarse; 4, output sockets for signal; 5, sinewave/squarewave output select; 6, frequency coarse or range selection; 7, outout fine adjustment control; 8, frequency fine adjustment control

Output amplitude or peak to peak value

The ability of the signal generator to provide signals of different peak to peak values is an important asset of the signal generator. It allows both sensitive circuits (i.e. circuits which require a very small signal input) and others to be tested.

Adjustment of the peak to peak value of the output is normally achieved through the use of two controls. One of these is usually marked 'attenuator' or 'output coarse' (3). This control is sometimes marked in decibels. The other is usually called 'output fine' or 'amplitude' (7). The attenuator selects a series of peak to peak output voltage levels between which the output of the generator can be set.

The type of output waveform (sine or square) can be selected (5). Other panel controls are simply on/off (2) and power indicator (1). The output is available across the terminals marked 4.

The fine control (7) provides a means of exactly adjusting the output peak to peak voltage to the required level.

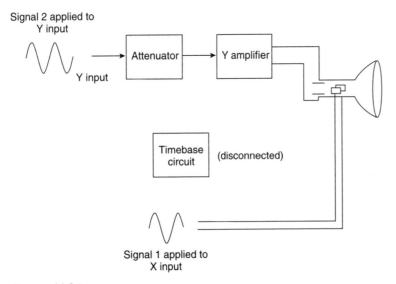

Figure 11.24

11.9 **Lissajou's figures**

Lissajou's figures are the names given to the shape that the oscilloscope trace assumes when the internal timebase is disconnected and, instead, the circuitry is driven from a signal generator connected to the X input as shown in Figure 11.24.

The display that results on the screen is a pattern the shape of which depends upon the ratio of the phases of the two applied frequencies and their individual peak to peak values and their frequencies.

If two sinewaves 90° (or 270°) out of phase with each other and of equal amplitude are applied to the X and Y inputs the resultant trace is a circle, as shown in Figure 11.25. Figure 11.26 illustrates the effect of other phase differences between the two input signals.

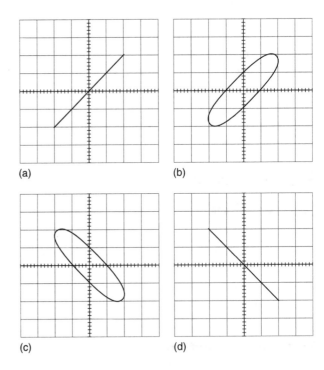

Figure 11.26 *Effect of phase difference on a Lissajou's figure: (a) 0° or 360°; (b) 30° or 330°; (c) 110° or 250°; (d) 180°*

Adjustment of the peak to peak values of the inputs whilst maintaining a phase difference results in the traces shown in Figure 11.27. Figure 11.28 illustrates the effect of different frequency ratios with equal peak to peak inputs.

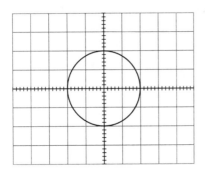

Figure 11.25 *Trace formed when two sinewaves 90° (or 270°) out of phase with each other are applied to the X and Y inputs*

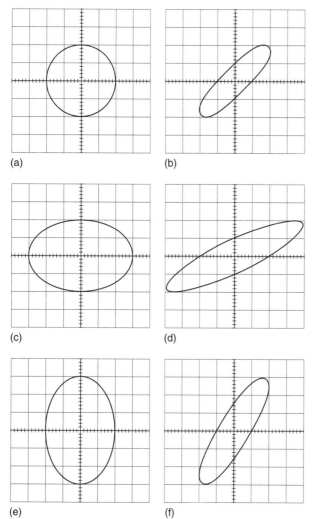

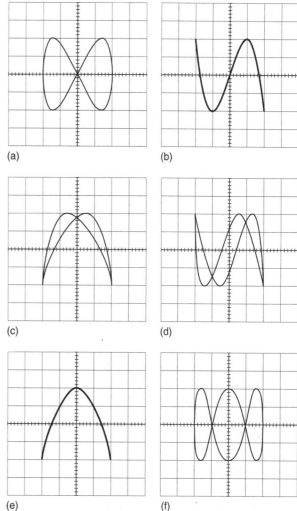

Figure 11.27 Effect of amplitude on a Lissajou's figure of constant phase: (a) 90° out of phase, horizontal and vertical amplitude equal; (b) 30° out of phase, horizontal and vertical amplitude equal; (c) 90° out of phase, horizontal amplitude greater than vertical; (d) 30° out of phase, horizontal amplitude grater than vertical; (e) 90° out of phase, vertical amplitude greater than horizontal; (f) 30° out of phase, vertical amplitude greater than horizontal

Figure 11.28 Effect of frequency on a Lissajou's figure at various phase differences:
(a) in phase, frequency 2:1 (vertical : horizontal);
(b) in phase, frequency 3:1 (vertical : horizontal);
(c) approximately 60° out of phase, frequency 2:1 (vertical : horizontal); (d) approximately 45° out of phase, frequency 3:1 (vertical : horizontal); (e) 90° out of phase, frequency 2:1 (vertical : horizontal); (f) 90° out of phase, frequency 3:1 (vertical : horizontal)

Multiple choice questions

1 In Figure 11.29 the resistor R is used
  (a) to damp the meter movement
  (b) to act as an impedance shunt
  (c) to extend the current range of the meter
  (d) to extend the voltage range of the meter.

Figure 11.29

2 A resistor incorporated in parallel with a meter is used
  (a) to enable currents greater than I_{FSD} to be indicated
  (b) to provide excess voltage protection
  (c) to calibrate known resistances
  (d) to replace conventional fusing.

3 In Figure 11.30 the meter will normally be calibrated to indicate
  (a) RMS AC voltages
  (b) average AC voltages
  (c) peak AC voltages
  (d) peak to peak AC voltages.

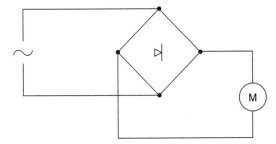

Figure 11.30

4 When selecting a multimeter it is better to choose one with
  (a) a low ohms per volt figure
  (b) a variable ohms per volt figure
  (c) a series ohms per volt figure
  (d) a high ohms per volt figure.

5 The main advantage of a digital meter is
  (a) its low impedance
  (b) its accurate digital display
  (c) its high impedance
  (d) its low current battery.

6 The oscilloscope should have
  (a) a multiplier probe
  (b) an associated frequency readout
  (c) as wide a bandwidth as possible
  (d) a low impedance input.

7 An oscilloscope displays the waveform in Figure 11.31. If the sensitivity is set to 20 mV/cm and the timebase to 2 μs/cm which of the following applies?
  (a) 20 mV peak to peak, 6 ms
  (b) 40 mV peak to peak, 0.006 ms
  (c) 40 mV peak, 600 μs
  (d) 20 mV peak to peak, 3 ms.

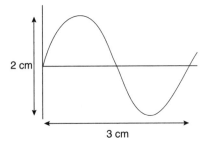

Figure 11.31

8 The control marked 'attenuator' on the front panel of a signal generator will
  (a) adjust the frequency of the output
  (b) adjust the peak to peak value of the output
  (c) adjust the periodic time of the output
  (d) reduce the input synchronising signal.

9 An oscilloscope will display
  (a) the RMS value of a waveform
  (b) the periodic time of a waveform
  (c) the frequency of a waveform
  (d) the average value of one cycle of a sinewave.

10 To remove a DC level and enable a trace to be displayed around a 0 V level the input select switch should be set to
  (a) DC
  (b) gnd
  (c) AC
  (d) AC/DC.

Index

Answers to multiple choice questions

Chapter 1
1 (d); 2 (b); 3 (a); 4 (b); 5 (a); 6 (c); 7 (b); 8 (a);
9 (b); 10 (a)

Chapter 2
1 (b); 2 (b); 3 (a); 4 (d); 5 (b); 6 (a); 7 (a); 8 (b);
9 (d); 10 (a)

Chapter 3
1 (b); 2 (d); 3 (d); 4 (a); 5 (a); 6 (d); 7 (b); 8 (a);
9 (b); 10 (b)

Chapter 4
1 (d); 2 (a); 3 (b); 4 (d); 5 (b); 6 (d); 7 (c); 8 (a);
9 (b); 10 (b)

Chapter 5
1 (a); 2 (c); 3 (d); 4 (d); 5 (d); 6 (b); 7 (b); 8 (d);
9 (a); 10 (c); 11 (c); 12 (a); 13 (b); 14 (d); 15 (b);
16 (d); 17 (b); 18 (d); 19 (a); 20 (d)

Chapter 6
1 (d); 2 (d); 3 (d); 4 (b); 5 (b); 6 (b); 7 (a); 8 (b);
9 (c); 10 (d)

Chapter 7
1 (c); 2 (a); 3 (d); 4 (b); 5 (a); 6 (d); 7 (b); 8 (b);
9 (a); 10 (c); 11 (c); 12 (a); 13 (c); 14 (c); 15 (d);
16 (a); 17 (a); 18 (b); 19 (c); 20 (c); 21 (a); 22 (d);
23 (b); 24 (d); 25 (c); 26 (c); 27 (c); 28 (b); 29
(d); 30 (b); 31 (a); 32 (d); 33 (b); 34 (d); 35 (a);
36 (a); 37 (c); 38 (c); 39 (b); 40 (d)

Chapter 8
1 (a); 2 (a); 3 (b); 4 (c); 5 (c); 6 (a); 7 (d); 8 (b);
9 (a); 10 (b)

Chapter 9
1 (d); 2 (b); 3 (c); 4 (a); 5 (a); 6 (b); 7 (d); 8 (b);
9 (a); 10 (d); 11 (a); 12 (d); 13 (b); 14 (b); 15 (a);
16 (d); 17 (c); 18 (b); 19 (c); 20 (b); 21 (b); 22
(b); 23 (c); 24 (a); 25 (d); 26 (a); 27 (d); 28 (c); 29
(b); 30 (a)

Chapter 11
1 (d); 2 (a); 3 (a); 4 (d); 5 (c); 6 (c); 7 (b); 8 (b);
9 (b); 10 (c)